TY MCSE Windows 95 in 14 Days, Second Edition

Covers MCSE Exam 70-64: Implementing and Supporting Microsoft Windows 95

Category: Planning

Objective	Sub-Objective	Location	Hands-on Material
Develop an appropriate implementation model for specific requirements.	Choosing a workgroup configuration or joining an existing domain	Workgroups Versus Domains, 192-194	Lab, 237-239
Develop a security strategy.	System Policies Profiles; File and Printer Sharing	Enforcing Corporate Policies, 268-280; Sharing Resources with Other Microsoft Clients, 201-206; Step-by-step, 203, 227	Step-by-step, 203, 227; Lab, 237-239; Lab, 288-294

Category: Installation and Configuration

Objective	Sub-Objective	Location	Hands-on Material
Install Windows 95.	Automated Windows setup; New Upgrade Uninstall; Dual boot combination with Microsoft Windows NT	Installation Options, 12-23	Exercises: Installation of Windows 95 Original Release and Installation of Windows 95 (OSR2), 35-38; Lab, 33-39
Install and configure the network components of a client computer and server.		Joining an NT Domain, 194-198; Installing the Microsoft Client for NetWare Networks, 220-222	Step-by-step, 198, 222; Lab, 237-239
Install and configure network protocols.	NetBEUI; IPX/SPX-compatible; Protocol TCP/IP; Microsoft DLC; PPTP/VPN	Network Protocols, 183-187; Installing IPX/SPX, 216-219; Priva͏ ͏ the I	Step-by-step, 216 Lab, 237-239; ͏e: Installing ͏, 257-258; ͏6-259; ͏-367

continues on page 2

Category: Monitoring and Optimization continued			
Objective	**Sub-Objective**	**Location**	**Hands-on Material**
Tune and optimize the system.	Disk Defragmenter ScanDisk DriveSpace	Disk Defragmentation, 158-160; ScanDisk Functions, 155-158	Exercise: 173, 160-162; Lab, 171-175

Category: Troubleshooting			
Objective	**Sub-Objective**	**Location**	**Hands-on Material**
Diagnose resolve installation failures.		Troubleshooting Installations, 29-32	Lab, 33-39
Diagnose and resolve boot process failures.		Troubleshooting Startup, 433	Lab, 452-453
Diagnose and resolve connectivity problems.	WinIPCfg; Net Watcher; Troubleshooting Wizards	TCP/IP Protocol, 244-255; Net Watcher, 285; Network Troubleshooting, 440-442	Exercise: Using WinIPCfg, 258; Lab, 256-259; Lab, 288; Lab 452-453
Diagnose and resolve printing problems.		Print Troubleshooting, 439-440	Lab, 452-453
Diagnose and resolve file system problems.		Troubleshooting File System Problems, 437-439	Lab, 452-453
Diagnose and resolve resource access problems.		Resource Arbitration, 116-118; The Device Manager, 118-123	Lab, 452-453
Diagnose and resolve hardware device and device driver problems.	MSD Add/Remove Hardware; Wizard	Microsoft Diagnostics, 446-449; Add New Hardware Wizard, 124-128	Lab, 452-453; Lab, 131-135
Perform direct modification of the registry as appropriate by using Regedit.		Software in the Registry, 94-99	Exercise: Editing the Registry, 105; Lab, 101-105

Category: Configuring and Managing Resource Access continued			
Objective	**Sub-Objective**	**Location**	**Hands-on Material**
Establish application environments for Microsoft MS-DOS applications.		Running Applications, 80-94	Exercise: Modifying an MS-DOS Program's Properties, 104; Lab, 101-105

Category: Integration and Interoperability			
Objective	**Sub-Objective**	**Location**	**Hands-on Material**
Configure a Windows 95 computer as a client computer in a Windows NT network.		Connecting to NT as a Client, 191-200	Lab, 237-239
Configure a Windows 95 computer as a client in a NetWare network.		Connecting to NetWare as a Client, 214-227	Lab, 237-239
Configure Windows 95 to access the Internet.		Domain Name System, 254-255	Lab, 256-259
Configure a client computer to use Dial-Up network.		Configuring the Dial-up Client, 335-345	Lab, 362-367

Category: Monitoring and Optimization			
Objective	**Sub-Objective**	**Location**	**Hands-on Material**
Monitor system performance.	Net Watcher System Monitor		Exercise: Monitoring the Processor, 424; Exercise: Installing the System Monitor, 423; Lab, 422-425

Category: Installation and Configuration   continued

Objective	Sub-Objective	Location	Hands-on Material
Install and configure hardware devices.	Modems; Printers	Installing a Modem, 336-339; Installing Printers in Windows 95, 305-310	Lab, 362-367; Lab, 322-325
Configure system services.	Browser	Browsing Microsoft Networks, 230-233	Step-by-step, 235; Lab, 237-239
Install and configure backup hardware and software.	Tape drives; The Backup application	Installing a Tape Drive, 165-166	Exercise, Installing a Backup, 173; Lab, 171-175

Category: Configuring and Managing Resource Access

Objective	Sub-Objective	Location	Hands-on Material
Assign access permissions for shared folders.	Passwords; User permissions; Group permissions	Using NT as Your Security Host, 208-213	Lab, 237-239
Create, share, and monitor resources.	Remote Network printers Shared fax modem Unimodem/V	Remote Administration, 281-285; Sharing Printers, 206-207; Sharing the Printer to the Network, 312-314; Exercise: Connecting to a Network Printer, 324; Sharing the Microsoft Fax, 389-390; Unimodem/V, 333-335	Exercise: Connecting to a Network Printer, 324; Lab, 237-239; Lab, 288-294; Lab, 322-325; Lab, 362-367; Lab, 395-398
Set up user environments by using user profiles and system policies.		The Benefits of User Profiles, 262-268	Step by step, 266, 268; Exercise: Profiles, 290; Exercise: Policies, 291-292; Alternate Exercise, 292; Lab, 288-294
Back up data and restore data.		Creating a Backup, 167-169	Lab, 171-175
Manage hard disks.	Disk compression Partitioning	Compressing Disks, 160-163; Partitioning, 138	Lab, 171-175

continues on page 3

Marcus Barton, MCT

Sams Teach Yourself

MCSE Windows 95

IN 14 DAYS

SAMS
PUBLISHING

Executive Editor
John Kane

Acquisitions Editor
Danielle Bird

Development Editor
Jeff Durham

Project Editors
Katie Purdum
Tom Lamoureaux

Copy Editor
Kelli Brooks

Technical Editors
Jason Shoults
Emmett Dulaney

Technical Reviewers
Brian M. Espinosa
Thomas M. Lane, Ph.D.

Indexer
Kelly Talbot

Cover Designer
Gary Adair

Book Designer
Gary Adair

Copy Writer
David Reichwein

Production Team Supervisor
Tricia Flodder

Production Team
Cyndi Davis-Hubler
Terri Edwards
Brad Lenser
Donna Martin
Sossity Smith

Overview

Contents

Appendix A Technical Glossary   476

Appendix B Answers to Review Questions   500

Acknowledgments

First and foremost, I would like to thank all the folks at Sams and Macmillan for providing me the opportunity to write this second edition. Danielle Bird, you are a wonderful person to work with and were extremely patient when I didn't always meet my deadlines. No matter where you go, you'll make friends. Continue to be you, and whatever you do, don't lose the accent. Jeff Durham, you are equally as patient and quite helpful in keeping me pointed in the right direction. Thanks for being so tactful. Emmett Dulaney, thank you for keeping me technically "in check." I would like to thank many more behind-the-scenes workers doing layout, cover design, and other aspects of the book with whom I don't come in direct contact.

Todd and Kim Hart, thank you for being such great friends. Todd, thanks for allowing me to bounce ideas off of you and take my frustrations out on you. You patiently listened when I just needed someone to talk to (or to play a game). You will go far, but not without the effort.

Brian Espinosa and Tom "Doc" Lane, thanks for all the help. You were instrumental in showing me the book from a reader's standpoint. We've been through a lot together; you two have proven that good friends are not *that* hard to come by. Thanks for sticking up for me when it counted.

I would like to thank my kids, Ashley, Aaron, and Jesslyn, for being so patient while dad was inaccessible and "serving my time" in my office. There were many days when you guys complained about my long stints of writing. You were constantly on my mind (thanks to thin walls and floors). Seriously, I love you all very much and you bring me endless joy.

Last and certainly not least, I would like to thank my wife, Alba, who put up with me while I was writing. I know there were times when I could be quite grouchy when there was too little sleep and too many deadlines. Thank you for being you.

About the Author

Marcus Barton is a Microsoft Certified Trainer, consultant, and lecturer currently employed by Interactive Business Systems, a consulting firm in Milwaukee, Wisconsin. In addition to training the MCSE track, he consults and lectures on the deployment, integration, and migration to Windows NT and other Microsoft BackOffice products. Marcus first started with networks while serving on active duty in the United States Air Force. You can contact Marcus at **http://www.bartonet.com**.

Interactive Business Systems, Inc. (IBS) is a full-service provider of information-technology consulting, offering quality resources to Fortune 1,000 companies across all markets since 1981. IBS has office locations in Chicago, Cleveland, Columbus, Cincinnati, Dallas, Detroit, Minneapolis, Atlanta, Denver, Milwaukee, and San Francisco. In addition to its locations in the United States, IBS also has offices in London, England, and Edinburgh, Scotland. For more information about IBS, see **http://www.ibs.com**.

Introduction

STOP and Read This

The fact that you are reading this probably means you are interested in becoming certified in Windows 95. Now, the reason for your interest probably varies from person to person. For some, this is their first step in the certification process; for others, it is another step towards their Microsoft Certified Systems Engineer certification.

If you picked this book up to learn everything there is to know about Windows 95, you picked the wrong book. This book is an Exam Preparation Guide and was designed and written specifically with the Windows 95 certification exam in mind.

If you are looking to become certified in Windows 95, it is usually because you're a network administrator wanting to know more about this popular operating system. Whether you are new to network administration or a seasoned professional, you will find this book helpful.

I became a network administrator not because I wanted to, but because I was volunteered for the job. If you have spent any amount of time in the military, you know what I mean. I have found this to be true in many instances in corporate America also. If you are anything like me, you were in the right (or wrong) place at the right (or wrong) time. Someone needed help, and you just happened to be the most knowledgeable person around. One day you're helping someone with a simple printing problem, and the next you're administering a network with an army of computers and numerous servers. Sound familiar?

Regardless of what may have compelled you to end up where you are or why you picked this book up, here's why it was a good choice that you did.

This book was designed specifically to assist you in passing the Microsoft Certification Exam 70-064. Many books out there claim to be preparation guides, exam study guides, and the like, but as a Microsoft Certified Trainer, I have found that many of these books have a lot of fluff and filler material. Even though they teach you about how to modify your screen colors or how to find one of the Easter Eggs (hidden programs created by the programmers), this information is hardly important come exam time. In this book, I've taken the fluff out.

Other books try to teach you everything there is to know about Windows 95. Don't get me wrong; these are excellent reference materials and many of them are part of my personal library, but they usually include countless pages of information that you are not tested on when taking the certification exam. For example, it might be important for you to know how to install the Novell 32-bit client for Windows 95 to support your job, but it isn't important when it comes to passing the exam. In a few spots, I provide additional helpful information such as this, but I try to keep it to a minimum and let you know via Test Tips when it is not relevant to the exam. Keep in mind that this book was designed and written for the sole purpose of preparing you for the certification exam.

The Quest for Information

After finding out that the Windows 95 exam would be changing in March 1998, we knew we had to write a second edition to meet the new exam guidelines. However, we had a little difficulty actually finding out what the new guidelines would be.

I contacted Microsoft and asked about the new guidelines. Within seconds, they were referring me to the Training and Certification Web site. After looking over these new guidelines, I was astonished to find many topics missing from the list (compared to the old exam guidelines). Not only were there things removed, but there were very few additions. I can sum up the additions with three main topics: Unimodem/V, PPTP, and VPN. If you don't know what they are right now, don't worry; they will be explained.

Everywhere I went, asking for questions about these new guidelines, I was told that they would probably not change very much, even after beta testing of the exam.

How to Use This Book

In this book, you begin with a list of the exam objectives. Don't worry if you only see one or two exam objectives for a 40-page chapter. It might be necessary to cover that much material about the topic to bring you up to speed on the topic being covered by the exam. These exam objectives at the beginning of the chapter are there to give you an idea of the area being covered.

Next, you will find a list of Fast Facts. These actually serve two purposes. These are usually facts that you need to know come test time. So glance over them before reading the chapter, even if they don't make a lot of sense to you when you read them the first time. After reading the chapter, read back over the Fast Facts as part of your review.

After the chapter comes a lab exercise that consists of review questions and/or a hands-on exercise. Remember that the questions are review questions. Some of them might look like questions you might find on the exam; however, they are not a good indicator of whether you are ready for the exam.

The last chapter is a sample exam. All of the questions have the same material and the same feel as the real exam. This can help you determine if you are ready. BE CAREFUL. The sample exam is a good tool for you to test yourself only the first time you take it. After that, you will begin to memorize the questions, answers, or both. So, try and save the practice exam for a day or two before you take the exam. This will make sure that it is effective.

The following table lays out the Microsoft exam objectives covered under each of this book's 14 days. You'll find a different version of this table on the tear out card at the front of this book (it's organized from the exam objective rather than from the chapter).

Table 0.1. Mapping of this book's content to the Microsoft exam objectives.

Day	Chapter	Objective	Sub-objectives
1	Planning for and Installing Windows 95	Install Windows 95	Automated Windows setup New Upgrade Uninstall Dual boot combination with Microsoft WindowsNT
		Diagnose and resolve Installation Failures	
2	Configuring and Personalizing Windows 95	None	
3	Windows 95 Blueprint: Internals and Architecture	Establish application environments for Microsoft MS-DOS applications.	Configuring and Managing Resource Access
		Perform direct modification of the registry as appropriate by using Regedit.	Troubleshooting
4	Plug and Play	Diagnose and resolve resource problems	Troubleshooting
		Diagnose and resolve hardware device and	Troubleshooting
			Add/Remove Hardware Wizard

Table 0.1. continued

Day	Chapter	Objective	Sub-objectives
5	Files, Folders & Disks	Install and configure backup hardware and software.	Tape Drives The Backup application
		Backup data and restore data.	
		Manage hard disks.	Disk Compression Partitioning
		Tune and optimize the system	Disk Defragmenter ScanDisk Compression Utility
6	Linking to Your Network	Develop an appropriate implementation model for specific requirements.	Choosing a workgroup configuration or joining an existing domain.
		Develop a security strategy.	File and printer sharing
		Install and configure the network components of a client computer and server.	
		Install and configure network protocols.	NetBEUI IPX/SPX
		Configure system services.	Browser
		Assign Access permissions for shared folders.	Passwords User Permissions Group Permissions
		Create, share and monitor resources.	Network Printers
		Configure a Windows 95 computer as a client in a Windows NT network	
		Configure a Windows 95 computer as a client in a NetWare network	

Day	Chapter	Objective	Sub-objectives
7	Linking to the World	Install and configure network protocols. Configure a Windows 95 computer to access the Internet.	TCP/IP PPTP/VPN
		Diagnose and resolve connectivity problems.	WinIPCfg
8	Locking Down the System: Profiles and Policies	Develop a security strategy.	System Policies Profiles
		Create, share and monitor resources. Set up user environments using profiles and system policies	Remote
		Diagnose and resolve connectivity problems	Net Watcher
9	Installing and Installation and Configuration	Install and configure hardware devices.	Printers
		Create, share and monitor resources.	Network Printers
		Install and configure network protocols.	Data Link Control (DLC)
10	Taking Windows 95 on the Road: Remote Services	Install and configure hardware devices, Configure a client computer to use Dial-Up networking for remote access.	Modems
		Install and configure network protocols.	PPTP/VPN
		Configuring and Managing Resource Access.	Data Link Control (DLC)
		Create, share, and monitor resources.	Unimodem/V
11	Exchange Messaging Services	Create, share and monitor resources	Shared fax modem

Table 0.1. continued

Day	Chapter	Objective	Sub-objectives
12	Monitoring and Optimizing Windows 95	Monitor system performance	Net Watcher System Monitor
13	Troubleshooting Windows 95	Diagnose and resolve installation failures. Diagnose and resolve boot process failures. Diagnose and resolve connectivity problems. Diagnose and resolve printing problems. Diagnose and resolve file system problems. Diagnose and resolve hardware device and device driver problems.	Net Watcher Troubleshooting Wizards MSD
14	Practice Exam	Combination of all categories	

Hardware Requirements

Much of this book addresses basic concepts of networking and does not require access to any particular hardware or software. Later chapters, however, do present some of the fundamentals of working with Windows 95 and Windows NT Server 4.0. Although not absolutely necessary, to get the most out of the exercises and examples presented in this book, you should have access to computers with both of these operating systems.

The hardware recommendations for running both Windows 95 and Windows NT Server 4.0 are listed in the following mini-tables.

Minimum recommended hardware for Windows 95	
Processor	386dx/ 33 (Pentium recommended)
Display	VGA (or better) video display adapter
Hard Drive Space	40MB (At least 100MB recommended)
Memory	4MB (16MB recommended)
Other	CD-ROM drive or network installation, mouse, at least one network interface card required for networked environment

Minimum recommended hardware for Windows NT Server 4.0

Processor	486dx/33
Display	VGA (or better) video display adapter
Hard Drive Space	125MB
Memory	16MB
Other	CD-ROM drive or network installation, mouse, at least one network interface card required for networked environment

In addition, readers will be required to have administrative rights on a Windows NT Server in order to complete some of the exercises in this book.

How to Contact Me

I am the first one to admit that no one can know absolutely everything there is to know about the Windows 95 operating system. I can surely attest to that. You need to realize that there were over 100 people involved in its design. So with that in mind, I would love to hear any comments, suggestions, tips, or tricks you have to offer. There are some extremely talented people out there, and you might be one of them.

I would also like to hear from you if you find any errors, omissions, or mistakes in this book. Because of the amount of people involved with the publishing of a book (take a look at the copyright page), there are bound to be mistakes. No one likes mistakes, especially authors, but to err is human. If there are any errors, I will place a page on my Web site dedicated to informing you of them. So, stop by at **www.bartonet.com** and check, just in case. Otherwise, if you would like to contact me, you can do so by emailing me at **marc@bartonet.com**. I look forward to hearing from you.

Enjoy the book and good luck on your path to certification.

Here's What Readers Are Saying About *Sams Teach Yourself MCSE Windows 95 in 14 Days*:

I just had to write regarding your book. It is so well written in plain English that the first time I opened the book, it drew me in and I blew through it in about a week. Although I had purchased other Windows 95 books to study for the Windows 95 certification, yours was the only book that I studied and I passed the exam with flying colors! Thanks for a great book! By the way, I recommended this book to my other colleagues, and they, too, passed the test within a three-week time frame.

—*Michael Limpahan, MCP (Win95/NT), Network Specialist Consultant*

Mr. Barton presented the material in a dynamic, logical style that simply made sense. I felt that he was personally walking me through the operation of Windows 95. I sat for the exam with confidence and understanding, and I passed on my first attempt. Mr. Barton's acumen in computers is quite evident, but his ability to relay that knowledge to others and foster enthusiasm—that's genius! Thank you!

—*John O. Gaetani, MCP, Systems Administrator, Aurora Concepts, Inc.*

Great book—I studied this book and passed. It was a great price and didn't overload me with a lot of material I didn't need for the exam. I liked the test tips that help point out specific things that I should know for the test. Great exam preparation.

—*Jacqueline A. Adkins, Network Administrator*

Sweet book—I passed the exam after finishing the book. The Fast Facts in the beginning of the chapters were helpful, especially before the exam. This book brought me up-to-speed very quickly.

—*Brian M. Espinosa, Technical Service Support Technician, Tushaus Computer Services*

Day 1

Planning for and Installing Windows 95

When it comes to testing, I like to come up with several little sayings that help me keep my mind on track. Call each saying a mantra if you like. The first one is, "Planning is good." Microsoft loves the idea of planning. Almost every exam I have taken has included some aspect of planning.

Always plan any sort or size of implementation. Whether it is large implementation of Windows 95 or just a handful of machines, planning ahead will save you time and reduce your headaches. Planning must come before implementation.

Implementation is not as simple as throwing the Windows 95 CD-ROM into the drive and firing up the setup program. Even though you could take that route, you should take a look at the aspects of Windows 95 implementation. First, you need to understand where Windows 95 belongs in the marketplace (as well as in the home) before you learn how to install it.

Keep in mind, however, that this is a guide to help you prepare for the exam. So, before I start tossing information at you, let's take a look at the exam objectives for which this chapter will prepare you.

Objectives

Microsoft publishes exam objectives for all its exams. Because this book was designed to prepare you for the Supporting Microsoft Windows 95 exam (Exam 70-064), I've listed the exam objectives that are current as of this writing. For more information about the Microsoft exams and the most current exam objectives, visit Microsoft's Web site at **http://www.microsoft.com/train_cert**. The exam objectives that are covered in this chapter are the following:

- Install Windows 95
- Automated Windows Setup
- New
- Upgrade
- Uninstall
- Dual boot
- Diagnose and resolve installation failures

1.1. Windows 95's Position in the Marketplace

The Microsoft family currently includes three operating systems. These three operating systems fill three separate roles in the marketplace. To understand the operating systems, you need to understand their roles. After you understand the roles, you can make a better decision as to where to use what.

The first role is the server. The server operating system must handle more than the file and print services of yesterday's servers. It must now manage not only files and printers, but email, applications, Web sites, remote administration, dynamic configurations, centralized security, and so on. Microsoft's Windows NT Server (NTS) is the one to handle such tasks.

Just below NTS is Windows NT Workstation (NTW). Whereas NTW doesn't have quite as many capabilities as NTS but more advanced capabilities than Windows 95, its place is as a high-end user machine. Basically, it's a high-end workstation OS with many of the advanced security and performance features of NTS. Let me clarify that. It is designed along the same concepts as NTS but not with some of the functions of NTS. It is designed and tuned for use as a workstation—hence, its name.

Notice that I said NTW has more advanced functions than Windows 95. Even though it might be more advanced than Windows 95, it doesn't overshadow the importance of Windows 95 in the Microsoft family. NTW is for power users with greater security needs, and Windows 95 is for everyone else. Windows 95 has some capabilities that NT Workstation lacks (such as Plug and Play).

Since its release in August 1995, Windows 95 has undergone some revisions. Like most other products that Microsoft kicks out, you can get these revisions from Microsoft, free of charge, via a service pack. Service packs are a way to make minor and sometimes even major modifications to a software package. Most of these modifications are designed to fix bugs that were found in the software. Sometimes they add functionality. As of this writing, there has been only one service pack released for Windows 95.

If you want to obtain a service pack for Windows 95, you can do so by downloading it or ordering it from Microsoft's Web site. As of this writing, you can visit www.microsoft.com/windows95 and find a link to the service pack.

The strange thing is that not only did Microsoft create a service pack for Windows 95, but they also released a version of Windows 95 dubbed OSR2, which stands for

OEM Service Release 2. OSR2 has picked up more nicknames and aliases than Billy the Kid. You might hear it also called Release 2, Second Release, 95B, B Version, and many more. Likewise, the original version has many names now also. First Release, Retail Version, Version A, and 95A are just a few names you might hear.

> *OEM: Original Equipment Manufacturer.* This term commonly describes companies that distribute software packaged with their product (usually software preloaded on computers).

As you might deduce, OSR2 is available only from Original Equipment Manufacturers like Dell, Compaq, and the like. If you are the end user buying Windows 95 off the shelf at your local software store, you need to install the service pack.

How can you tell what you have? Go to the Control Panel and open the System option. (If you don't have Windows installed yet, check this out after you install it.) The window that pops up gives you basic information. Look for the version number (see Figure 1.1).

Figure 1.1.

The System Properties sheet can tell you what version of Windows 95 you are running.

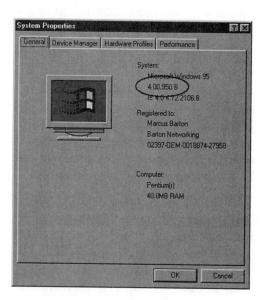

What you have installed boils down to this:

- 4.00.950—Original Release
- 4.00.950A—Original Release with Service Pack 1 installed
- 4.00.950B—OSR2

Throughout the book, I will point out some of the subtle differences between the first and second releases of Windows 95. Otherwise, just assume that we are talking about both versions. Let's take a more in-depth look at some features of Windows 95.

1.1.1. Features and Functions of Windows 95

The first thing you notice is the interface. Microsoft has moved away from the traditional Program Manager and Program Groups of its 3.x family members. It still has the traditional desktop but without the cumbersome Program Manager. Everything starts with the Start button and fans out into a series of menus and submenus. We'll talk more about the interface in Chapter 2, "Configuring and Personalizing Windows 95."

Another commonly discussed feature is the capability to save your files using *long file names* (*LFNs*) . You no longer have to put up with eight-character names, making it difficult to figure out what's what. LFNs in Windows 95 can now extend up to 255 characters long. Of course, with everything good comes something bad. In Chapter 5, "Files, Folders, and Disks," I'll discuss long filenames further (no pun intended).

Windows 95 was built upon the concept of multimedia. (I know you might be justifying to your boss that you need Windows 95 so that you can put together an advanced presentation using sound and graphics for that next board meeting. But what you really want Windows 95 for is to take advantage of some of the new 32-bit, high graphics, surround-sound games. You can't pull a fast one over on me.) You can incorporate some powerful presentations using embedded video, sounds, animation, and the like. With all these capabilities, Windows 95 gives you more ways to get your point across.

Unlike its 16-bit predecessors, Windows 95 not only has the capability to run 16-bit programs, but 32-bit programs as well. Windows 95 has both 16-bit and 32-bit code present in the operating system code. This gives it true, backward compatibility. Long gone is the traditional memory model that is segmented into conventional, expanded, and extended sections. Now a flat, linear model designed after Windows NT has arrived.

Preemptive multitasking is another way that Windows 95 is different from older versions of Windows. In Windows 3.x products, applications are *cooperatively*

1

multitasked—that is, programs have to take turns sending threads of code to the processor. They cooperate with each other, allowing only one program to talk at a time. Preemptive multitasking gives all the programs the capability to send threads to the processor at the same time. Windows 95 cooperatively multitasks 16-bit programs and preemptively multitasks 32-bit applications. Additionally, unlike the 16-bit programs that can only send single threads of code, 32-bit applications are multithreaded. This basically means that they can do more, in less time. This is an exciting capability that I'll discuss further in Chapter 3, "Windows 95 Blueprint: Internals and Architecture."

Also implemented into Windows 95 is the technology of *Plug and Play (PnP)*. Although PnP won't be present until later versions of Windows NT, it is alive and well in Windows 95. The capability to support *hot docking* of laptops (placing laptops in or out of a docking station with the laptop fully powered) and configuration of hardware with little or no intervention from the user is here.

The subject of hot docking brings up the topic of mobile users. Windows 95 supports mobile users better than any other operating system out there. Through the implementation of dial-up networking, users can now connect to anyone in the world from anywhere in the world. Through built-in telephony functions (integrating your computer and your telephone), users can now send email, transfer files, and browse the Web from anywhere.

Telephony not only integrates dial-up networking but built-in fax services as well. With Microsoft Exchange messaging, you can not only send and receive email, but faxes, too. With Microsoft Fax, you can turn your PC into a fax machine, faxing documents directly from Microsoft Word or some other word processing application. Windows 95 integrates them all.

Instead of implementing networking as an add-on such as: Windows for Workgroups, Windows 95 was built from the ground up with networking capabilities. It can act as a client for many network operating systems, such as Microsoft Windows NT and Novell NetWare. Now you can control who accesses files on a Windows 95 machine across the network using pass-through authentication. Sound interesting? Check out Chapter 6, "Linking to Your Network," for more.

1.1.2. Windows 95 and NTW Head to Head

Up to now, I've made a few comparisons between Windows 95 and Windows NTW. As I described earlier, Windows NT is a network operating system that consists of a server and client system appropriately named Windows NT Server (NTS) and

Windows NT Workstation (NTW). The server half is, of course, the server end of the two with NT Workstation being the client.

Now, not only can you have NTW as a client to NTS, but Windows 95 can act as a client as well. You might be asking yourself, "When should I use Windows 95 over Windows NTW, or vice versa?" Well, ask yourself the following questions:

- **Does the user need a secure desktop machine, such as in finance or other environments where information privacy is a must?** When users need an operating system that lets them secure files stored locally on their machines, they pick NT. The National Security Agency (NSA) has certified Windows NT with a Class C2 secure system rating as a standalone machine.

- **What will the user be doing on the computer?** If it's basic word processing, graphics, spreadsheets, and such, there is no need to go overboard with NTW. But, if users will be doing computer-aided design (CAD), drafting, and other high-end, processor-intensive programs that need the capability to handle more than one processor, you'd better vote for NTW.

- **What about the hardware requirements?** Well, we will talk more about Windows 95's hardware requirements in the next section, but Windows 95 and Windows NT have one major difference in their respective hardware requirements: RAM. The minimum requirement for Windows 95 is 4MB of RAM as opposed to 12MB for Windows NT.

- **Will users be spending large amounts of time away from the office but still relying on a personal computer for keeping track of their work?** You'd better go with Windows 95. It supports mobile users better with its PnP capability that allows for use with laptops and docking stations. Not to mention, Windows 95 has lower hardware requirements than Windows NTW.

As you can see, quite a few differences exist between the two. Take a look at Table 1.1 for a summary of the differences to help you make a decision.

Table 1.1. Windows 95 and Windows NTW 4.0 comparison.

Description	Windows 95	Windows NTW
MS-DOS programs run	Yes	Most (see note)
16-bit programs run	Yes	Yes
32-bit programs run	Yes	Yes
Can use MS-DOS device drivers	Yes	No
Can use Win16 device drivers	Yes	No

Description	Windows 95	Windows NT
Supports multiple file systems (HPFS, NTFS, & FAT)	No	Yes (only 3.51 supports HPFS)
Supports multiple processors	No	Yes
Supports Intel platforms	Yes	Yes
Supports RISC, MIPS, DEC Alpha, & PowerPC platforms	No	Yes
Supports Plug and Play	Yes	No (as of 4.0)
Largest hard disk partition	2GB	16EB (exabyte)

> **Note**
>
> You might be wondering what I meant by stating that Windows NTW only ran some MS-DOS programs. No, I wasn't off my rocker; I meant it. You see, some MS-DOS programs like to have control of the hardware, such as a communications port, LPT port, and so forth. When they do that, it is called a *direct hardware call*. NT does not like programs that try to bypass all of its advanced security and access the hardware directly. Therefore, when a DOS program attempts to make a direct hardware call, it simply shuts the program down, foiling would-be security violations.

If you want more information on the differences between Windows 95 and Windows NTW, the best place to find it is on the Microsoft Web site. Just take a gander at http://www.microsoft.com/windows95, and you will find plenty of comparison information. Just look for anything that mentions evaluating Windows 95.

1.2. Planning for Hardware and Software Requirements

The first step to implementation of Windows 95 is to make sure that the machines meet the minimum hardware requirements. Remember, planning is good.

On the exam, expect at least two questions that ask you about the hardware requirements. The question could be in the form of a list of machines, asking you to pick all the machines that meet the requirements, or a troubleshooting scenario, asking you what part of the machine doesn't meet the requirements.

1.2.1. Minimum Installation Requirements

With any operating system, program, application, or whatever, there comes hardware requirements. The company that produces it sets it forth. As with any of the products mentioned, the company states the minimum hardware requirements but also usually states a recommended hardware list. Basically, "This is what it takes to run our product, but we prefer you use this." As for the exam, be prepared to know both.

Table 1.2 states both the minimum and recommended hardware requirements as stated by Microsoft. I'll discuss them a little more in detail after the table.

Table 1.2. Windows 95 minimum and recommended hardware requirements.

Description	Minimum Required	Recommended
Processor	386DX or higher	486/25MHz
Memory	4MB	8MB
Floppy/CD-ROM (for installation)	Floppy	CD-ROM
Disk Space	40MB	50-55MB
Video Display	VGA	SVGA
Pointing Device		Mouse
Others		Modem/Fax Modem

Processor

You can run Windows 95 on a 386DX, but you can probably guess that it's not a pretty sight. Microsoft's Web site (http://www.microsoft.com) states that you should run Windows 95 on a 486 or higher processor running at least 25MHz or faster. This is not as bad as it might seem. I currently run Windows 95 on a Compaq Contura laptop, which is a 486.

 Note

Most people do not understand the difference between a 486SX chip and a 486DX chip. They believe that the 486SX chip doesn't have a math coprocessor and the 486DX chip does. The 486SX chip does have a math coprocessor, but it's just disabled (talk about a marketing ploy).

With Windows 95 installed on a 486SX and a 486DX of the same MHz, the difference is minimal. As a matter of fact, the average user usually doesn't notice the difference between a 486SX and a 486DX.

I have successfully installed Windows 95 on a 386DX and a 386SX (even though the minimum requirement is a DX chip). The 16-bit I/O buffers of the SX chip greatly reduced the performance of the machine. I just wanted to see if it could be done.

Memory

If you want to make Windows 95 happy, give it lots of RAM. Once again, it's not pretty on 4MB, but it will run. Microsoft recommends 8MB, but if you really want to see it perform, I recommend 16MB. As a matter of fact, the Compaq Contura that I mentioned is at 24MB. When it comes to RAM, the more, the merrier.

Floppy/CD-ROM

This requirement is mainly for installation. Even though you can install Windows 95 without either of these (via a network), life is better with both of them. You can buy the Windows 95 media either on floppy (yuck) or CD-ROM. You'll want the CD-ROM not only for installation, but for multimedia purposes also. If you choose to go the floppy route, be prepared to do the old floppy shuffle. Need I say more?

Disk Space

Once again, I quote the Microsoft Web site in stating that the minimum disk requirement for Windows 95 is 40MB. That is the barebones minimum. If you choose to install some of the optional components, be prepared to set aside 50 to 55MB depending on which options you choose to install.

Video Display

The minimum requirement is VGA or better. So get rid of all your monochrome monitors. The recommended is Super VGA or better. Windows 95 can do some pretty neat graphics, and plenty of programs designed for Windows 95 are out there ready to exploit the capability. Go with Super VGA.

Pointing Device

This should be a requirement, but it's not. Have you ever tried getting around Windows 95 without one? It is possible, but not fun. Give it a whirl sometime.

Modem/Fax Modem

These are not necessary, but if you want to take advantage of the dial-up networking and fax functions built into Windows 95, you'll need one. The fax modem would be the modem of choice. Someone once asked me whether I had a particular speed of choice. That is actually a battle right now. I guess the answer to that question (as of this writing) is 28.8Kbps. You might be wondering why 28.8 when there are 33.6 and even 56.6 modems out there. Actually, you might find it hard to find an Internet service provider who supports above 28.8. Additionally, modem manufacturers are currently in a battle to determine which company will create the standard for 56.6 modem technology. Until an industry standard exists, you might be better off waiting rather than getting stuck with a modem that might not be supported at a later date.

1.2.2. Software Requirements

When it comes to software requirements, I'll spend the majority of the time talking about upgrading, but let me briefly mention the requirements for a fresh (non-upgrade) installation.

For a brand-new installation, you need at least version 3.2 of MS-DOS already loaded on the machine. Microsoft recommends, however, that you use at least version 5.0 because of heavy modification of pre-5.0 versions by OEMs.

1.3. Installation Options

The last part of the exam's Planning portion deals directly with installation. You need to know several things about the installation process for the exam. The four main topics (as gathered from the exam objectives) deal with the installation methods, dual-boot systems, setup switches, and troubleshooting.

1.3.1. Installation Mediums

Even though there are many ways of going about the task of installing Windows 95, there are just a few ways to actually get the installation files to the computer on which you want to install them on. The three ways are floppy disks, CD-ROM, and via a network server.

Floppy Disks

The floppy disk shuffle is by far the slowest way to install. It is relatively simple: Just pop in the number one disk, access the drive, and type **Setup**. You can run Setup from MS-DOS or from within Windows.

If you are performing a new installation from a full (non-upgrade) version of Windows 95, you'll be doing a floppy install. As discussed earlier, the full version is not available on CD-ROM (unless of course it's an OEM version).

CD-ROM

CD-ROM installation is the most popular installation. It is faster than the floppy installation but is executed in the same manner. You pop the CD-ROM in, access it, and run Setup.

One advantage to the CD-ROM installation over the floppy installation is that the CD-ROM comes with some remote administration tools and extra utilities, which mainly deal with administration, such as the Policy Editor (see Chapter 8, "Locking Down the System: Profiles and Policies").

Network

Using this option, you set up the Windows 95 files on a server to be shared out to the network. By selecting a network setup during the setup process, it expands and copies the Windows 95 files down to the hard disk and marks them as read-only. By doing so, you do not create a working copy of Windows 95, only one that you can use to do installs. This is for situations when you want to copy the necessary files to a server. For example, if you want to copy them to a Windows NT server, you should use this option. Obviously, you don't want to create a working copy (thus reinstalling your server).

This provides some obvious advantages. If you only have one CD-ROM and need to install tons of machines, there's no waiting until one machine is done. You can install multiple machines at the same time from this network share. The other advantage is that you can use this to create a shared installation of Windows 95.

1.3.2. Installation Options

After you have decided how you will distribute the files, you must plan what type of installation that you want to perform. There are many options available: a new installation (which is an installation "from scratch," so to speak), an upgrade form Windows 3.x, or a dual boot with Windows NT.

New

A new installation, as dubbed by Microsoft, is an installation when there is no operating system currently installed on the machine. When this is the case, you need to partition and format the hard disk. For more information on partitioning and formatting, see Chapter 5, "Files, Folders, and Disks."

This section covers the following exam objective: Install Windows 95–New.

After the hard disk is partitioned and formatted, you need to install whatever drivers or software are needed to access the installation files. If you have chosen to install from a floppy, then no extra drivers are needed.

If you are installing from a CD-ROM, then you need whatever CD-ROM drivers are necessary to access the CD. For example, in my case, I am using an NEC CD-ROM drive. I have the MS-DOS drivers installed and the appropriate lines in the AUTOEXEC.BAT and CONFIG.SYS files that are necessary to make my CD-ROM usable.

Last, if you are installing via the network, you need some sort of network client installed. I have installed many machines by simply partitioning and formatting the hard disk using a system disk created from another Windows 95 machine. After the hard disk is set up and bootable, I install the Microsoft Network Client for DOS that is available on the Windows NT Server CD-ROM.

You can create a floppy system disk on another Windows 95 computer by formatting the floppy using the Explorer. When formatting, place a check mark in the Copy System Files option towards the bottom of the Format dialog box. After the disk is formatted, copy FDISK.EXE (for partitioning) and FORMAT.COM (of course, for formatting) from the Windows\command directory to the floppy disk.

When you can access your CD or network share of the files, simply run the SETUP.EXE from the WIN95 folder.

Automated (Batch)

The batch setup is automated. Basically, the administrator specifies the settings in advance using INF (information) script files. When the batch installation method is used along with the script files, the administrator is not prompted for input. Instead, it receives all the setup information from the script file. For this reason, this setup option is sometimes referred to as an *unattended setup*. This is great when you have a ton of machines to install. The only problem is that you need to know all the setup information up front. Then, you need to spend some time making the script files.

This section covers the following exam objective: Install Windows 95–Automated Setup.

A utility that comes with the Windows 95 Resource Kit simplifies the creation of the setup scripts. It's called BATCH.EXE, and it's a Windows-based program designed to make it easy to create the scripts needed for using the Batch installation method. Check out Chapter 5 of the Resource Kit for more information on this program.

Shared

A shared installation is not as complicated as it might sound. First, you need to use the network option (as described previously) to set up the network shared copy of Windows 95. Then at the workstation, you run Setup from the shared copy using the minimal installation option. Basically, this installs the least amount of files necessary to get the workstation up and running, whereas most of the operating system resides on the server that has the shared copy.

This method has some apparent advantages. First off, the only place that an administrator needs to perform an upgrade is on the server where the shared copy resides. Second of all, multiple machines can use this single shared copy. (No, this is not a way around licenses.)

The disadvantages of the shared method include increased network traffic and slower workstations. Another big problem is the availability of the server. If the server where the shared copy resides goes down, you'll have some unhappy Windows 95 users.

The quickest and easiest way to set up a shared installation is by using a program called NetSetup.

NetSetup

The Windows 95 CD-ROM contains a program that allows you to perform a server-based setup. Although this program performs the same tasks as the network setup described previously, this program tends to be a simple one-stop solution to setting up a shared installation.

To run this program, locate the \admin\nettools\netsetup folder on the Windows 95 CD-ROM. In this directory, you will find NETSETUP.EXE.

Note

The Admin folder is not included with the version of Windows 95 that comes on floppy disks.

NetSetup is a three-step process. As you can see in Figure 1.2, the first step is to set the server install path. This is where you specify the source path (where you are getting the files) as well as the server path (where the shared files will be).

Figure 1.2.

The Server Based Setup screen.

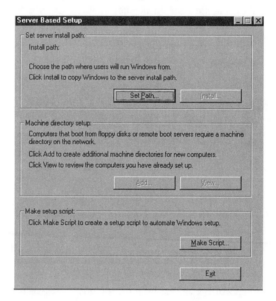

The second step is to specify where the machine directory will be. For a shared installation on each computer that starts from a floppy disk or a remote-boot disk image, the machine directory is a required network directory that contains the particular files required for that specific configuration. The machine directory contains WIN.COM, the full Registry, and startup configuration files such as SYSTEM.INI.

Note

If you have several machines with an identical hardware setup (same network cards, video cards, and so on), they can share the same machine directory.

The third step of the server-based setup is making a setup script. Setup scripts aid you during the installation process by allowing you to specify information before-hand that you normally have to specify during setup. You can even create a totally automated setup. Server-based setup can create a default setup script automatically by storing the setup options you specify in an MSBATCH.INF file that is placed with the Windows 95 source files on the server. You can use this default setup script to install Windows 95 on individual computers or as a template to create other versions of the setup script.

> **Note** The NetSetup program can be run only from a computer running Windows 95. You cannot run Server-based Setup from Windows 3.1, Windows for Workgroups, Windows NT, or MS-DOS.

To perform a server-based setup, follow these steps:

1. Insert the Windows 95 CD in the CD-ROM drive. Then switch to the ADMIN\NETTOOLS\NETSETUP directory.

2. In Windows Explorer, double-click NETSETUP.EXE.

3. Click the Set Path button and specify the shared folder where you want to copy the shared files. Click OK.

4. Click the Install button.

5. Specify where you want the files to be located (see Figure 1.3):

   ■ **Server**—Allows only shared installation of Windows 95. Select this option if client computers will use the source files on this server to run a shared copy of Windows 95.

   ■ **Local Hard Disk**—Allows installation only on a local hard disk. Select this option if all Windows 95 files are to be stored on each computer's local hard disk.

   ■ **User's Choice**—Prompts the user to specify either shared or local instal-lation. Select this option if you are allowing users to choose whether to run a shared installation or if you are using setup scripts to install differ-ent types of installations using the same source files.

6. Specify the location of the source files. In this scenario, I am installing from my CD-ROM in drive E.

7. Click OK.

8. NetSetup asks if you want to create a default script. This is the MSBATCH.INF discussed previously. You can create individual scripts later using the Make Script option. Click the Create Default button and specify a storage location.

9. Specify the script options and click OK.

Figure 1.3.

Specifying the source and install paths.

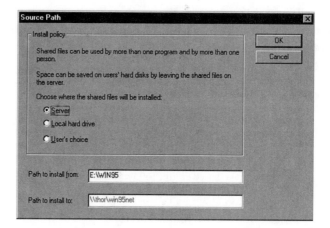

The setup script box (Figure 1.4) allows you to specify options that are normally prompted during Windows 95 setup. Specifying them beforehand allows for a more automated installation that prevents you from having to baby-sit the computer.

Figure 1.4.

Creating a default setup script.

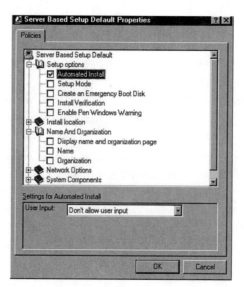

1

After installing the files and creating a default script (optional), you can create a machine directory. Creating a machine directory is as simple as clicking the Add button from the Server Based Setup screen (refer to Figure 1.2) and specifying the computer name along with the path to the machine directory.

Note

Creating a machine directory is not necessary if the installation will be to the local hard disk. Machine directories are needed for shared installations.

After you have finished transferring the files, creating a setup script, and setting up your machine directory (if necessary), you can use your setup script to start the installation process by using the setup script parameter at the command line at the beginning of setup. An example might be

SETUP A:\STANDARD.INF

In this example, I created a setup script and saved it to a floppy disk. The setup script can be on a floppy, local hard disk, or network drive.

1.3.3. Dual-Boot Systems

You can install Windows 95 on machines running other operating systems and have the capability to boot up to either operating system. This end result is called *dual booting.*

Test Tip

This section covers the following exam objective: Install Windows 95– Dual Boot.

MS-DOS

When you install Windows 95 onto a machine that already has MS-DOS 3.2 or later on it, it creates a dual boot automatically. During setup, if you install Windows 95 into an existing Windows 3.x directory, Setup deletes any MS-DOS files that might conflict with Windows 95. It is not necessary to know which files it deletes for the exam. If you want to know which files it deletes, check Chapter 6 of the Windows 95 Resource Kit. If you don't install into an existing Windows 3.x directory, all MS-DOS files are retained.

During setup, Windows 95 renames the files in Table 1.3 for future use during dual booting.

Table 1.3. MS-DOS file names changed during Windows 95 setup.

MS-DOS filename	Changed to
COMMAND.COM	COMMAND.DOS
CONFIG.SYS	CONFIG.DOS
AUTOEXEC.BAT	AUTOEXEC.DOS

At system start, when you see the words, "Starting Windows 95", you can press F8, which gives you an option to boot to a previous version of MS-DOS. When selecting that option, the files in Table 1.4 are renamed to those indicated. At that time, the files with the DOS extension are renamed to their original names, and the machine continues to boot up the original files.

Table 1.4. Windows 95 filenames changed during dual bootup.

Windows 95 filename	Changed to
COMMAND.COM	COMMAND.W40
CONFIG.SYS	CONFIG.W40
AUTOEXEC.BAT	AUTOEXEC.W40

After rebooting the machine, the MS-DOS files are renamed back to their DOS extensions, and files having the W40 extension are renamed to their original names. Then, Windows 95 boots up as normal.

Note

If you press F8 and do not see an option to boot to the previous version of DOS, it is because of a missing setting in the MS-DOS.SYS file. You can edit the MS-DOS.SYS by typing

```
attrib -s -r -h ms-dos.sys
```

After changing the attributes, edit it using any text editor. You should ensure that there is the following line under the Options heading:

```
BootMulti=1
```

When you are finished editing the MS-DOS.SYS, be sure and change the attributes back by typing

```
attrib +s +r +h ms-dos.sys
```

Not only can you dual boot your Windows 95 computer with MS-DOS, but you can also dual boot it with Windows 3.*x*. Follow the same guidelines as you would with MS-DOS (because MS-DOS is the OS, not Windows 3.*x*).

The only catch is where you install Windows 95. If you want to dual boot with Windows 3.*x*, make sure that you install Windows 95 into a separate directory. By installing Windows 95 into the same directory as 3.*x*, you will be upgrading (covered later in this chapter), not dual booting.

Windows NT

In Windows NT, you can format hard disk partitions with one of two file systems: FAT or NTFS. You can install Windows 95 on a machine already running Windows NT as long as it is in a separate directory as Windows NT. This installation has to be on a partition formatted with the FAT file system. Any NTFS partitions are not accessible from Windows 95. If the FAT partition that Windows 95 resides on is converted to an NTFS partition, Windows 95 will no longer run.

This section covers the following exam objective: Install Windows 95—Dual Boot with Windows NT.

If you are planning on a dual-boot machine, I suggest that you set up Windows 95 first and then install Windows NT. This is mainly because of how Windows 95 modifies the boot sector of the hard disk.

If you already have NT on the machine and want to install Windows 95 after the fact, reboot the Windows NT machine. At system startup, choose MS-DOS from the boot menu, and then install Windows 95. By doing this, the machine boots up to a file called BOOTSECT.DOS. Any modification that Windows 95 setup makes to the boot sector is made to this file and does not affect the boot sector information that Windows NT needs.

If you install Windows NT 3.5*x* into the same directory as Windows 95, you will no longer be able to use Windows 95. This is because Windows NT 3.5*x* uses DLLs similar to those in Windows 3.*x*. These DLLs replace existing ones in the System directory.

continues

> If you install Windows NT 4.0 into the same directory as Windows 95, you will no longer be able to use Windows 95. This is not only because of the device drivers but also because the registries between Windows NT 4.0 and Windows 95 are different.

After you have successfully installed Windows 95 as a dual boot with Windows NT, you have to reinstall any existing applications already installed in Windows NT in Windows 95 so that you can make the appropriate Registry entries. Also, you have to install any new applications twice, once inside each operating system.

OS/2

Dual booting with OS/2 is supported. Windows 95 must be installed on a FAT partition. If any HPFS partitions exist, they will not be accessible from Windows 95. It cannot be installed into the same directory as OS/2. Also, Windows 95 cannot migrate the desktop or any other settings from OS/2.

Because Windows 95 Setup cannot run from within OS/2, you need to start it from an MS-DOS prompt. If you have the OS/2 Boot Manager installed, Windows 95 disables it. After setup is complete, use the OS/2 boot disk and run the OS/2 version of FDISK. This restores the Boot Manager and Windows 95 will operate normally. Once again, you must reinstall all applications for Registry changes to take effect.

DR DOS

DR DOS is a disk operating system created by Novell. When you install Windows 95, it is upgraded and cannot be made to dual boot with Windows 95.

1.3.4. Common Setup Switches

In Figure 1.5, you see some common Setup switches. *Switches* are basically variations of how a program executes. These particular switches pertain to the setup of Windows 95.

The switches that you have available for use when running Setup from MS-DOS differ from those available to you when running Setup from within Windows. Table 1.5 summarizes the setup switches for both MS-DOS and from within Windows.

Figure 1.5.

The Windows 95 Setup switches.

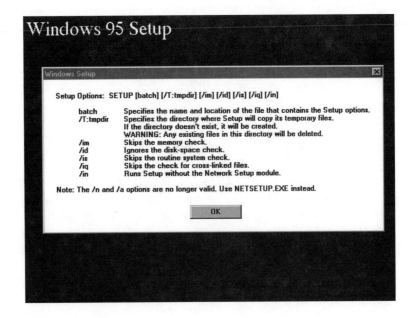

Table 1.5. Windows 95 Setup switches.

MS-DOS Switch	Windows Switch	Function
/C		Does not load SmartDrv.
/ID	/ID	Does not check for disk space.
/IL		Installs Logitech mouse driver.
/IM	/IM	Ignores conventional memory check.
	/IN	Does not run Network Setup module.
/IS	/IS	Skips the routine system check.
/IQ	/IQ	Skips check for cross-linked files. This switch is used if the /IS is used.
/T:<PATH>	/T:<PATH>	Installs the temporary setup files to location specified. The directory that you specify must already exist before you run Setup.
<BATCHFILENAME>		Specifies the name and location of the batch script file that contains the setup options. This option is used without a /.
/?	/?	Help.

You will want to know these command-line switches like the back of your hand. It is very common to see *at least* one exam question on them.

1.4. Upgrading from Windows for Workgroups

If you choose to do a new installation, be prepared to do the floppy shuffle. The full version of Windows 95 is not available on CD-ROM. The only way to get it on CD-ROM is to buy the upgrade version. Most people that have dealt with software know that, in most instances, the upgrade version and the full version of software have few differences. The upgrade version of Windows 95 searches for software that meets the upgrade requirements. If it does not find an upgradable product, it prompts the user to insert a disk from one of the qualifying products to verify that the user does have a copy. If not, Windows 95 does not install.

This section covers the following exam objective: Install Windows 95—Upgrade.

After you start the setup program, Windows runs ScanDisk to check for hard drive errors. After ScanDisk completes, Setup searches the hard disk(s) for any previous versions of Windows 3.*x* or later. If it finds a version of Windows, if prompts the user whether it is OK to start this version of Windows (if Setup was not executed within Windows already).

The Windows setup program is actually a Windows-based application. This means that you need Windows to be running for Windows to use the setup process. Sound confusing? Well, if you already are running setup from a previous version of Windows (3.11 for example), then you're all set. However, if you are installing from MS-DOS, or if an existing version of Windows is not found, Setup copies the necessary files to get a minimal copy of Windows 95 up and running. After it starts the protected-mode (Windows) portion of Setup, the License Agreement is displayed. After the user has agreed to the License Agreement, the Upgrade Check follows. The

1

user is then alerted that an upgradable product was not found and that Setup will search for the product. If one is not found, the user is then prompted for the setup disk of the upgradable product.

So you have an upgradable product (Windows 3.*x*) and you want to upgrade to Windows 95. After you've passed the License Agreement and Upgrade Check, you see the Welcome to Setup screen in Figure 1.6. This screen gives you a quick overview of the installation process.

Figure 1.6.
The Welcome to Setup screen.

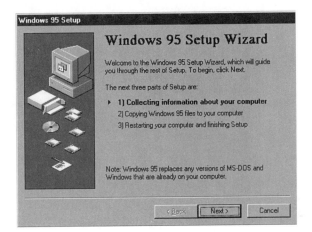

1.4.1. Incorporating User Preferences

After clicking Next, you see a screen (see Figure 1.7) that asks you where you would like to install Windows 95. Simply specify the directory in which the previous version of Windows exists. Setup converts any existing Program Groups to folders on the Start menu, and any icons in those groups become shortcuts within those folders. After the conversion, the Program Group files (GRP extension) that contain the groups' settings remain so that the Windows 3.*x* Program Manager will still function.

1.4.2. Importing INI File Settings

When Windows 95 is installed, the Registry replaces the majority of the INI files of Windows 3.*x*, but the WIN.INI, SYSTEM.INI, and WINFILE.INI files still remain in the Windows directory. Even though Windows 95 doesn't need these files to run, they are maintained for backward compatibility. Think of it this way: If you install a 16-bit program that was developed before Windows 95 was around, it doesn't understand that it needs to put information into the Registry. It starts looking around for those INI files. Any programs installed still have the old INI files there if they need to put configuration information in them.

Figure 1.7.
The Choose
Directory screen.

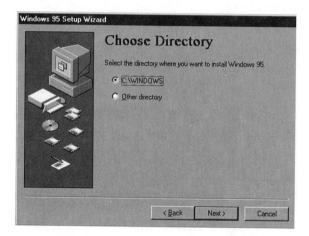

If you install Windows 95 over the top (in the same directory) of Windows 3.*x*, the settings in the WIN.INI, SYSTEM.INI, and WINFILE.INI are automatically copied to the Registry.

1.5. Installation Steps

When starting the installation process, it might differ from installation to installation depending on what installation methods you choose and what type of operating system the computer already has on it. For example, let's say you need to install two machines. One machine has Windows 3.11 and the other MS-DOS. The first machine also needs to be on your company network. The other, because you will be using it for training, does not need to be on the network. Another way they might differ depends on what components of Windows 95 you want installed on the different machines. For example, you might want to remove the games from the training computer, but go with the standard options with the first. These are just a few things you might need to think about that can make the installation process differ (ever so slightly) from machine to machine.

Additionally, you might see different setup processes between the first release of Windows 95 and the OEM Service Release 2 (OSR2). Although the differences are minimal, I just thought I'd warn you up front.

Because this might differ slightly, I will show you the steps necessary after you have passed all the initial stages of setup and after you have reached the Choose Directory screen (refer to Figure 1.7).

After you have chosen your directory, Setup prompts you with four choices. These choices (see Figure 1.8) allow you to specify what components of Windows 95 to install. There are three pre-configured options: Typical, Portable, and Compact.

Typical setup is what most people choose. It gives the most commonly wanted components. That's why they call it typical.

Portable setup is most commonly used for laptops and notebook computers. It gives some additional functionality such as being able to suspend the laptop as opposed to shutting it down.

If you are limited in the amount of disk space, or if you only want a minimum number of files copied to your hard disk, you can select the Compact option.

The last option, Custom, allows you to define which components to install.

Figure 1.8.

The Setup Options screen.

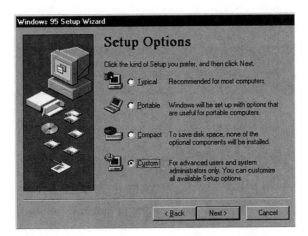

I am choosing the Custom option. The next thing that Windows 95 wants you to provide varies between the first release and OSR2. I will walk you through the steps of installing each version in the lab exercise. For now, I'll skip over to the Select Components screen (see Figure 1.9).

In this dialog box, you can specify exactly which components you want Windows 95 to install. If you had selected any other option besides the Custom option, you would not have been shown this dialog box. If you want to change this later, you can do so from within Windows 95 by selecting the Add/Remove Programs applet in the Control Panel.

Figure 1.9.

The Setup Options screen.

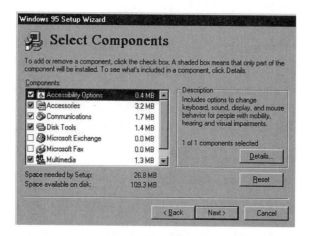

Another option that comes with the Custom setup is selecting which network components you want installed. In Figure 1.10, you see what components Windows 95 automatically selected for me. I will discuss networks, protocols, and other related components in Chapter 6.

Figure 1.10.

The Setup Options screen.

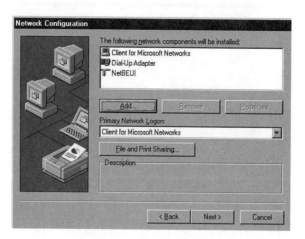

The rest of the setup is a relatively straightforward process. You should become familiar with installing Windows 95. In the lab exercise, you will find step-by-step instructions for installing a Windows 95 computer using either the original release or OSR2.

1.6. Uninstalling Windows 95

If you need to remove Windows 95, you can certainly do so. Let's say, for example, that you prefer to go back to your old operating system, such as Windows 3.11. Another example might be that you prefer to install a different operating system, such as OS/2. Rather than attempt to upgrade Windows 95 to OS/2, you would rather uninstall Windows 95, return to Windows 3.11 (or other previous operating system), and then upgrade the older operating system to OS/2.

There are several ways to remove Windows 95; some easier than others, and some more destructive than others. If you had Windows 95 save your previous configuration, and you have a Windows 95 system disk (sometimes called the emergency boot disk), you are in luck.

 This section covers the following exam objective: Install Windows 95–Uninstall.

If you did specify that Windows 95 save a copy of your previous operating system, boot up to the Windows 95 system disk and run `uninstal.exe`. This determines which files should be replaced or deleted and starts the process. If you're not sure that you have the previous version saved, try it anyhow. If you do not have the proper files, it does not run and prompts you with an error message similar to Figure 1.11.

Figure 1.11.

Uninstall error message.

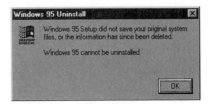

If you receive this error, or one like it, you have to take more drastic measures.

1.7. Troubleshooting Installations

There are two main aspects of troubleshooting installations: troubleshooting when things go wrong during setup and troubleshooting when things go wrong directly after setup.

This section partially covers the following exam objective: Diagnose and resolve Installation Failures.

1.7.1. Problems During Setup

The main problem you might run across when setting up Windows 95 is the system crashing or hanging up during Setup. Some measures are already in place that allow the Windows 95 Setup program to recover from these problems automatically. If a system crashes during setup, a binary file called DETCRASH.LOG is created, but the DETCRASH.LOG does not work alone. Setup also creates a text-based SETUPLOG.TXT file. This file lists everything that took place during setup and whether it was a success or not. In case of a crash, Setup uses both the SETUPLOG.TXT and DETCRASH.LOG files to ensure it doesn't crash twice on the same thing (causing an endless loop).

If the machine crashes during setup, do not warm boot the machine. In other words, stay away from Ctrl+Alt+Del. A warm boot does not allow ISA devices to reinitialize. Cold boot the machine by completely turning it off.

Even though the system might crash several times, continue to restart the machine. Setup continues to bypass whatever caused it to crash in the previous crash and moves the setup right along.

Another file created during setup is a text-based file called DETLOG.TXT, which contains a listing of all hardware detected during setup. Because this is a text-based file, you can use it to determine which components were successfully detected and which ones were not. With that information, you can narrow down a possible hardware problem.

Do not delete any of these files during your process of troubleshooting. Deleting them only causes more problems when you attempt to rerun Setup. Deleting the files causes the system to crash due to the same reasons; these files provide the Windows 95 setup with information about

1

what caused the crash, thus allowing it to avoid the same problem twice.

1.7.2. Problems After Setup

Two things usually go wrong with Windows 95 at Startup after the initial installation. The first problem results from the wrong programs starting automatically at bootup. The second problem usually is more drastic: Windows 95 doesn't start. Let's take a look at both.

Wrong Programs Start at Windows 95 Bootup

Windows 95 includes a startup option very similar to that of Windows 3.*x*. Any programs and/or batch files that are contained in the Startup folder automatically start at bootup. An example of this might be a virus scanning utility.

The Startup folder's default location is in the Start Menu folder, which is in the Windows folder. Therefore, by double-clicking the Windows folder in the Explorer, you should be able to find the Start Menu folder. Double-clicking the Start Menu folder should reveal the Startup folder. Simply delete any reference to the program that you do not want to start up automatically.

If that doesn't fix the problem or if the programs do not appear in the Startup folder, you can take a look at this Registry entry using the Registry Editor:

```
Hkey_Current_User\Software\Windows\CurrentVersion\Explorer\Shell Folders
```

The value of that entry should be

```
Startup=<WinDir>\Start Menu\Startup
```

I used *WinDir* as a variable. You should replace it with the drive and directory where you installed Windows 95. If the entry doesn't point to that directory, there's your problem. Believe it or not, I have run across machines that somehow mysteriously had this key pointing to the Microsoft Office directory. Yep, you guessed it; when the machine started up, all of the Office apps started automatically.

Windows 95 Will Not Boot Up

Even though numerous things can cause Windows 95 not to boot up at all, very few things cause it to happen shortly after setup. One of the most common reasons is missing Registry files.

The Windows 95 Registry consists of two files that are required for startup. These files are SYSTEM.DAT and USER.DAT. The SYSTEM.DAT contains all information specific to the system (machine), whereas the USER.DAT contains user-specific settings such as desktop, colors, and so on. Both of the files are automatically backed up with duplicate file names having a DA0 extension.

The USER.DAT isn't as important as the SYSTEM.DAT when it comes to starting up the machine. If the SYSTEM.DAT file is missing, one of two things will happen. First, Windows 95 attempts to restore the missing file automatically by replacing it with the file that has the DA0 extension.

Second, Windows 95 starts up in Safe Mode and displays a dialog box informing you of the Registry problem. The dialog box has only one button: Restore From Backup and Restart. By clicking this button, Windows 95 attempts to restore from the DA0 file(s).

If both the SYSTEM.DAT and SYSTEM.DA0 are missing, the same message as mentioned in the previous paragraph appears, but because both files are missing, Startup can't restore them from backup. To fix this problem, you must either restore the Registry files from backup or run Setup again.

Warning

Do not use the Registry files from another computer; the SYSTEM.DAT is machine-specific. Restore it only from a backup of the computer you are attempting to restore.

Note

You might see a similar error message stating that the Registry is missing even if the files are there and not corrupted. If you do, check the WinDIR= entry in the MSDOS.SYS file. Its value should be the directory on the hard disk where Windows exists.

I will discuss troubleshooting more throughout the book and specifically in Chapter 13, "Troubleshooting Windows 95."

Lab

The lab consists of review questions pertaining to this chapter and provides an opportunity to apply the knowledge that you've learned with this chapter. You can find answers to the review questions in Appendix B.

Questions

1. Which of the following machines do not meet the minimum guidelines for Windows 95? Choose all that apply:

   A. 386DX, 8MB RAM, 320MB Hard Drive

   B. 386DX2, 4MB RAM, 400MB Hard Drive

   C. 386SX, 16MB RAM, 850MB Hard Drive

   D. Pentium, 8MB RAM, 400MB Hard Drive

2. Which of the following Setup options does not create a working copy of Windows 95?

   A. Floppy

   B. CD-ROM

   C. Network

   D. Shared

   E. Batch

3. A company has asked you to help determine which operating system to migrate to in its different workcenters. The company has already decided that it will be either Windows 95 or Windows NT. It has four workcenters. In the first workcenter, four people will do word processing, spreadsheets, and other general administrative work. In the second workcenter, 20 people will be working with accounting information, payroll, and accounts payable. They will also be doing some minimal word processing. In the third workcenter, around six to ten people will be working with computer-aided design and graphics. The fourth workcenter will consist of ten machines shared by manufacturing personnel who will need them from time to time to do word processing and basic spreadsheets.

Using this scenario, which operating system would be appropriate for the first workcenter?

A. Windows 95

B. Windows NT Workstation

4. Using the scenario given in Question 3, which operating system would be appropriate for the second workcenter?

A. Windows 95

B. Windows NT Workstation

5. Using the scenario in Question 3, which operating system would be appropriate for the third workcenter?

A. Windows 95

B. Windows NT Workstation

6. Using the scenario in Question 3, which operating system would be appropriate for the fourth workcenter?

A. Windows 95

B. Windows NT Workstation

7. Which of the following files would contain useful information about hardware found during Windows 95 setup?

A. DETCRASH.LOG

B. SETUPLOG.TXT

C. DETLOG.TXT

D. HARDWARE.LOG

8. To upgrade the desktop settings and program groups from Windows 3.11 to Windows 95, copy all files having GRP and INI extensions to the folder containing the Windows 95 files.

A. True

B. False

9. Which of the following statements are true about installing Windows 95?

   A. Windows 3.1 can be upgraded to Windows 95 by installing into the same directory.

   B. Windows 3.11 can be upgraded to Windows 95 by installing into the same directory.

   C. Windows NT Workstation 3.51 can be upgraded to Windows 95 by installing into the same directory.

   D. Windows NT Workstation 4.0 can be upgraded to Windows 95 by installing into the same directory.

Exercises

This lab assumes that you have a machine that meets the minimum requirements including a CD-ROM. Some of the options you learned about in this chapter will be applied in subsequent labs. Also, it is assumed that you have an Ethernet network card installed for subsequent labs.

Whenever you are prompted for a logon name and password, use a valid user name and password for your network.

In this lab, you will install Windows 95.

Installation of Windows 95 (Original Release)

1. Insert the CD-ROM and access it.

2. Type **SETUP** and press Enter.

3. If you are running setup from MS-DOS, press Enter to begin ScanDisk.

4. After ScanDisk is complete and all errors, if any, are repaired, click Continue to begin setup.

5. Read the Software License Agreement and click Yes to continue.

6. The Windows 95 Setup Wizard dialog box appears. Click Next to continue.

7. If you are upgrading an existing version of Windows, choose the appropriate directory by clicking the Other Directory option. Otherwise, click Next to accept the default directory.

8. Select Custom in the Setup Options dialog box and click Next.

9. Put in your name and the name of your company, if any.

10. Type in the CD-ROM key number for your CD-ROM. This is usually on the back of the CD-ROM case.

11. Allow Setup to detect installed hardware by clicking Next.

12. Setup then asks you if you would like for it to scan for additional hardware such as a sound card. Click the appropriate boxes pertaining to hardware that you have installed and click Next.

13. The Get Connected dialog box appears. At this time, we are not going to install any of the options, so click Next to continue.

14. View what the default options are in the Select Components box and click Next.

15. In the Network Configuration dialog box, view what hardware it detected. Ensure that your network card was found and appropriately installed. If TCP/IP was installed, select it and click Remove (this will be installed in a later lab). Click Next to continue.

16. Type in a name for your computer to use on the network (computer names on a network must be unique). Choose defaults for other options by clicking Next.

17. The Computer Settings dialog box appears. This box contains all basic information about your computer. Click Next to continue.

18. We will create a startup disk. This startup disk contains files that will help you recover Windows 95 in the event of a system crash. You need a blank, formatted 1.44 3 1/2-inch disk. Click Next.

19. Windows 95 Setup informs you that it will begin to copy files to the hard disk. Click Next to begin copying.

20. Setup informs you to insert a disk into the floppy drive to create the startup disk. Click OK.

21. After Setup has finished creating the startup disk, it informs you to remove the disk. Click OK, and files transfer.

22. When the files are transferred, Setup restarts the computer. Click Finish to restart.

23. Choose the appropriate time zone, date, and time and click Close.

24. The Add Printer Wizard appears. We will be adding a printer later, so click Cancel.

25. Setup is complete. Click OK to restart the computer.

1

Installation of Windows 95 (OSR2)

1. Insert the CD-ROM and access it.

2. Type **SETUP** and press Enter.

3. If you are running setup from MS-DOS, press Enter to begin ScanDisk.

4. After ScanDisk is complete and all errors, if any, are repaired, click Continue to begin setup.

5. Read the Software License Agreement and click Yes to continue.

6. The Windows 95 Setup Wizard dialog box appears. Click Next to continue.

7. If you are upgrading an existing version of Windows, choose the appropriate directory by clicking the Other Directory option. Otherwise, click Next to accept the default directory.

8. Select Custom in the Setup Options dialog box and click Next.

9. Put in the OEM Certificate number.

10. Allow Setup to detect installed hardware by clicking Next.

11. Setup then asks you if you would like for it to scan for additional hardware such as a sound card. Click the appropriate boxes pertaining to hardware that you have installed and click Next.

12. View what the default options are in the Select Components box and click Next.

13. In the Network Configuration dialog box, view what hardware it detected. Ensure that your network card was found and appropriately installed. If TCP/IP was installed, select it and click Remove (this will be installed in a later lab). Click Next to continue.

14. Type in a name for your computer to use on the network (computer names on a network must be unique). Choose defaults for other options by clicking Next.

15. The Computer Settings dialog box appears. This box contains all basic information about your computer. Click Next to continue.

16. We will create a startup disk. This startup disk contains files that will help you recover Windows 95 in the event of a system crash. You need a blank, formatted 1.44 3 1/2-inch disk. Click Next.

17. Windows 95 Setup informs you that it will begin to copy files to the hard disk. Click Next to begin copying.

18. Setup informs you to insert a disk into the floppy drive to create the startup disk. Click OK.

19. After Setup has finished creating the startup disk, it informs you to remove the disk. Click OK, and files transfer.

20. When the files are transferred, Setup restarts the computer. Click Finish to restart.

21. Choose the appropriate time zone, date, and time and click Close.

22. The Add Printer Wizard appears. We will be adding a printer later, so click Cancel.

23. Setup is complete. Click OK to restart the computer.

Day 2

Configuring and Personalizing Windows 95

Sporting a drastically different interface, Microsoft has improved Windows 95 leaps and bounds over the older Windows 3.*x* products. The interface is not the only change, however. As the title of this chapter may imply, users can now customize their Windows product better than ever.

Objectives

Customization comes in many formats through many different avenues in Windows 95. In this chapter, I will show you many of these. As for the exam, there aren't any direct exam objectives covered in this chapter. However, Microsoft does expect you to be familiar with the interface. In addition, some of the concepts learned in this chapter will be used throughout the book and, therefore your understanding of these concepts will have some effect on you passing the exam.

2.1. Maneuvering Through Windows 95

Getting around in Windows 95 is much easier than its predecessors. The interface no longer has the cluttered look of the Program Manager. The user of Windows 3.*x* could very easily lose a window and become confused. After a window had dropped behind the Program Manager, it was lost forever in the user's eyes. One big addition to keep the user from losing things is the *taskbar* (see Figure 2.1).

Figure 2.1.

The Windows 95 taskbar.

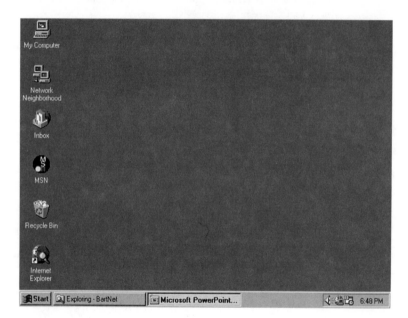

The Windows desktop has changed in several ways. The most familiar change is the addition of the Start button. As the Windows 95 rollout approached, the Start button became famous with the use of catchy tunes and big ads. Even today, you can still find a full- or two-page ad in a magazine or other periodical sporting the Start button.

2.1.1. Everything Is an Object

Almost everything in Windows 95 is an object. Some examples of objects include:

- A document
- A folder
- A shortcut

■ The desktop

■ A thread

Not only is almost everything an object, but every object has properties. The properties of most objects can be modified through the use of a property sheet. This property sheet is a way for you to change what an object can do or what can be done to it. So in essence, you can modify an object's behavior through the use of its property sheet.

By using the secondary mouse button (for most of you, that's the right one), you can bring up a shortcut menu on an object. (Do not confuse this with the shortcut I discuss later.) The reason I call this a *shortcut menu* is because it allows you to save some time. Here are a few items that you can get on a shortcut menu:

■ **Open**—Opens an object with its associated program.

■ **Print**—Prints an object with its associated program.

■ **Quick View**—Views an object without opening its associated program.

■ **Cut**—Removes an object and places it on the Clipboard.

■ **Copy**—Copies an object to the Clipboard.

■ **Delete**—Sends an object to the Recycle Bin (or deletes where appropriate).

■ **Properties**—Opens an object's property sheet.

If you hold down the Shift key when right-clicking the object, you might get a few different or additional items on the shortcut menu. For example, right-clicking a file in the Explorer results in getting an Open option. Clicking Open opens the file with whatever program is associated with that particular file type. If you hold the Shift key down while right-clicking the file (the file has to be selected first), you see an Open With option that allows you to open the file with an alternate program.

The mouse button that you normally use to select items or move items is called the *primary mouse button*. The other button is called the *secondary mouse button*. This might cause confusion because some people (namely, left-handed people) have their mouse buttons swapped so that they're just the opposite. To avoid confusion, whenever I say *right-click*, I mean click the *secondary mouse button*.

If you would like to modify an object's property sheet, point to it with the mouse, right-click, and select Properties from the shortcut menu. After you click on Properties, you see the property sheet of that object.

Property sheets vary from object to object. Some property sheets cannot be modified and only provide information on the object. Take a look at Figure 2.2 for an example of a property sheet.

Figure 2.2.

A property sheet.

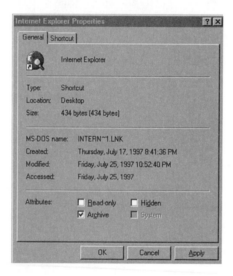

2.1.2. The Start Button

As mentioned earlier, the Start button takes the place of the Program Manager from the Windows 3.*x* products. As you can see from Figure 2.3, you have several options from which to choose. You can also refer to this menu as the Start menu.

The very top option, Programs, contains various program folders and icons. There is no need for double-clicking. Click the Start button, point to the folder you would like to open, and another menu opens up to show that folder's contents. When you are pointing to the icon of a program, just click once to start.

Note

> Want to pull up the Start menu, but your mouse isn't working? No problem. Press Ctrl and Esc simultaneously and Start pops up. From there, you can use your arrow keys to maneuver and Enter to start an application.

Figure 2.3.

The Windows 95
Start Menu.

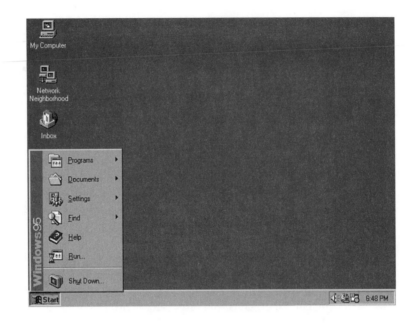

2

Unlike the program groups of earlier Windows products, you can have menus (folders) inside of folders. In Windows 3.*x*, you couldn't have a program group inside of a program group.

The Documents option points to a hidden folder called Recent that contains shortcuts to the most recently used files. By default, the Recent folder is a subfolder inside the Windows folder.

This location differs if you have profiles enabled. For more information on profiles, see Chapter 8, "Locking Down the System: Profiles and Policies."

The Settings options gives you quick and easy access to the Control Panel, the Printers Folder, and settings for the taskbar, which I'll discuss next.

Finding things in Windows 95 is easier. It really surprises me how some network administrators plop a new machine down on a user's desk with Windows 95 on it and give him or her a quick, five-minute tour of the Start button without explaining the Find option. You can perform filename, date, time, and content searches with Find.

You should know how to find files or folders for the exam. Be sure to know all the options available in the Find applet. Also, be aware that the settings of the three tabs work together to allow you to be very specific with your search.

Help has been revamped and improved. The Help option on the Start menu gives you help with Windows 95 topics, of course.

If you would like to execute a command line, choose the Run option. The Run option also sports a Browse option that allows you to look for the command, if you do not know it right off the top of your head. It also features a pull-down list of cached commands that you have run in the past.

The last option is Shut Down. It's never been easier to show the user how to shut down his or her PC. What's even better, when you select the Shut Down the Computer option from the Shut Down Windows dialog box (see Figure 2.4), the computer shuts down and turns the power off. Your PC must support it in the BIOS, of course. Also, notice the Close All Programs and Log On as Different User option.

Figure 2.4.

The Shut Down Windows Dialog Box.

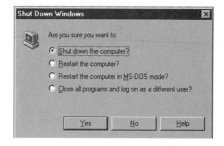

The Close All Programs and Log On as a Different User option is relatively self-explanatory. When you need to log on as someone else or someone would like to use your computer, you can log off using this option. Be aware that all programs shut down.

Other options of the Shut Down command are Restart the Computer and Restart the Computer in MS-DOS Mode. The first option reboots the computer for you and returns to Windows 95. The latter allows you to reboot the computer to a DOS prompt.

2.1.3. The Taskbar

The Start button resides on the taskbar. It displays buttons for all programs and Windows that are open at any time. The user can see what is open by glancing at the taskbar. Figure 2.5 gives an example. This keeps the user from losing a window in the shuffle. If the user does lose track of one, he can bring it back on top by simply clicking the button for that window that resides on the taskbar.

Figure 2.5.

The Windows 95 taskbar appears at the bottom of the window.

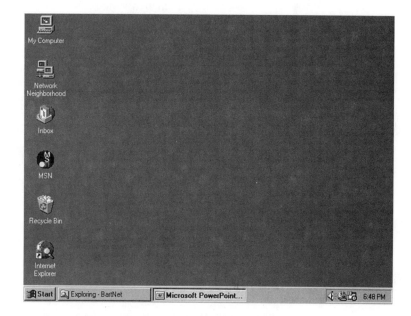

On the right side of the taskbar, you see a clock displayed by default. Changing the time on your computer is as simple as double-clicking the clock. The right side of the taskbar can also display icons that represent different things. For example, in Figure 2.5, you see three icons representing (from left to right) sound volume, the Personal Web Server, and the System Agent.

You can modify the taskbar by bringing up its property sheet. (Remember, it is an object too.) Options on the property sheet include:

■ **Always on top**—Keeps the taskbar in sight.

■ **Auto Hide**—Drops the taskbar out of view when not needed. Taking the mouse to the bottom of the screen pops it back up.

■ **Show small icons on Start menu**—Large icons become small.

■ **Show Clock**—Keeps your eye on the time.

In the sample screen above the options, you can see what effect each one of these options has. You can also get to the taskbar properties by right-clicking a blank area of the taskbar. This menu not only gets you the properties but also gives you a few options about window arrangements.

Note

During my assistance in Windows 95 deployment, I have come across several instances where new Windows 95 users have made their taskbars disappear and couldn't find them.

You might be thinking that they had Auto Hide on, but that's not the case. You see, you can resize the taskbar. It's a handy option if you have more than five or six windows open. It allows the buttons on the taskbar to resize so you can read their labels. It's simple. Just point to the top border of the taskbar and you will see a double-headed arrow. Click, hold, and resize.

In the case of the missing taskbar, it was resized downward so that it was just a thin strip. In most cases, it was actually off of the monitor screen. A little screen adjustment and resizing, and it was back.

2.1.4. Application Shortcuts

An *application shortcut* is just what the name implies. A shortcut is an icon that points to the executable file of a program or even to a folder. Shortcuts can reside on the desktop or in a folder.

Creating a shortcut is relatively simple. One way is by right-clicking the desktop and selecting New and then Shortcut. The Create Shortcut Wizard walks you through creating a shortcut. I prefer the drag-and-drop method. You can open a window, such as the Windows 95 Explorer (which I discuss in 4.2.1), point to the executable program, hold the primary mouse button down, and drag it to the desktop. When you let go, it automatically creates a shortcut. Be careful; this only works with EXE and COM files. With all other files, it performs a move by default. If you would like to create a shortcut to a document, for example, you must hold the Ctrl and Shift keys down while performing the operation.

I think that probably needs some clarification. In Figure 2.6, you see me dragging an executable file from the Explorer to the desktop (dragging it from left to right). Notice the arrow next to the mouse pointer. This represents that I am creating a shortcut. It simply creates an icon that points to the actual executable file.

Figure 2.6.

Creating a shortcut on the desktop.

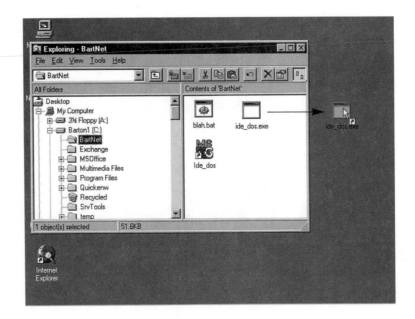

2

If the icon has a plus sign instead of an arrow, you are performing a copy. This means that a copy of the file still resides in its original location, but now a copy also resides on the desktop.

If the mouse pointer has neither the arrow nor the plus sign, the operation is a move. Moving a file means that it no longer resides in its original location, but only where you are dragging it.

The neat thing about shortcuts is that they can be temporary. Say, for instance, you are working with a contract for the next few days, and you want to create a shortcut to it so you don't have to trudge through a File-Open dialog box. Create the shortcut on the desktop and leave the file wherever you want to store it. When you're done with the contract, you can delete the shortcut without affecting the file.

You can also create folders directly on the desktop. Folders allow you to store things in them such as shortcuts, documents, or other folders. Right-clicking the desktop and pointing to New reveals several options of things that you can create directly on the desktop. The types of things that show up under the New option depend on what applications you have installed. Take a look at Figure 2.7 to see what my options are.

Figure 2.7.

Creating an item on the desktop.

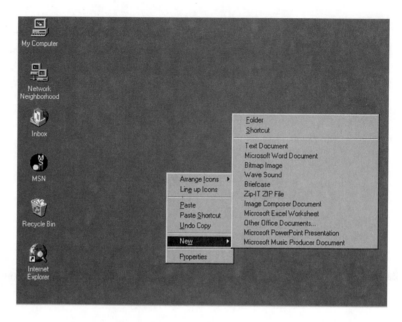

If you're wondering where items on the desktop are really stored, they do equate to an actual hard disk location. The default location is a hidden folder called Desktop that is within the Windows folder where you installed Windows 95. Within that folder, you can see the shortcuts (they have LNK as their extension).

 Note   This location differs if you have profiles enabled. For more information on profiles, see Chapter 8.

Because shortcuts are considered objects, you can modify a shortcut's properties by right-clicking the shortcut and selecting Properties. By selecting the Shortcut tab, you can modify numerous things. Some examples are these:

■ **Target**—What executable file the shortcut points to.

■ **Start in**—What folder to start in (this is the equivalent to the working directory).

■ **Run**—Whether to run the shortcut in a window, full screen, or minimized.

2.1.5. Modifying the Start Options

One part of customizing Windows 95 involves customizing the Start menu. Like most Microsoft products, there is more than one way to accomplish it. Before I tell you how, let me clarify the fact that program icons on the Start menu are nothing more than shortcuts. Creating an icon on the Start menu is identical to creating a shortcut. The submenus are nothing more than folders. Creating a submenu is the same as creating a folder.

The first way to customize the Start menu is through the taskbar settings, so from the Start menu, point to Settings and click Taskbar. At the top of the Taskbar Properties dialog box, you see Start Menu Programs as a tab. Selecting this tab produces something similar to Figure 2.8. In that box, you have three options:

- Add
- Remove
- Advanced

Figure 2.8.

The Start Menu Programs dialog box.

If you want to add or remove items from the Start menu, I think the first two options are self-explanatory. They walk you through the process using a series of simple screens.

The Advanced option shows you the entire layout of the Start menu in a folder and subfolder hierarchy in the Windows 95 Explorer similar to Figure 2.9.

Figure 2.9.

Advanced editing of the Start menu.

I prefer using the Explorer to modify the Start menu, simply because I enjoy working with the Explorer, but I do not prefer going through the Taskbar properties to get to it. If you look again at Figure 2.9, you'll see that Programs is at the top of the hierarchy. You'd have to open another window to drag an EXE into the Start menu to create a shortcut.

The Start menu coincides with an actual folder on the hard drive. It is for that reason that I choose to open a copy of the Windows 95 Explorer and modify the Start menu there. Notice the full path of the Start menu in Figure 2.10, which is a snapshot of the Explorer. Opening it this way allows me to drag and drop shortcuts from anywhere in the Explorer onto the Start menu without opening several windows. Once again, creating a submenu is as simple as creating a folder.

Another quick and easy way to add an item to the Start menu is by dragging an item and dropping it on the Start button. Doing so produces something similar to what happened when I dragged a Microsoft Word document and dropped it on the Start button. See Figure 2.11 for the results.

2.2. Exploring in Windows 95

There are several ways to get around the Windows 95 interface. To get to the files in Windows 3.*x*, you were pretty much stuck with using the File Manager. Not with Windows 95; not only do you have the Explorer (which replaces the File Manager), but you also have the My Computer and Network Neighborhood icons on the desktop.

Figure 2.10.

Exploring the Start menu.

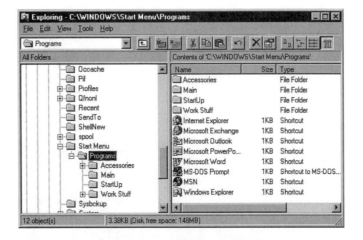

Figure 2.11.

The First Quarter item added to the Start menu.

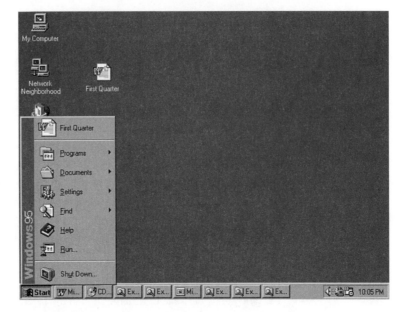

2.2.1. The Explorer

My first taste of the Windows 95 Explorer was not a good one. I was an avid Windows 3.11 user and liked the File Manager. But after using the Explorer for a while, I realized how much more flexible the Explorer is—the Explorer can do so much more than the File Manager can.

In Figure 2.12, you see a sample of the new Explorer. At first glance, it's similar to the File Manager. You have the tree on the left and the contents on the right, but all drives appear simultaneously on the left. In File Manager, your drive letters appeared at the top. To see the different drives, you had to open several Windows. Not only do local drives show up, but all network drives also show up. Notice also that the Network Neighborhood, Control Panel, and Printers Folder are present in the Explorer.

Figure 2.12.

The Windows 95 Explorer.

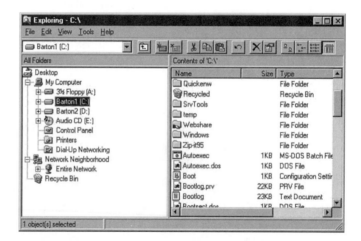

One example of an advancement that I like is the capability to expand the tree on the left without affecting what is being viewed on the right. For example, I want to drag a file that is in C:\Bartnet to a folder such as C:\Windows\Start Menu\ Programs\Accessories to create a shortcut on my Start menu. Notice on the right in Figure 2.13 that I am viewing the contents of C:\Bartnet (I simply clicked the folder), but on the left, I clicked the plus signs to expand the tree to my destination location. Now all I have to do is drag and drop (from right to left).

Note

When dragging a file or folder around in the Explorer, it is important to know the consequences of dropping it. When you are dragging a file or folder to another folder on the same hard disk, by default, you perform a move of the files if you drop them. If you hold down the Ctrl key while dropping it, though, the files are copied and left in their particular position.

Moving from one drive to another is another story. By default, it copies by holding the Shift key to move the files.

Note

If you have been using the Explorer and are experienced with the File Manager, you might be wondering where the Expand All option is (as in expand all directories). Well, you won't find it under any menu.

Click the folder (or drive) you would like expanded and press the asterisk (only the 1 on the number pad will work).

2

You can customize the Explorer in a multitude of ways. The majority of this customization relies on how you view the information within Explorer. With that in mind, take a look at Figure 2.14 at the View menu options.

You might notice that the first two options are on/off options. In other words, the toolbar and status bar are either viewed or not, depending on whether there are check marks by them.

The next four options are Large Icons, Small Icons, List, and Details. Choosing one of the four determines how the files are viewed in the contents (right) pane of the Explorer. Try them all out to see which you prefer. As you can see, Details is my favorite.

Figure 2.13.

Dragging an item in the Explorer.

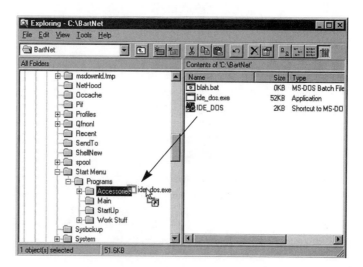

Figure 2.14.

The Explorer View menu.

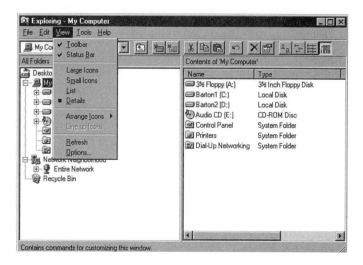

Beneath that, you have a few ways of arranging those icons along with a Refresh option.

That brings us to Options. Selecting Options produces a dialog box (see Figure 2.15) that gives you several more configuration options. At the top is the capability to either show all files or to hide some of the more common system files. This is a handy option to have on users' machines. Out of site, out of mind, and away from the Delete key.

Figure 2.15.

Explorer's View Options.

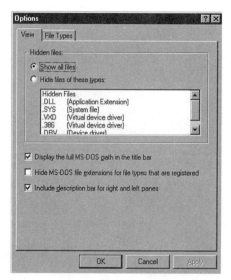

The three options at the bottom are self-explanatory. As you can see, I like to see my file extensions. For those of you who are used to MS-DOS and Windows 3.*x*, the fact that Explorer hides the extensions by default can be annoying.

The File Types tab (see Figure 2.16) lets you associate files with their parent applications. It does so by associating the file's extension with that particular application. I find it easier to right-click the file in the Explorer and choose Open With. The Open With option, automatically associates the file to the application you pick (if it is not already associated with another application).

Figure 2.16.

Explorer's File Types Options.

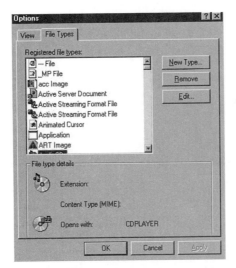

Working with folders (directories) couldn't be easier. Because folders are also considered objects, you can bring up the properties of folders by right-clicking them and selecting Properties. Notice that, when you right-click a file, you also see items such as Cut, Copy, and Paste as a part of the menu. Moving and copying folders is as simple as cutting, copying, and pasting text in a word processor. You might also notice a Rename option. By selecting Rename, you can easily rename a folder. Try that in your Windows 3.*x* File Manager. Of course, you also have the same old drag-and-drop functionality you had in File Manager.

Another way that you might consider customizing the Explorer is through the use of command-line switches. You can use these command-line switches through the Run option of the Start menu or through the use of shortcuts. Take a look at Table 2.1 for a list of the switches and syntax.

2

Table 2.1. Windows Explorer command-line switches.

Switch	Action
/n	Opens a new window for each item selected.
/e	Opens an Explorer view similar to the File Manager.
/root,<object>	Specifies the root level, the level to begin. For example, the root would be a computer name or drive.
/select,<sub object>	The folder to be opened upon execution of the Explorer command.

Syntax would be as follows:

```
EXPLORER.EXE [/n] [/e] [/root,<object>] [/select,<sub object>]
```

Example:

```
EXPLORER /n /root,\\xserver
```

You can reach the Explorer in several ways. Not only can you use the shortcut from the Start menu, but you can also use the Explore option available when you right-click the My Computer icon, the Network Neighborhood icon, or the Start button.

The folder that receives emphasis (is opened upon opening Explorer) depends on which object you click. My Computer and Network Neighborhood receive emphasis when clicked. When you click the Start button, it automatically opens up to the Start menu in the Explorer.

2.2.2. Navigating the Local System

Another way of getting to the files and folders, among other things, is through an icon sitting on the desktop called My Computer. Although it may serve the same purpose as the Explorer, it has a little different look and feel.

By double-clicking the My Computer icon, you see something similar to Figure 2.17. There are separate icons for each local drive, the Control Panel, the Printers folder, and the Dial-Up Networking folder (if installed). If there are any mapped network drives, they appear in the My Computer window also.

When you open up another object in My Computer, it creates a separate window with the contents (see Figure 2.18). If you would like to have it stay within the same window, you can select Options from the View menu and change the Folder option (see Figure 2.19). Your choices are these:

Figure 2.17.

The My Computer window.

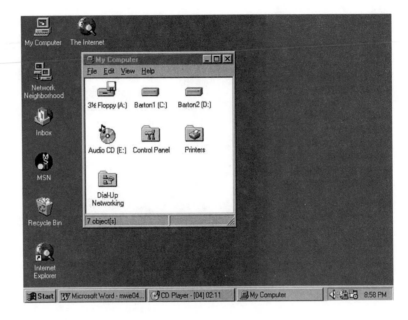

- Browse folders using a separate window for each folder.
- Browse folders using a single window that changes as you open each folder.

Other options from the View menu are very similar to the View menu in the Explorer.

2.2.3. Navigating the Network Neighborhood

If you have network components installed, a Network Neighborhood icon appears on the desktop. The Network Neighborhood icon is similar to the My Computer icon. They both open separate windows for each level that you navigate through. They are different in content. The contents of the Network Neighborhood are just what the name implies. It shows computers on the network at the first level (see Figure 2.20). When you double-click one of the computers, you can see which folders and/or printers that it is sharing out (see Figure 2.21). More aspects of networking and interoperability are covered in Chapter 6, "Linking to Your Network."

Now the Network Neighborhood is organized so that you only see computers that are in your particular workgroup at the first level. Then, if you want to browse other computers, you can see them through the Entire Network option.

Figure 2.18.

The My Computer and C drive windows.

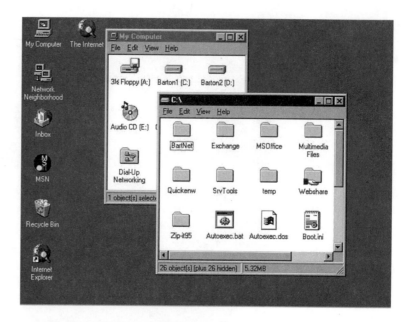

Figure 2.19.

The My Computer Folder options.

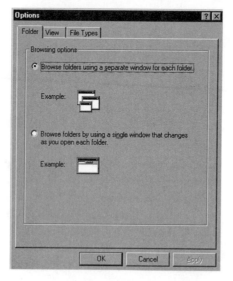

Another way of browsing the Network Neighborhood is through the Explorer. Below all the local and mapped network drives appears a Network Neighborhood icon. By clicking the plus signs next to it, you can easily browse the contents of the network. Figure 2.22 shows the same computer's network shares as does Figure 2.21.

Figure 2.20.
The Network Neighborhood.

Figure 2.21.
A computer's network shares.

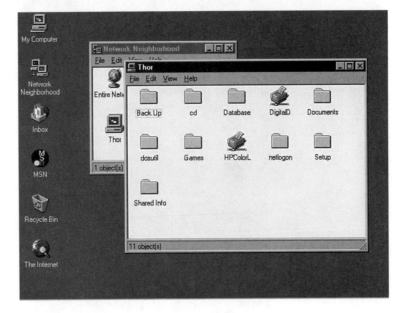

Figure 2.22.

A computer's network shares in Explorer.

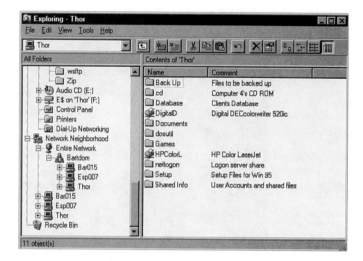

2.3. Establishing Desktop Preferences

You can set the desktop preferences with ease. There are two basic ways to reach the desktop settings. One way is through the Control Panel by clicking the Display icon. Another way is by right-clicking an empty area of the desktop and selecting Properties. Either way produces the dialog box in Figure 2.23.

Figure 2.23.

The Display Properties dialog box.

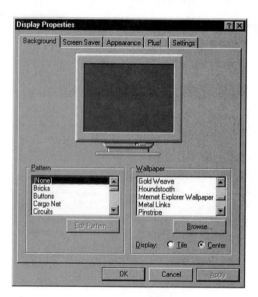

Normally, this box only contains four tabs, but I have installed Microsoft Plus for Windows 95. Also, some OEM versions of Windows 95 will have several more tabs.

The first option is Background. You have several backgrounds to choose from, but any bitmap (BMP) file will do. As long as it is located in the Windows folder, it shows up automatically. There is also a Browse option that allows you to specify a file at another location. Additionally, it allows you to specify not only BMP files but also DIB files.

Screen Saver is self-explanatory. It has several styles to choose from with various settings for each. Also located at this tab are settings for Energy Star-compliant monitors, which are usable if your machine supports this activity.

The Appearance tab has all the settings for the windows themselves. This includes fonts, colors, and sizing. There are several prefabricated color schemes available, or you can set specifics for each item.

The Plus! tab only appears if you have installed the Microsoft Plus software. This software package contains a lot of features and utilities that were intended for Windows 95 but did not make it into the final release because of time constraints. The Plus! tab allows you to change the desktop icons, font smoothing, and other features.

The Settings tab is where you set the number of colors, screen resolution, and which drivers are to be used for your video card. Most computers have advanced enough hardware that allows changing the resolution without restarting the machine as long as the number of colors isn't changed.

Note

This is the first instance in this book where the Apply button actually makes a difference. It brings up a good point. I have heard numerous people battle over the purpose of the Apply button.

Some people believe that you *have* to press the Apply button before pressing OK when you have made changes; otherwise, the changes won't get applied.

Wrong. The Apply button is there for one reason. If you want to apply the changes you've made without closing the window (to preview the changes, for example), click the Apply button. Otherwise, simply pressing the OK button *does* apply the changes as the window closes.

Lab

This lab consists of review questions pertaining to this chapter and provides an opportunity to apply the knowledge that you've learned with this chapter. You can find answers to the review questions in Appendix B.

Questions

1. You can modify the behavior of a Windows 95 object through its _____.

    A. settings

    B. attributes

    C. switches

    D. property sheet

2. What keyboard keys do you press to access the Start menu?

    A. Alt+Tab

    B. Shift+Enter

    C. Ctrl+Esc

    D. Shift+Up Arrow

3. A user is experiencing problems navigating through the Start menu. She is having difficulty opening up an application that she uses daily because she has to go through a series of menus to get to it. How would you make it easier for her to get to her application?

    A. Create a shortcut on the desktop that points to her application.

    B. Drag the icon representing the program directly from a window and drop it on the Start button.

    C. Create an icon for it on her taskbar.

    D. Both A and B.

    E. Both A and C.

4. You want to modify the Start menu. What two paths can you take to access it in order to edit it?

    A. Click Start, point to Settings, and select Taskbar. Then, select the Start Menu Programs tab.

B. Open the Explorer and navigate to its default path, C:\Windows\Programs Menu.

C. Right-click the Start button and click Explore.

D. Both A and B.

E. Both A and C.

5. When you delete a shortcut, it also deletes the application (or other object) that it points to.

A. True.

B. False.

6. What ways can you access the Control Panel?

A. Click Start, point to settings, and select Control Panel.

B. Open the Explorer and navigate to Control Panel.

C. Double-click the My Computer icon.

D. All of the above.

E. Both A and C.

7. A user complains that he has lost his taskbar. Upon investigation, you find that his taskbar is visible when no applications are open, but the minute one is, it disappears and the application is full screen. Taking the mouse to the bottom of the screen does not result in a reappearing taskbar. What could be the best possible solution to the problem?

A. Click the Restore button for the application.

B. In the Control Panel, double-click Display. Remove the check mark from Hide Taskbar.

C. Right-click the taskbar and select Properties. Remove the check mark from Auto Hide.

D. Right-click the taskbar and select Properties. Place a check mark in Always on Top.

8. You have just installed Windows 95 on an end user's machine. You would like to configure the computer so that common system files are out of view from the user in the Explorer without affecting the operability of the files. What is your best possible solution?

A. Do nothing.

B. Select the files that you want hidden, right-click them, and select Properties. In the Properties dialog box, place a check mark in the box next to Hidden.

C. Select the files that you want hidden, right-click them, and select Properties. In the Properties dialog box, click the Miscellaneous tab and select Administrative view only.

9. Jack, a user on your network, prefers using the My Computer instead of the Explorer to view his files, but he doesn't like how many windows he has open after getting to the file he wants. What way would be the best solution to Jack's problem?

A. Open My Computer. From the View menu, select List.

B. Right-click My Computer and select Properties. In the properties dialog box, select the Folders tab and click next to Browse folders by using a single window that changes as you open each folder.

C. Open My Computer. From the View menu, select Options. In the Options dialog box, select the Folders tab and click next to Browse folders by using a single window that changes as you open each folder.

D. Open My Computer. From the View menu, select Details.

10. You have installed a new video card in a Windows 95 machine and have installed the new drivers. Where is the appropriate place to do so?

A. Click Start, point to settings, and select Control Panel. Double-click the Drivers icon.

B. Right-click the desktop. Click the Settings tab. Click the Change Display Type button.

C. Click Start, point to settings, and select Control Panel. Double-click the Display icon. Click the Settings tab. Click the Change Display Type button.

D. Both B and C.

E. Both A and B.

11. A user has a shortcut to a document on the desktop and would like to know an easier way to print it. What would be the best answer?

A. Double-click the icon and select the printer icon from the toolbar.

B. Right-click and select print.

C. Open the My Computer icon and drag the shortcut on top of the print-ers folder.

D. Both B and C.

Exercises

In this lab, you will make some basic configuration changes to Windows 95. This will help you prepare for the exam by meeting the exam objectives:

- Use the Windows 95 interface to create, print, and store a file.
- Add items to the Start menu.
- Configure shortcuts.
- Customize the desktop for a specified set of criteria.
- Configure the taskbar.
- Configure the property sheet for an object.

Start this exercise at the desktop without any other programs running:

1. Right-click the desktop. Point to New and select Text document. Title the new document **text1**.

2. Double-click the new text document and modify it. Save the changes.

3. Right-click the desktop. Point to New and select Folder. Title it **Documents.**

4. Drag the text document and drop it on top of the new folder.

5. Open the folder by double-clicking it.

6. Is the text document there?

7. Add the document to your Start menu by dropping a copy of it on top of the Start button.

8. Open the Explorer. Navigate to the Windows folder.

9. Navigate to the Start menu folder.

10. Click the Start menu folder.

11. Remove the text document by deleting the shortcut.

12. Close the Explorer.

13. Is the document still in the folder?

14. Open the Control Panel.

15. Double-click Display.

16. Modify the wallpaper and screen saver options.

17. Change the resolution from 640×480 to 800×600.

18. Click OK.

19. Right-click the taskbar.

20. Click Properties.

21. Click Auto Hide.

22. Click OK.

As you can see, we covered many topics in a relatively short exercise. You should familiarize yourself with these procedures. In addition, you might want to try accomplishing the same tasks in different ways such as moving files to and from the desktop using the Explorer versus drag and drop.

TEST DAY
FAST FACTS

At exam time, you should have a general understanding of applications and memory and Windows 95. Additionally, you should be sure when it is appropriate or inappropriate to use Regedit to modify the Registry. A general understanding of the Registry is also needed. Here are a few fast facts for you to look over, not only as an introduction to the chapter, but as a great last minute study tool:

- A virtual machine simulates an entire computer's resources to an application.

- All system processes, Windows 16-bit applications, and Windows 32-bit applications run in a single virtual machine called the *system virtual machine*.

- Each MS-DOS program runs on a separate virtual machine called an *MS-DOS virtual machine*.

- A 16-bit application can send the processor only one thread of code at a time for execution.

- A 32-bit application can send the processor multiple threads of code at a time for execution.

- When one 16-bit application stops responding, all 16-bit applications might stop responding. The 32-bit applications are not affected. Ending the hung up application will cause other 16-bit applications to respond once again.

Day 3

Windows 95 Blueprint: Internals and Architecture

An architect is a person who designs and oversees the construction of a building. It is said that no one knows a building like the person who designed and built it. Likewise, with Windows 95, no one knows it better than the programmers who created it. However, you can gain a better appreciation and understanding of Windows 95 by taking a look behind the scenes at the internals and architecture.

I won't try to teach you everything about Windows 95 that the programmers who built it know (I couldn't if I tried). Instead, we'll discuss how memory, applications, and the infamous Registry work in Windows 95. In supporting Windows 95, it is important that you have a basic understanding of how it works. Knowing how it works will not only make it easier for you to understand when something goes wrong, but also how to possibly fix that problem. Additionally, having a better understanding of the internals will help you determine when to deploy a certain type of application over another. These are but a few of the reasons why this information should be on the exam. Let's take a look at the exam objectives.

Objectives

When taking a look at the Microsoft exam objectives covered in this chapter, you will find a quite considerable difference in the objectives from prior Windows 95 exams. Even though there are only two exam objectives listed here, there are many other topics within this chapter that are important when it comes to exam time. Here are the Microsoft exam objectives covered in this chapter:

- ■ Establish application environments for Microsoft MS-DOS applications.

- ■ Perform direct modification of the Registry as appropriate by using Regedit.

3.1. Ring Architecture

Processors that rely on the design of the Intel X86 processor, including AMD and Cyrix brand processors, use Intel ring architecture. Each software component runs within one of four rings numbered from 0 to 3. The lower the number, the more critical that software component is to the system.

Think of each ring as a group. An application, which can be a member of one of these groups, is provided a certain amount of protection by the processor. When applications run, they require a memory space to store their information, transfer data, and so on. Occasionally, some applications try to overtake or write information in the memory address space of other programs. This usually results in either corrupted information or crashing of one or both of the applications. In the attempt to prevent this, the processor tries to protect these applications from each other.

Additionally, the processor gives each group certain privileges to certain system resources. What level of protection and privileges the processor provides depends on which group (or ring) the program is a member of. The lower the number, the more protection and privileges the program receives from the processor.

Whenever the processor needs to run an application in the different ring, it must switch between the rings. Switching between these different rings takes processor time and a considerable amount of memory. Because there is enough protection provided with just two rings, Windows 95 only uses two: Ring 0 and Ring 3. This also accounts for some of the speediness of Windows 95 by cutting out the two inner rings. Let's take a look at what components of Windows 95 are implemented into these two rings.

3.1.1. Ring 0

The main components of Windows 95 run in Ring 0. Within this ring, the processor provides the most protection against other programs and the most privilege to system resources. Such components as the Kernel, GDI, and User Interface (discussed in 3.3) run within Ring 0. Because these very important functions run within Ring 0, if any components crash within Ring 0, they can cause the entire system to crash.

3.1.2. Ring 3

Most other components and software run within Ring 3. Within this ring, the processor doesn't provide any protection. That means the software is on its own, because the processor offers no protection in this ring. If there is going to be any protection provided, they will have to provide it themselves. However, because the processor doesn't provide that protection, Windows 95 steps up for the job and provides this protection.

3.2. Windows 95 Internal

Windows 95 consists of many components, but the three main components are the User, kernel, and graphical device interface (GDI). Each of these core components consists of two DLLs, one of which is 16-bit and the other 32-bit. This means that Windows 95 has 16-bit code as a main part of the operating system.

The reason for this is to ensure backward compatibility and better performance. It keeps the older 16-bit code where needed for backward compatibility, but has newer 32-bit code for increased performance.

The kernel, which handles most virtual memory functions, I/O services, and task scheduling, is predominately 32-bit to ensure that the main core of Windows 95 is fast and reliable.

The GDI takes care of anything that is placed on the screen. Because graphics are nothing more than complex calculations, most of them became 32-bit in Windows 95, but some portions of the code that are smaller functions, such as window management, remained 16-bit for compatibility with older applications.

The User portion manages keyboard, mouse, and other input or output devices. Most aspects of the User portion are still in 16-bit code.

Because you have both 16-bit and 32-bit portions of code that compose the Windows 95 operating system, how do these devices communicate with each other? The kernel provides a service called *thunking* to translate between 16-bit and 32-bit code. This provides the capability of being able to run MS-DOS based, 16-bit, and 32-bit applications at the same time. Thunking translates a 16-bit call into an equivalent 32-bit call.

3.3. Windows 95 Memory Management

One problem with Windows versions prior to Windows 95 was the way they handled memory. Let's think back to when we had only 1MB of usable memory in computers. Remember that? It was segmented into several layers. Figure 3.1 shows a typical setup of the MS-DOS memory model.

Figure 3.1.
The MS-DOS memory model.

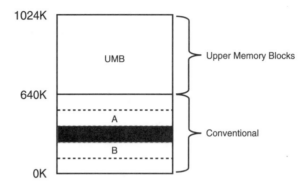

Granted, my job here is to prepare you for the Windows 95 exam, but I think a basic understanding of how things used to be will give you a greater understanding of how the Windows 95 memory model works. With that in mind, I will go a little in-depth with my explanation of memory, but I'm not going to go into great detail telling you about the MS-DOS memory model, such as explaining hexadecimal addressing. In other words, I won't be explaining everything there is to know about memory.

First of all, we started with 1MB of memory. It was segmented into a range of 0K to 640K to be used by applications, and the upper 384K for system use. Portions of the top 384K, called *upper memory blocks* (UMBs) could be used for loading some type of driver because some reserved areas were not always used. You can see an example of this with areas of upper memory that were reserved for CGA monitors (who uses them anymore?).

Then came Lotus, which needed more than 1MB memory. With the help of Intel, they created what we call *expanded memory* (also called *LIM memory*, short for Lotus-Intel memory). In Figure 3.2, you'll see that this was separate from the conventional memory and used a portion of the reserved area to page pieces of information between the conventional memory area and the expanded memory area. To do this, they needed a software program to do the paging, an *expanded memory manager*. The most common one was EMM386.SYS, and later it became EMM386.EXE. You may not be familiar with the term *paging*. Think of it as paging someone over a loudspeaker. The expanded memory manager calls for the information and stores it in the expanded memory area. When the information is needed, the expanded memory manager once again calls for the information for retrieval.

Developers soon realized that this fix could only be a temporary one once more, and more programs started to require more and more memory. Then came along the extended memory specification. Any memory above the 1MB limit would be known as extended memory (see Figure 3.3). For this higher memory to exist, developers needed another software implementation called HIMEM.SYS. In my example, the computer has 16MB of RAM.

Figure 3.2.

The expanded memory area.

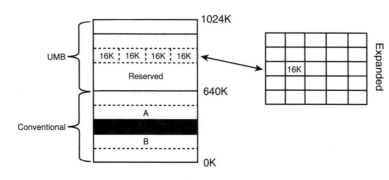

Figure 3.3.

The extended memory area.

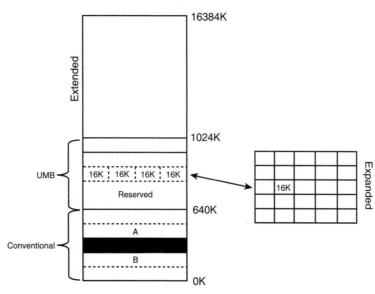

The old memory model had several problems. First of all, information in memory was stored in 64K blocks; therefore, wasted memory was a big problem. If you wanted to load a driver that required 12K of space, it was allocated 64K whether it used it all or not. In that particular scenario, 52K would go unused. I realize that by today's standard, 52K is nothing, but remember, we are talking about way back when we thought we would never need more than 1MB of RAM.

The second and probably more obvious problem was that of segmentation. In Figure 3.3, you'll see two blocks labeled A and B. Let's say that those two blocks are the only two blocks we have that are unused. If we attempted to load a 128K driver, even though those two spaces add up to 128K, we would see an Out of Memory error message. This is because, for programs to be loaded into memory, they had to be loaded contiguously (in spaces right next to each other). Some of you die-hards would say that I needed to move some things around and free up the space contiguously. Short of explaining hexadecimal addresses and such, you're right, but I'm here to tell you about the Windows 95 memory model, and it's just an example.

The last problem was the biggest to fight. The model never had enough memory. The more programs and drivers we wanted to run, the more we were fighting the battles explained in the previous two paragraphs. The end problem always boiled down to not having enough.

By now, you are probably wondering why I went through so much trouble explaining how things *used* to work. Well, I wanted to make you understand the differences between Windows 95 and previous Microsoft operating systems. This will help you better understand why the Windows 95 virtual memory model is different. Many of my students understand the Windows 95 memory model when it is explained to them; however, they always end up with one question: Why? So now that you understand how things used to be, let's take a look at how they are now.

With Windows 95, most of the problems were resolved. The Windows 95 memory model in Figure 3.4 was taken from the Windows NT memory model. Windows 95 tells every loaded application that it has 4GB of memory available. You heard it right. That 4GB of memory is broken down into 2GB of usable space by the application and 2GB reserved as system addressable.

Keep in mind that this 4GB of RAM is *virtual memory*. There are different components that reside in this 4GB address space. Take a look at Table 3.1 for a detailed explanation of what the different components are and where they are stored.

Table 3.1. Components loaded into virtual memory.

Range	Contains...
3GB-4GB	Ring O Components
2GB-3GB	Core system components, shared DLLs; other shared objects, Win16-based applications
4MB-2GB	Win32-based applications
640K-4MB	Free
0-640K	Real mode drivers and terminate-stay resident programs

Figure 3.4.

The Windows 95 virtual memory model.

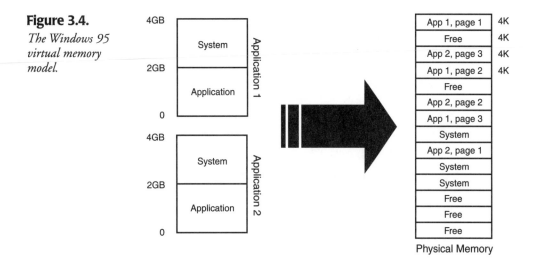

The *virtual memory manager* (*VMM*) takes the information from virtual memory addresses of the applications on the left and maps them to actual spaces in physical memory. It tricks the applications into thinking that their information is stored somewhere that it isn't. For instance, if you run two MS-DOS applications at the same time, they both want 0 to 640K. Windows 95 gives them both 0 to 640K, but whenever the applications tell the VMM that they want to store information there, the VMM really puts it where it sees fit to, all the while hiding where it's really stored from the applications.

Think of it this way. If you hire a household goods storage company to store some furniture for you, you couldn't care less where they put it, as long as you get it back when you ask for it. When you get your furniture (or your data) back, you want it in the same condition as when you saw it last. They could tell you that your belongings are stored in Chicago, when all the while they're really stored in Milwaukee. That's kind of what the VMM does.

Let's talk about the problems that this 32-bit, flat, linear model fixed. The first problem was the wasted memory. In the MS-DOS model, the blocks were 64K in size; in the new Windows 95 model, they are 4K in size. Smaller chunks mean less wasted space.

Another problem was that, to load a program, the spaces used had to be contiguous. The new memory model no longer requires this. In Figure 3.4, you can see that the applications and free space are spread out noncontiguously. The Virtual Memory Manager handles it all.

3.3.1. Paging Memory

The new memory model still needed to solve one problem: not enough memory. The new memory model was created to tell the applications that they had 4GB of memory available, with up to 2GB that was usable. Who was going to back up what the application was being promised? After all, the minimum requirement for RAM was 4MB. Where was this 4GB going to come from? Believe it or not, it would come from the hard disk. I know, I know, not everyone in this day and age has 4GB hard drives yet. Hear me out.

Think about this concept: Windows 95 can allocate more memory than is physically installed in the computer. Even though you may run several applications at one time, it doesn't mean that the applications need things loaded into memory at the same exact time. Take a look at Figure 3.5. When an application needs information loaded into memory, the VMM puts it into physical RAM. When another application needs physical memory space, the VMM takes information that is loaded in physical memory but not currently in use and pages it to the hard disk. It places the information in a file called a *swapfile*. This frees up space in physical memory to be used elsewhere. When the application with information that was paged to disk needs its information back, the VMM moves the information back into physical memory. This process of memory swapping is also called *demand paging*. When an application demands it, the VMM takes care of it.

Figure 3.5.

Demand paging.

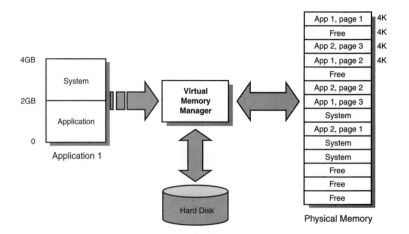

So how does the VMM keep track of this? Actually, it's quite simple: The VMM uses what is called a *paging table* to keep track of what information is stored on the hard disk and what information is in physical memory (see Figure 3.6).

Figure 3.6.

The paging table.

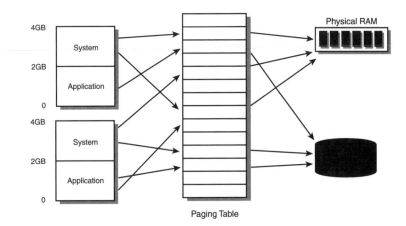

Virtual memory and this idea of paging to the hard disk involve a slight problem. Let's say that every available space in physical memory is being used. To load information that is currently in the swapfile into physical memory (paged in), something currently in physical memory needs to be swapped to the hard disk (paged out) to free up the space. Sounds like musical chairs, doesn't it?

Even though Windows 95 was designed for paging information in and out of memory, the time comes when enough is enough. Too much of this swapping causes the system to become slow and unresponsive, not to mention that it takes a toll on the hard drive. This is what is called *excessive paging*. You'll know when your computer is excessively paging. The computer runs slow, and you hear high activity from the hard drive (*thrashing*). The fix for excessive paging is simple: Add more RAM.

You should know that the fix for excessive paging (hard disk activity and slow system response) is to add more RAM. This makes for an excellent test question where the true answer, adding more RAM, seems too simple to be the correct answer. Don't let more complicated choices throw you off.

I have found that Windows 95 runs smoothest with at least 16MB of RAM. The 4MB minimum is definitely not enough to make you happy with the performance.

3.4. Running Applications

Supporting Windows 95 does not only mean supporting the operating system itself; it also means supporting applications that will be used with Windows 95. Even though we can't even begin to talk about every application that will run in a Windows 95 environment, we can talk about how to support applications in a general sense. In doing so, we can break it down into three types of applications:

- MS-DOS applications
- Windows 16-bit (Win16) applications
- Windows 32-bit (Win32) applications

3.4.1. Virtual Machines

The Windows 95 architecture is implemented through the use of *virtual machines*. A virtual machine (VM) is a way that Windows 95 can trick the application into thinking that it is running on a computer with full access to all of that computer's resources. If you have two applications running and they are in separate VMs, they think they have an entire computer all to themselves.

> Note
>
> A virtual machine is the simulation of an entire computer's resources that is accomplished by an operating system.

> Test Tip
>
> This section covers the following exam objective: Compare and contrast the memory usage of a Microsoft MS-DOS–based application, a 16-bit Windows-based application, and a 32-bit Windows-based application operating in Windows 95.

There are two basic types of VMs. The first type is called a *system virtual machine* (*system VM*). Windows 95 contains one, and only one, System VM. All the base components of Windows 95 run inside the system VM, including the interface, GDI, and kernel. Also, all Win16 applications and Win32 applications run in this system VM.

However, all Win16 applications share the same memory address space. The main reason for this is backward compatibility. Some Win16 applications transfer information to each other by the way of this shared address space. Because they share memory with each other, they all have access to each other's information.

Win32 applications are independent from one another because each Win32 application runs in its own separate memory address space. Take a look at Figure 3.7. This does not mean that Win32 applications cannot share information. Instead, they use the more advanced *object linking and embedding* (*OLE*) capability to share information.

Figure 3.7.

The system virtual machine.

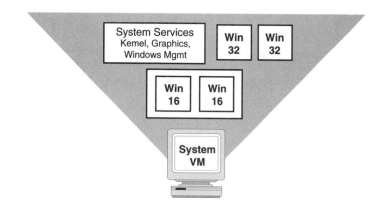

The other type of VM is an MS-DOS VM. Each MS-DOS application runs in its own separate MS-DOS VM (see Figure 3.8). The reason behind this should be clear already. Before there was Windows, all we had was MS-DOS. Back in those days, we couldn't run two MS-DOS applications at once. This mainly was because MS-DOS applications were written with the idea that they would have full control over the computer's resources. If you remember my definition of a VM, you'll see that the way we give an MS-DOS application the full control that it wants is to run it in its own VM.

You will almost definitely be asked to identify the number of virtual machines in a given scenario on the exam. For example, if you were running three 16-bit applications, two 32-bit applications, and three MS-DOS applications, how many virtual machines are in use? The correct answer is four virtual machines—one system virtual machine for the Windows applications and one for each MS-DOS application.

Figure 3.8.
The MS-DOS virtual machine.

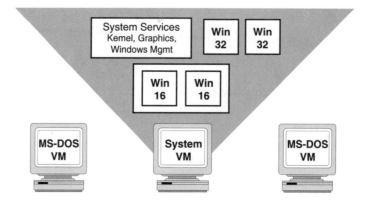

3.4.2. Processes and Threads

Understanding applications means understanding how the actual process happens. In understanding how the process happens, think for a minute about what a process is. Think of a *process* as a project that an application wants to accomplish. To complete a project, you can break the project down into smaller tasks; the faster you can accomplish those smaller tasks, the faster the project is completed. If a process were a project, we would call those smaller tasks *threads*.

So simply, a *process* comprises at least one thread, and a *thread* is a unit of code to be executed. As long as you understand that basic terminology, understanding the different applications is a breeze.

Let's talk about how Windows 95 uses these processes and threads. Windows 95 has a way that it controls these processes and threads through what is defined as a *message passing model*. A *message* could consist of some function such as an interrupt (click of a mouse) or information to be transferred. These messages are used to send information from the application to the rest of the system, whether it is from one program to another, to the processor, or to the screen.

These messages are passed through one of several message queues. These message queues are similar to a print queue. If you print something out, you have to wait until earlier print jobs are done before you see your latest printout. Likewise, messages in the same message queue have to wait to be processed until earlier messages are processed.

The number of message queues that you have is directly proportionate to how many and what types of applications you have running.

MS-DOS applications do not use a message queue because they are not designed for message passing.

Because all Win16 applications share a common address space, they all share the same message queue. All threads of code to be executed from these applications have to go through one message queue. Therefore, if one Win16 application becomes hung up for some reason, it clogs the message queue and prevents any other Win16 applications from responding. After the hung-up application has been terminated, the message queue resumes with the next message in line. In Figure 3.9, you see two Win16 applications running. See how they all share the same message queue?

Figure 3.9.

The Windows 95 message queue.

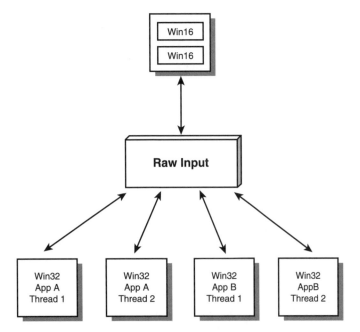

Win32 applications are a different breed altogether. Not only does each application run in its own separate memory address space, but also every thread of code gets its own message queue. Also in Figure 3.9, you will see two Win32 applications running. These applications can send multiple threads simultaneously, each thread having its own message queue.

3.4.4. 32-Bit Versus 16-Bit Applications

So far, we've talked about Win32 and Win16 applications in how they use the message queues, memory address spaces, and such. Let's contrast the two by talking about the difference between preemptive and cooperative multitasking. *Multitasking* is defined as being able to accomplish more than one task at a time. In Windows, it means that we can run more than one application at a time; but there are two kinds of multitasking: *preemptive* and *cooperative.*

Preemptive

In a multitasking environment, threads are assigned a priority. They are then executed in the order of the priority that they hold. With preemptive multitasking, each thread is run for a preset amount of time, or until another thread with a higher priority comes along. This prevents one thread from taking control of the processor and keeping it all to itself.

Because Win32 applications run in their own separate memory address space and MS-DOS applications run in their own separate MS-DOS VM, they are preemptively multitasked in Windows 95.

Cooperative

With cooperative multitasking, a thread can control the processor until the processor is done with it. The program that is sending the thread controls how long the thread has control of the processor and when it should relinquish it. Therefore, a Win16 application that is not well-written can attempt to take total control of the system.

Win16-based applications are the only applications that are cooperatively multitasked in Windows 95.

Contrasting

Win32 applications are *multithreaded.* A single Win32 application can send multiple threads simultaneously to the processor to be processed. When you couple that with the idea that each Win32 thread has its own message queue, you can see how these applications can do more, faster. Therefore, Win32 applications can be preemptively multitasked. They can all send out multiple threads at the same time to be processed.

Unlike Win32 applications, Win16 applications can kick out only one thread at a time. Also keep in mind that all Win16 applications running in Windows 95 share the same message queue; therefore, they have to wait on one another. This is why Win16 applications are cooperatively multitasked. They must cooperate with each other when sending out threads from the message queue.

Figure 3.10 gives an overview of how the whole process works.

Figure 3.10.

Multiprocessing in Windows 95.

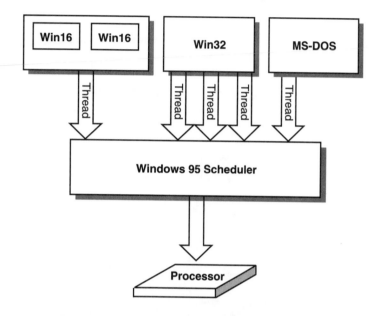

3.4.5. Running MS-DOS Applications

All Windows-based applications have information stored in the executable file of the program that tells Windows what resources it needs, how much memory it needs, and other attributes about the program.

MS-DOS applications do not have this type of information, however. You can modify the behavior of MS-DOS applications by pulling up the property sheet for that application. To obtain the property sheet of an application, right-click the EXE file in the Windows Explorer and select Properties.

The property sheet consists of several tabs that I will explain. After you've modified the information in the property sheet, a *program information file* (*PIF*) is created automatically. By default, the file created uses the same name of the executable file and has PIF for the extension. Any time you execute that application, the information stored in the PIF will be set for that application.

The PIF must reside in the same directory as the executable (EXE) file. You can create more than one PIF for the same program and, therefore, different settings. Simply copy the PIF and rename it. When you want to execute the program, simply double-click the PIF, not the EXE. If you use a shortcut to execute the program, make sure the shortcut points to the PIF and not the EXE.

Figure 3.11 shows the first tab, the General tab, of the property sheet for an MS-DOS application. As you can see, this tab is common to all files in Windows 95 and contains pretty basic information.

Figure 3.11.

The MS-DOS Properties sheet, General tab.

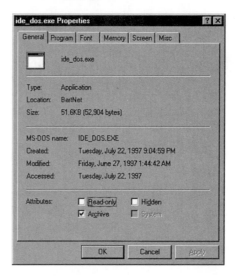

The Program tab contains information such as the command line, the working directory, and shortcut keys, if applicable (see Figure 3.12). Also on this tab, you can specify that a certain batch file run prior to the execution of the application. At the bottom, you see two buttons, one titled Advanced and the other Change Icon. I think Change Icon is self-explanatory, but I will cover the Advanced button toward the end of this section.

The Font tab is the next tab in line. In Figure 3.13, you see that you can change the size and style of font used in the program. I think this option is relatively self-explanatory.

The Memory property sheet lets you tightly control the memory on an application. I've come across several instances where someone was trying to run an MS-DOS application and was having difficulty. The user simply assumed that the application wouldn't run in Windows 95 and gave up. With a little tweaking here, you can run many applications that you might have thought wouldn't. Keep in mind that these settings are only for that specific application and not for the entire machine. This basically sets up the memory configuration for the MS-DOS VM. Figure 3.14 shows a picture of this tab.

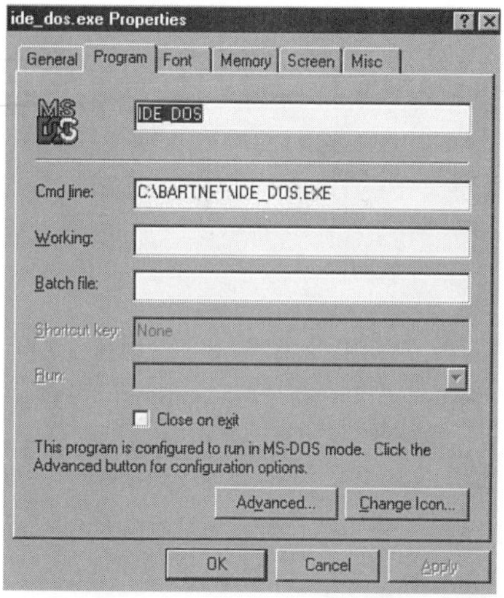

Figure 3.12.

The MS-DOS Property sheet, Program tab.

Figure 3.13.

The MS-DOS Property sheet, Font tab.

3

The Conventional Memory setting specifies how much conventional memory is required for this application to run. I have yet to come across an instance where Auto hasn't worked.

The Initial Environment setting specifies how much memory you want to set aside for COMMAND.COM or settings in batch files such as SET variables. *SET variables* are things like the PATH statement, TEMP folder, and the like.

Figure 3.14.

The MS-DOS Property sheet, Memory tab.

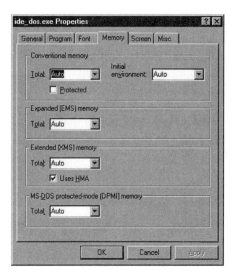

You should check the Protected check box if you do not want the information stored in memory for this application to be paged to the hard disk. Be prepared for a performance drop if you select this option.

The Expanded (EMS) Memory setting is where we did some tweaking. This setting specifies how much expanded memory you want to limit this application to. If you set it at Auto, the sky's the limit. Some applications have difficulty when they can't see the limit. If so, set this to 8MB (8192K).

The Extended (XMS) Memory setting is like the expanded memory setting. This is where you set a limit as to how much extended memory you are going to allow this application to have. Auto is the setting where there is no limit. If you have to tweak the expanded memory setting, there's a pretty good chance you'll have to tweak this one. Once again, set it to 8192K if the application doesn't like the Auto setting.

DPMI stands for *DOS protected-mode interface.* This is also a maximum setting. Unlike the previous settings, Auto does not leave it as no limit. If you leave it on Auto, Windows specifies a setting based on the machine's current configuration.

In Figure 3.15, you see the Screen tab. This tab is also relatively basic. The settings at the bottom—Fast ROM Emulation and Dynamic Memory Allocation—usually throw most people off.

The Fast ROM Emulation is checked by default. When checked, it allows the program to use the ROM drivers in protected mode. This can increase video performance by speeding up the rate in which the program can write information to the screen. If your program has difficulty writing to the screen, try removing the check mark in this box.

Figure 3.15.

The MS-DOS Property sheet, Screen tab.

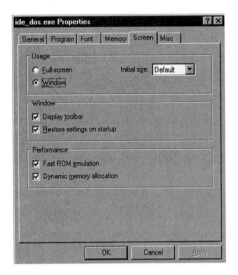

3

As for Dynamic Memory Allocation, with the check mark on (default), it allows the program to control the amount of memory set aside for displaying graphics. Make sure this check mark is on if the program frequently switches between graphics and text. Remove the check mark if you are running Windows on a machine with very little RAM. This allows Windows to manage the memory and allocate to the program as Windows sees appropriate.

The Misc tab (see Figure 3.16) contains all the misfit settings not appropriate for other tabs. Once again, some settings here are self-explanatory.

Idle Sensitivity is how long you want Windows 95 to wait before it suspends (pauses) the application for inactivity. If you have an application that appears to be idle but isn't, Windows suspends it. This causes some MS-DOS applications to crash. If so, set this to its lowest level.

The QuickEdit Mouse setting allows for cutting and pasting inside an MS-DOS program when the program is running in a window. Deselect this option if the MS-DOS application uses a mouse.

Exclusive Mode locks the mouse inside the MS-DOS application window. If your MS-DOS program uses a mouse and you run the application in a window, you'll find this option handy. If the mouse cursor loses synchronization when you move it in and out of the application window, select this option. It can be a little frustrating at first.

Figure 3.16.

The MS-DOS Property sheet, Miscellaneous tab.

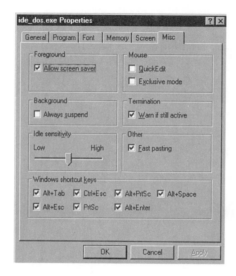

The Windows shortcut keys area at the bottom of this window specifies which Windows 95 shortcut keys are enabled in this program. If your MS-DOS application uses any of these shortcut keys, deselect them here so that the keystroke stays within the program instead of going to Windows 95.

Using MS-DOS Mode

This section covers the following exam objective: Distinguish between MS-DOS mode and the standard method for running MS-DOS–based applications.

Let's go back to the Program tab. Clicking the Advanced button on the bottom pulls up a dialog box similar to Figure 3.17.

Some MS-DOS programs are written to detect whether they are running in a Windows environment. These programs react differently depending on whether they are running in Windows or in an MS-DOS environment. If you would like to hide the Windows environment from the MS-DOS program, place a check mark in the first setting.

Figure 3.17.

*The Advanced
Program Settings
dialog box.*

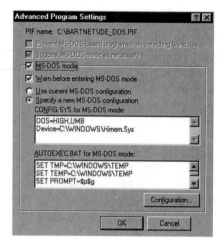

The next setting, if checked, allows Windows to determine whether you should use
MS-DOS mode for this particular application. This setting is checked by default.
(These figures are grayed out in the figure because I have selected to run in MS-
DOS mode.)

This section covers the following exam objective: Determine when you
should run an application in MS-DOS mode.

If your program will absolutely not run in Windows 95, you can choose to run it in
MS-DOS mode. Most examples that I can come up with are games. I do have a couple of games (yes, I believe in having fun, too) that require MS-DOS mode. Not
sure what MS-DOS mode is? Allow me to explain.

Let's say you specify that you want a particular program to run in MS-DOS mode.
When you execute that program, Windows 95 shuts down and the computer restarts
in MS-DOS mode (Windows 95 is not loaded). The program then executes automatically. When you exit the program, the machine restarts in Windows 95.

After you have specified that your machine start in MS-DOS mode, you have two
choices of how to configure the machine for that application. Looking again at
Figure 3.17, you see that I have already specified that this program run in MS-DOS
mode. The two choices you have are these: Use Current MS-DOS Configuration
and Specify a New MS-DOS Configuration.

If you choose the Use Current MS-DOS Configuration, the default settings of the computer are used. If you choose the Specify a New MS-DOS Configuration, you can specify any CONFIG.SYS and AUTOEXEC.BAT settings in the provided boxes. With this option, you can specify specific settings on a program-by-program basis. You can even take it a step further and create several PIFs for one application and specify different settings in each PIF.

Note

I have actually put MS-DOS mode to use in a dual-boot configuration with Windows 3.11. The customers needed to use both Windows 3.11 and Windows 95 environments.

Windows 95 was their predominate environment, but they wanted a quick and easy way to drop completely out of Windows 95 and into Windows 3.11.

With the machine installed with Windows 3.11 and Windows 95 in separate directories (so changing one wouldn't in any way affect the other), we created a shortcut on the desktop. The shortcut's command line pointed to the WIN.COM of Windows 3.11. We configured it to start in MS-DOS mode with specific CONFIG.SYS and AUTOEXEC.BAT settings.

When they wanted to drop down to Windows 3.11, they simply double-clicked the shortcut icon. The machine reboots and starts in Windows 3.11. After they're done with Windows 3.11, they simply exit Windows. The machine reboots again and starts back up in Windows 95.

By default, a check mark is placed in the Warn Before Entering MS-DOS Mode setting. This option, upon executing the program, displays the message in Figure 3.18.

Figure 3.18.

The MS-DOS Mode warning.

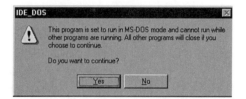

3.4.6. When an Application Goes Bad

When the term *crashed application* is used, it usually means different things to different people. For those of us who are familiar with Windows 3.*x*, it usually means the appearance of the infamous general protection fault error message. For others, it may mean the application no longer responds to keystrokes or mouse clicks. Well, in actuality, both are correct.

General Protection Faults

A *general protection fault* (*GP fault*) is not a thing of the past with the creation of Windows 95, but you will see fewer of them. A GP fault basically occurs when a program attempts to violate system integrity. This is classified as an application failure. The way Windows 95 handles applications that attempt to violate system integrity depends on what type of application it is.

 This section covers the following exam objective: Resolve general protection faults.

If an MS-DOS application fails, a GP fault error appears. Clicking OK terminates the program. The program that fails is the only program affected by the failure because MS-DOS applications run in their own separate VM.

When a Win16 application fails, a GP fault error message appears stating which application has failed. Until this application is terminated, all other Win16 applications stop responding. If you remember from 3.2.3, Win16 applications are cooperatively multitasked. After the failed application terminates, all other Win16 applications resume.

Win32 applications are a little different. Because they each run in their own separate memory address space (refer to 3.2.3), they don't affect other applications when they fail. A GP fault error message is displayed notifying you what program failed.

Hanging an Application

No, by "hanging an application," I am not talking about getting the noose out for those notorious applications. I'm talking about when an application stops responding to the system. Most people think that because the application that they have in the foreground has hung up, Windows 95 is hung up as well; this is a fallacy. Usually, this results in the user pressing Ctrl+Alt+Del about 30 times at an alarmingly fast rate or just as badly reaching for the infamous power button. These actions are not warranted because there is an easier (and safer) way.

 This section covers the following exam objective: Determine the appropriate course of action when the application stops responding to the system.

Pressing Ctrl+Alt+Del once (and only once) performs a *local restart*. Despite what the name might imply, the computer does not restart. In fact, it pulls up the Close Program dialog box. This box informs you which program has hung up by placing the words *Not Responding* next to it. To terminate the program, simply click it, and click the End Task button.

Program Resources

When you terminate an application, what happens to the resources? Well, that depends on whether the application is an MS-DOS-based, 16-bit Windows, or a 32-bit Windows application.

When you terminate an MS-DOS-based application, its virtual machine is also terminated. This returns all resources to the system.

If the application is a 16-bit Windows application, things are a little more complicated. The 16-bit Windows applications might use resources without Windows 95 being aware of them. Additionally, they might also use resources that other 16-bit Windows applications are using because all 16-bit applications share the same memory address space. Therefore, when you terminate a 16-bit Windows application, the resources that it was using are not returned to the system until all 16-bit applications are no longer running. After the last 16-bit application is closed, all resources are returned to the system.

With 32-bit Windows applications, things are tracked more closely. When a 32-bit Windows application is terminated, its resources are returned to the system.

In Windows 3.*x*, 16-bit applications many times crashed the computer because Windows 3.*x* was 16-bit. Windows NT has a capability to run 16-bit applications in their own separate memory address space so that they do not affect other applications or resources.

3.5. Software in the Registry

Most people think the Registry would be covered in a chapter that covers configuration. Although the Registry is a configuration tool, it is generally thought of as the bowels of Windows 95. You should think of the Registry as part of the internals of Windows 95.

This section covers the following exam objectives:
- Define the purpose of the Registry.
- Determine where the Registry is stored.
- Identify situations in which it is appropriate to modify the Registry.
- Perform modification of the Registry as appropriate using Regedit.

The *Registry* is a hierarchical database where Windows 95 keeps its configuration of hardware, software, user specific settings, and so on. It replaces the need for AUTOEXEC.BAT, CONFIG.SYS, and INI files. Windows 95 still maintains a copies of these files for backward compatibility. Additionally, Windows 95 will load any real-mode drivers mentioned in these files that weren't converted during setup.

The Registry contains two files: SYSTEM.DAT and USER.DAT. The SYSTEM.DAT contains all system-specific information. Likewise, the USER.DAT contains all the user-specific information. If profiles have been enabled, each user who logs on to Windows 95 will have his own individual USER.DAT created.

As mentioned in Chapter 1, "Planning and Installing Windows 95," the SYSTEM.DAT and USER.DAT are automatically backed up as SYSTEM.DA0 and USER.DA0. You can find these files in the Windows directory. If profiles have been enabled, each user will have a directory created to store his settings. That person's copy of the USER.DAT is stored in that directory. I'll talk more about profiles in Chapter 8, "Locking Down the System: Profiles and Policies." You can view and edit the Registry directly by using the program REGEDIT.EXE.

You might be asked how to invoke the Registry Editor on the exam. You should know that REGEDIT.EXE is the command line for starting it.

Be careful with the Registry Editor. When you make changes in it, most of them are dynamic. In other words, the change takes effect immediately.

continues

If you can modify the configuration through some other means, such as the Control Panel or the System Policy Editor, you should do so. Only use the Registry Editor to modify the configuration when you have to.

It isn't like the old INI files where you can experiment and see what happens. Modifying the Registry incorrectly could have systemwide effects that you might only be able to repair by reinstalling Windows 95.

3.5.1. How Applications Use the Registry

Applications store their configuration information in the Registry. When they are written specifically for Windows 95, they update the Registry automatically upon installation.

Earlier applications, such as Win16 applications that still need the INI files such as WIN.INI and SYSTEM.INI, are handled a little differently. If you upgraded Windows 3.*x* with Windows 95 (installed it into the same directory), Windows 95 took the settings in the INI files and updated them into the Registry. If you installed Windows 95 into a separate directory, you need to reinstall all applications for them to be stored properly in the Registry.

3.5.2. Structure of the Registry

You can see by Figure 3.19 that the Registry is broken down into six keys of information called the *root keys*. These root keys have a similar look and feel of a directory structure. There are subkeys inside of subkeys similar to subdirectories inside of subdirectories. Table 3.2 provides a breakdown of what each key contains.

Figure 3.19.

The Microsoft Registry Editor.

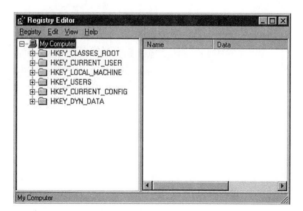

Table 3.2. Windows 95 Registry Keys.

Key	Contains...
HKEY_CLASSES_ROOT	OLE and file associations.
HKEY_USERS	Information about all users of this computer.
HKEY_CURRENT_USER	User-specific information about the currently logged on user. This key is created at logon.
HKEY_LOCAL_MACHINE	Machine-specific information: drivers, hardware, and so on.
HKEY_CURRENT_CONFIG	Storage of multiple configurations such as when a laptop docked or undocked in a docking station.
HKEY_DYN_DATA	The dynamic status of devices. Used for Plug and Play configuration. Created at bootup and not part of either of the Registry files.

Even though you do not need to memorize every single piece of information that is stored in the Registry and where it's stored, it is important that you know what each HKEY contains.

3.5.3. Storing Registry Values

In Figure 3.20, you see the configuration of the user who's currently logged onto this machine. I've expanded several of the subkeys on the left so that you can see the directory-like structure. On the right, you see some sample values of that subkey. The three values at the top are legitimate, whereas I plugged in the three at the bottom, beginning with the word *sample*, to show you the three types of values. The values consist of a value name and the actual data of that value.

Figure 3.20.

Adding values in the Microsoft Registry Editor.

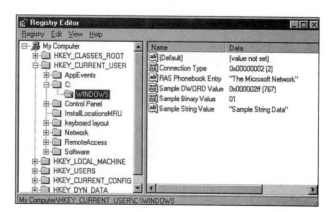

The Binary value is, of course, a binary number. The DWORD value is also a binary value, but the data of a DWORD value is hexadecimal. A program or hardware device sets both of these types of values. Even though you can edit them, it's a good idea to leave them alone.

A String value, however, can be helpful in troubleshooting and configuration. In the next section, I'll give you an example.

3.5.4. Searching the Registry

If you haven't by now, expand out some of the keys and see just how overwhelmingly big the Registry is. Finding a specific value that you need is like looking for a needle in a haystack. Like most Microsoft programs, a search option helps. By clicking the Edit menu option (see Figure 3.21), you see the Find option.

Figure 3.21.

The Find option of the Registry Editor.

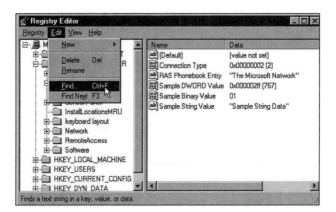

Using the Find option, I am going to search for the string sourcepath. This particular search provides the result that you see in Figure 3.22. Notice the path to this particular key at the bottom of the dialog box.

3.5.5. Editing the Registry Values

Once again, I must caution you on editing the Registry. Change the values only if you know what the outcome will be.

Editing the Registry values is as simple as double-clicking them. When I double-click the source path value, the dialog box in Figure 3.23 appears. As you can see, you can change the string value simply by typing in the new value. The editing dialog box that appears varies depending on the type of value that you are editing.

Figure 3.22.
Results of the Registry search.

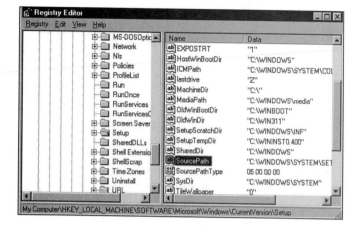

Note

By the way, the source path is where Windows 95 looks for the installation files. This is a very handy thing to change. Did you install from a CD-ROM? If so, do you hate it whenever you make a change that requires the CD-ROM and you have to go hunting for it?

If so, copy the contents of the WIN95 folder from the CD-ROM down to the hard drive. Then, change this key to point to that new location. From then on, Windows 95 will get the required software from that directory.

Figure 3.23.
Editing a string value in the Registry.

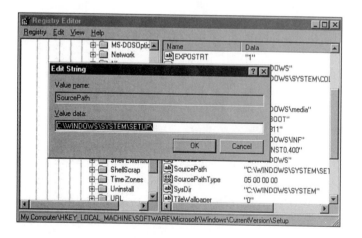

3.6. Common System Drivers

Drivers provide the link necessary for Windows 95 and the hardware to communicate. Call them translators, if you will. Windows 95 supports three basic types of drivers: MS-DOS, real-mode Windows, and protected-mode Windows.

MS-DOS drivers load prior to Windows starting. They are placed in the CONFIG.SYS and AUTOEXEC.BAT. These drivers usually have a SYS extension. You can still use them, but they are not your best choice.

Real-mode Windows drivers are drivers that are drivers similar to MS-DOS drivers except they are usually loaded in the SYSTEM.INI and end in DRV. They are designed to run under MS-DOS. They are mostly older 16-bit drivers designed to run in Windows 3.*x* (hence the SYSTEM.INI).

Protected-mode drivers are 32-bit drivers designed to take advantage of Windows 95 and the protected-mode architecture of 386 and higher processors. Usually ending with VXD, they are called *virtual device drivers*. These are the drivers of choice because they are faster and do not use the conventional memory, as do older real-mode drivers.

Lab

This Lab consists of review questions that pertain to this chapter and gives you an opportunity to apply the knowledge you've learned with this chapter. You can find the answers to the review questions in Appendix B.

Questions

1. What type of application can have multiple threads per process?

   A. An MS-DOS application

   B. A Windows 16-bit application

   C. A Windows 32-bit application

2. A user is working on a 486DX2 with 16MB of RAM. He is working in several 16-bit Windows-based applications when the one he is currently using stops responding to the keyboard and the mouse. What would be his proper course of action?

   A. Restart the computer.

   B. Press Ctrl+Alt+Del twice to bring up the Close Program dialog box and terminate the proper application. All other 16-bit applications will resume normal operation.

   C. Press Ctrl+Alt+Del to bring up the Close Program dialog box and terminate all programs. Restart the programs as appropriate.

   D. Press Ctrl+Alt+Del to bring up the Close Program dialog box and terminate the proper application. All other 16-bit applications will resume normal operation.

3. What key in the Windows 95 Registry stores information such as which drivers are loaded, what hardware is installed, and how ports are mapped?

   A. HKEY_CLASSES_ROOT

   B. HKEY_LOCAL_MACHINE

   C. HKEY_DYN_DATA

   D. HKEY_CURRENT_CONFIG

3

4. You are running three Win16 applications, two Win32 applications, and two MS-DOS applications on a Windows 95 computer. How many virtual machines are running on that computer?

   A. 3

   B. 4

   C. 5

   D. 7

5. Windows 95 Virtual Memory allocates memory in what size blocks?

   A. 2K

   B. 4K

   C. 16K

   D. 64K

6. A user calls you and complains that her computer is running sluggishly. You inquire and find out that her hard drive is almost constantly active. You investigate to find that she has plenty of free disk space available to last her for quite some time. What would be the proper fix for this problem?

   A. Monitor the hard disk. A possible disk failure may be approaching.

   B. Have her use fewer applications at once.

   C. Remove any unneeded applications.

   D. Add more RAM.

7. Which applications in Windows 95 are preemptively multitasked?

   A. MS-DOS applications

   B. Win16 applications

   C. Win32 applications

   D. Both A and C

8. A user who is having problems with his MS-DOS application contacts you. It appears that his machine runs fine in MS-DOS mode, but he needs the capability to cut and paste between this application and a Windows-based application. The application runs inside Windows 95, but behaves differently. Which of the following would you suggest?

A. From the Properties dialog box of this application, go to the Miscellaneous tab and set the Idle Sensitivity at its lowest level.

B. From the Properties dialog box of this application, go to the Program tab. Click the Advanced button and place a check mark in the box titled Prevent MS-DOS–Based Program from Detecting Windows.

C. From the Properties dialog box of this application, go to the Program tab. Click the Advanced button and place a check mark in the box titled Suggest MS-DOS Mode as Necessary.

D. From the Properties dialog box of this application, go to the Screen tab. Click the Advanced button and place a check mark in the box titled Fast ROM Emulation.

9. Which one of the following statements is true?

   A. A process contains only one thread.

   B. A process consists of at least one thread.

   C. A process contains two threads.

   D. A process consists of at least two threads.

10. You are running an MS-DOS application, two 16-bit Windows applications, and a 32-bit Windows application. The MS-DOS application fails. Which of the following statements is true?

   A. Only the MS-DOS application is affected.

   B. The MS-DOS application and the 16-bit applications will stop responding.

   C. The MS-DOS application and the 32-bit applications will stop responding.

   D. All applications will stop responding.

Exercises

In this lab, you will modify the properties of an MS-DOS program and modify the Registry. This will prepare you for the exam by meeting the following objective: Establish application environments for Microsoft MS-DOS–based applications.

Modifying an MS-DOS Program's Properties

1. Double-click My computer.

2. Double-click the C: drive.

3. Locate the file COMMAND.COM.

4. Drag the file to your desktop. (This should create a shortcut to MS-DOS prompt.)

5. Close the My Computer and C: drive windows.

6. Double-click the shortcut you've just created. (An MS-DOS prompt window should open.)

7. At the prompt, type **MEM** and press Enter.

8. Write down the amount of EMS memory and XMS memory that is used and available.

9. Type **EXIT** and press Enter.

10. Right-click the shortcut and then select Properties.

11. Click the Memory tab.

12. Change the amounts of EMS and XMS memory to None.

13. Click OK.

14. Double-click the Shortcut icon.

15. At the prompt, type **MEM** and press Enter.

16. How much EMS and XMS memory is used and available now? Compare to previous values.

    The memory changed because of the amounts that you specified in the properties.

17. Open another MS-DOS window by clicking Start, pointing to Programs, and selecting MS-DOS Prompt.

18. At the prompt, type **MEM** and press Enter.

19. Compare values with those in previous MS-DOS window.

    The values are different because they are separate virtual machines. Also, by modifying the properties of one, it does not affect the other because of separate PIFs.

20. Close both windows.

Editing the Registry

In this lab, we will create a logon banner to be displayed at each Windows logon. This will prepare you for the exam by meeting the following exam objective: Perform direct modification of the Registry as appropriate by using Regedit.

1. Click Start and select Run.

2. Type **REGEDIT** and press Enter.

3. Expand HKEY_LOCAL_MACHINE by clicking the plus sign next to it.

4. Expand Software.

5. Expand Microsoft.

6. Scroll down and expand Windows.

7. Expand CurrentVersion.

8. Scroll down and click the folder next to Winlogon.

9. From the menu, click Edit.

10. Point to New and click String Value.

11. Type **LegalNoticeCaption** (do not put spaces) and press Enter.

12. Double-click LegalNoticeCaption.

13. Type the word **Caution** into the Value data field and click OK.

14. From the menu, click Edit.

15. Point to New and click String Value.

16. Type **LegalNoticeText** (do not put spaces) and press Enter.

17. Double-click LegalNoticeText.

18. Type in the phrase **Authorized users only.** into the Value data field and click OK.

19. Close the Registry Editor and click the Start button.

20. Click Shut Down, select Close all Programs, and log on as different user.

21. Click OK.

22. Log back on.

Did you see the caption?

If not, repeat these steps again, and be careful to watch punctuation.

You can delete the caption by repeating steps 1 through 8, clicking LegalNoticeCaption and LegalNoticeText, and pressing the Delete button on the keyboard.

3

Here are a few fast facts for you to breeze through before test time. Be sure to know the resource arbitration process:

- The goal of Plug and Play is to allow changes in the configuration of a computer without intervention of the user.

- A *legacy device* does not meet any PnP component specifications.

- The resource arbitrator's job is to work closely with the Configuration Manager and resolve conflicting resource assignments that may occur when more than one device attempts to use the same resource (such as an IRQ).

- The main four resources concerned in the arbitration process are IRQs, I/O port addresses, DMA channels, and memory regions.

- With the Device Manager, you can manually configure devices in the event that Windows 95 cannot successfully resolve conflicts.

- The Configuration Manager oversees all parts of the configuration process and all components involved.

Day 4

Plug and Play

The Plug and Play (PnP) idea was designed to make configuring computers easier. It is a set of specifications that defines how computer architecture should work in order to configure the computer automatically without intervention from the user. These specifications were not created by Microsoft and are not proprietary to anyone.

With PnP, you should be able to insert a new card, dock or undock a laptop, or plug in a printer, and the system should be able to make the necessary changes automatically. The system can then take advantage of the new devices.

In this chapter, I will discuss PnP, its design, and its relation to Windows 95.

Objectives

When it comes to the exam, a whole lot about PnP isn't involved, but you should still be familiar with the concept. If you had one thing to remember from this chapter, it should be how to arbitrate resources. Even though it is not in the exam objectives, you will see it on the exam, trust me. Speaking of the exam objectives, here they are.

- Diagnose and resolve resource problems (such as IRQ assignments).
- Diagnose and resolve hardware device and device driver problems.
- Add New Hardware Wizard.

4.1. Defining Plug and Play

PnP is a philosophy and a set of specifications for manufacturers of PC components (including hardware, the BIOS, and operating systems) to follow to ensure PnP compatibility. Because so many companies make components, it is imperative that they all follow the same guidelines, or the whole PnP process does not work properly. We are only now beginning to see some of the true benefits of PnP. This is mainly due to the vast amount of legacy devices still on the market and in computers. Legacy devices are devices that do not meet the PnP standard.

The reason for PnP is simple. The goal is to make it as simple as possible to make changes to a computer. Those changes include installing new devices, replacing devices, or changing the environment.

Installing new devices or replacing them should be as simple as inserting or replacing the component. One example of these components is PCMCIA cards (PC cards). You should be able to insert a new PC card, and the machine should automatically detect it and configure the device.

Changing the environment includes things such as docking or undocking a laptop. Even though its video card, network card, and the like might change, the computer should automatically detect that a change has occurred and reconfigure itself accordingly.

One amazing PnP example can be seen with the use of a printer with an infrared port. When you enter into a room with a laptop that also has an infrared port, it should "see" the printer and automatically configure itself so that you can use the printer.

For all of these amazing feats to work properly, the machine has to be PnP-compliant. This compliance is measured with three main areas in mind: the BIOS, the operating system, and the hardware.

4.1.1. The BIOS

The BIOS in a PnP-compliant machine must do more than a BIOS of the past. First, it should be able to configure all of the devices on the motherboard. This happens prior to the operating system starting.

After configuration, it should maintain all of this information for future use. After the operating system is up and running, the BIOS should report the information about the configuration of the system board devices to the operating system.

Lastly, the BIOS should report any changes in configuration to the operating system. These are in the form of dynamic changes, such as docking of a laptop computer. The BIOS needs to be able to handle these dynamic events so that the computer can be reconfigured with restarting the computer.

4.1.2. The Operating System

The operating system must also be PnP-compliant. It should take the information gathered by the BIOS and store that information for future reference. This information is usually stored in memory and is called a *hardware tree* (which I'll explain in section 4.3.2).

The OS must also include some sort of configuration manager. This manager's job makes sure that the configuration process happens smoothly. It should keep track of each device in the system that is part of the configuration process. Something needs to find all the devices in the system and inquire about their resource needs. These resources are such items as IRQ and DMA (all of which I explain a little later in section 4.3.5). The Bus Enumerator has to do this by bus. An example bus is the ISA bus where all ISA devices reside. For example, extending off of an ISA bus might be a sound card, a network card, and a modem. All these devices reside in the same bus. So which device resolves these conflicts? This sounds like a job for the Bus Enumerator.

> **Note** | *ISA* stands for *integrated systems architecture.* I discuss ISA and the bus in the next section (4.2).

After the Bus Enumerator figures out what devices are present and what resources they would like (the Bus Enumerator politely asks for their orders), something should be in charge of passing out the rations of resources. This is done by the resource arbitrator. The arbitrator makes sure that, as it assigns resources, it doesn't promise the same resource to more than one device.

The operating system must also be able to use existing hardware. If it supported only PnP devices, all the existing legacy hardware would be useless.

4.1.3. The Hardware

The hardware plays a vital role in the PnP process. It is one of the main reasons that PnP has problems (if it has problems). This occurs because so many legacy devices are already in place and still being sold. You will see the main disadvantage of legacy devices when I discuss resource arbitration in section 4.4.6.

PnP-compatible devices should identify themselves to the system. They should also specify the capabilities they possess and any requirements for resources and/or drivers that they might need. When inserted into the system, the device notifies the operating system of such information so that it can make the necessary changes.

4.2. Riding the Bus

Windows 95 supports many different types of busses. A *bus* is nothing more than the interface between the device and the motherboard. In other words, if you want to install a PCI network adapter card, you slide it into a PCI slot. The group of PCI slots located on the motherboard composes the PCI bus. If this seems confusing, or if you're not sure what PCI stands for, don't worry. Let's take a look at the different types of components that Windows 95 supports, including PCI.

4.2.1. ISA

ISA stands for *industry standard architecture*, which is one of the older technologies for computer architecture when comparing what we are discussing in this section. ISA was designed for the IBM PC/AT and comes in 8-bit (older) and 16-bit devices. Windows 95 is backward compatible and supports these devices. Some of the newer ISA devices are PnP, but even more are out there that aren't. These legacy ISA devices can coexist with their PnP-compatible counterparts.

During the detection of ISA devices, the devices are usually polled (or queried) for configuration information, or the user is prompted to specify the device's setting(s). When the settings for these devices are stored in the Registry, they are stored as static devices. This makes them exempt from dynamic changes to the system.

4.2.2. EISA

EISA or *extended industry standard architecture* is a design for x86 computers. This specification is newer and is upwardly compatible (compatible with newer components) from ISA. These devices conform more closely to the PnP standards than ISA devices, mainly because EISA devices use software mechanisms for identification and configuration stored in nonvolatile RAM on the card. Windows 95 includes a Bus Enumerator that makes this information accessible to the operating system.

4.2.3. PCMCIA

PCMCIA cards are most common in portable computers. *PCMCIA* stands for *Personal Computer Memory Card International Association.* The more common name for PCMCIA cards is *PC cards,* which is nothing more than a shortened version of PCMCIA. PC cards are standard credit card-sized interface cards that support full PnP functionality and are used in portable computers and many types of small computers like handheld PCs. Windows 95 provides many features for PC cards such as automatic installation, real-mode and protected-mode support, and hot swapping of cards. *Hot swapping* means being able to remove or insert the card while the computer and Windows 95 are up and running. After the card is inserted, the functionality of the card is immediately available, or if it is removed, its functionality is immediately unavailable.

Note: Not all PCMCIA cards can be hot swapped. With some older laptops, the PCMCIA controller doesn't like its cards disappearing all of a sudden. With these older laptops, swapping a card while the computer is up and running can produce strange results, sometimes even locking Windows 95. Most newer laptops have slots that allow the cards to be hot swapped. If in doubt, ask your laptop manufacturer or reseller.

4.2.4. PCI

The *PCI* (or *peripheral component interconnect*) local bus is one of the newer component technologies available in computers. The PCI bus is standard in most Pentium machines and offers 32-bit access to the device.

The PCI bus is fully PnP-compliant, but another problem exists. Because so many ISA and EISA components exist, most computers incorporate an ISA or EISA bus along with a PCI bus all in the same machine. The problem is that many times the PCI bus is usually a secondary bus in these cases.

For example, you might have ISA and PCI slots in your computer. However, sometimes this means that the ISA bus is the "parent" for the PCI bus. In this case, if the ISA bus is not fully PnP-compliant (which it usually isn't), you lose the full PnP functionality of the PCI bus.

4

4.2.5. SCSI

The *small computer standard interface* (SCSI) allows you to chain multiple devices of different types together on the same interface, such as CD-ROMs, hard disks, tape devices, and so on.

With SCSI, there is a host adapter card that is assigned resources such as an IRQ and DMA channel. The devices are then attached to the adapter via a SCSI data cable. Each device attached must be assigned a unique ID, and both ends of this cable must be terminated.

Prior to Plug and Play, most users did not know how to configure SCSI devices properly. With its advent, the knowledge level of the user did not increase, but the user does not need to know the specifics. Using the Plug and Play capabilities of Windows 95, anyone should be able to plug in a SCSI component, and Windows 95 can take care of the rest.

4.3. Windows 95 PnP

Windows 95 is the first PnP-compliant operating system that Microsoft has rolled out. Its components include the standards of PnP as discussed earlier.

4.3.1. Bus Enumerators

Windows 95 includes *Bus Enumerators*, which are responsible for assigning a unique identification number to each device on its bus. That is where the term *enumerating* originates. A *bus* is simply a way for several devices to communicate. Because several different types of devices exist, there are several types of buses. Most computers have several types of buses. Here is a list of the most common:

- Motherboard/BIOS bus
- Keyboard controller bus
- Display controller bus
- ISA bus
- SCSI bus
- PCI bus

Each bus has its own numerator and its own driver. The Bus Enumerators also retrieve device configuration information from each device on its bus.

4.3.2. Hardware Tree

The hardware tree is nothing more than information about your current system configuration stored in RAM. It is *volatile,* meaning that the tree is re-created every time the computer is started. The information is then stored in memory and makes up part of the Windows 95 Registry (the SYSTEM.DAT file).

This information is made available to other PnP components and programs that need hardware-specific information. Because this information contains all configuration settings for the hardware, it replaces the need for *.INI files used in Windows 3.*x.*

> The hardware tree is rebuilt every time the computer is started and is stored in the SYSTEM.DAT file of the Registry.

The information is stored in the SYSTEM.DAT file under two keys. The first is the HKEY_LOCAL_MACHINE where the device information is stored. Under the HKEY_DYN_DATA hive, information about dynamic changes such as IRQ and DMA is stored.

4.3.3. Configuration Manager

The Configuration Manager monitors all aspects of configuration. It takes control of the configuration process any time the BIOS notifies it of any dynamic changes or when it receives the system board configuration data at initial boot of the machine.

The Configuration Manager is in charge of coordinating the flow of information between the different Bus Enumerators, hardware tree, Registry, device drivers, and resource arbitrators. It establishes a working configuration by working closely with these components. It also notifies device drivers of any changes that are present or pending.

When a device driver is loaded, the Configuration Manager instructs the driver to wait for a resource assignment. The Configuration Manager then works with the resource arbitrators for resource allocation. It continues reconfiguration until a working configuration is determined and then notifies the device drivers of the resource assignment. It initiates this process of reconfiguration any time the BIOS or any of the Bus Enumerators inform it of a system change, such as adding or removing a PC card.

4.3.4. The Plug and Play Process

Each time you start Windows 95, it polls the hardware for identification and specification of the requirements it needs. Additionally, any time a new device is added to the system, the device gives Windows 95 the same information dynamically. Then, Windows 95 takes care of the configuration.

The actual step-by-step process for the PnP process at startup is as follows:

1. The Configuration Manager invokes the PnP logic on all the PnP cards. This puts them in configuration mode.

2. The cards are then isolated one at a time and assigned a "handle" that is used to select each card.

3. Each card's specifications are then read to determine its resource requirements—in other words, what type of IRQ, DMA, and so on that it needs. The card is also queried to find out what capabilities it possesses. This is because some cards such as sound cards provide several functions such as sound, CD-ROM, and joystick functions. Each of these functions are considered separate logical devices and are configured separately.

4. The Resource Arbitrator then assigns resources to the cards. It is imperative that the arbitrator assigns resources without conflicts. Conflicts arise when more than one device is assigned the same resource (such as an IRQ). Devices cannot share the same resources. If they do, the devices usually do not work properly, if at all.

5. After the resources have been assigned, the cards are then removed from configuration mode and activated.

Until all devices are PnP, you will probably end up with a mixture of PnP and non-PnP legacy devices in the same machine. Because these devices have no way of informing Windows 95 of their requirements and specifications, Windows 95 uses an invasive polling routine to identify these devices. If additional information is needed, the user is prompted to provide the additional information.

PnP devices are usually flexible in the resources that can be assigned to them. For example, you might have a PnP network card that could use IRQs 3, 5, and 10. You might also have a legacy sound card that requires IRQ 5. Because most legacy devices are not as flexible as PnP devices, the legacy devices are assigned resources first. I'll explain the Resource Arbitrator more in depth in section 4.3.6.

4.3.5. Resources

There are four main resources with which you need to concern yourself. Hardware devices use these resources to communicate with the processor. The Resource Arbitrator assigns these resources during its phase of configuration. The resources are interrupt request, direct memory access, input/output ports, and memory.

Interrupt Request (IRQ)

Whenever a device needs to let the operating system or application know that it has information, it needs to interrupt them. Each device in the system is assigned its own interrupt number. These numbers come from one of two *programmable interrupt controllers* or *PICs*.

With the original IBM PCs, only one PIC had eight interrupt numbers. With more devices being added to the computer, you soon ran out of IRQ numbers to give out. So with the invention of the PC/AT computer, came a second PIC. This second PIC cascaded from the first PIC, giving you 16 possible IRQs.

As more PC/ATs came out, conventions on how the IRQs are assigned were created. Table 4.1 is a list of IRQs and the most common usage of those IRQs.

Table 4.1. IRQ assignments.

IRQ	Use
0	System Timer
1	Keyboard
2	Cascade to second PIC
3	Comm Port 2, 4
4	Comm Port 1, 3
5	Parallel Port 2
6	Floppy Disk Drive
7	Parallel Port 1
8	Real Time Clock
9	Open for use
10	Open for use
11	Open for use
12	PS/2 Mouse (if installed); otherwise, Open for use
13	Math coprocessor
14	Open for use
15	Open for use

4

You might want to memorize some of the most common assignments of IRQs. Chances are very good that you will see a question or two about IRQs on the exam. Microsoft assumes that these assignments are common knowledge.

Direct Memory Access

Normally, if any device or program wants to use memory (RAM) in a computer, it must go through the processor for access. This tends to slow things down a bit. To speed things up, eight DMA channels were created. Devices might access memory directly by using one of these channels. This eliminates the processor "middle-man" and speeds things back up. Like IRQs, the numbering for DMA channels begins at 0 and goes through 7, but not all of them are available right away. Channel 4 is used for the DMA controller chip, so it's taken. Additionally, the second DMA channel is normally used for the floppy disk controller.

Input/Output (I/O) Ports

When you have devices in your computer that need to perform input and output functions (such as a network card or modem card), they are allocated a space in memory called an *IO Port*.

These address spaces are referred to using hexadecimal addresses such as 0-FFFF.

Memory Regions

Some devices reserve memory addresses for storage. Still others might have their own onboard memory. A lot of legacy devices might still map memory to the old location below the 1MB cutoff. Newer devices now use protected memory above 1MB. Even though these devices use that memory in the higher region, they might still map to the lower range in the 384K area.

4.3.6. Resource Arbitration

The resource arbitrator takes the resources mentioned in the previous section and resolves any conflicts that arise when two devices ask for the same resource.

When two devices ask for the same resource, the arbitrator gathers information from each resource pertaining to alternate resources that are assigned. It then provides this new information to the operating system, where it is stored in the Registry. Resource arbitration can happen at system startup or any time a dynamic configuration change takes place.

For example, take a look at Figure 4.1. There are four devices. Each device reports to the resource arbitrator which resources it needs and which alternate resources it can use. In this particular case, I am using interrupt requests as an example. The modem can use IRQs 3, 5, or 7; the sound card wants IRQ 5 (and is obviously a legacy device); the network card can use IRQs 5 and 9; and the printer can use IRQs 3, 5, or 7.

Figure 4.1.

Different devices might want the same resource. The resource arbitrator assigns the resources.

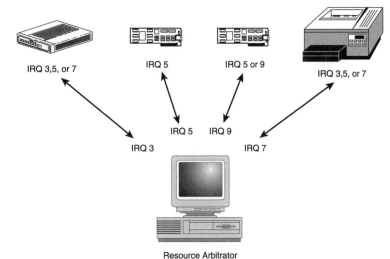

Resource Arbitrator

4

Because some of the devices want the same IRQ, the resource arbitrator must determine which resources can be assigned to the devices without causing a conflict by assigning the same IRQ to two devices. In this particular scenario, the modem is assigned IRQ 3, the sound card is assigned IRQ 5, the network card is assigned IRQ 9, and the printer is assigned IRQ 7.

The sound card was the only legacy device in this scenario. Because the other devices were all PnP-compatible, they were flexible enough to be assigned different IRQs. Even though some legacy devices might have the capability to be set to different IRQs, this usually entails having to change jumper settings on the card or running a software utility to change the setting stored on the card. In that case, the card is not considered PnP-compliant. A true PnP-compliant device can accept different IRQ settings (and any other resource settings) that the resource arbitrator assigns to it without intervention from the user.

The resource arbitrator assigns resources in a set pattern. Any devices required to allow the machine to boot are assigned their resources first. If the boot drive is an IDE drive, it is assigned its resources first. If the drive is a SCSI, the SCSI adapter is given its IRQ first.

After boot devices are given their resources, legacy devices are assigned resources. Legacy devices tend to be less flexible than PnP devices. Usually they are configured for specific resources. As an example, a network card can be configured using *jumpers* (small plastic devices used to connect two wire posts together so that an electronic current may flow). If so, the jumpers on the card can be jumpered (connected) for a specific IRQ. Because they are less flexible, legacy devices are assigned resources first, and then the remaining devices (which are PnP devices) are assigned their resources.

The resource arbitrator attempts to configure all the devices, but in some situations the resource arbitrator might not be able to do so. This can usually be attributed to one of two scenarios. The first occurs usually because too many legacy devices are used. Because the legacy devices are less flexible, it is more difficult to make sure that each device is set to use different resources, and they almost always require user intervention.

The other situation that can cause a problem is becoming a more common one: limited IRQs. It is not uncommon today to find a computer with a sound card, modem, network card, and many other devices. Because each device needs its own IRQ, it is relatively easy to run out of IRQs. The solution is either to get more IRQs or simply leave a device or two out of the system. Unfortunately, you can't get more IRQs, so you are usually left with removing devices to resolve the conflict.

It is also not necessary to have the devices assigned the resources as the arbitrator sees fit. You can manually configure which resources Windows 95 uses for the devices. To do so, you must use the Device Manager.

4.3.7. The Device Manager

Sooner or later, you will have to intervene and manually configure a device. There are actually several different reasons why you might need to do this; here are two:

- Windows 95 does not detect a legacy device.
- The Configuration Manager and resource arbitrator cannot resolve a resource allocation conflict.

The first reason usually results in going to the Add New Hardware option in the Control Panel, installing the device manually, and specifying the type and manufacturer of the device.

 Test Tip This section covers the following exam objective: Diagnose and resolve resource problems.

You can repair the latter of the two reasons by manually configuring the resources for the device(s). Enter the Device Manager, which is nothing more than a tool that lets you view and modify the configuration of the devices that are installed in your machine. You can reach the Device Manager by clicking the System option in the Control Panel. The second tab is appropriately marked. Selecting the Device Manager tab allows you to view the devices that are currently configured. The interface has an Explorer-style interface. You can click the plus signs to expand and see the devices (see Figure 4.2). Whenever a device is not working properly, the Device Manager automatically expands to it and the device is labeled with a yellow exclamation point on your screen (unfortunately, the color disappears in the following black-and-white figure).

4

Figure 4.2.

Viewing devices in the Device Manager tab of the System Properties window.

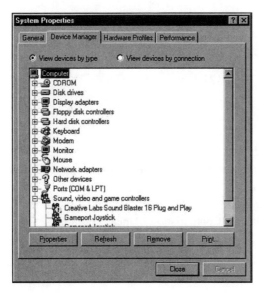

Note   You can also reach the Device Manager by right-clicking the My
        Computer icon located on your desktop. Selecting Properties in the
        shortcut menu takes you right to it.

You can manually change the configuration of the devices by locating the device in the Device Manager, selecting the device, and then clicking the Properties button.

The Properties sheet for the device seen in Figure 4.3 shows why my device is not working properly. The first tab gives general information about the device. The second tab (see Figure 4.4) gives a list of drivers that the device currently has installed, along with an option to change the driver(s).

Figure 4.3.

The Properties sheet of a device causing a resource conflict shows the telltale signs.

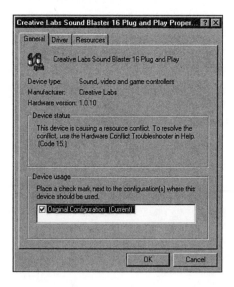

If you would like to configure what resources a device uses manually, you can do so by selecting the Resources tab at the top of the System Properties sheet. In my particular situation, Windows cannot determine which resources the device needs. Therefore, the only option under the Resources tab for me to select (as you see in Figure 4.5) is a Set Configuration Manually button.

Figure 4.4.

You can change the drivers that a device uses by selecting the Driver tab.

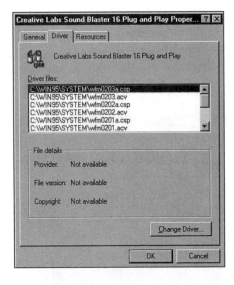

Figure 4.5.

Manually setting the configuration on a legacy device.

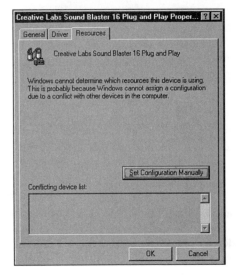

4

After you click the Set Configuration Manually button, you can then see the default settings of the resource. You also see a list of any devices with which the current settings might cause conflicts. In Figure 4.6, you see that my device, which is a sound card, is currently causing an IRQ conflict with the network card and an I/O Port conflict with the gameport joystick. You can change the settings by clicking the resource in the upper portion of the window and then clicking the Change Setting button.

Figure 4.6.

Viewing the conflicting resources and devices.

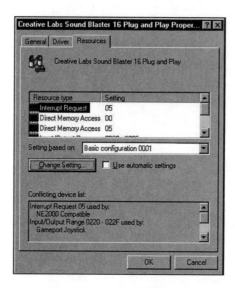

By clicking the Change Setting button, you can change the setting for that particular resource (see Figure 4.7). Notice that the bottom of the window shows which devices are already assigned to which resources so that you don't assign the same resource to two devices by mistake.

Note

You might need to remove the check mark from the Use Automatic Settings option on the Resources tab (refer to Figure 4.6) before Windows 95 will allow you to change the settings.

After completing any changes to the devices settings, you might be prompted to restart or shut down the computer (see Figure 4.8). For most legacy devices, the computer must be restarted or shut down to reassign resources.

Figure 4.7.

Changing the resource assignment of a device.

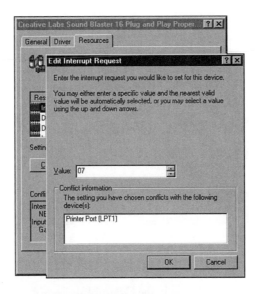

Figure 4.8.

Restarting the computer for changes to take effect.

4

Note

Stop and take the time to notice what the message says that pops up on your screen. If you have been working on computers for a while, you probably fall into the trap of ignoring these messages. Believe me, I do. In this particular case, it is important whether you completely shut the computer down or simply press Ctrl+Alt+Del. Sometimes it is necessary to power the machine off completely to ensure that the PnP BIOS and other devices have a chance to reset completely.

It is not necessary to bring up the property sheet for every device to view the allocation of resources. At the Device Manager screen, you can click Computer at the top of the list and then click the Properties button. This displays the entire list of resources currently assigned (see Figure 4.9). The resources are grouped into four areas: IRQ, I/O port, DMA channel, and memory. You can view the different groupings by clicking the different radio buttons at the top of the window.

Figure 4.9.

You can view all of the resources assigned by bringing up the Computer Properties sheet.

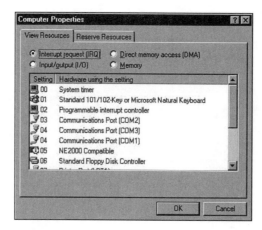

4.4. Add New Hardware Wizard

The Add New Hardware icon in the Control Panel opens a wizard that helps you install new hardware devices on your computer. Windows uses Plug and Play technology to make this process easier, even for legacy devices that do not support Plug and Play.

This section partially covers the following exam objective: Diagnose and resolve hardware device and device driver problems—Add New Hardware Wizard. More information on this exam objective can be found in Chapter 13, "Troubleshooting Windows 95."

4.4.1. Installing New Hardware

After installing the hardware into the computer, simply start Windows 95 and double-click the Add New hardware icon in the Control Panel. After clicking Next, you are prompted whether to allow Windows 95 to detect your hardware or not (see Figure 4.10). For the most part, you should allow Windows to detect the hardware (unless specified not to by the manufacturer of the hardware, support personnel, and so on). Windows uses Plug and Play methods to determine if new hardware has been added to the machine or not, and what the settings of the new hardware might be.

Figure 4.10.

Starting the New Hardware Wizard.

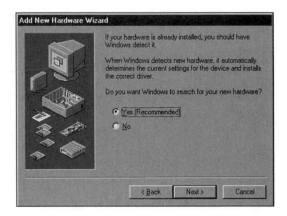

To have Windows attempt to detect the hardware, ensure that Yes is selected and click Next. A dialog box appears, warning you that all programs should be closed during the process and what to do if your computer should stop responding (see Figure 4.11). After clicking Next, another box appears showing you the status of the detection process (see Figure 4.12).

Figure 4.11.

The New Hardware Wizard warning message.

After the detection process is complete, you are notified whether Windows detected any new hardware or not. In my particular case, Windows did find new hardware. By clicking the Details button, I can view what hardware was detected (see Figure 4.13).

Figure 4.12.

Viewing the status of hardware detection.

Figure 4.13.

The hardware detected after running the wizard.

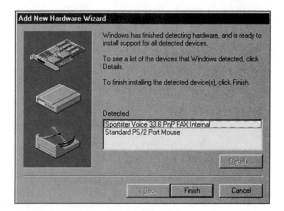

By clicking the Finish button, you complete the setup process by supplying the software that Windows 95 needs. For the most part, this consists of the Windows 95 setup files from the CD. On some occasions, you might be prompted to provide drivers from the manufacturer of the particular piece of hardware.

4.4.2. What If My Hardware Isn't Detected?

There will be times that the New Hardware Wizard won't detect the hardware that you just installed. The reasons for this can vary. Perhaps there is a resource conflict or the hardware is relatively new and is not recognized by Windows 95. If it does not detect your new hardware, you can specify what new hardware you have. You can do this before attempting to detect by selecting No at the first screen (refer to

Figure 4.10). If you allow Windows to attempt the detection of hardware and it does not find any, the next dialog box that appears is one similar to Figure 4.14.

Figure 4.14.

Specifying which type of hardware to install.

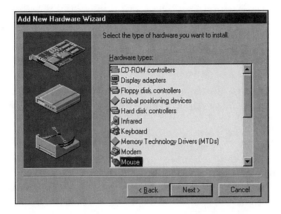

In this box, you can specify the type of device. In this example, I am installing a mouse. After specifying that I want to install a mouse and clicking Next, I am prompted to specify which manufacturer and type of mouse that I want to install (see Figure 4.15). This process is similar with any type of hardware device you choose.

Figure 4.15.

Here I specify the manufacturer and type of mouse I am installing.

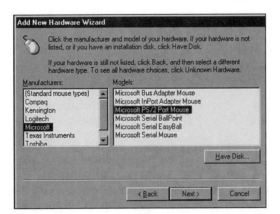

In Figure 4.15, you might notice that you have a button labeled Have Disk. This option allows you to specify a newer device and driver that you might have received from the manufacturer.

If you have a driver disk that came with the piece of hardware, you should consider using the Have Disk option. This ensures that the driver being installed for the device is the correct one. Before doing so, ask yourself two questions:

1. Is the driver a Windows 95 driver?

2. Is the driver newer than the version of Windows 95 you have installed?

If you answer Yes to both questions, use the Have Disk option. There is a good possibility that the driver that comes with the device is more current.

To continue, click Next. After supplying the software that Windows prompts you for, you are prompted to restart the computer. When you restart, the device is installed.

4.5. Portable Features

In addition to the PnP features mentioned previously, Windows 95 also supports many features that relate directly to the use of Windows 95 on portable computers. These features make Windows 95 the best operating system available for use on portable computers. The three main features are:

- Support for docking stations
- Support for power management features
- Support for PC cards

These features might not seem all that great or like they separate Windows 95 from other operating systems you might see installed on portable computers, but read further to gain a better understanding of what these features have to offer.

Be careful not to confuse the terminology when talking about the different types of smaller computers that are available. The term *portable* refers to what some might refer to as laptop or notebook computers. It does not, however, refer to handheld computers (HC). These computers run a ROM-based version of Windows 95 called *Windows CE* (*Compact Edition*). They are also sometimes referred to as *palmtops*.

4.5.1. Docking Stations

Computing while traveling usually entails the use of a portable computer or laptop. As convenient as these computers are, they still do not offer the comfort of a nice big monitor, normal-sized keyboard, and a real mouse.

In the past, if you wanted the niceties of a desktop machine but the convenience of a portable, you were forced to put up with having two computers. The invention of the *docking station* takes care of this problem, though.

Docking stations are designed to be placed on the desktop, connected to a normal monitor, keyboard, and so on. Additionally, this docking station might have its own network card, modem, or other device(s). When you get back to your office with your portable in tow, all you need to do to get the functionality of these devices is to "dock" the portable in the docking station.

Windows 95 supports docking stations. As a matter of fact, it supports docking stations quite fabulously. It supports three different types of docking:

- **Cold Docking**—The computer must be completely shut down (powered off) before it can be docked or undocked.
- **Warm Docking**—The computer can be docked or undocked during a suspended or sleep mode (reduced power).
- **Hot Docking**—The computer can be docked or undocked while completely up and running.

Test Tip

Understand the difference between cold, warm, and hot docking as described in the previous paragraph.

The type of docking really depends on the manufacturer of the hardware. You can configure Windows 95 for the different configurations based upon whether the computer is docked or undocked. For example, you might have a PC card modem in the portable that you would like to use for communication when the portable is undocked, but the docking station has a faster modem that you want to use for communications instead of the PC card modem while the computer is docked.

To work properly, the devices must be PnP-compliant. Additionally, the programs installed must be able to handle the removal or addition of devices. Some programs don't like the idea of devices just disappearing.

Different types of docking systems are also available. The first is an auto-eject, VCR-style docking station. When I say, *VCR-style*, I mean that the docking station can eject the portable computer using a motorized ejection system. With this system, Windows 95 prompts the user about saving files or closing resources prior to ejection.

The second type uses a manual ejection. Because Windows 95 has no idea of when an ejection is about to happen, you must take the responsibility of saving files and closing resources prior to ejecting the portable.

4.5.2. Card Insertion and Removal

Windows 95 allows for dynamic changes to the computer. This includes the insertion or removal of PC cards. As long as all PnP requirements are met, you can insert and remove PC cards, and Windows 95 automatically sets up or removes the device without any interaction from you.

Once again, the computer's BIOS or PC card socket component should be able to notify the Configuration Manager so that the new device can be configured properly. Additionally, the programs in use must be able to support hot swapping of PC cards. They should be able to start using the device, if necessary, or stop using the device (stop making calls to the device) should it be removed.

Lab

The lab consists of review questions pertaining to this chapter and provides an opportunity to apply the knowledge that you've learned with this chapter. Answers to the review questions can be found in Appendix B.

Questions

1. What type of docking requires that the portable computer be in a suspended or sleep mode?

   A. Hot docking

   B. Warm docking

   C. Cold docking

   D. Boat docking

2. Legacy devices cannot be used in a PnP computer.

   A. True

   B. False

3. Which of the following components is in charge of handling all aspects of the configuration process?

   A. Configuration Manager

   B. Resource arbitrator

   C. Bus Enumerator

   D. Registry

4. Which of the following components resolves conflicts between devices?

   A. Configuration Manager

   B. Resource arbitrator

   C. Bus Enumerator

   D. Registry

4

5. Which of the following components is responsible for building the hardware tree?

    A. Configuration Manager

    B. Resource arbitrator

    C. Bus Enumerator

    D. Registry

6. Which of the following components is used to manually intervene in the event of an unresolved resource conflict?

    A. Configuration Manager

    B. Device Manager

    C. Registry editor

    D. Configuration editor

7. A user solicits your assistance. He has just installed a new component in his machine and seems to be having problems. He has the following devices installed that can use the listed IRQs:

    Mouse on COM 1

    Floppy Drive

    Printer on LPT1

    Modem that can use IRQ 3, 4, or 5

    Network card that can use 5 or 7

    Sound card that can use 3 or 5

    IDE controller that can use 14 or 15

    All the devices are legacy devices. Can the resource conflict be resolved?

    A. Yes

    B. No

8. Which component is responsible for creating the hardware tree?

    A. BIOS

    B. Device Manager

    C. Bus Enumerator

    D. Resource Arbitrator

9. As part of the Plug and Play operating system, certain resources need to be assigned to devices so that they can communicate with the processor. Which of the following are they? Choose all that apply.

   A. Direct Memory Access (DMA) channels

   B. Interrupt Requests (IRQ)

   C. Peripheral Component Interconnect (PCI) numbers

   D. Input/Output (I/O) ports

   E. Memory

   F. Small Computer Standard Interface (SCSI) ID numbers

10. Which component is responsible for allocating specific resources and resolving conflicts when two or more devices request the same resource?

    A. BIOS

    B. Device Manager

    C. Configuration Manager

    D. Resource Arbitrator

11. For a computer to be Plug and Play–compliant, its BIOS must be able to do which of the following? Choose all that apply.

    A. Notification of dynamic changes in system configuration

    B. Creation of the hardware tree

    C. Allocation of IRQs

    D. Configuration of system boot devices

Exercise

This chapter has a lot of theory-based information in it. You might not need to know everything in this chapter for the exam or for real-world applications, but that should not overshadow the importance of understanding the PnP standards and processes. Now, you can be a little less frustrated when Windows 95 does not assign the proper resources to a conflict device because you have the background knowledge on how the process works.

Take this knowledge and apply it to becoming familiar with changing resource assignments in the Control Panel. You should practice resolving conflicts manually until you are comfortable with the procedure. If this means that you need to memorize the resources that are commonly assigned throughout the industry (floppy drive, LPT ports, and so on), make it so.

MCSE

Day 5

Files, Folders, and Disks

Windows 95 comes with many disk tools to manage your files and hard disks. It has been enhanced with new improvements to its disk support and filing system. Users no longer are limited to eight-character file names as with older versions of Windows and MS-DOS.

Added administration and troubleshooting come with these added capabilities. You must understand how long file names work and how to use the new disk utilities. Additionally, you need to know how to troubleshoot problems with the file system and disks. This chapter will explain how to do just that.

Objectives

The exam objectives for this chapter are short and sweet. The main theme for this chapter covers the simple knowledge of running the different disk utilities and a few basics for disk and file management, including:

- Managing hard disks
- Disk compression
- Partitioning
- Tuning and optimizing the system
- Disk defragmenter
- ScanDisk
- Compression utility
- Installing and configuring backup hardware and software
- Tape drives
- The Backup application
- Backing up and restoring data

5.1. File Systems Versus Operating Systems

Microsoft has created many operating systems over the years, but most people do not understand the history of the file system that most Windows operating systems use and how it has evolved.

In its first operating system, MS-DOS ran using an 8-bit file system called *file allocation table (FAT)*. Later, this file system was upgraded to use a 16-bit FAT. I won't bore you with the full explanation of what composes the FAT and how it works. The FAT basically maps out to the operating system where the files physically reside on the hard disk.

With Windows 3.*x*, the FAT file system still remained because these versions of Windows needed MS-DOS to run. Because Windows 95 is its own operating system, though, FAT has been replaced with *VFAT*, which is a *virtualized file allocation table* that is 32-bit, unlike its 16-bit predecessor. I'll come back to VFAT in a moment.

5.2. Partitioning and Formatting

Before you can use a hard disk, it must be partitioned and formatted. Windows 95 includes a utility called `FDISK.EXE` that was also included in previous versions of Windows and MS-DOS. This command-line utility is used to partition hard disks. Another command-line utility, `FORMAT.COM`, is included for formatting the hard disk after you have partitioned it.

 This section covers the following exam objective: Manage Hard Disks—Partitioning.

5.2.1. Partitioning

Partitioning your hard disk is the simple process of logically breaking up the hard disk into smaller sizes. I like to think of partitioning a hard disk as something similar to what more and more corporations are doing today with office space. They rent this huge area of office space, and instead of putting up permanent walls, they simply break it up into smaller offices using cubicles or modular furniture.

To partition a hard disk for use with Windows 95, you must use a utility such as FDISK.EXE. To use FDISK, you need to understand a few basic terms. If you don't, you can become easily confused with using the FDISK program. Later in your certification path, this information will prove to be valuable after you begin studying for Windows NT exams.

A partitioned hard disk consists of at least one *primary partition*. With early versions of MS-DOS, you could have only one primary partition. Beginning with MS-DOS 5.0, you can have up to four.

Because you had to have at least one and only one primary partition with early versions of MS-DOS, how could you have more than one partition? After creating your primary partition, you could create a *secondary partition*. But wait, there is one small problem. With those early versions of MS-DOS, you could have only one secondary partition. This brings me to my next rhetorical question.

How can you divide your disk into more than two sections with early versions of MS-DOS when you could have only one primary and one secondary partition? Well, you could divide the secondary partition into *logical drives*. Logical drives are just another way for you to split up the hard disk into separate smaller drives. Confused yet? Let me give an example that may help. In Figure 5.1, you see an example hard drive divided into two partitions, a primary and secondary. However, the secondary partition is divided into two logical drives, resulting in a total of three drive letters.

All three items—primary partitions, secondary partitions, and logical drives—can be created using FDISK.EXE.

5.2.2. Windows 95A Versus Windows 95B (OSR2)

I want to bring two issues to your attention. These are not necessarily on the test, but valuable enough that I choose to cover it. If you are only concerned with what is on the exam, skip to section 5.2.3., "Using FDISK." There are differences between the first release of Windows 95 and release 2 (OSR2). The first issue is partition size, and the second is cluster size.

Windows 95 OSR2 provides an updated version of the file allocation table file system, called *FAT32*. The main differences between the original version of Windows 95 and OSR2 when it comes to the hard disks are the maximum size of partitions and the cluster sizes.

5

Figure 5.1.

An example of a partitioned drive.

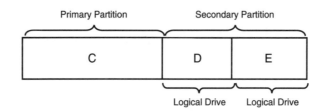

Note

You can determine whether you are running the original version or OSR2 by double-clicking the System option in the Control Panel. If your version number is 4.00.950B, you have OSR2. If the B does not exist, you are running the original version.

Partition Size

With the original release of Windows 95, partition sizes can be a maximum of 2GB. If your hard disk is larger than that, you have to partition it into 2GB or smaller partitions.

The FAT32 of OSR2 allows your partitions to be up to 2 tetrabytes in size, but simply installing OSR2 on your computer that previously contained the original version Windows 95 will not give you the FAT32 capability. (No, you cannot upgrade the first release with OSR2.) You must use an OSR2 startup disk that has a new and improved FDISK and FORMAT programs to repartition your hard disk so that you can employ the new capabilities.

Warning

As with most advantages, there come some disadvantages. FAT32 does have some disadvantages. As of this writing, Windows 95 OEM Service Release 2 is the only operating system capable of accessing FAT32 volumes. MS-DOS, the original version of Windows 95, and Windows NT do not recognize FAT32 partitions and are unable to boot from a FAT32 volume. Additionally, FAT32 volumes cannot be accessed properly if the computer is started using another operating system (for example, a Windows NT or MS-DOS boot disk).

However, Windows 95 OSR2 can still be booted to real mode (for example, to run a game or other MS-DOS based program) and can use FAT32 volumes.

Cluster Size

When you format your hard drive or floppy disk, it is divided into *sectors*. These are divisions of the hard disk. If the hard disk were a pie, this would be the equivalent of cutting it into slices. *Clusters* are groups of sectors. How big your clusters are depends on how big the partition is. Why does your cluster size matter? Well, it determines how much of your hard disk is wasted.

When you write a file to the hard disk, it takes at least one cluster, no matter what the size. If your cluster size is 32K and the file is only 2K, it is still allocated one cluster. That means 30K is wasted. Even though all your files may be larger than 32K, you still could have wasted space because two files cannot share the same cluster.

For example, let's say you store a file that is 50K in size. Two clusters are allocated for its storage (64K). That means that one cluster is filled, leaving the other cluster still wasting 14K. When you multiply this times the amount of files you may have stored on your computer, you can see how much space can possibly be wasted.

How big your clusters are depends on which version of Windows 95 you have. Table 5.1 outlines the cluster sizes for the first release.

Table 5.1. Cluster sizes for Windows 95 (first release).

Drive Size (MB)	Sectors per cluster	Cluster Size
0-15	8	4K
16-127	4	2K
128-255	8	4K
256-511	16	8K
512-1023	32	16K
1024-2048	64	32K

The cluster sizes with OSR2 are significantly smaller, resulting in 10 to 15 percent more efficient use of disk space. Table 5.2 outlines the cluster sizes for OSR2.

5

Table 5.2. Cluster sizes for Windows 95 (OSR2).

Drive Size	Cluster Size
1-512MB	n/a
513MB-8GB	4K
8GB-16GB	8K
16GB-32GB	16K

To find out what your cluster size is, run ScanDisk. When the results screen comes up, take a look at the bytes in each allocation unit line. That is your cluster size.

5.2.3. Using FDISK

Whenever I use FDISK, I usually boot up to a floppy disk that contains not only FDISK.EXE, but also FORMAT.COM and any other important files such as an AUTOEXEC.BAT, CONFIG.SYS, and any drivers that I may need to get the machine up and running. These drivers may include, but are not limited to, disk drivers (for SCSI hard disks, for example), CD-ROM drivers, network card drivers, and more.

Many times, this disk can be a system disk created in another Windows 95 loaded computer, or a startup disk created during a previous Windows 95 installation.

If you are running the updated FDISK that comes with OSR2, the first thing that you see is the warning in Figure 5.2. By selecting Yes to this message, you enable the advanced FAT32 functions that I mentioned in section 5.3.2.

Using FDISK, you can create primary partitions, secondary partitions, and logical drives (see Figure 5.3). Additionally, you can partition more than one hard disk at one time.

Deleting partitions using FDISK results in loss of all data on that partition.

Figure 5.2.

The OSR2 large hard disk support screen.

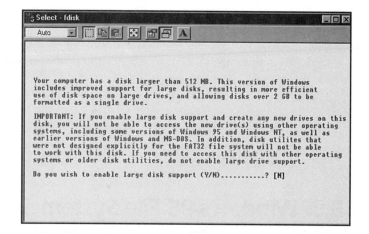

Figure 5.3.

The main FDISK screen.

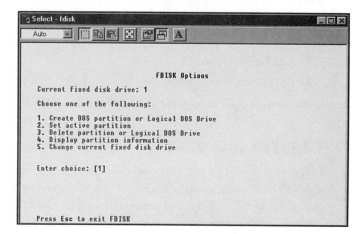

5

A step that is often overlooked is setting *an active partition*. After you have created your partition(s), you must set one to be the active partition. This is simply telling the computer which partition to use when it looks for the system files (the files that it needs to boot up). When it comes to active partitions, there can be only one.

If you are using only one hard drive and create only a single partition, then the active partition is set automatically to that partition. However, if you create more than one, you must set it using FDISK (refer to Figure 5.2). Usually, whichever partition is designated as the C drive becomes the active partition.

5.2.4. Using FORMAT

After you have your partitions created, you need to format them before they can be used. When formatting the C drive, which is usually the active partition, you should use the following command line:

```
FORMAT C: /S
```

This not only formats the drive, but it also transfers the system files from the floppy and makes the C drive bootable. Be sure that whichever operating system you want to be on the hard disk is the one that is on the floppy that you booted up to.

5.3. Windows 95 File System Support

Windows 95 incorporates the use of the Installable File System (IFS) Manager to allow interoperability of the different components that handle files. Installable File Systems include such items as:

- **VFAT**—Virtualized FAT
- **CDFS**—CD-ROM File System
- **Network redirectors**—Allows access to files on the network

5.3.1. FAT and VFAT

Disk drivers control access to the hard disk. Real-made drivers are usually associated with MS-DOS and are usually loaded prior to Windows starting. These drivers are part of the operating system and are either 16-bit or 32-bit. They are also either *real-mode* or *protected-mode drivers*. For the most part, 16-bit drivers are usually real-mode drivers; likewise, 32-bit drivers are protected-mode drivers.

Real-mode drivers are access to the hard disk. These drivers are part usually associated with MS-DOS and are usually loaded prior to Windows starting. Real-mode drivers are usually specified in the CONFIG.SYS and are not as robust and stable as protected-mode drivers.

Protected-mode drivers are loaded within Windows. They get their name from the fact that protected mode components are loaded in memory in such a way that they are protected from corrupting each other. The 32-bit components are preferred because they tend to be more robust and more stable than their 16-bit counterparts.

The FAT file system of MS-DOS is 16-bit and real-mode. The VFAT file system of Windows 95 is 32-bit and is protected-mode. It only provides 32-bit access to hard disks because other components like CD-ROMs have their own installable file system.

VCache

VCache is a utility that takes the place of SmartDrive of MS-DOS and Windows 3.1. If you are not familiar with SmartDrive, it is a utility that allowed for disk caching. What is *caching*, you might be asking? There are actually two types.

Read-ahead

The first type is called *read-ahead.* When you install a program to the hard disk, the computer writes the files to the first available free space. Assuming that the free space was contiguous, the files that made up this program would be right next to each other on the hard drive. What does this have to do with read-ahead caching? Take a look at Figure 5.4.

Figure 5.4.

Read-ahead caching allows the computer to cache information that the program might need in the near future.

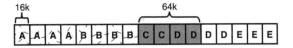

In the figure, let's assume that that the blocks represent 16K of disk space, and each letter represents a different file on the hard disk. Notice that the files take up more than one 16K block of space.

Well, when you use the program, the computer reads the files from the hard disk. In this scenario, the program makes a call for the computer to read files A and B. With read-ahead caching, the computer reads more information than the program requests. In our scenario, we have the read-ahead caching set at 64K. Therefore, when the program requests files A and B, the computer reads ahead 64K and loads the information into memory. When and if the program needs file C, it can obtain it faster because it is already loaded into RAM.

5

This entire process just speeds up the program. Accessing information in RAM is much faster than reading information from the hard disk. (Keep in mind that hard disks work in milliseconds and RAM works in nanoseconds.) The computer assumes that if you are reading information from a particular area of the hard disk, there is a good possibility that you will need more information from the same area, so it reads ahead.

Note Remember that read-ahead caching is optimized when the files are contiguous. In other words, it works well when the hard disk is defragmented. I'll cover defragmentation later in this chapter.

You can modify how much the computer reads ahead. Follow these steps:

1. Double-click the System option in the Control Panel.
2. Select the Performance tab.
3. At the bottom of the Windows, click the File System button.
4. Select the Hard Disk tab.

You will see a screen similar to Figure 5.5. You can modify two settings in this window. The first setting is the role of the computer. The role determines how much RAM will be set aside for caching. The more RAM that is set aside for caching usually means that less is available for applications.

The settings include the following:

- **Desktop computer**—Small cache size
- **Mobile or docking system**—Medium cache size (more caching means less power is needed for hard disk reading)
- **Network server**—Large cache size

Don't worry: no sizes are specified because Windows 95 allocates the memory automatically. The amount it allocates is based upon how much memory is actually available. There is no need for you to specify an amount like with previous versions of Windows.

Figure 5.5.

*Modifying the hard
disk read-ahead
caching.*

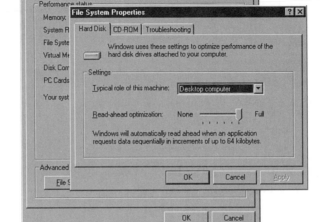

In addition to modifying the role of the computer, you can modify how far ahead
the computer reads ahead. The increments are no read ahead, 4K, 8K, 16K, 32K,
and 64K.

Write-behind caching

The second type of caching available through VCache is write-behind caching. This
type of caching can actually be harmful, but it is only harmful if not used properly.

Write-behind caching mainly allows you to regain control of the computer faster.
For example, with Windows 3.1, when you were using a word processor and you
wanted to save a large file, you had to wait until it was completely saved and written
to the disk until you could do anything else. That's not the case with Windows 95.

In Windows 95 with write-behind caching enabled (it is by default), you can save a
file and continue with your work. You can do this because Windows 95 tells the
application that the file is saved so that the application returns control to you, the
user. This file may not actually be saved, however. Windows 95 holds the saved file
in memory until it is not as busy, and then it writes it to the disk. The amount of
time that it waits depends largely on what is currently being done on the computer;
but for the most part, it's merely seconds.

This can still be dangerous, though. I've seen users shut down a word processing
application at five o'clock, with their finger on the power button, waiting for the
application to say the file was saved. The second the application reports its save is

5

complete, the user powers off the machine. This same user comes to work the next day and wonders why his file is not there, not current, or worse yet, is corrupt. Apparently, no one educated this user that before powering off the machine he should shut down Windows 95 properly (which is the only sure way that cached files are saved).

Write-behind caching can also be dangerous in situations where you have flaky power when outages or surges are a common occurrence. If you want to turn off the write-behind, follow these steps:

1. Double-click the System option in the Control Panel.
2. Select the Performance tab.
3. At the bottom of the window, click the File System button.
4. Select the Troubleshooting tab.

You are given a list of options to turn on or off that allow you to modify the behavior of the system (see Figure 5.6). To disable the write-behind option, place a check mark in the box next to Disable Write-Behind Caching for All Drives. You might notice that you do not have the option of disabling for individual drives.

Figure 5.6.

Disabling write-behind caching for all disk drives.

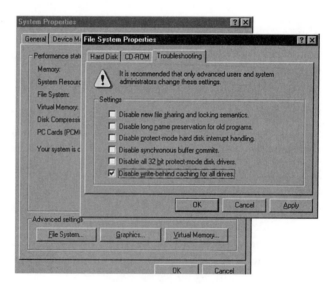

5.3.2. CDFS

The *CD-ROM File System* (*CDFS*) is another virtual file system that supports CD-ROMs in the same manner as VFAT supports hard disks. It is a protected-mode version of the MSCDEX.EXE most familiar with MS-DOS and previous versions of Windows.

Likewise with VFAT, CDFS has improved the performance of reading CD-ROMs by adding a caching capability through VCache. Caching is called *supplemental caching* with CD-ROMs and is used for caching path table, directory, and file information. Caching this information lets multimedia, such as video and multimedia presentations, run more smoothly.

You can modify the parameters by following these steps:

1. Double-click the System option in the Control Panel.
2. Select the Performance tab.
3. At the bottom of the window, click the File System button.
4. Select the CD-ROM tab.

At the CD-ROM tab (see Figure 5.7), you can modify the cache size in two ways. The first way is to use the slide bar to modify the size; the second is through the use of specifying the speed of your CD-ROM. Notice the fastest is Quad-speed or Higher.

Figure 5.7.

The CD-ROM Cache settings.

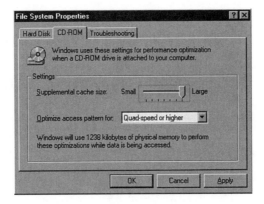

5

5.3.3. Long and Short File Names

Windows 95 supports file names as long as 255 characters. It also allows the use of spaces and other special characters that were not normally supported under MS-DOS, but this support only extends to 32-bit programs. Windows 95 automatically truncates these long file names for 16-bit programs that do not understand them.

> The path and file name together may not contain more than 260 characters. This might limit the actual length of the file name. For example, if the directory is C:\WINDOWS\SYSTEM\ (which is 18 characters), the file name cannot be more than 242 characters.

Long file names are not case-sensitive, but they do preserve the case you specify. Whenever you create a long file name, Windows 95 automatically creates an 8.3 alias so that older 16-bit programs will be able to read the files. When the 16-bit programs modify and save the files, the long file names are preserved.

> Some 16-bit programs can erase long file names. When saving files with these programs, it first deletes the existing file and then resaves the file with the same name instead of overwriting or appending the existing file. When the existing file is deleted, the long file name is lost.

The truncated files maintain an 8.3 format that the 16-bit programs understand. The files are truncated using an algorithm that incorporates the use of a tilde (~).

The algorithm takes the first six characters of the long file name and places a tilde after them. Then it adds a number (1-9) at the end to make the eight character name. The number is to identify files that may have a very similar file name when it comes to the first six characters. For example, MY LONG FILENAME.TXT and MY LONG STORY.TXT are similar names when truncated. When the tenth like file name is reached, the file name uses the first five characters, the tilde, and then a number (10-99). Likewise, when you reach the one hundredth like name, it uses the first four characters.

The three character extension is the same as the first three letters of the long file names extension. If the long file name has multiple extensions (multiple period separators), the three-character extension comprises the first three letters after the first period separator. In addition, the long file name alias is placed in all uppercase letters.

You should be careful with long file names in the root directory of a hard disk. The root directory has a hardcoded limit of 512 directory entries in the FAT table. These directory entries contain information such as the file name, extension, attributes, time and date the file was last modified, the starting cluster number, and the file size. Each directory entry uses 32 bytes to store this information. Because the root directory is 16K in size, it can contain a maximum of 512 directory entries, which are 32 bytes each.

> With the second release of Windows 95 (OSR2), you can overcome this limitation by creating a FAT32 drive. The root directory on a FAT32 drive is an ordinary cluster chain, so it can be located anywhere on the drive. For this reason, the previous limitations on the number of root directory entries no longer exist.

Because long file names can be used with Windows 95, you might reach the 512 entry limit sooner than you anticipate. This might occur because, when a file name exceeds 13 characters, an additional directory entry is used for storing the file name. For every 13 characters, an additional entry is used. Also, when the file name exceeds 13 characters, an additional entry is used to store the 8.3 alias. If the file name does not exceed the 13 character limit, only one directory entry is used. Take a look at Table 5.3 for some examples.

Table 5.3. Sample long file names and their 8.3 aliases.

Long file name	Possible 8.3 alias	Directory entries used
FILENAME.TXT	FILENAME.TXT	1
FileName.txt	FILENAME.TXT	2
LFN TEST.TXT	LFNTES~1.TXT	2
My Long File Name.TEST	MYLONG~1.TES	3
My Very Long File.Name. test	MYVERY~1.NAM	4

> Almost all exams have a question on the proper alias name for a long file name.

For only one directory to be used, long file names must be 8.3-compliant. This not only means that the file names be eight characters long with a three character extension, they must also not contain any special characters, spaces, or a combination of upper- and lowercase letters.

When an 8.3 alias does not produce a unique file name using 1-9 after the tilde, it then uses the long file name's first five characters, the tilde, and then a double-digit number (10-99). It is followed by a period separator and the three character extension. This process continues with three digit numbers, if necessary, until a unique file name is generated.

If you don't like the use of the tilde (~), you can disable it. To do so, add the value NameNumericTail=0 to the following Registry key:

Hkey_Local_Machine\System\CurentControlSet\Control\FileSystem

Also be careful when accomplishing duties at the command prompt. If you're not careful, you could trash your long file names. One example is with the rename (REN) command. If you rename a file using its 8.3 alias at the command prompt, you not only rename its 8.3 alias, but its long file name as well. For example, let's say you have a file called Long File Name.txt (LONGFI~1.TXT), and you decide to rename it at the command prompt. If you type the command

```
REN LONGFIL~1.TXT SHRTFI~1.TXT
```

not only would its 8.3 alias be SHRTFI~1.TXT, but so would its long file name. The proper way to rename it is something along the lines of the following:

```
REN "LONG FILE NAME.TXT" "SHRT FILE.TXT"
```

So you see, whenever you want to specify a file's long name, you must use quotes for spaces. If there are no spaces, you can simply use the REN command and type the entire long file name out. Because MS-DOS separates its commands with spaces, you need to designate that the spaces are part of the file name by surrounding the file name with quotes.

Disabling Long File Name Support

You might want to disable long file name support on your Windows 95 computer. Reasons behind this decision can stem from needing to use a utility that does not understand long file names or other reasons. Examples of utilities are any disk utility not specifically designed for Windows 95. This includes ScanDisk, Defrag, or other disk utilities created for MS-DOS or previous versions of Windows. Utilities such as Norton Utilities and PC-Tools are more examples.

Generally, utilities not designed for Windows 95 should not be used, but if you must, you can disable long file name support temporarily using a utility called *LFNBK*. This utility can back up the long file names and then disable them. After running your utility, you can then use the LFNBK utility to restore the long file names.

The LFNBK utility renames the long file names to their respective aliases and then backs up the long file name information to a file called LFNBK.DAT. If you delete the LFNBK.DAT file, you lose the capability to restore the long file names.

To use the LFNBK utility, you must copy the LFNBK.EXE file from the Windows 95 CD-ROM to your Windows directory. It does not install onto the hard disk during install (for good reason). It is located in the \ADMIN\APPTOOLS\LFNBACK folder on the CD-ROM.

Microsoft highly recommends that you use the built-in utilities such as ScanDisk and Defrag or third-party utilities specifically designed for Windows 95 for disk management and backup. Using older utilities is not recommended.

Additionally, the LFNBK utility is considered an advanced tool, and only experienced Windows 95 users should use it.

5

To back up and disable long file names, follow these steps:

1. Double-click the System option in the Control Panel.
2. Select the File System tab.
3. Select the Troubleshooting tab.
4. Place a check mark in the box next to Disable Long Name Preservation for Old Programs and click OK.
5. Click OK in the System Properties box.
6. Close all programs.

7. At the command prompt, type **lfnbk /b** *c:* to back up and remove long file names (where *c:* can be replaced with a different drive letter).

8. Restart the computer and run the utility of your choice.

After you have run the necessary utilities that don't support long file names, you should re-enable the long file name support. To do so, follow these steps:

1. At the command prompt, type **lfnbk /r** *c:* to restore the long file names.

2. Double-click the System option in the Control Panel.

3. Select the File System tab.

4. Select the Troubleshooting tab.

5. Remove the check mark from the box next to Disable Long Name Preservation for Old Programs and click OK.

6. Click OK in the System Properties box.

7. Restart the computer.

If for whatever reason, you need to disable long file name support permanently, you can do so very simply. Follow the steps necessary to disable the long file names as discussed previously. Before restarting the computer, you need to make a Registry change. Change the value of Win31FileSystem to 1. You can find the value at:

Hkey_Local_Machine\System\CurrentControlSet\Control\ Filesystem

Long File Name Support for Servers

Windows NT workstations and servers support long file names, but older clients such as Microsoft LAN Manager or Windows for Workgroups cannot use shared folders with names longer than eight characters.

Long file name support on Novell NetWare servers is supported as long as the OS/2 name space has been loaded on the NetWare server. This is a module that is loaded at the NetWare server console. It, in essence, makes the NetWare server understand long file names. Without it, you must use conventional 8.3 file names.

5.4. Using Disk Utilities

Do you remember when you wanted to run utilities such as ScanDisk and Defrag and had to exit Windows to do it? Well, those days are long gone. The problem with older versions of Windows was that the file system didn't allow those utilities to have exclusive access to the disk on which it was being used. Therefore, you had to exit Windows and run the utility from MS-DOS.

With Windows 95, the enhanced file system allows these utilities to have exclusive access. Additionally, the utilities are protected-mode versions that support long file names. This means that you can use these versions in Windows while accomplishing other tasks. Additionally, third-party utilities written to the same APIs as the Microsoft utilities can also take advantage of these capabilities.

5.4.1. ScanDisk Functions

ScanDisk is a utility that fixes problems with hard disks, floppy disks, RAM drives, and memory cards. For the most part, the utility is used primarily for hard disk and floppy disk errors. The problems that it fixes include the following:

- File allocation table
- File system structure
- Directory tree structure
- Physical surface
- Compressed volumes
- Long file names

This section covers the following exam objective: Tune and optimize the system—ScanDisk.

ScanDisk was designed to repair three main problems. Two of these problems are logical and one is physical. The two logical problems are *crosslinked files* and *lost clusters*. Both of these problems are considered FAT errors and are usually interrelated.

When you store files on a hard disk, they make an entry into the FAT. The FAT identifies the starting cluster where the file begins and then points to the next cluster. Each cluster points to the next one in the chain. In Figure 5.8, you can see a very basic example.

5

Figure 5.8.

This is an example of a crosslinked file leaving lost clusters.

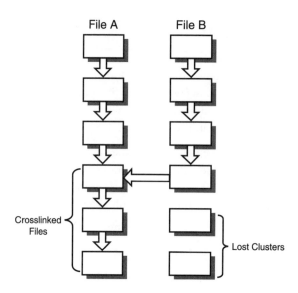

Crosslinked files are files that attempt to use the same cluster(s). The data in a crosslinked cluster is usually only correct for one of the crosslinked files or is incorrect for both. It will probably never be correct for both. By default, ScanDisk makes copies of the information for both files, but this usually corrupts one of the files. You can specify that ScanDisk delete the crosslinked clusters.

Lost clusters (sometimes referred to as lost file fragments) can contain useful data. Most of the time they are only taking up free space. By default, ScanDisk converts these lost fragments to files so that you can view them to determine if the data is worth being salvaged. The files are saved as File0000 and so on in the root directory of the disk being scanned. You can specify that ScanDisk convert these lost fragments to free space.

The physical problem that ScanDisk can fix is *bad sectors*, which are caused by normal wear and tear of the disk or by mishandling. In actuality, ScanDisk can't really fix bad sectors. ScanDisk can attempt to recover data from bad sectors and move it to another area of the disk. Then, it can mark the bad sectors to prevent them from being used.

To run ScanDisk, click the Start button, select Run, and type **ScanDisk**. If it is installed as part of Windows 95, it should appear under the Start menu at \Programs\Accessories\System Tools. Additionally, you can click any disk drive with your secondary mouse button in the Explorer or My Computer interfaces and select Properties. Then by selecting the Tools tab, you will have the option of checking for errors on the drive. When you run ScanDisk, you have two basic options (see Figure 5.9).

Figure 5.9.

The ScanDisk screen allows you to set basic options.

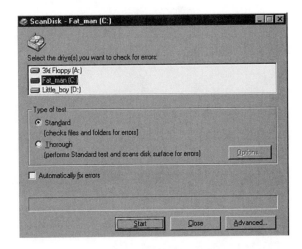

The first option, Standard, only checks files and folders for errors. This includes the FAT and long file names. The second option, though, performs the same as the Standard scan but also checks the physical aspects of the drive. Clicking the Advanced button allows you to specify what ScanDisk does when it comes across logical errors (see Figure 5.10).

Figure 5.10.

You can specify what you would like ScanDisk to do when it comes across logical errors.

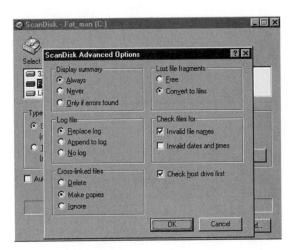

5

After you tell ScanDisk to perform a Thorough scan, you can click the Options button to specify what areas you would like ScanDisk to scan and what to do when it comes across Physical errors (see Figure 5.11).

Figure 5.11.

You can also specify what areas to scan and what you would like ScanDisk to do when it comes across physical errors.

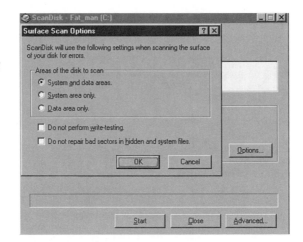

5.4.2. Disk Defragmentation

Disk fragmentation is a process that happens over time with normal use of the hard disk in Windows 95. When files are written and removed from the hard disk, they can become fragmented. This is because, with the FAT file system, files are not written contiguously. In other words, when a file is written, Windows 95 does not attempt to find a continuous block of free space to write the entire file. It writes the file in the first available free spaces. Those spaces might not be contiguous, and therefore fragments of the file might be written in several different locations on the hard disk. The information is still written, but it just might take longer to access it when it is fragmented. This is because the hard disk read/write head must search several different physical locations for the entire file.

This section covers the following exam objective: Tune and optimize the system—Disk Defragmenter.

In Figure 5.12, you see a very basic representation of what happens during a normal operation of adding and deleting files that can lead to fragmentation. Each block represents a block where data can be stored physically on the hard drive. The actual size of the blocks is not important for this explanation. In the first step, you see four files written contiguously to the hard disk represented by the letters A through D. In step 2, you see that file C is deleted, leaving two blocks of free space. In step 3, file E needs four blocks of space and is written in the first available free areas. Here you see the first signs of fragmentation as file E is written in two separate areas. Step 4 shows file D being deleted, once again revealing free space. In the last step, file F is written. It only needs two blocks, leaving one block open. You can see the trend happening. Currently, we have fragmented files and free areas between files.

Figure 5.12.

File fragmentation happens during normal disk operations.

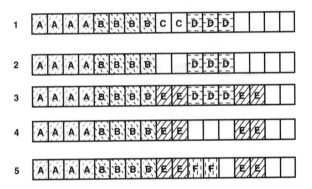

Defragmenting the drive not only puts the files back together so that they are in contiguous blocks, but it also consolidates the free spaces together after all of the files. Like ScanDisk, you can start the Defragmenter in several ways. You can run the command Defrag by selecting it from the Start menu at `\Programs\Accessories\System Tools` or by bringing up the property sheet of the drive and selecting the Tools tab. After you have executed the program, you see a very simple dialog box that allows you to select the drive(s) you want to defragment (notice the All Drives option). After you have selected a drive and clicked OK, you are prompted to start the process (see Figure 5.13).

5

Figure 5.13.

Defragmenting the hard disk.

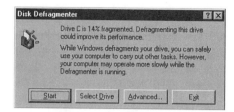

You can start the defragmentation process, however, by clicking the Advanced button, where you can modify what the program does (see Figure 5.14). Using the previous analogy, the options should be self-explanatory.

Figure 5.14.

You can select the options for defragmentation by clicking the Advanced button.

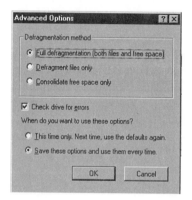

After you start the defragmentation, you can view the progress by clicking the Show Details button (see Figure 5.15).

Note

Even though the Disk Defragmenter was designed so that it can be run during normal operation of Windows 95, it is best if you close all programs and let the Disk Defragmenter do its thing. Anything that causes a change to the contents of the drive (programs that might be running) cause the defragmentation process to start over. Trust me, let it run by itself and get yourself a cup of coffee. It takes forever otherwise (depending on the size of your disk and how bad it's fragmented).

5.4.3. Compressing Disks

If you are running out of hard disk space, you have two options. Either you upgrade your machine, or you compress the hard disk. Windows 95 supports disk compression including Microsoft DriveSpace, Microsoft DoubleSpace, and Stac Electronics Stacker.

Figure 5.15.

Defragmenting a hard disk.

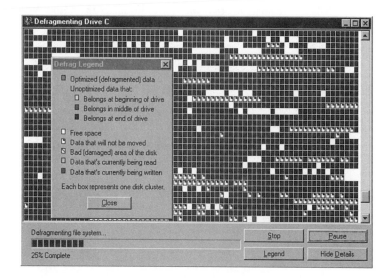

This section covers the following exam objective: Tune and optimize the system—Compression utility.

Compressing a hard disk is actually taking the contents of the hard disk and compressing it into one large file. The file is called a *compressed volume file* (*CVF*) and is named something similar to DRVSPACE.000. The disk to be compressed is called the *host drive*. When a drive is compressed, for example, the C drive (host drive) actually is assigned a different letter, such as H. Then the compressed file is viewed as the C drive. From then on, any time you write or read a file from the C drive, you are actually reading or writing that file to the CVF file.

Do not alter, move, copy, or otherwise tamper with the CVF file. Remember that everything is contained in that file. If you corrupt it, you'll possibly lose everything contained within it.

Compressing a Floppy

You can also compress removable media such as floppies. This is a handy option when that single file that you want to transfer to another Windows 95 computer is just a little bit over 1.44MB.

You can compress a floppy drive by following these steps:

1. From the Start menu, select Programs, Accessories, System, Tools.

2. Select DriveSpace.

3. Select the A drive (see Figure 5.16).

4. From the menu, select Drive and then Compress.

5. Click the Start button (see Figure 5.17).

Figure 5.16.

Selecting which drive to compress.

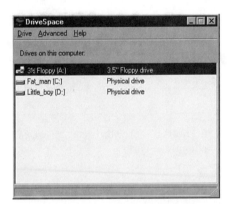

Figure 5.17.

Starting the compression process.

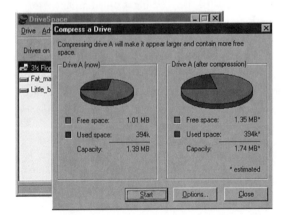

Drives compressed using the Windows 95 DriveSpace are not compatible and cannot be accessed by Windows NT or OS/2. This includes floppy disks. If you plan to dual-boot your Windows 95 computer, you have to decompress the drive for Windows NT to install.

Compressing a Hard Disk

Compressing a hard disk drive is very similar to compressing a floppy disk, only it's on a larger scale—except you can choose to compress the entire disk or just part of it. With the DriveSpace that comes with Windows 95, you can compress hard disks that are 512MB or smaller. Only with Microsoft Plus installed can you compress drives that are 2GB or smaller. Additionally, the Microsoft Plus version allows for many different levels of compression. They include Hipack and Ultrapack.

It is important that you know the DriveSpace disk size limitations for the exam.

Buy another hard disk and upgrade your computer. Using disk compression only slows your computer down and increases the chances of losing data (if the CVF file becomes corrupt). Besides, as of this writing, hard drive prices were still dropping. Trust me, it'll be worth it.

You can also uncompress drives that were previously compressed. You can do so by running DriveSpace and then selecting Uncompress from the Drive menu, but you must have enough free space for the files when they are uncompressed.

5.4.4. System Agent

The System Agent is a utility that comes as part of the Microsoft Plus package. This utility is used for scheduling programs to be run automatically at times and dates that you specify. By default, the System Agent runs the Disk Defragmenter, Microsoft Backup, ScanDisk, and the Compression Agent; but it can run any programs that you specify. Some programs were designed for use with the System Agent. These applications are called *System Agent-aware applications*. Special settings are usually configurable for System Agent-aware applications.

5

Scheduling an Application

You can use the System Agent to run just about any executable program on a schedule. Follow these steps:

1. Open the System Agent from the Programs, Accessories, System Tools option of the Start menu.

2. Select Program from the menu and select Schedule a New Program.

3. Type in the path to the executable file or use the Browse button (see Figure 5.18).

4. Click the When To Run button, specify the time and days you want the program to run (see Figure 5.19), and click OK.

Figure 5.18.

Specifying the path for a program to run in the System Agent.

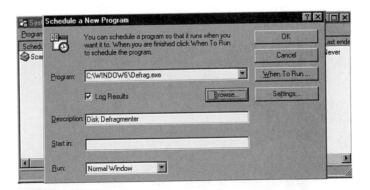

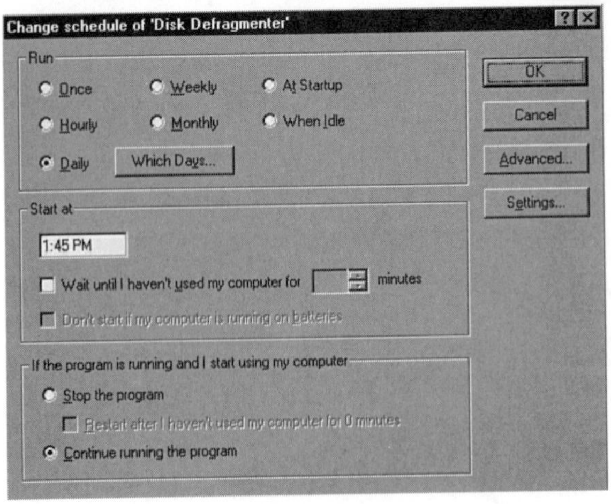

Figure 5.19.

Configuring when and how often the program should run.

You can remove programs just as easily by selecting the program and selecting Remove from the program menu.

5.5. Backing Up the System

If you have ever lost important information from a hard disk crash, you know the importance of a good backup system. The average person believes that the hard disk should never fail. This is the same type of person who doesn't carry a spare tire in the trunk of his car.

Windows 95 includes a good backup utility that allows for backing up the files on the computer to tape, another hard disk, a floppy, or even a mapped network drive.

Be careful: the backup utility included with Windows 95 is not compatible with earlier backup utilities that came with previous versions of Windows or MS-DOS. It will not read backups created with older versions.

5.5.1. Installing a Tape Drive

Even though Backup allows you to back up to floppies, hard disk, or mapped network drives, you might want to use a backup drive to back up your files on tape. If so, you need to know how to install a tape drive.

This section covers the following exam objective: Install and configure backup hardware and software—Tape drives, The Backup application.

5

Installing tape drives differs depending on the manufacturer and type of tape drive. Before you purchase your tape drive, you should be sure that it is compatible with Windows 95.

There are many backup programs available for Windows 95 that support a wide variety of backup media. However, the Windows 95 Backup program supports only the following tape backup units and manufacturers: QIC 40, QIC 80, and QIC 3010 tape drives made by the following companies, and connected to the primary floppy disk controller:

- Colorado Memory Systems (CMS)
- Conner
- Iomega

- Wangtek (only in "hardware phantom mode" or "Drive B sharing mode")
- CMS QIC 40, QIC 80, and QIC 3010 tape drives connected to a parallel port.

The following items are not compatible with Backup:

- Drives connected to a secondary floppy disk controller or to an accelerator card
- Archive drives
- Irwin AccuTrak tapes
- Irwin drives
- Mountain drives
- QIC Wide tapes (Backup supports QIC Wide drives using QIC 80 tapes.)
- QIC 3020 drives
- SCSI tape drives
- Summit drives
- Tape drive controllers of any type
- Travan drives

 Note Some floppy-controller-driven tape backup units require firmware revisions to work properly with the Windows 95 Backup program.

Just because your tape drive might not appear on the preceding compatibility list does not mean that you can't use it with Windows 95. It simply means that you can't use it with the Windows 95 Backup utility. Many third-party vendors sell tape drives that come with backup software that you can use in Windows 95.

In a test machine that I am using for this book, I am using a Colorado 1400 tape drive (something I had lying around).

The first step to your installation, of course, is to install the hardware into your computer. Plug and Play software does not detect tape drives. As a result, the only tape drives that appear in Device Manager are SCSI tape drives, which appear as either an unknown device or a tape drive. Most backup programs, however, do detect tape drives, so don't be concerned if your tape drive does not appear in Device Manager. If your backup software does not detect your tape drive, contact the company that wrote the software.

After starting Windows 95, you should install Microsoft Backup. To do so, follow these steps:

1. From the Control Panel, double-click Add/Remove Programs.
2. Select the Windows Setup tab.
3. Select Disk Tools (do not put a check in the box).
4. Click Details.
5. Place a check mark in the box next to Backup.
6. Click OK.
7. Click OK again.

When you start Microsoft Backup (Start, Run, Accessories, System Tools), you see your tape drive listed in the Backup window. If not, select Redetect Tape Drive from the Tools menu. If Backup doesn't detect your drive, follow the instructions.

5.5.2. Creating a Backup

Running the backup utility is a fairly simple and straightforward process. You can access Backup from the command line by typing **Backup** at the Start, Run command line. Additionally, you can access the Backup utility from the Tools tab of a disk drive's property sheet as well as from Accessories in the System Tools folder.

This section covers the following exam objective: Backup data and restore data.

5

After you start the utility, you see an interface that is similar to Windows Explorer. The difference is the addition of the check mark boxes (see Figure 5.20). You tell the program which files you would like to back up by placing check marks next to the files and/or folders that you would like to back up. Notice that the grayed box means that not all files and folders beneath it are selected, whereas the white box with a check mark means that all files and folders are selected.

The next step in the backup process is to click the Next Step button (pun intended). Then you select where you want to back the files up. Notice in Figure 5.21 that I am choosing a mapped network drive (great option to use if you do not have a tape drive).

Figure 5.20.

Selecting which files to back up.

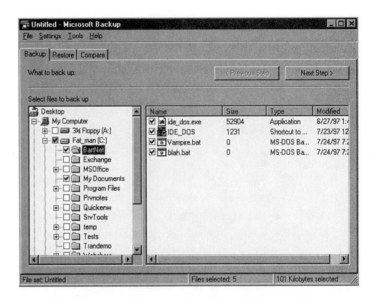

Figure 5.21.

Choosing a backup location.

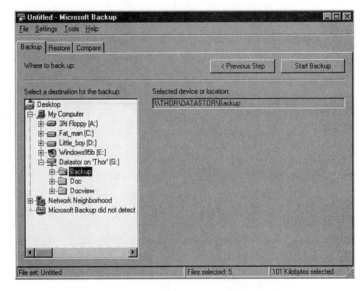

After you have specified the location, you can start the backup. You are prompted to give the backup set a name. Now you have your important files backed up in case of an emergency.

Restoring the files is as simple as reversing the process. You start the backup program and click on the Restore tab. You must then specify the location of the backup set. After you have specified the location of the backup set, you see an Explorer type hierarchy. The exception is it shows only the files that you backed up (see Figure 5.22).

Figure 5.22.

Restoring files from a backup set.

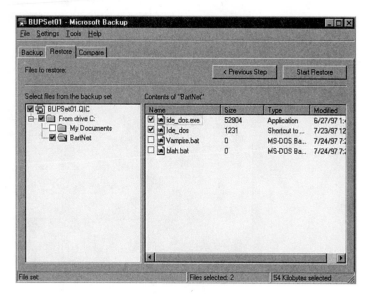

The next step in the process is to click Start Restore. The Backup utility automatically restores the files to their original location.

5.5.3. Ensuring Backup Integrity

The Compare tab allows you to compare copies of the of the files included in the backup set with their counterparts on the hard disk. This is handy in situations where you suspect that files on the hard disk and backup differ. The last thing that you want to happen is to restore an older file on top of a newer one. Additionally, this is a way for you to ensure that the files you just backed up match the files on the hard disk.

You can have the Backup utility automatically perform this function for you. To do so, follow these steps:

1. From the menu, click Settings.
2. Click Options.
3. Select the Backup Tab.

5

4. Place a check mark in the box next to Verify Backup Data by Automatically Comparing files after backup is finished (see Figure 5.23).

Figure 5.23.

Ensuring backup integrity by having backup automatically compare files.

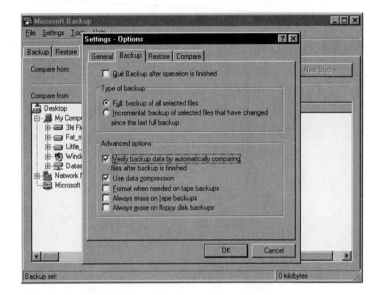

Similarly, if you want the Backup utility to compare before restoring the files, you see a similar option under the Restore tab of Settings—Options.

Lab

The Lab consists of review questions and exercises pertaining to this chapter and provides an opportunity to apply the knowledge that you've learned with this chapter. Answers to the review questions can be found in Appendix B.

Questions

1. What program takes the place of SmartDrive in Windows 95?

    A. DrvSpace

    B. VCache

    C. DiskCache

    D. DiskSpace

2. When renaming a long file name that contains spaces at the command prompt, what should you use before and after the file name to designate that the spaces are part of the file name?

    A. Asterisks

    B. Number Signs

    C. Quotes

    D. Parentheses

3. In order to support long file names, what additional component(s) must be loaded on a Windows NT server? Choose all that apply.

    A. OSR2 Name Space

    B. OS/2 Name Space

    C. LFNBK

    D. Nothing

4. In order to support long file names, what additional component(s) must be loaded on a Novell NetWare server? Choose all that apply.

    A. OSR2 Name Space

    B. OS/2 Name Space

    C. LFNBK

    D. Nothing

5. A user comes to you and states that she just ran ScanDisk and Defrag to optimize her system, but she also states that her files no longer have long file names and some of her files are corrupt. What could she have possibly done wrong?

   A. She ran ScanDisk before she ran Defrag and should have run Defrag first.

   B. She shut her system down while one of the utilities was running.

   C. She ran the utilities in Windows when she should have run them in MS-DOS mode.

   D. She used 16-bit real-mode versions and should have used the 32-bit protected-mode versions.

6. With the Windows 95 Backup program, you can back up to what type of devices? Pick all that apply.

   A. Floppies

   B. Another hard disk

   C. Mapped Network Drive

   D. Tape Drive

7. A file name in Windows 95 can be how many characters long?

   A. 250

   B. 255

   C. 256

   D. 260

8. What is the largest partition that can be compressed with Windows 95 without any additional software installed?

   A. 256MB

   B. 512MB

   C. 1GB

   D. 2GB

9. What is the largest partition that can be compressed with Windows 95 with Microsoft Plus software installed?

   A. 256MB

   B. 512MB

   C. 1GB

   D. 2GB

Exercises

Exercise 5.1.

You should definitely spend some time becoming familiar with how long file names react to different situations. Practice renaming the files at the command prompt using quotes and without using quotes. Additionally, practice deciphering how the 5.3 aliasing works. Here is an exercise to help:

1. Open the Explorer.

2. Navigate to the C drive.

3. From the menu, select File, point to New, and then select Folder.

4. For the folder name, type: **A Folder with a Long Name**.

5. Press Enter.

6. Open the newly created folder.

7. Create the following text documents by selecting File, New, and then Text Document:

   My First Document.txt

   My First Duck.Rubber.txt

   My First Spreadsheet.txt

   Rubber Ducky in a tub.txt

8. Notice how the files are listed in the Explorer.

9. Go to an MS-DOS prompt.

10. Change to the root directory of C.

11. Do a directory listing.

12. Notice how the folder is listed.

13. Change to the new folder by typing **cd\"a folder with a long name"** and pressing Enter.

5

14. Do a directory listing. Notice the 8.3 alias names and compare them with their long file name counterparts.

15. Type **ren rubber~1.txt rubber~2.txt.**

16. Press Enter.

17. Do a directory listing.

18. Notice how the long file name also becomes the same as the alias. This is because quotation marks were not used.

19. Type **ren "My First Spreadsheet.txt" "My Last Spreadsheet.txt".**

20. Press Enter.

21. Do a directory listing.

22. Notice how the long file name is changed, and the alias also changes accordingly.

Exercise 5.2.

In this exercise, you run ScanDisk. This prepares you for the exam by covering the following exam objective: Tune and optimize the system—ScanDisk. Note: Do not do this exercise if your computer has a dual-boot configuration with Windows NT.

1. Click Start.

2. Select Programs.

3. Select Accessories.

4. Select System Tools.

5. Select ScanDisk.

6. Click the Advanced button.

7. Under Cross-linked files, select Delete.

8. Under Lost file fragments, select Free.

9. Click OK.

10. Click Start.

11. When summary is displayed, click Close.

12. Click Close Again.

You might want to take this exercise a little further. Because you are taking the time to run ScanDisk, take a little more time to fully optimize the disk by running Defrag also.

Exercise 5.3.

In this exercise, you install Backup. This prepares you for the exam by covering the following exam objective: Install and configure cakup hardware and software—The Backup application.

1. From the Control Panel, double-click Add/Remove Programs.
2. Select the Windows Setup tab.
3. Select Disk Tools (do not put a check in the box).
4. Click Details.
5. Place a check mark in the box next to Backup.
6. Click OK.
7. Click OK again.
8. Click Start.
9. Select Programs.
10. Select Accessories.
11. Select System Tools.
12. Select Backup.

You can take this exercise a little further. You might want to practice backing up files and restoring them. Depending on your hardware setup, you might want to try backing up to a floppy, another hard disk, mapped network drive, or tape drive.

Additionally, be sure to become familiar with the different reasons that the caching methods help and hurt. This includes the good and the bad consequences of having caching enabled.

5

TEST DAY FAST FACTS

Listed here are some fast facts about this chapter. Be sure to know the purposes of the different protocols for the different-sized networks. Take a few minutes to review these handy facts before test time:

- The main difference between NDIS 3.0 and NDIS 3.1 is that 3.1 supports Plug and Play.

- The three main protocols used by Windows 95 on networks are NetBEUI, IPX/SPX, and TCP/IP.

- NetBEUI is good for small networks because of the small overhead. Additionally, it cannot be used for larger networks because it does not support routing.

- IPX/SPX is a routable protocol designed by Novell that works well for medium- to large-sized networks.

- TCP/IP is a routable protocol used for connecting to the Internet and for connecting dissimilar systems.

- Windows-based networks use server message blocks (SMB) to communicate.

- A workgroup is a logical grouping of computers that, when used in a peer-to-peer environment, offers very little security.

Day 6

Linking to Your Network

Windows 95 was designed with connectivity in mind. This connectivity for the most part takes place through networking to a local area network.

Connectivity with Windows NT networks and Novell NetWare networks is built right in. You can connect Windows 95 to these types of networks without any additional software. Acting as a client is not the only thing that Windows 95 can do on Windows NT and NetWare networks. It can also share information and services to the network acting as a server.

Objectives

The exam objectives are relatively cut and dried when it comes to the topic of networking. Microsoft clearly sees that Windows 95 will not only be used on Microsoft networks but also on Novell networks. This is clearly shown in the exam objectives:

- Develop an appropriate implementation model for specific requirements
- Choose a workgroup configuration or join an existing domain
- Develop a security strategy
- File and print sharing
- Install and configure network components of a client computer and server
- Install and configure network protocols
- NetBEUI
- IPX/SPX
- Configure system services
- Browser
- Assign access permissions for shared folders
- Passwords
- User Permissions
- Group Permissions
- Create, share, and monitor resources
- Network Printers
- Configure a Windows 95 computer as a client on a Windows NT network
- Configure a Windows 95 computer as a client on a NetWare network

6.1. Windows 95 on the Network

When the marketplace began to move to a client/server PC network, a need arose for a client-based operating system. Microsoft had already developed a good network server with the making of Windows NT 3.51, but Windows 3.11 just didn't do the job very well. It was basically Windows 3.1 with some networking components tacked on. Microsoft needed a better operating system for connectivity, not only to the Microsoft Windows NT server but to other operating systems as well.

Windows 95 fits that category. It includes support for several existing network operating systems. The following networks are ones that Windows 95 supports:

- Artisoft LANtastic 5.0 and later
- Banyan VINES 5.52 and later
- DEC Pathworks
- Microsoft LAN Manager
- Microsoft Windows for Workgroups 3.x
- Microsoft Windows NT
- Novell NetWare 3.11 and later
- Sunsoft PC-NFS 5.0 and later

Windows 95 includes support for a wide range of transport protocols and industry-standard communication protocols as well. There are several benefits to using Windows 95 as a client. Some of these benefits include the following:

- **Plug and Play networking.** Installing network adapter cards couldn't be easier. Most network cards are detected, and the proper software is installed automatically using Plug and Play. If you are using Windows 95 on a laptop or notebook PC, you can insert and remove PCMCIA network cards while the computer is up and running. Additionally, if you disconnect the network cable, the computer continues to function. With some older versions of Windows and other network clients, this can cause the system to crash.

- **Roving users.** When using Windows 95 as a client to a Novell NetWare server or a Windows NT server, you can set up user profiles. This allows the user's settings to be available at whatever Windows 95 computer that he logs on to.

- **Better lock-down capabilities.** With the use of system policies (discussed in Chapter 8, "Locking Down the System: Profiles and Policies"), you can lock Windows 95 computers down to keep users from messing around with some things. This is easily configured and administered by using a NetWare or Windows NT server.

- **Long filenames.** Windows 95 not only lets you save files using long filenames locally on the computer, but it also supports saving files using long filenames on the network. Windows NT server already supports this option. With Novell NetWare, you must install the OS/2 name space on the server.

- **Automatic recovery of lost connections.** If you lose a server connection while using Windows 95, the next time you attempt to use the resource, Windows 95 automatically attempts to restore the connection. In most cases, you are unaware of the lost connection.

- **32-bit client components.** The client for Microsoft networks and NetWare networks are 32-bit, protected-mode clients. This means they use no conventional memory and can be twice as fast as the real-mode DOS clients used by Windows 3.*x.*

- **16-bit client support.** Windows 95 also supports the older 16-bit clients that you might be using with Windows for workgroups; but, if available, use a 32-bit one and increase your speed.

Windows 95 was designed not only to work well with Windows NT, but also with the one network server that had the greatest market share, Novell NetWare. Let's take a look at how it's done.

6.2. Network Architecture Overview

One important aspect of networking is the idea that computers can communicate with each other. This would be extremely difficult, however, if someone did not set a standard of how things were done. If everyone just simply made their own operating systems, software applications, network cards, and so on without thinking about how they would communicate with other components, you'd expect to have compatibility problems. A standard must be created for everyone to follow to ensure compatibility.

6.2.1. The OSI Model

The International Standardization Organization (ISO) developed a standard called the *open systems interconnection (OSI) model,* which is the most widely accepted standard for network architecture. Although it is not important to know this material for the exam, it will help you gain a better understanding about how Windows 95 compares with other network operating systems. Expect to see much more about the OSI model on other MCSE exams.

6

It is not necessary to know the OSI reference model in depth for the exam. However, if you would like more information about the OSI model, pick up a copy of *Sams Teach Yourself MCSE Networking Essentials in 14 Days* by Walter Glenn and Mark Sportack.

The OSI model consists of several layers. This layered approach helps programmers, designers, and the like create a product designed to operate in that layer. Before I explain this further, take a look at Figure 6.1.

Figure 6.1.

The OSI reference model defines the standard of networking components.

As you can see in the figure, the OSI model comprises several layers. In Table 6.1, there is a brief description of each of these layers.

Table 6.1. The OSI model.

Layer	Description
Application	When you use an application, it communicates to the operating system using this layer, which prevents the application from caring whether the resource is coming from the computer locally or whether it is coming from the network.
Presentation	This layer takes the information from the application and changes it into a usable form. It presents the information to the operating system and to the network in a form that it understands.
Session	This layer's job makes sure the communication process doesn't break down. It keeps track of the network session and ensures synchronization of the communication process.
Transport	This layer's sole purpose is to make sure that the information arrives safely and that the information that arrived is indeed the correct information that was sent.

Layer	Description
Network	This layer is in charge of addressing the information and ensuring that the information is sent to the correct destination.
Data Link	This layer consists of network protocols and network card drivers. The protocols ensure that the information is sent in the correct form and is error-free. The network card driver communicates with the network card to deliver and receive information from the protocols.
Physical	The network card resides at this layer. This is where the information from the computer is generated into electricity to be communicated to the network wire.

This layered approach makes it easier to create parts of the network. For example, the creator of a network card driver couldn't care less about the application. Instead, she only has to design the network card driver to run in the Data Link layer. The only other layers she needs to be concerned with are the layer above (Network) and the layer below (Physical) the Data Link layer. As long as the driver can communicate with the surrounding layers, it will work.

Now let's take a look at how Windows 95 fits into the OSI model.

6.2.2. The Windows 95 Network Architecture

Windows 95 meets the OSI standard. Once again, it is not necessary to memorize this information for the exam, but the more familiar you are with it, the better you will understand Windows 95. And, the better you understand Windows 95, the more likely you will pass the exam. In Figure 6.2, you can see how Microsoft implemented Windows 95 by using the OSI model.

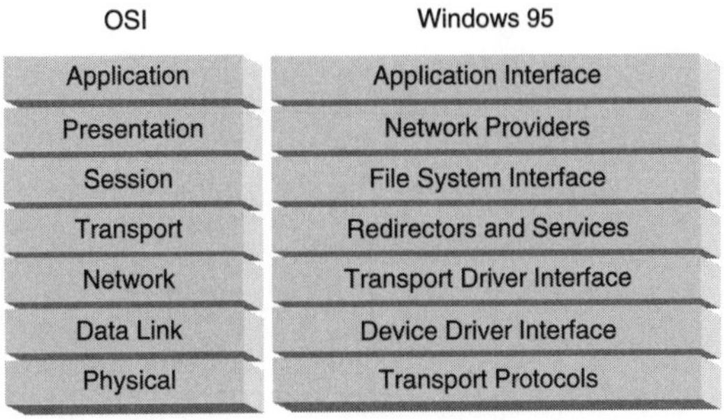

Figure 6.2.

How Windows 95 stacks up to the OSI reference model.

OSI	Windows 95
Application	Application Interface
Presentation	Network Providers
Session	File System Interface
Transport	Redirectors and Services
Network	Transport Driver Interface
Data Link	Device Driver Interface
Physical	Transport Protocols

6

Microsoft ensured that Windows 95 met the OSI model by creating its own layered approach to Windows 95. Table 6.2 illustrates these layers.

Table 6.2. The Windows 95 model.

Layer	Description
Application Interface	This is the way applications access the network. This layer makes the network independent of the application. This allows programmers to write applications regardless of the type of network they will run on. This layer consists of the Win32 WinNet Interface, which allows access to resources, and the Win32 Print API, which gives access to network printing functions.
Network Providers	This level consists of WinNet16, Windows NP/PP, and the NetWare NP/PP. WinNet16 allows 16-bit access to the network for backward compatibility with older Windows-based programs. The Windows Network Provider/Print Provider gives 32-bit access for newer applications to servers who use the server message block (SMB)-based sharing protocol. The NetWare Network Provider/Print Provider gives 32-bit access to NetWare-based servers.
File System Interface	The installable file system (IFS), which resides at this level, directs traffic. It routes calls that are made by the application to the appropriate destination. For example, it determines that a call to retrieve a file should be to the local hard drive or sent across the network.
Redirectors and Services	When you use Windows 95 on a network, it can share and access information. The Redirector allows you to connect to others. The Services portion of this layer allows others to connect to you. Although you can install several services onto Windows 95, the most common are File and Print services, which allow you to share files and printers from your Windows 95 computer.
Transport Driver Interface	This layer provides a uniform way of communication with the network. This layer includes both the NetBIOS interface and Windows Sockets interface.
Transport Protocols	This layer encompasses the network protocols and allows Windows 95 to use multiple protocols at once. The three major protocols that would reside at this layer are NetBEUI, IPX/SPX, and TCP/IP.

Layer	Description
Device Driver Interface	This layer provides a set way for the protocols to communicate with the network card. Windows 95 supports both NDIS-compliant and ODI specifications. NDIS is an industrywide standard of how the protocols should work (bind) with the network card. The ODI specification was defined by Novell.

Note

Windows 95 supports many versions of NDIS that range from version 2.0 to 4.0.

Version 2.0 is real-mode and thus is 16-bit. Version 3.0 is protected-mode and 32-bit. Version 3.1 supports Plug and Play. Version 4.0 adds several features to include support for point-to-point tunneling protocol (PPTP).

Version 4.0 is available only with the OEM Service Release (OSR2) (also known as Release 2) version of Windows 95. Most recent books I have seen mention version 4.0, but I have seen tons of systems out there still running the original version of Windows 95. It doesn't mean that NDIS 4.0 is not important; it only means that until new machines start to replace the older ones, OSR2 will not be in great numbers in the networks. You can only get OSR2 on new machines.

6.2.3. Network Protocols

You've seen the OSI model and how Windows 95 compares to it. I will explain more about the Windows 95 components as the chapter goes along. Let's take a more in-depth look at the three major network protocols that can be used with Windows 95.

First of all, let me explain what a protocol is. If you look up *protocol* in a dictionary, you probably won't find anything that makes any reference to a computer. You'll see things like formal documents and etiquette; but if you think about the word *protocol* and how it is used in those situations, you'll understand that it means a standard of how things are to happen. In computer terms, *protocol* is the standard way in which computers exchange information on a network. This is mainly to ensure that all computers involved understand the information.

Three main protocols can be used with Windows 95: NetBEUI, IPX/SPX, and TCP/IP. Although you can install many third-party protocols, I focus on these three because third-party protocols are not covered on the exam. The decision of which

6

protocol(s) to use is entirely up to you and what you will be doing with the computer. Even though Windows 95 might automatically install certain protocols when you install a network card, you are not required to use them. You can remove them and use the ones that you choose. I have dubbed the three protocols the small, medium, and large network protocols for simplicity.

I have seen numerous people have difficulty with this. For the hardened network veteran, it's easy as pie; but the new kid on the block usually gets frustrated with protocols.

To communicate on the network, a networked computer must have at least one protocol installed on it. With Windows 95, you can load multiple protocols. For example, in Figure 6.3, if computer A has NetBEUI and IPX/SPX installed, it can talk to computer B, which has only NetBEUI installed, and computer C, which has only IPX/SPX installed. Computer B and computer C cannot communicate with each other, however, because they don't have a common protocol installed.

Figure 6.3.

Using more than one protocol.

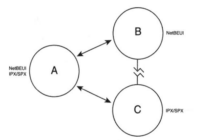

In the old days (when protocols were loaded into conventional memory), the biggest problem with managing protocols was managing where they were loaded into memory. Today, Windows 95 protocols are 32-bit and run in protected mode. In other words, they fire up after Windows has started, so they can take advantage of the new flat, linear memory model of Windows 95. And, of course, because they are 32-bit, they run much faster than the 16-bit ones from way back when.

The other problem we were presented with was configuration of these protocols. We don't need to change INI files or other configuration files. All configurations are handled through the Control Panel with the Network applet. The three protocols (what I call the *Big Three*) that accompany Windows 95 are 32-bit implementations of NetBEUI, IPX/SPX, and TCP/IP.

The following sections will discuss the different protocols and how to determine which ones to install.

Microsoft NetBEUI

NetBEUI is actually an acronym inside an acronym. It stands for *NetBIOS extended user interface.* IBM introduced it into the network world back in 1985. It is the fastest of the Big Three, is predominately self-tuning, and needs little configuration from the administrator. People experienced with NetBEUI might disagree with me here, but it's true. This is not the same old NetBEUI from our Windows 3.*x* days. It is much faster than those older versions, especially over slower links.

There is one major problem with NetBEUI, though. It was designed back when experts thought that networks would be segmented into smaller departmental LANs. These departmental LANs were supposed to communicate through the implementation of gateways (or routers). Therefore, NetBEUI was not designed for use with routers, thus giving it the designation as a nonroutable protocol. You will want to know that NetBEUI is nonroutable for the exam. Hint, hint. Wink, wink. Say no more.

I dub NetBEUI the *small network protocol.* The actual size of the network doesn't matter. The minute you begin to segment your network or connect two networks together using routers, you lose—or never gain—the capability to communicate across the routers if all you are running is NetBEUI. There is no need to uninstall NetBEUI; just add a routable protocol to the stack. Remember that you can run more than one protocol simultaneously.

Microsoft IPX/SPX

This protocol is the Microsoft protocol compatible with Novell's IPX/SPX. The acronym *IPX/SPX* stands for *internetwork packet exchange/sequential packet exchange.*

There are a couple of reasons to use this protocol. First of all, IPX is a routable protocol. It solves the headache of communicating over routers that you might have with NetBEUI. Its configuration isn't nearly as difficult as TCP/IP, and most configurations (such as Frame Type) are automatic.

The second reason you might want to use IPX/SPX is pretty obvious. If you need to connect to any Novell NetWare servers on the network, it's a must. This is a 32-bit version, so it will definitely run faster than the 16-bit real mode version that Novell supplies. I dub IPX/SPX the *medium-sized network protocol.* The reason should be obvious: It has the capability to work across routers, so you can use it on larger networks than NetBEUI. It doesn't have the capabilities of TCP/IP, which is clearly designed for large networks.

6

Note I don't mean to ruffle any feathers out there. You can get a 32-bit client from Novell to install on a Windows 95 machine. It is fast and works relatively well, but it doesn't work quite as well when connecting to Windows NT servers that are also running IPX/SPX. Also, it's not necessary to know about the Novell 32-bit client for the exam.

TCP/IP

This protocol is a full implementation of the *transmission control protocol/Internet protocol* that has become famous with the wildfire of the Internet, but it's not just for the Internet. First of all, unlike NetBEUI and IPX/SPX, which are single protocols, TCP/IP is a suite of protocols and utilities. It is, by far, the most widely used protocol. Let's take a look at how it came to be.

Back in the '70s when the Department of Defense was developing the ARPAnet, it needed some way for computers to communicate. TCP/IP fulfilled this need and later became part of the Berkeley Standard Distribution (BSD) UNIX. Ever since, it has been distributed as part of UNIX, and it has become the most widely used with the Internet craze. Like the Internet, no one owns TCP/IP (unlike NetBEUI and IPX/SPX).

So why would you need to use it with Windows 95? Allow me to sum it up:

- It includes support for the Internet.
- It allows you to connect dissimilar systems, such as Windows NT to UNIX, Open VMS, and IBM mainframes.
- Configuration of TCP/IP can be a breeze if you use it along with Windows NT dynamic host configuration protocol (DHCP) servers.
- Many utilities common to other networks come with the Microsoft implementation of TCP/IP such as PING, FTP, Telnet, and NETSTAT.

Explaining the full capabilities of TCP/IP in a few paragraphs is impossible. As a matter of fact, explaining TCP/IP would take more than just one book. My job here is simply to help you make a decision whether to use it with Windows 95. I will discuss how to install and configure TCP/IP further in Chapter 7, "Linking to Your World."

Keep in mind that you can install more than one protocol simultaneously. For example, if you need access to NetWare servers but also need access to TCP/IP printers and Windows NT servers running TCP/IP, you can add both the IPX/SPX and TCP/IP protocols.

6.3. Securing the System

When you install Windows 95 onto a network, you need to think about several things. If that machine is going to share anything out to the network for others to use (a printer or files, for example), the first thing you should ask yourself is how you are going to secure them. You can set up security through the Control Panel using the Network applet. Using the Access Control tab, as shown in Figure 6.4, you have two options: Share-level and User-level.

Figure 6.4.

The Access Control tab of the Network applet.

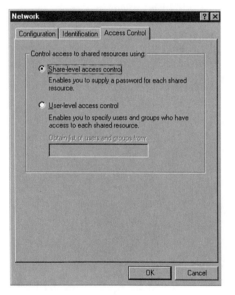

6.3.1. Share-Level Security

With Windows 3.x, you had very few choices. Let's say, for instance, that you have a folder (directory) that you want to share out to the network on a Windows 3.11 machine. Your choices of security are Full Control, Read-Only, or Depends on Password. This is called *share-level* security, and it is still available in Windows 95.

With share-level security, your options are limited. With full-control (now just called Full in Windows 95), anyone can access the share and do anything he wants to it (including delete). I think that Read-Only should be self-explanatory, but Depends on Password can be a little confusing. You can share out a folder by right-clicking the folder in the Explorer (see Figure 6.5) and choosing the Sharing option. Then the Properties dialog box of that particular folder with the Sharing tab appears already selected. When you select the Depends on Password option, you can see, as shown in Figure 6.6, that you have two options: Read-Only Password and Full Access Password. You control access by regulating who knows the password. The more folders you share, the more passwords they need to remember. The more passwords you give out, the harder it is for you to keep track of who has what kind of access to which folders. Sound like a nightmare? It is. As you can see, this is not the smart way to handle security on larger networks. That is not to say that it does not work well for small, peer-to-peer networks. Personally, I would set the limit at 10 computers. I have managed larger groups, but more than 10 computers configured with this scheme is administratively overwhelming.

Figure 6.5.

The folder shortcut menu.

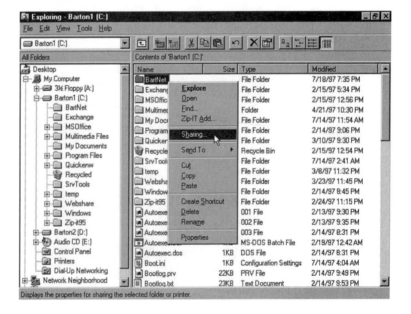

Figure 6.6.

The Sharing tab of the folder Properties dialog box.

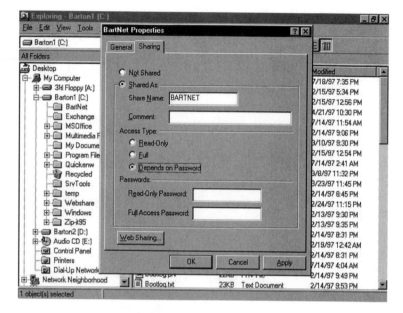

6.3.2. User-Level Security

A better way of handling security is through the implementation of user-level security. With user-level security, you don't have to remember any passwords (other than your logon password). Here is where you need a security provider (usually a server) to provide you with a list of users on the network. You can use one of the following types of machines as a security provider for Windows:

- Windows NTW 3.5 or later
- Windows NT Server 3.5 or later
- Windows NT Server 3.5 or later (installed as a domain controller)
- Novell NetWare 3.x
- Novell NetWare 4.x (running bindery emulation)

6

Note

> Windows 95 also supports the NDS services of NetWare 4.1, but not with the original release of Windows 95. Microsoft MS-NDS 32-bit, protected-mode support for NDS is additional software available in Windows 95 service pack 1 or OSR2. See Section 6.5.1, "Connecting to NetWare as a Client."

The reason you need one of these machines is simple: Windows 95 does not have the capability to keep a database of users. When you share something (such as a folder) while using user-level security, you can choose what users have what type of access. In Figure 6.7, you can see that in the left pane Windows 95 retrieves a list of users from the security provider. On the right, you can give different users different levels of access to the same share. You are also not limited to just Full Access and Read-Only. By clicking the Custom button, you can choose what type of access to give (see Figure 6.8). We'll discuss sharing folders and security further in the next two sections.

Figure 6.7.

Controlling access from the Add Users dialog box.

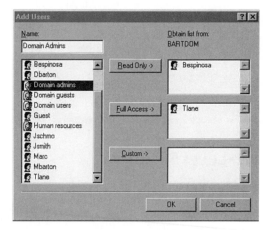

Figure 6.8.

Sharing a folder in Windows 95.

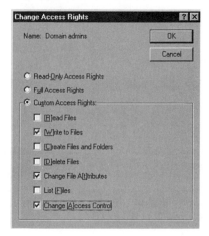

6.4. Interoperability with Windows NT

Windows NT is Microsoft's version of a network operating system. As I explained earlier, Windows NT Server is the server version of Windows NT. Throughout this chapter, when I refer to Windows NT, I am referring to the server version of the operating system.

It is not necessary to have an in-depth knowledge of Windows NT for the Windows 95 exam. The more that you have, however, the better off you are. For more information about Windows NT Server, pick up a copy of *Sams Teach Yourself MCSE Windows NT Server 4 in 14 Days* by David Schaer, et al.

Windows NT server offers tremendous advantages to a network. These advantages span more than just file and print services of other network operating systems; but security is one of the main advantages. Windows 95 was designed with Windows NT in mind. It was designed to take advantage of the services that Windows NT provides.

6.4.1. Connecting to NT as a Client

Windows NT servers communicate using *server message blocks* (SMBs), which allow Windows clients the capability to request services such as file sharing from Windows NT servers. To communicate with Windows NT servers and other Microsoft networking systems, you must install the client for Microsoft Networks that enables the Windows 95 computer to communicate with other computers using SMB-based communications on the network. The client for Microsoft Networks also supports, on a limited basis, communication with other SMB-based servers such as IBM LAN Server, DEC Pathworks, AT&T StarLAN, and LAN Manager for UNIX. The client for Microsoft Networks can also be used in a peer-to-peer networking environment common with Microsoft Windows for Workgroups.

This section covers the following exam objective: Configure a Windows 95 computer as a client on a Windows NT network.

6

Workgroups Versus Domains

On a network, Windows 95 can act both as a client and a server. In other words, it can access information on other computers, but it can also share information. Windows 95, however, has no way of validating users onto the network and cannot act as a security host. When Windows 95 is on a network with no servers (ones capable of being a security host), the network is called a *peer-to-peer network*. When you browse for network resources (I discuss browsing more later), you can see a list of the computers that are sharing resources on the network. If your peer-to-peer network consists of several hundred computers, all the computers could easily overwhelm you when looking for a resource.

This section covers the following exam objective: Develop an appropriate implementation model for specific requirements—choosing a workgroup configuration or joining an existing domain.

What you really need is a way to divide up this list of computers. Organizing them into smaller groups makes resources easier to find. In the Microsoft arena, these smaller groups are called *workgroups*.

Becoming a member of a workgroup, or creating your own workgroup, is simple. After double-clicking the Network option in the Control Panel, you see the Network dialog box. You might also notice that you have three tabs at the top of the window. Select the Identification tab. The other two tabs—Configuration and Access Control—are discussed throughout this chapter and in 6.4.3. By selecting the Identification tab, you see that you have three options (see Figure 6.9).

Another way to get to the Network dialog box (other than through the Control Panel) is by right-clicking the Network Neighborhood icon on the desktop and selecting Properties.

The three things that you can change at the Identification tab are:

- **Computer Name**—A computer name is how a computer is identified on the network and is also known as its NetBIOS name. This name must be unique on the network and can consist of up to 15 characters.

- **Workgroup**—The workgroup name is the workgroup to which you want to belong. This can also be up to 15 characters long.

- **Computer Description**—When browsing the network, information in this block is placed next to the computer name as a description. Notice that I used spaces in my description.

Figure 6.9.

Changing the workgroup you belong to is done at the Identification tab of the Network applet.

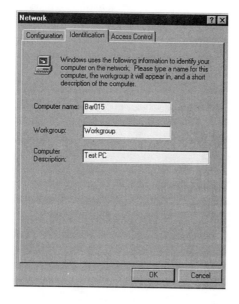

Changing your workgroup membership is as simple as typing in a new or existing workgroup name. By default, Windows 95 makes you a member of a workgroup originally titled Workgroup.

Workgroups have one small problem: There is little control over security. Computers in workgroups do not share security with other computers on the network. Security is managed at each individual computer. In my opinion, this can be an administrative nightmare when more than 10 computers are involved.

With Windows NT on a network, the computers can be organized into another type of logical grouping called a *domain*. A domain is a logical grouping of computers for administrative purposes. By becoming a member of a domain, you can let the Windows NT server (Domain Controller) control access to your computer's resources. A centralized list of user accounts is used for network logon validation and resource access. I'll explain security more in-depth later (predominately in 6.4.3); for now, Table 6.3 gives you a quick comparison of workgroups versus domains.

6

Table 6.3. Workgroups versus domains.

Workgroups	Domains
Decentralized Security (No Server)	Centralized Security (Provided by Security Provider)
Decentralized Administration	Centralized Administration
Decentralized Resources (Each computer shares resources)	Centralized Resources (file and print services are on the server)

Note If you are one of the unlucky individuals who has not yet tried Windows 95 on a Windows NT environment, do it. Many Windows 95 features are designed specifically for the Windows NT environment. Give it a try.

Joining an NT Domain

Joining a Windows NT domain is a simple task. When you open the Network applet of the Control Panel, you see what networking components, if any, that you already have installed. In Figure 6.10, you see my configuration. Notice that I have a network adapter and a dial-up adapter. I already have NetBEUI installed as protocol, but I have no Client software installed as of yet.

Test Tip This section covers the following exam objective: Install and configure network components of a client computer and server.

The Network dialog box is where you'll go for most of the network configuration options. The first step to joining the domain is to add the proper client software to access the network. Installing components in the Network dialog box is done by clicking the Add button. You then can choose which type of network component you want to install (see Figure 6.11).

You can see by the figure that you can choose from the following components:

- **Client**—Installs client networking software for different types of networks. This includes both 32-bit and 16-bit clients. You are limited to only one real-mode networking client at a time. There is no limit to the number of 32-bit clients installed simultaneously.
- **Adapter**—Installs drivers for network adapter cards.

- **Protocol**—Installs network protocols such as NetBEUI, IPX/SPX, and TCP/IP.
- **Service**—Installs services such as backup agents or services for sharing files and printers.

Figure 6.10.

The Network applet of the Control Panel shows my current configuration.

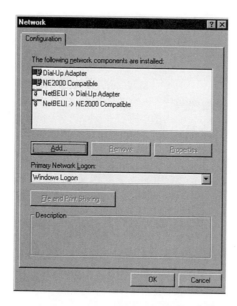

Figure 6.11.

You can choose which type of network component to install by clicking the Add button.

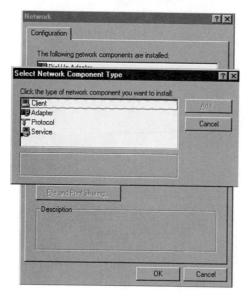

6

By selecting the Client option, Windows 95 produces a list of manufacturers that produce networking operating systems (as you can see in Figure 6.12). Also notice in the figure that I have already selected Microsoft under the list of manufacturers and Client for Microsoft Networks under the list of network clients.

Figure 6.12.

Adding the Client for Microsoft Networks software.

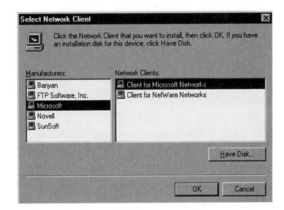

Clicking OK takes you back to the Network dialog box. Notice that you now have the client showing in the Network dialog box (see Figure 6.13), but you're not done yet.

Figure 6.13.

The client is now displayed in the Network dialog box.

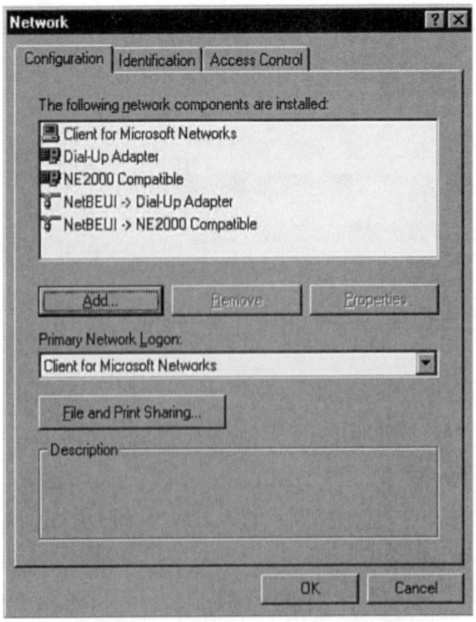

If you stopped right here, you would be adding the Client for Microsoft Networks without specifying which Windows NT domain you want to join. Basically, you have set up Windows 95 to act on a peer-to-peer network. You will not be validated by a server and, therefore, not become a member of a domain.

To continue linking to the Windows NT server, you must specify the domain you want to join. To do so, select the Client for Microsoft Networks from the list of installed components and click the Properties button. Doing so produces Figure 6.14.

Figure 6.14.

Specifying which domain to log on to using the Client for Microsoft Networks.

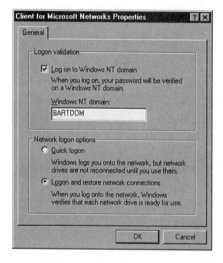

Place a check mark in the box next to the Log On to Windows NT Domain option. Next, specify the name of the domain by typing it in the Windows NT domain box. Notice the two network logon options at the bottom of the dialog box:

- **Quick logon**—Windows logs you on to the network, but network drives are not reconnected until you use them.

- **Logon and restore network connections**—When you log on to the network, Windows verifies that each network drive is ready for use.

6

After you have specified the information needed by this dialog box, click OK to return to the Network dialog box. After you click OK in the Network dialog box, Windows 95 needs the original installation files. Depending on how you installed Windows 95, you might or might not be prompted to provide the disk. After the software is transferred, you are prompted to restart the computer for the changes to take effect. You become a member of the domain the next time the computer starts.

Let's review the steps needed to join a Windows NT domain:

1. Double-click the Network option in the Control Panel.
2. If the Client for Microsoft Networks already exists, go to step 6.
3. If not, click the Add button.
4. Click Client and click Add.
5. Click Microsoft under the list of manufacturers and click Client for Microsoft Networks; then click OK.
6. Click the Client for Microsoft Networks in the list of installed components and click Properties.
7. Place a check mark in the box next to the Log On to Windows NT Domain option.
8. Specify the name of the domain by typing it in the Windows NT Domain box and click OK.
9. Click OK from the Network dialog box.
10. Restart the computer when prompted.

> **Note** If you plan to use profiles and/or polices with this Windows 95 computer where the profiles and/or policies will be placed on the server, you must specify the Client for Microsoft networks to be the Primary Network Logon in the Network dialog box.

Connecting to NT Resources

You can connect to resources on a Windows NT server in several different ways. The first and probably easiest way is to browse for them using the Network Neighborhood. The second way is through the mapping of network drives using Universal Naming Conventions.

Double-clicking the Network Neighborhood and then double-clicking the Entire Network reveals the contents of my test network (see Figure 6.15). You see two groups of computers. Even though the icons are the same, they are two different logical groupings. The Workgroup icon represents my Windows 95 workgroup, whereas the Bartdom icon represents my Windows NT domain. Double-clicking the

Bartdom icon reveals my Windows NT server Thor. If I double-click Thor's icon, I can then see the resources that are shared from that server (see Figure 6.16). The Network Neighborhood is also available in the Windows Explorer interface.

Figure 6.15.

Viewing the Entire Network contents of the Network Neighborhood displays the two groups of computers on my test network.

Figure 6.16.

The resources that are shared on my server can be viewed through browsing the Network Neighborhood.

The main problem with exploring for the resources is that you have to trudge your way through the same tree to get to the resources each time. If you need access to the resources on a regular basis, it is just as simple as mapping a network drive to those resources. When you map a network drive to a resource on a server, you are basically assigning a drive letter to that resource. From then on, when you want to access the resource, simply use the drive letter to refer to it.

You can map a network drive in two basic ways. One way is simply by right-clicking the resource when browsing for the resource as described previously. You get a short-cut menu similar to Figure 6.17.

By clicking the Map Network Drive option, you can specify what drive letter you want to assign to the resource. Additionally, you can also specify that Windows 95 reconnect this network drive to this resource the next time you log on to Windows 95 (see Figure 6.18).

The second way to map a network drive is a little more difficult, and guess what? You will need to know it for the exam. It's not complicated at all. Because every

Windows-based computer must have a computer name on a network, you can use that computer name to connect to it. Not only do you need to know the name of the computer that you would like to connect to, but you also need to know the name of the resource that is shared (its share name). For example, in Figure 6.18, I was mapping drive G: to \\thor\datastor. Thor is the name of the Windows NT server, and datastor is the share name of the resource. The two backslashes designate that this is a call to the network and not to the local hard drive. This naming convention is called Universal Naming Convention or UNC.

Figure 6.17.

Mapping a network drive when browsing network resources is as simple as right-clicking the object.

Figure 6.18.

Specifying the drive letter and whether to reconnect at logon.

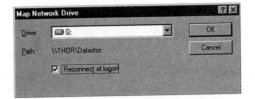

You might see some information about this on the exam. When asked how to connect to a resource on a Windows NT network using UNC naming, the correct response should be \\server\share or \\server\sharename.

I prefer using UNC naming to map network drives as opposed to browsing. You can very easily map a network drive by right-clicking either the My Computer or Network Neighborhood icons located on the desktop. You will find Map Network Drive as an option on both menus.

6.4.2. Sharing Resources with Other Microsoft Clients

Windows 95 computers can also act like servers on the network. A basic definition of a server is a computer that contains resources that it can share with others on a network. When someone mentions a server, you might think of Windows NT server or Novell NetWare. Don't get me wrong; Windows 95 by far does not have the capabilities as these advanced network operating systems, but it does meet the criteria of being able to share network resources.

 This section covers the following exam objective: Develop a security strategy—file and print sharing.

When you share resources on a Windows 95 computer with other client computers on a network, it can be called *peer resource sharing*, which is simply sharing files and printers with each other on a network, even without the use of a server. The first step to sharing resources is installing a compatible client. In this section, we will be using the Client for Microsoft Networks.

First, let's discuss sharing resources with other clients, or peer resource sharing. The first step to this process is to install the proper client. In this particular situation, the Windows 95 computer that will be sharing the resource must have the Client for Microsoft Networks installed. The computers that will be connecting to it must have a compatible client—one that can communicate with the Client for Microsoft Networks. If you remember linking to NT servers in 6.4.1, we talked about how Microsoft computers use SMB to communicate on the network. A compatible client is one that also communicates using SMB. For this particular section, let's assume you are connecting using another Windows 95 computer also running the Client for Microsoft Networks.

The next step to sharing resources is to install the File and Print Sharing for Microsoft Networks service. There are two basic ways to install the service. After double-clicking the Network option in the Control Panel, you might notice a File and Print Sharing button. After you click that button, you see a window similar to that shown in Figure 6.19.

This only enables file and print sharing for the Client for Microsoft Networks. To ensure you are installing the right option, I prefer clicking the Add button and adding a Service. After you get the list of services (see Figure 6.20), you can choose

6

Microsoft from the list of manufacturers. Notice under the list of Network Services that you can choose File and Printer Sharing for both Microsoft and NetWare Networks. By choosing File and Printer Sharing for Microsoft Networks and then clicking Add (see Figure 6.21), the service is added into the list of installed components.

Figure 6.19.

Enabling file and print sharing using the button in the Network dialog box.

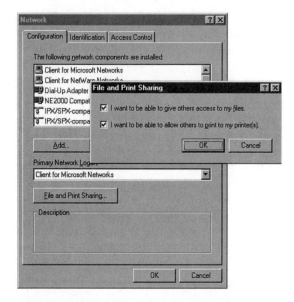

Figure 6.20.

Adding the File and Printer Sharing for Microsoft Networks using the Add, Service option.

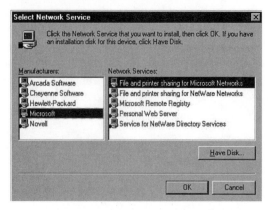

Figure 6.21.

Viewing the list of installed components after adding the File and Printer Sharing for Microsoft Networks.

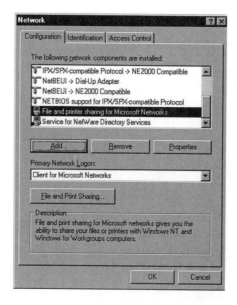

After clicking OK and restarting the computer, you can then share your files and printers with the rest of the network. Let's review adding the File and Printer Sharing for Microsoft Networks by taking a look at the step-by-step procedures:

1. Double-click Network in the Control Panel.

2. Click the Add button.

3. Click Service and click Add.

4. Select Microsoft from the list of manufacturers.

5. Select File and Printer Sharing for Microsoft Networks and click OK.

6. From the Network dialog box, click OK.

7. Restart the computer when prompted.

Sharing Folders

You can share folders with the rest of the network either through the My Computer or Explorer interfaces. The only difference is how you get to the folder that you want to share. I prefer the Explorer, because I can view multiple resources without having a series of windows open, which is the case with using the My Computer interface (by default).

6

After you locate the folder that you want to share, simply right-click the folder. You will see Sharing as one of the options in the shortcut menu. Selecting Sharing produces a dialog box like Figure 6.22.

Note

If you do not see Sharing as an option on the shortcut menu, it is because you do not have file and print sharing enabled.

Figure 6.22.

Specifying the sharing parameters of a folder is as simple as right-clicking the folder and selecting Sharing.

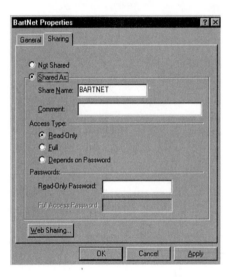

At the top of the dialog box, you see two options, Not Shared and Shared As. Choosing the radio button next to Shared As allows you to change the rest of the parameters. Under Shared As, you find the following options:

- **Share Name**—This is the name people on the rest of the network see when browsing for resources. Additionally, this is the name used in UNC naming where \\computer\sharename is an example.

- **Comment**—This appears as a comment that others see when using the Details option when browsing for the resource. The Details option can be invoked under the View menu of the utility (Network Neighborhood or Explorer) that you are using to browse for the resource.

The Share Name defaults to the directory name. You can create whatever name you like for the share name up to 12 characters long including spaces.

If you use spaces in share names, MS-DOS–based network clients will be unable to connect to the resource because MS-DOS–based clients use UNC names to connect and do not understand the use of spaces. All Windows-based clients will still be able to connect, though.

After you have completed the Share Name and Comment sections, you can then add security to your share. There are two basic kinds of security that you can specify on your share: share-level security and user-level security. I discuss user-level security in 6.4.3.

 When you share a folder on a Windows 95 computer, users accessing this folder from across the network will have access to not only the folder that you shared but any subfolders it contains.

Share-level security is simply the security option where you can set three basic levels of security:

- **Read-Only**—Users accessing the resource via the network can only read and/or execute the files in the folder. They cannot delete, change, or move the files.
- **Full**—Users accessing the resource via the network can modify, delete, or otherwise control the file.
- **Depends on Password**—This option sets a password for both read-only and full access to the folder.

The first two options are self-explanatory, but Depends on Password might need some clarification. I know I explained it earlier in the chapter, but I will reiterate it for the purpose of comparison with user-level security (explained later in this section). You can set separate passwords for read-only and full access to the folder. The way you control who has what type of access to the files is by controlling who has knowledge of which password. When the user attempts to connect to the resource, he is prompted for a password to complete the connection. Which password he types in determines which type of access he receives.

This type of access is called share-level security because security is set separately at each resource. Let's say, for example, that you have two folders—one called Sales and

6

one called Finance. You also want to give two people access to the folders—Bob and Jane. Let's also say that you would like Bob to have read-only access to Sales and full access to Finance, and you want to give Jane read-only access to Finance and full access to Sales.

This presents a problem if you had planned on using only two passwords for all the folders you had planned on sharing. Now you have to assign different passwords for the resources.

Note

Keep in mind that share-level security should only be used in peer-to-peer networks where there is no advanced server such as Windows NT or NetWare.

If you think about this concept of each individual computer having shared resources (each resource having its own passwords), you'll understand that this provides the great possibility of giving an administrator nightmares. The more computers and shares you have, the more difficult it becomes to administer.

Sharing Printers

Sharing a printer is very similar to sharing a folder. You must have the File and Printer Sharing for Microsoft Networks installed if you are to share your printer with other Microsoft clients. Secondly, you must have the printer properly installed on your Windows 95 computer that will be sharing the printer. I discuss proper installation of a printer more in depth in Chapter 9, "Installing and Configuring Printers."

Test Tip

This section covers the following exam objective: Create, share and monitor resources—Network Printers

After you have the printer properly installed, from the Printers folder, right-click the printer. You will see Sharing on the shortcut menu of that printer (see Figure 6.23). Choosing the Sharing option allows you to configure the sharing options for this printer. If you do not see the Sharing option on the shortcut menu, you possibly don't have the file and printer sharing service installed.

Figure 6.23.

Sharing a printer is very similar to sharing a folder: Simply right-click the printer and choose Sharing.

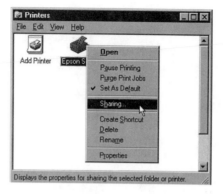

In Figure 6.24, you see the printer sharing options for the Epson printer I have installed. You have three options:

- **Share Name**—This name is seen by the users on the rest of the network when they are browsing for resources. Additionally, this is the name used in UNC naming where *computer**sharename* is an example.

- **Comment**—Other users see this when using the Details option when browsing for the resource. The Details option can be invoked under the View menu of the utility (Network Neighborhood or Explorer) that you are using to browse for the resource.

- **Password**—This is the password to access the printer. If you do not type in a password, everyone can access the printer. If you do type in a password, users are prompted for that password when they attempt to connect to the resource.

After you have specified the proper information, click OK. The printer is then shared to the network. Connecting to shared printers is also discussed further in Chapter 9.

6.4.3. Implementing NT Domain Security Controls

Windows NT was designed to add security to your network. Think of a Windows NT server (a primary domain controller) as the police force on the network. Users are validated on the network at logon and whenever they access resources on the network. Additional security services such as user policies and profiles can also be used with Windows NT servers.

6

Figure 6.24.

Sharing a printer to the network.

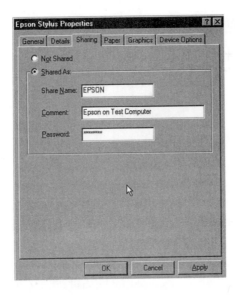

Using NT as Your Security Host

In the previous section, we discussed how to share resources on a Microsoft network. So far, I have only talked about using passwords for each share for security, hence the name *share-level security*. If you haven't figured it out by now, sharing with share-level security has the possibility of growing to a level where it can no longer be managed properly. Every time a computer is added or begins to share resources, the complication of administration grows. If you can't get away from sharing resources on the client computers altogether, you can tame the administration headache a little by implementing a different security scheme called *user-level security*.

This section covers the following exam objective: Assign access permissions for shared folders.

- Passwords
- User Permissions
- Group Permissions

User-level security is, simply put, better security than share-level using some type of security provider (in this case Windows NT Server). User-level security takes away the need for passwords at each share. As a matter of fact, users only have to remember one password, which is their logon password.

When you introduce a Windows NT server to the network, you have an operating system designed to keep track of users. With Windows NT server, you create a list of users. When resources are shared, instead of assigning a password to that resource, you specify which users can have which type of access. When the users attempt to access the resource, Windows 95 asks Windows NT to validate the user. After Windows NT verifies the user, Windows 95 grants the type of access specified. This is called *pass-through authentication*. Let's configure your Windows 95 computer to take advantage of user-level security and discuss it further.

You can use one of four types of computers with user-level security:
- Windows NT Server (installed as a PDC)
- Novell NetWare
- Windows NT Server (installed as a member server)
- Windows NT Workstation

The main thing that is common to all four is the capability to maintain a list of users. For all of the Windows 95 security functions to work properly, Windows NT Server (PDC) or NetWare should be used.

The first step is to enable user-level security. To do so, double-click the Network option in the Control Panel. In the Network dialog box, there are three tabs (see Figure 6.25). Under the Access Control tab, you find these options:

- **Share-level control**—Enables you to supply a password for each shared resource.

- **User-level access control**—Enables you to specify users and groups who have access to each shared resource.

- **Obtain list of users and groups from**—Specifies who the security provider will be and what computer will validate the users (requires user level security).

By choosing the User-Level Access Control radio button, you invoke user-level security. You must tell Windows 95 whom it will get the list of users from because Windows 95 does not have the capability of maintaining a user database. For Windows NT, you should put in the name of the domain from which you will be obtaining the list (see Figure 6.25).

6

Figure 6.25.

Switching to user-level security.

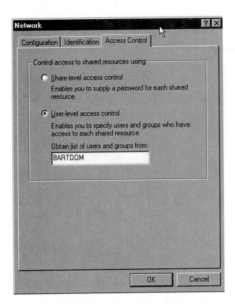

You can specify the computer name of the primary domain controller to obtain the list of users, but it is better to specify the name of the domain. When you have one or more backup domain controllers, they can also validate the users for access to the resource if you place the domain name rather than the computer name of the PDC.

After clicking OK, you are prompted with the message in Figure 6.26 which basically means that all the things you have shared already will not be shared because you are switching the security scheme. Click OK, and you are prompted to restart the computer for the changes to take effect.

With user-level security enabled, sharing a resource looks a little different. When you share a folder (see Figure 6.27), you no longer assign passwords to the resources; you assign users.

By clicking the Add button, you see a list of users and three types of access that you can grant them (see Figure 6.28). You grant access simply by clicking the user or group's name and then clicking the button that corresponds with the type of access. The three types of access are:

- Read-Only
- Full Access
- Custom

Figure 6.26.

After changing the security scheme, you are warned that all previously shared components will no longer be shared.

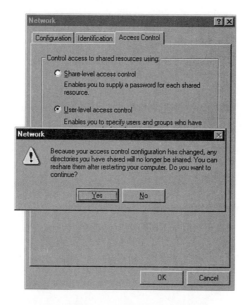

Figure 6.27.

Sharing a folder using user-level security.

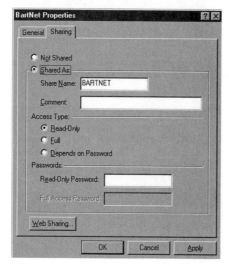

6

You should be careful giving several different groups different types of access. When a person is a member of two or more groups in which you have given access, that person's effective access rights are the combination of all groups. For example, let's say Bill is a member of the Accounting and Sales groups. You gave Accounting read access to a folder. Then you gave Sales write access to the same folder. Because Bill is a member of both groups, his effective access is the combination of the two groups (read and write).

Figure 6.28.

Defining share access for users and groups.

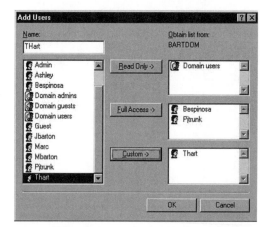

The first two types of access are self-explanatory, but custom access usually deserves a little further explanation. With custom access, you can get very definitive with the type of access users have on your resources. Adding someone to the Custom box doesn't seem to accomplish anything until you click OK.

After you click OK, Windows 95 pops up the Custom Access Rights dialog box, which allows you to specify what access rights that you give the users and/or groups that you specified to have custom access (see Figure 6.29).

The custom access rights that you can define are:

- **Read Files**—Users can read and/or execute files.
- **Write to Files**—Users can edit files already in the folder.
- **Create Files and Folders**—Users can create new files and subfolders in the existing folder.
- **Delete Files**—EEK! Users can delete files and folders.

- **Change File Attributes**—Users can change attributes of files and folders (Read-Only, Hidden, and so on).
- **List Files**—User can see contents of folder and subfolders.
- **Change Access Control**—EEK! Users can change security settings.

Figure 6.29.

Defining custom access rights.

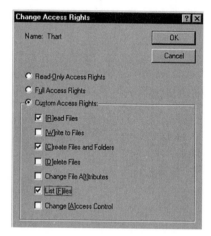

After specifying the type of custom rights, click OK. Notice that with the new users in the folder's property dialog box. Users with custom rights have their rights listed with one-letter abbreviations. These abbreviations designate what rights that they have. Click OK and the resource is now shared with the new access rights.

Server-Based Policies

Without user-level security, you cannot take advantage of group policies.

You can use system policies to lock down the computer on a per user, per group, or per computer basis. Even though the system policy can figure out your computer name and user logon name, it cannot figure out group membership. If you want to specify a policy using groups that you already have created on the Windows NT server, you must have user-level security enabled. When enabled, follow the directions in Chapter 8, "Locking Down the System," to enable group policies.

Additionally, you can store your CONFIG.POL file on the Windows NT server. This keeps you from having to have a copy of the policy file on every Windows 95 computer where you want to enforce policies. With user-level security enabled, by default Windows 95 looks to the NETLOGON share of the domain controller that validates the user. The Windows NT local path to the NETLOGON share is %systemroot%\system32\repl\import\scripts where %systemroot% is the drive and directory where Windows NT is installed.

Note

If you have a primary controller, and one or more backup domain controllers, you might run into a problem with the policy being enforced. With several domain controllers in a domain, any of the domain controllers can validate the user onto the network. The `CONFIG.POL` needs to be copied to each of the domain controllers' `NETLOGON` share to ensure that the policy is enforced no matter which controller validates the user. Windows NT also has the capability of automatically copying them. It is called directory replication.

6.5. Interoperability with Novell NetWare

NetWare is a server operating system created by Novell. Unlike Microsoft, Novell does not make a graphical user interface client for its NetWare network operating system. Therefore, other companies like Microsoft create client operating systems to connect to NetWare servers. NetWare is one of the most popular network operating systems and, as of this writing, has the largest installed base of PC server operating systems.

6.5.1. Connecting to NetWare as a Client

You can connect Windows 95 to a NetWare server in several ways:

- Built-in, 32-bit, protected-mode Microsoft Client for NetWare Networks
- Novell NetWare 3.*x* real-mode networking client using NETX (additional software obtained from Novell)
- Novell NetWare 4.*x* real-mode networking client using VLM (additional software obtained from Novell)
- Novell NetWare Client 32 protected-mode client supporting NDS (additional software obtained from Novell)
- Microsoft MS-NDS 32-bit, protected-mode support for NDS (additional software available in Windows 95 service pack 1 or OSR2)

Test
Tip

This section covers the following exam objective: Configure a Windows 95 computer as a client on a NetWare network.

Windows 95 has built-in capabilities to be a client to versions 2.*x*, 3.*x*, and 4.*x* NetWare servers. The Microsoft Client for NetWare Networks is a 32-bit, protected-mode client that supports all of the 16-bit NetWare 3.*x* and most of 4.*x* command-line utilities.

NetWare servers communicate using *NetWare Core Protocol* (NCP). To communicate with NetWare servers and other NetWare clients, you must install a client capable of communicating using NCP. The Client for Microsoft Networks enables the Windows 95 computer to communicate with other computers using NCP-based communications on the network.

> **Test Tip**
>
> For the exam, you should know that Microsoft networks use SMBs and NetWare networks use NCPs.

NetWare 2.*x* and 3.*x* servers store users, groups, and other information in a bindery. The bindery is accessed to obtain security information and validation. One disadvantage to the bindery is the fact that it is server-centric. This means that security information cannot be shared between servers. If you need to access resources on two different servers, you need user accounts on both servers.

With NetWare 4.*x* servers, the NetWare Directory of Services (NDS) takes care of the disadvantage of a bindery. The NDS is not server-centric, which allows better administration of resources, but as of this writing, very few applications are still NDS-aware. Therefore, NetWare 4.*x* servers can emulate a bindery allowing it to operate very similarly to previous versions of NetWare.

With the different options of accessing NetWare servers, your choice of which to use might be difficult. Using 16-bit, real-mode clients is a bad idea. These usually have to be loaded in the AUTOEXEC.BAT file and take up conventional memory. Additionally, they don't work well in multiple environments. By that I mean when you might need the capability to connect to Windows NT and NetWare servers simultaneously. You can only use one real-mode client at a time, but you can run multiple protected-mode clients simultaneously.

Both Microsoft and Novell have 32-bit clients. In the past, if you needed support for NDS, your choice was easy because, in the first release of Windows 95, the Microsoft client did not support NDS, whereas the Novell Client 32 did. With Service Pack 1 for Windows 95 or if you are running Release 2 of Windows 95 (OSR2), however, you can install an additional service that gives you NDS support with the Microsoft Client for NetWare Networks. This service is called Microsoft MS-NDS. It is also available for download from the Microsoft Web site (www.microsoft.com).

6

Note

If you have no reason to connect to a Windows NT server, I suggest the Novell Client 32. If you also need connectivity to Windows NT servers using the Client for Microsoft Networks, I suggest using the Microsoft Client for NetWare Networks along with the Microsoft MS-NDS service.

The main reason to use the NetWare-supplied client is to support VLM or NETX functions. The Microsoft Client for NetWare does not support any NETX or VLM functions. Remember that NETX and VLM are part of real-mode clients made by Novell.

Installing IPX/SPX

The first step to connecting to a NetWare server is installing the IPX/SPX-compatible protocol, which is required for connectivity to NetWare. If you choose to install the Microsoft Client for NetWare Networks first, the IPX/SPX protocol is installed automatically.

Test Tip

This section covers the following exam objective: Install and configure network protocols—IPX/SPX.

To install the IPX/SPX-compatible protocol, follow these steps:

1. Double-click the Network option of the Control Panel.
2. Click the Add button.
3. Click Protocol and click Add.
4. Select Microsoft from the list of manufacturers, select IPX/SPX from the list of protocols (see Figure 6.30), and click OK.
5. Click OK from the Network dialog box and follow the prompts.

After you restart the computer, the IPX/SPX-compatible protocol is installed, but you can modify the parameters of the protocol prior to completing step 5. To modify the protocol, simply select it from the list of installed components and click the Properties button. In Figure 6.31, you see the Properties of my IPX/SPX-compatible protocol.

The Advanced tab of the IPX/SPX protocol contains several options. The main option you need to be concerned with from a troubleshooting and exam perspective is Frame Type.

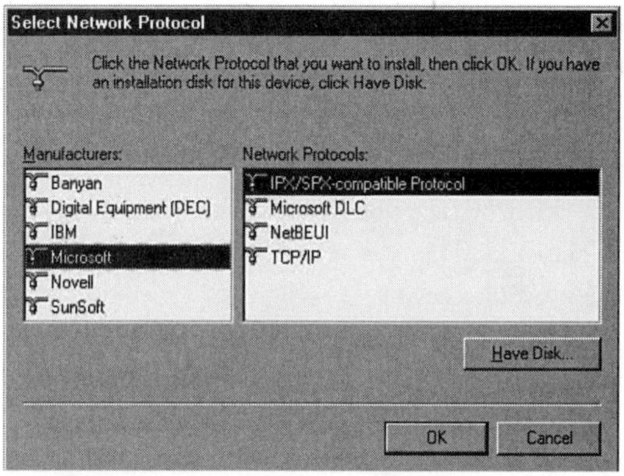

Figure 6.30.

Selecting the IPX/SPX-compatible protocol from the list of Microsoft protocols.

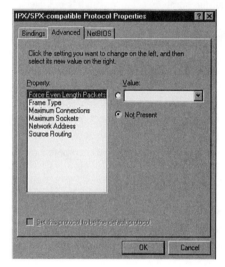

Figure 6.31.

The IPX/SPX-compatible protocol properties.

If you thought of the IPX/SPX protocol as the language spoken on the network, the frame Type option would be considered the dialect of that language. The different frame types available are:

- Ethernet 802.2
- Ethernet 802.3
- Ethernet II
- Token Ring
- Token Ring SNAP

6

As you can see, three of the frame types deal with Ethernet networks, and the other two deal with token ring networks.

You can specify any of these frame types that might be in use on your network. Because the most common topology today is Ethernet, you will probably set your frame type to either 802.2 or 802.3; NetWare uses one of those two types by default on Ethernet networks. The type you should use depends on which version of NetWare you need to access.

If you are using NetWare version 3.11 or earlier, the standard frame type is 802.3. If you are using NetWare version 3.12 or later, use 802.2.

Note

Don't let the numbers confuse you. It is not like software versions where the bigger the number, the newer the version.

802.2 and 802.3 are just two different standards. 802.3 uses a *carrier-sense multiple access with collision detection* (*CSMA/CD*) format on the network; 802.2 uses a *logical link control* (*LLC*) format.

You can also configure Windows 95 to detect the frame type on the network automatically and use the type that it detects when Windows 95 starts by sending out a message on all frame types. If it does not get a response or gets multiple responses, it defaults to 802.2.

If Windows does not receive a response on 802.2 but does get a response on other frame types, it picks a frame type from one of the types that gave responses. Windows picks a frame type in the following order:

- Ethernet 802.2
- Ethernet 802.3
- Ethernet II

For example, if Windows did not receive a response for Ethernet 802.2 and did receive a response for Ethernet 802.3 and Ethernet II, it would use a frame type of Ethernet 802.3.

Note

I have personally experienced problems with Windows 95 not detecting the correct frame type on several occasions. When this happens, the symptoms are simple. You can't connect to other computers running IPX/SPX. I suggest manually setting the frame type.

Other settings under the Advanced tab of the IPX/SPX-compatible protocol include the following:

- **Force Even Length IPX Packets**—Use this option for Ethernet 802.3 situations where odd-length packets cause problems.
- **Maximum Connections**—Maximum number of connections IPX allows.
- **Maximum Sockets**—Maximum number of IPX sockets that IPX assigns.
- **Network Address**—Specifies the network address as a four-byte value.
- **Source Routing**—Used in token ring networks, this option specifies the cache size to use with source routing.

 This information is not necessarily needed for the exam, but the information is still important in troubleshooting situations.

The NetBIOS tab allows you to enable the NetBIOS option to be used with IPX. You use this option when you need to communicate with other computers using NetBIOS over IPX. One example of this might be Lotus Notes. NetBIOS is used to establish logical names on the network, establishing sessions between computers using logical names and the like.

In general, you should enable this option if you will be communicating with other computers that might also be using NetBIOS over IPX. Additionally, if you will be connecting to other Microsoft-based computers, such as Windows NT and Windows for Workgroups, it is a good idea to enable NetBIOS over IPX.

 Here's a strange situation. Let's say you have a Windows NT 3.51 computer and a Windows 95 computer. They both have IPX/SPX loaded as a protocol, but neither has the NetBIOS over IPX option enabled. You can connect the Windows 95 computer to a resource shared on the Windows NT 3.51 computer, but you cannot connect the Windows NT 3.51 computer to a resource shared on the Windows 95 computer.

To make it work, you must enable NetBIOS over IPX on the Windows 95 computer.

6

Installing the Microsoft Client for NetWare Networks

Because the exam only covers material relating to the Microsoft Client for NetWare networks, that is the client that I concentrate on in this section. Because Release 2 contains the Microsoft MS-NDS, I also cover installing it in this section.

> This section covers the following exam objective: Install and configure network components of a client computer and server.

Installing the Microsoft Client for NetWare Networks is very similar to that of installing the Client for Microsoft Networks. You start by double-clicking the Network applet in the Control Panel. After the Network dialog box is available, click the Add button. You see a list of the network components that you can install. Click the Client button and click Add. From the list of manufacturers, choose Microsoft, then choose Client for NetWare Networks from the list of clients (see Figure 6.32), and click OK.

> If you are installing the Microsoft version of the NetWare client, make sure that you choose Microsoft in the list of manufacturers.
>
> If you choose Novell as the list of manufacturers, you get a list of the following installable components:
>
> - Novell NetWare (Workstation Shell 3.x [NETX])
> - Novell NetWare (Workstation Shell 4.0 and above [VLM])
> - Novell NetWare Client 32
>
> When choosing one of these options, Windows prompts you for the install disk from Novell. These clients are not included with Windows 95.

After you have clicked OK to install the client, you are returned to the Network dialog box. Also similar to the install of the Client for Microsoft Networks, it is easier to set any parameters in the Network dialog box prior to clicking OK. If you go ahead and click OK, you are prompted for the installation files (depending on how you installed Windows 95). Then, you are prompted to restart the computer. Upon doing so, you can then return to the dialog box to set parameters, but with most modifications in the network dialog box, you are prompted to restart. Setting the parameters at the time you install the client saves you an extra reboot.

Figure 6.32.

Installing the Microsoft Client for NetWare Networks is very similar to installing the Client for Microsoft networks.

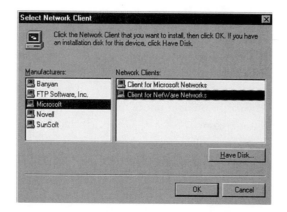

You can modify the parameters of your newly installed NetWare client by selecting it from the list of installed components and then clicking the Properties button, producing the dialog box in Figure 6.33.

Figure 6.33.

Modifying the Microsoft Client for NetWare.

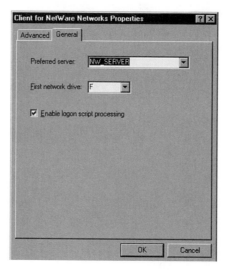

There are basic parameters to the Microsoft Client for NetWare. Looking at them, you can see that the settings are based upon a NetWare bindery and not the NDS of NetWare 4.*x*. The settings include:

- **Preferred server**—Bindery-based server by which you want to be validated.

- **First network drive**—The first drive letter available for use as a mapped network drive.

6

■ **Enable login script processing**—Toggle to determine whether you want the user login script to run.

By selecting the Advanced tab, you can specify whether to retain the case of your file names when you store files. Upon installing the Client for Microsoft Client for NetWare Networks, you might notice that both clients appear in the list of installed components (see Figure 6.34).

Figure 6.34.

By looking at the Network dialog box, notice that both clients can coexist.

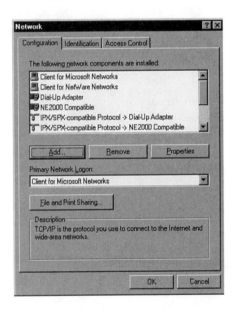

Let's review the install of the Microsoft Client for NetWare Networks:

1. Double-click the Network option in the Control Panel.
2. If the Microsoft Client for NetWare Networks already exists, go to step 6.
3. If not, click the Add button.
4. Click Client and click Add.
5. Select Microsoft from the list of manufacturers, select Microsoft Client for NetWare Networks, and click OK.
6. Select the Microsoft Client for NetWare Networks from the list of installed components and click Properties.
7. Specify the configuration information as necessary.
8. Click OK from the Network dialog box.
9. Restart the computer when prompted.

Installing Microsoft NDS support

In 1996, Novell built a brand new business around Novell Directory Services (NDS). NDS is a global, distributed information database that maintains information about every resource on the network including users, groups, printers, volumes, and other devices in a hierarchical tree structure.

With the original release of Windows 95, the Microsoft Client for NetWare Networks did not support the NetWare Directory Services of NetWare 4.*x.* As part of Service Pack 1 for Windows 95 and included with Release 2 (many times referred to as OSR2 or version B) of Windows 95, there is a service that you can install called Microsoft MS-NDS. MS-NDS does give the Microsoft Client for NetWare Networks that capability. Even though this information is not needed for the exam, it will help you better understand connecting to NetWare servers.

Keep in mind that the Microsoft Client for NetWare Networks has not changed from Release 1 to Release 2 (the part that supports NDS at least). To give it the NDS functionality, you must install both the client software and the MS-NDS service. If you install the MS-NDS service without having the Microsoft Client for NetWare networks installed, it installs the client automatically.

If you don't have Service Pack 1 or Release 2, you can still install the MS-NDS service. You can obtain the MS-NDS service from the Microsoft Web site free of charge.

To install the service, follow these steps:

1. Double-click the Network option in the Control Panel.
2. Click the Add button.
4. Click Service and click Add.
5. Click the Have Disk button and specify the location of the service installation files.
6. Click OK.
7. A dialog box appears with the service listed (see Figure 6.35); click OK.
8. Click OK from the Network dialog box.
9. Restart the computer when prompted.

The configurable options for the MS-NDS service are the Default tree and the default context for the workstation you are at (see Figure 6.36).

6

Figure 6.35.

Installing the Microsoft MS-NDS service.

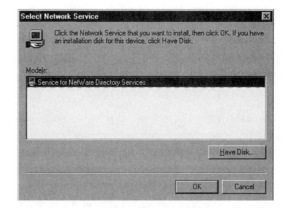

Figure 6.36.

Configuring the NDS parameters of the Microsoft MS-NDS service.

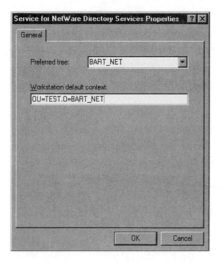

Note

With the Microsoft Client for NetWare Networks installed, it is not necessary to drop down to an MS-DOS prompt to run the WHOAMI utility to find out who you are logged in as or to what server.

You can check this very easily by double-clicking the Network Neighborhood icon located on the desktop. On the shortcut menu, you find Who Am I as an option. Selecting it reveals the information you seek.

Additionally, with the MS-NDS service installed, it also gives you NDS information.

Connecting to NetWare Resources

Connecting to NetWare resources can be very similar to connecting to resources on a Windows NT server. The reason that I say *can* be similar depends on whether the NetWare server is a bindery-based server. It also depends on how you go about connecting to that resource.

Once again, you can connect to a resource by browsing the Network Neighborhood. I am running version 4.11 of NetWare on my test network. In the previous section, I installed the Microsoft MS-NDS so that I could access the NDS of my server. Also, to show you bindery-based servers, I am also running bindery emulation on my NetWare server. In Figure 6.37, you can see what the Entire Network option of my Network Neighborhood looks like.

Figure 6.37.

Viewing the contents of the Entire Network in my Network Neighborhood after installing the Microsoft Client for NetWare and MS-NDS.

Notice that, in addition to the Windows 95 Workgroup and the Windows NT domain Bartdom, you see another group called Bart_Net and a computer called Nw_server. The Bart_Net group is not a group at all; it is the NDS Tree. The Nw_server is the NetWare server. Here is where most people get confused.

The Nw_server and the Bart_Net tree are actually both the same NetWare server. Because I installed the MS-NDS, you can see the NDS tree Bart_Net. You see Nw_server because my NetWare server is running bindery emulation. Both icons represent the same computer as far as the resource that I want to access (which is the SYS volume on my NetWare server). However, they (the icons) are two different ways of accessing the resource (whether you access it through the bindery or the NDS tree). Take a look at Figure 6.38 for a little more clarification.

Notice how the Nw_server is shown both directly under the Entire Network of the Network Neighborhood and under the Bart_Net NDS tree. If I expand out further so that I can view the SYS volume under the Nw_server and map a network drive to it, it shows a UNC name for the mapping (see Figure 6.39).

6

Figure 6.38.

Viewing my NetWare resources through the Explorer.

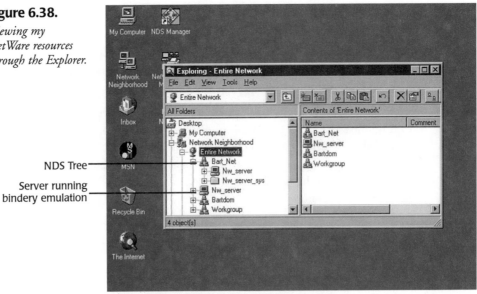

NDS Tree

Server running bindery emulation

Figure 6.39.

Mapping a network drive to a bindery-based NetWare server.

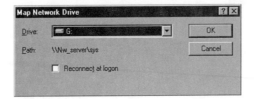

Note

UNC naming is slightly different between Microsoft shares and NetWare bindery-based shares. With Microsoft shares, the syntax is

`\\servername\sharename`

UNC naming with NetWare servers is slightly different. The syntax for NetWare shares is

`\\servername\volumename`

This is relatively unimportant because Windows 95 shares folders in the same manner. The only difference is how you connect to them. It really boils down to different terminology.

If I map a network drive to the Nw_server_sys which falls directly from the NDS tree Bart_Net, you will see that I am no longer mapping to a UNC name but rather to an NDS object (see Figure 6.40).

Figure 6.40.

Mapping a network drive to an NDS object (SYS volume of the Nw_server).

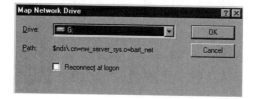

Also, notice that you have the option of automatically reconnecting the mapped network drive the next time you log on to the Windows 95 computer.

6.5.2. Sharing Resources with Other NetWare Clients

Windows 95 has the capability to act like a NetWare server on a NetWare network. This, in all actuality, is almost identical to what we just accomplished in the previous section. Windows 95 can share files and printers on a NetWare network and use a NetWare server as a security host.

First, you must install a NetWare client. In this section, let's assume that you have the Microsoft Client for NetWare networks installed. Second, you must install the File and Printer Sharing for NetWare networks service. This is done almost identically to installing the same service for Microsoft networks.

> Only one File and Printer Sharing service can be installed at one time. If you have the File and Printer Sharing for Microsoft networks installed, you must remove it before installing the File and Printer Sharing for NetWare networks (or vice versa).

6

To install the File and Printer Sharing for NetWare networks, follow these steps:

1. Double-click Network in the Control Panel.
2. Click the Add button.
3. Click Service and click Add.
4. Select Microsoft from the list of manufacturers.

5. Click File and Printer Sharing for NetWare Networks and click OK.

6. From the Network dialog box, click OK.

Using NetWare as Your Security Host

File and printer sharing for NetWare networks does not function using share-level security. For it to work properly, user-level security must be installed. If you haven't configured user-level security previously, you will receive the error message in Figure 6.41 when you click OK in step 6.

Figure 6.41.

The share-level security error message you get if you haven't configured user-level security before.

If you have installed user-level security before but have it configured for a Windows NT computer as your security host, you will receive the error message in Figure 6.42.

Figure 6.42.

The user-level security error message you get if you have previously configured user-level security with a Windows NT.

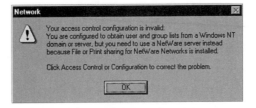

Selecting the Access Control tab at the top of the Network Configuration dialog box allows you to request a list of users from the NetWare server. After you have specified your NetWare security host, you can click OK and restart the computer when prompted.

After restarting the computer, you can share folders in the same manner as previously discussed. Now, when you add users to the list of users who might access the share, you obtain a list of users from the NetWare server (see Figure 6.43).

To other computers running the Microsoft Client for NetWare networks, the shared folders and printers appear as any other shared resources on the network. For other clients that might be running NETX- or VLM-based NetWare clients, however, the shared folders appear as NetWare volumes and the shared printers appear as NetWare print queues.

Figure 6.43.

Obtaining a list of users from a NetWare server.

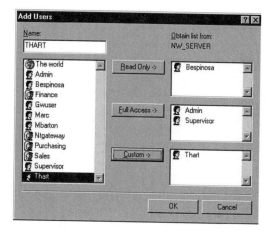

Microsoft File and Printer sharing for NetWare networks does not work with Novell's Client 32.

You must have SAP Advertising enabled for NETX- and VLM-based clients to find your resources on the network.

Server-Based Policies

You can also use a NetWare server with Windows 95 system policies. Group policies can be enforced using predefined groups on the NetWare server. For them to work properly, you must have the NetWare server as your security provider.

If you want to store the CONFIG.POL file on the NetWare server for central administration, you should store it in the SYS;PUBLIC directory. If you are concerned with users accessing this file, simply assign read-only access rights to it for the users. Follow the steps outlined in Chapter 8 for setup of policies.

6

> **Note**
>
> Access to SYS;PUBLIC is read-only to all users by default. Modifying or deleting the CONFIG.POL shouldn't be a concern for the administrator.

6.6. Browsing the Network

Browsing the network is basically the process of looking through a list of servers and viewing a list of their resources being shared. How is this accomplished? If there were no browsing capabilities, users would have to know the servers' names and share names to connect to them. This would be cumbersome for the user and time-consuming for the administrator.

So how do we fix this problem? It depends on the type of network you are running. So far, we have discussed two types of sharing for Windows 95 computers: File and Printer Sharing for Microsoft networks and that of NetWare networks. Which service you have installed (remember, only one can be installed at a time) determines how the browsing process happens. First, let's talk about Microsoft networks, and then we'll discuss NetWare networks.

6.6.1. Browsing Microsoft Networks

We could configure the computers to broadcast constantly what resources were available, but this option would quickly flood the network with traffic. To alleviate this problem, a list must be made of the servers and the resources that they are sharing. You can then browse this list to find the resource you seek. This list is appropriately called the *browse list*, which must also contain the address of this server. For simplicity, think of the browse list as a phone book.

Someone must make this list, though. If you had to create this list, you would have a full-time job trying to keep it up-to-date as servers went down, when servers came online, or when resources were shared or unshared. With Windows, this list is created and updated automatically.

If each computer on the network maintained a copy of this list, network traffic would increase just to keep this list up-to-date. Therefore, a central copy of this list is created and maintained by a computer called the Browse Master.

When a computer comes online, it sends a broadcast looking for a Browse Master. By default, all computers with File and Printer Sharing enabled have the capability to become Browse Masters. There is always one Browse Master per workgroup or domain.

So how does the process work? Well, when a computer comes online, it sends out a broadcast looking for a Browse Master. When it finds one, the computer sends its information to the Browse Master including what resources it has to share to the network. The Browse Master then adds the computer to its browse list. Because the computer coming online now knows who the Browse Master is, any time it needs to see the browse list (when you start browsing via the Network Neighborhood for example), it contacts the Browse Master (or one of the Backup Browsers, explained next).

To keep the Browse Master from becoming overwhelmed by all these requests, computers with File and Printer sharing enabled can become Backup Browsers. Once again, this happens automatically. So how many Backup Browsers are there? Well, if only one computer is on the network, there are no Backup Browsers because the single computer is the Browse Master (but you don't really have a network with only one computer). With two to 32 computers on the network, there is one Backup Browser. After that, an additional Backup Browser is created for every 32 computers.

So, you can see that computers on a Windows network can have many roles. Which computer has which role is determined through an election process to ensure that the computers with the best credentials become the Browse Master and Backup Browsers. The first credential that comes into play is the type of operating system a computer has. Computers with higher operating systems are determined in this order of precedence:

- Windows NT Server (installed as a PDC)
- Windows NT Server
- Windows NT Workstation
- Windows 95
- Windows for Workgroups

If two computers are competing for the role as Browse Master and both are running the same type of operating system, the computer with the newest version is elected. If both computers have the same version, the computer that has been online longest (which is usually already the Browse Master) remains the Browse Master.

It might seem that this is a long complicated process, but it is relatively fast and works well. Besides, in a Windows NT domain, the election process is usually cut short when the PDC enters the election. The PDC wins the election not because of the version and type of the operating system, but because of its configuration. This

6

brings me to the next role that a computer can have on the network: Preferred Browse Master.

The Preferred Browse Master, as you can probably figure out, has an edge in the election process. A Windows 95 computer can also be configured as a Preferred Browse Master.

 This section covers the following exam objective: Configure system services—Browser.

To configure what role the Windows 95 computer has in the browse process, follow these steps:

1. Double-click the Network option in the Control Panel.
2. Select File and Printer Sharing for Microsoft networks from the list of installed components.
3. Click the Properties button.

After you have the properties for the service, you see two options: Browse Master and LM Announce. For the Browse Master setting, you can specify three options (see Figure 6.44):

- **Automatic**—The computer can become a Browse Master or Backup Browser.
- **Enabled**—The computer is a Preferred Browse Master.
- **Disabled**—The computer does not participate in elections but can still share files and/or printers.

 Here is where I want to give you my opinion on File and Printer Sharing for Microsoft networks. Personally, I think that the file and print services should be left to the network operating systems like Windows NT and NetWare on larger networks.

By all means, on small networks, this service is great, so use it. On larger networks, though, it increases the network traffic for elections and makes your browse list huge.

There is a quick and easy solution to prevent a Windows 95 computer from participating in the browse elections and to keep it off the browse list. Simply don't install (or remove) the File and Printer Sharing for Microsoft networks service.

Figure 6.44.

You can configure the Browse Master setting for Microsoft networks by modifying the properties of the File and Printer Sharing for Microsoft networks service.

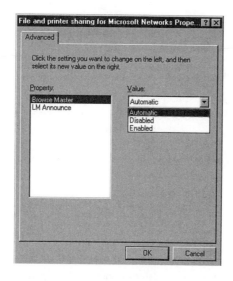

The LM Announce option is used for older LAN Manager networks. If you are not using LAN Manager, this option should be set to No. If set to Yes, the computer announces itself periodically using broadcasts.

You should keep a couple of other things in mind with the browse process. If you recall, a computer is added to the browse list when it comes online and contacts the Browse Master (if it has file and printer sharing enabled). So how do the Backup Browsers get this information? The Backup Browsers are notified by the Browse Master any time it has changes to the master copy of the browse list. The Backup Browsers then contact the Browse Master for a list of changes. Also, to ensure that the Backup Browsers have an up-to-date browse list and to notify the Browse Master that they are still online, the Backup Browsers contact the Browse Master every 15 minutes.

Also keep in mind that when you browse the list, your computer randomly contacts one of the browsers. If it contacts one of the Backup Browsers, you might not see a computer that has recently come online. Because the Backup Browsers contact the Browse Master every 15 minutes, a computer might not appear on the browse list for that 15-minute period of time.

So how do computers get removed from the browse list? This is an important question to answer. Computers should be removed from the list when they are taken offline. It really depends on how the computer is shut down.

6

If the computer is shut down properly by selecting the Shut Down option from the Start menu, it sends a message to the Browse Master telling it to remove it from the list. Once again, because the Backup Browsers are updated every 15 minutes, it might still appear on browse lists for up to 15 minutes.

If you ask most uneducated users if they know how to shut down their computers properly, the majority of them say, "Sure. I press the power button." You and I both know that this is not the proper way, so educate them how. Anyhow, if this event does happen, the computer can potentially show up on the browse list for 45 minutes.

> **Note**
>
> This is another reason to remove the File and Printer Sharing for Microsoft networks when you don't need it. Every computer that has it installed also contacts the Browse Master every 15 minutes to give and receive updates (increased network traffic). If the computer has not contacted the Browse Master for three of these periods (45 minutes), the Browse Master automatically removes it from the list.

6.6.2. Browsing NetWare Networks

The browsing process on NetWare networks is a little different. NetWare servers use an option called Server Advertising Protocol (SAP) to make other computers aware of the resources.

Every NetWare server broadcasts a SAP packet every 60 seconds. This packet contains the name of the server and the resources it is sharing. As you can see, as you increase the number of servers, you also increase the amount of network traffic because of SAP advertising.

You can configure Windows 95 to advertise itself using SAP when you install the File and Printer Sharing for NetWare networks. By default, when you do install File and Printer Sharing, SAP advertising is turned off (and for good reason). Without SAP advertising, the Windows 95 computer does not show up on the browse list of other NetWare clients.

If other NetWare clients (ones running Novell's real-mode client software) need access to the Windows 95 computer that has File and Printer Sharing installed, SAP advertising must be turned on for the NetWare clients to see the computer when browsing for resources. You can still connect to the resource using UNC naming; however, you just can't browse for it.

To enable SAP advertising for the Windows 95 computer, you must first have the File and Printer Sharing for NetWare networks installed. After it's installed, to enable the SAP advertising, follow these steps:

1. Double-click the Network option in the Control Panel.
2. Select File and Printer Sharing for NetWare networks from the list of installed components.
3. Click the Properties button.

You see two options: SAP Advertising and Workgroup Advertising. SAP Advertising can be enabled by the pull-down option on the right (see Figure 6.45).

Figure 6.45.

You can enable SAP Advertising through the File and Printer Sharing for NetWare networks.

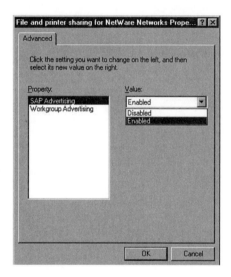

Workgroup Advertising accomplishes the same tasks as the Browse Master options discussed in Browsing NT networks. If you do not enable some form of workgroup advertising, Microsoft-based computers (ones *not* running Novell's real-mode stack) do not see the Windows 95 computer on the browse list. The options (see Figure 6.46) allow you to specify the computer's role in the browse elections.

6

Figure 6.46.

The Workgroup Advertising options.

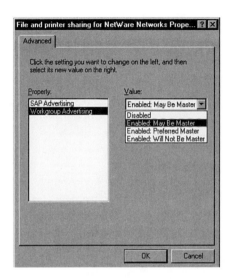

Lab

This lab consists of review questions pertaining to this chapter and provides an opportunity to apply the knowledge that you've learned with this chapter. Answers to the review questions can be found in Appendix B.

Questions

1. The naming convention used to connect to resources is called what?

    A. Universal Naming Convention

    B. Universal NetBIOS Connection

    C. United Name Convention

    D. Underling Naming Correction

2. Windows 95 supports which of the following network protocols? Choose all that apply.

    A. Net1

    B. TCP/IP

    C. IPX/SPX

    D. NetBEUI

    E. NetX

3. Windows 95 can use which of the following computers for security hosts? Choose all that apply.

    A. Windows 95

    B. Windows NT Workstation

    C. Windows NT Server

    D. Novell NetWare

4. When connecting to a Windows NT server, which UNC name would be used?

    A. `\\sharename\directory`

    B. `\\servername\sharename`

    C. `\\servername\volumename`

    D. `\\volumename\directory`

6

5. When connecting to a Novell NetWare server, which UNC name would be used?

   A. `\\sharename\directoy`

   B. `\\servername\sharename`

   C. `\\servername\volumename`

   D. `\\volumename\directory`

6. You can have File and Printer Sharing for Microsoft networks and File and Printer Sharing for NetWare networks installed simultaneously.

   A. True

   B. False

7. Security that is based on a password at each resource is called what?

   A. Resource-level security

   B. Password-level security

   C. Share-level security

   D. User-level security

8. John has a network consisting of ten Windows 95 computers and two Windows NT servers. Several printers are attached to the Windows 95 computers. He would like to share the printers so that others can use them, but he wants to set security so that not everyone has access to all printers (for example, check printers). He would like to have the highest level of security available to him but with the easiest administration. What type of security should he use?

   A. Resource-level security

   B. Password-level security

   C. Share-level security

   D. User-level security

9. With the frame type of IPX/SPX set to automatic, what frame type will be used if Windows 95 cannot detect the frame type?

   A. 802.2

   B. 802.3

   C. Ethernet II

   D. Token Ring

Exercise

Windows 95 was made with a client in mind. Take what you have learned in this chapter and connect a Windows 95 computer to a NetWare server and a Windows NT server using the steps indicated in the chapter.

I do not include step-by-step instructions for you to follow here due to the variety of configurations of Windows NT and NetWare servers. If you have a Windows NT and/or NetWare server available, contact your network administrator for details on their configurations. After you have the necessary configuration information, you can use the step-by-step instructions within the chapter to practice and familiarize yourself with it.

Connecting to a Windows NT version 4.0 server and a NetWare version 4.1 server has the greatest benefit. Windows NT 4.0 has DNS capabilities that 3.51 doesn't. Additionally, using NetWare 4.1 allows you to get some NDS experience under your belt. You can see some of the complications when using bindery emulation also.

6

Day 7

Linking to Your World

With Windows 95 connectivity, the design did not stop with local-area networks, but continued to connect to the world's largest network, the Internet.

Windows 95 was built with the Internet in mind. With the vast growth of the Internet, more and more users need access to it. Windows 95 has built-in Internet utilities and functions.

One important aspect of connectivity with the Internet is the use of the TCP/IP protocol. This chapter discusses installation and configuration of TCP/IP.

Objectives

Connecting to the Internet is an important aspect of Windows 95. Even though only two Microsoft exam objectives pertain to the Internet, they cover a very broad aspect of Windows 95.

- Install and configure network protocols
- TCP/IP
- Configure a Windows 95 computer to access the Internet
- Diagnose and resolve connectivity problems
- WINIPCFG

7.1. Internet Basics

Windows 95 was built with the Internet in mind. Whether you will use dial-up networking (Chapter 10, "Taking Windows 95 on the Road: Remote Services") or your corporate network to connect to the Internet, Windows 95 works like a charm. In this section, I assume that we are talking about the latter of the two. This section not only discusses the Internet, but TCP/IP as a protocol as well. You can use TCP/IP on your LAN or WAN with excellent results.

There are actually two terms that most people get confused. The Internet (notice the capital *I*) is the worldwide network of networks that has been the latest craze. An internet is usually several departmental LANs in a company that are connected together to form a WAN (or a network of networks). The Internet and an internet have very similar characteristics. They both comprise smaller networks that are interconnected via routers, but most companies refer to their internetworks as WANs. At any rate, I will be talking about both when I discuss TCP/IP.

Do not let the Internet overshadow the importance of why it was created. That reason was to connect dissimilar systems. You can use TCP/IP on your network and never touch the Internet. You might be using it to communicate between your Windows PC network and your UNIX network. Windows 95 has TCP/IP built into it not only for connectivity to the Internet, but also so that it can be used in scenarios where connectivity to dissimilar systems is a need.

7.1.1. Internet History

As an Air Force veteran, I have had the opportunity to work with computers on both the Internet and ARPAnet, but where did these terms come from and what are they?

The Department of Defense (DoD) buys all kinds of computers from all kinds of manufacturers. The computers are not just different from service to service (Army, Navy, Air Force, Marines, and so on) but also within each service. In the Air Force, I've seen various mainframe systems, as well as PC systems. The problem is that each organization or base usually had its own type of networks and no effective way to exchange communication. The problem was that each network had its own proprietary protocols and communication processes.

Around 1969, all the military branches decided to interconnect all of these smaller networks into one large network—a network of networks, so to speak. It really ended up being one huge WAN. This network was called ARPAnet because it was designed primarily by the Advanced Research Projects Agency. It not only connected military organizations but other federal agencies, numerous research organizations, and universities.

The neatest thing about the ARPAnet is that it used a common protocol so unlike systems could communicate. This protocol was called *NCP,* or *network core protocol,* which was redefined repeatedly until it actually became two separate components called *transmission control protocol (TCP)* and *internet protocol (IP).* We know this protocol today as *TCP/IP.*

The ARPAnet eventually evolved into what we now know as the Internet, but it didn't happen overnight. The Internet really wasn't born on a certain date. Portions of the Internet were still in use when I was in the Air Force that were called the ARPAnet, even though it used TCP/IP. The ARPAnet was a major way for us to transfer information from base to base.

7.1.2. Internet Functionality

So what actually makes up an internet? Well, to understand that, you need to understand some terminology. In Figure 7.1, you see a sample internet. Notice the three segments comprised of three computers per segment. In an internet, these segments are called *subnets.* To make it easier to understand, I gave each computer a person's name. I will refer to each of the computers by its name.

Computers in the same subnet can communicate with each other, but computers cannot communicate with computers on other segments. For example, Bill cannot communicate with Kim without the help of a router. A *router* is a device used to connect the two subnets together. A router might be a hardware device or a computer, such as Windows NT. Whenever a computer in one subnet wants to communicate with computers in another subnet, it must send its messages to the router to be forwarded.

Note | Windows NT is the only operating system in the Microsoft family that can act as a router.

Another neat feature of the Internet can be demonstrated with my internet in Figure 7.1. For example, if Bill wants to communicate with Don, he would normally connect through router 1, but if router 1 is down, he can forward the message via router 3 and, in turn, to router 2. Then, router 2 would relay the message to Don.

7

Figure 7.1.

An internet is several small network segments joined via routers.

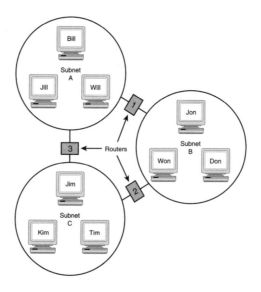

7.2. TCP/IP Protocol

The Internet and other internets use TCP/IP as the network protocol. TCP/IP is not a single network protocol; it is actually a suite of protocols and utilities that are used for various purposes. I won't go into all of them, simply because it is not necessary for the exam. Secondly, if I did, this book would probably be three times as thick as it is now. If you would like more information on TCP/IP, you can pick up a copy of Sams *Teach Yourself MCSE TCP/IP in 14 Days* by Robin Burke.

 This section partially covers the following exam objective: Diagnose and resolve connectivity problems—WinIPCfg.

Microsoft TCP/IP includes utilities such as:

- **FTP**—File transfer protocol, allows files to be transferred between dissimilar systems. Windows 95 can download files from any type of computer running TCP/IP and FTP software.

- **TelNet**—Allows you to connect to mainframes by emulating a terminal.

■ **WINIPCFG**—Command-line utility that gives full TCP/IP configuration and status information.

■ **NetStat**—Command-line utility that displays the network status.

■ **Ping**—Packet Internet groper, a command-line utility that allows you to test connectivity.

■ **Route**—Command-line utility to configure routing.

■ **Tracert**—Command-line utility to check the route to another computer.

■ **ARP**—Address resolution protocol, displays and modifies the IP address to physical address translation.

■ **SNMP**—Simple network management protocol, allows computers and devices to be managed by a standard set of network tools.

■ **UDP**—User datagram protocol, gives a computer the capability to send information without actually establishing a connection between computers.

7.2.1. TCP/IP Basics

So how does TCP/IP work? Well, we'll start by examining the two components. IP, in particular, can be confusing, so I'll cover it first.

Internet Protocol (IP)

The IP portion of TCP/IP takes care of all addressing. When using TCP/IP, each computer must be assigned a unique address. This address is referred to as an *IP address*. This address is a 32-bit address represented in four sets of numbers like:

207.68.156.16

This example, by the way, is an IP address of Microsoft's Web site. Now, that might not look like a 32-bit number, but it is; it's just in decimal format. If you converted it to binary, it would be

11001111 1000100 10011100 00010000

Normally, the number does not have spaces, but I wrote it that way to distinguish between the different parts of the address. The 32-bit number is divided into four chunks, separated by periods. This format is sometimes referred to as dotted decimal format. Each chunk is called an *octet*. Therefore, the 207 in the address is considered the first octet.

7

Note

I'm not going to bore you with the equation that it takes to convert binary to decimal format, even though you should learn how to use it sometime. You need to know how to use it if you are planning to take the TCP/IP exam as one of your MCSE electives. The reason I don't explain it here is because you don't need it for the Windows 95 exam. However, there is an easy way to convert the numbers. All you need is the calculator that comes with Windows 95.

Open the calculator, select View from the menu, and choose Scientific. You need to use two radio buttons, BIN and DEC. For example, if you would like to convert a decimal number to binary, make sure the DEC button is on. Punch in the number and click BIN (or press F8). You now have the binary equivalent. If you want to convert binary to decimal, just do the opposite (F6 is the keystroke for decimal).

If you will be connecting your network to the Internet, you can't just make these addresses up. Remember that IP addresses must be unique. An organization called InterNIC, or just NIC (which stands for Network Information Center), manages which IP addresses are in use and by whom. You can contact the NIC at www.internic.net (or at 703-742-4777). More commonly, your Internet service provider (ISP) will assign you IP addresses. Regardless of whether you get your IP addresses from the NIC or an ISP, they must be unique.

Note

If you are not connected to the Internet, you can make your IP addresses up as you go along, but I have seen numerous network administrators use that philosophy only to reconfigure all the computers after their Internet connection was established. If you see that you will be connected to the Internet in the future, take the necessary steps up front and get IP addresses assigned. Therefore, when your Internet connection is established, you won't have to reconfigure much, if anything at all.

IP addresses are divided into classes of IP addresses. In the past, you would be assigned a certain class of IP address based upon how many computers would need an IP address. Now, the NIC has devised a new way of assigning addresses called *CIDR* (Classless Inter-Domain Routing) to prevent wasting large numbers of addresses.

You need to know the different classes for the exam.

The first octet determines which class of address it is. The NIC also assigns part of the address and leaves the rest up to you to determine how it should be assigned. The part that NIC assigns cannot be changed. This is to ensure that the IP addresses are unique. Table 7.1 gives you a summary of the different classes.

Table 7.1. IP address classes.

Class	First Octet	Possible # Networks	Possible # Hosts	Part by NIC (X)
Class A	1-126	126	16,777,254	XXX.000.000.000
Class B	128-191	16,384	65,534	XXX.XXX.000.000
Class C	192-223	2,097,152	254	XXX.XXX.XXX.000

Numbers in the first octet of Class A addresses range from 001 to 126. Notice that I skipped 127. That's because 127 is reserved for diagnostic reasons. If you send a message to 127.0.0.1 (called the *loopback address*), it will be returned to you. Therefore, only 126 Class A addresses can exist. NIC assigns the first octet and leaves the rest of the IP address for you to assign to each computer. If you do the math, you'll see that each Class A network can have up to 16,777,254 computers on it. Unfortunately, because there is a limited number of Class A networks (126 of them), they have been taken already—most of them by large companies, universities, and, of course, the Department of Defense (DoD).

The NIC has assigned the first two octets of Class B networks. That leaves the last two octets for you to assign. The first octet's numbers range from 128 to 191, and the second octet's numbers range from 0 to 255. Table 7.1 shows you the statistics of the number of networks and number of hosts per network. Once again, all Class B addresses have already been assigned.

Class C networks are still available, though. The NIC assigns the first three octets, leaving the last octet for you to modify. The first octet includes from 192 to 223. The second and third octets include from 0 to 255. This gives you the possibility of 254 addresses that you can assign.

7

Note You might be wondering how I came up with 254 hosts if the address range is 0 to 255. Well, in actuality, you can't use 255. It is reserved for broadcasts. Yes, broadcasts do happen on a TCP/IP network. All computers in the same subnet (same network ID) establish the communication process. For example, let's say you have a Class C address of 192.107.101.0, where the first three octets are assigned and the last octet is open for you to use. The address 192.107.101.255 is reserved for broadcasts on that particular network. Also, neither the network ID nor the host ID can be all zeros.

Previously, I mentioned that you distinguish between the network portion and the host portion of the IP address through the use of a subnet mask. The default subnet masks are as follows:

Class A—255.0.0.0

Class B—255.255.0.0

Class C—255.255.255.0

For example, with the network address of 192.107.101.0, my subnet mask would be 255.255.255.0, by default. Let's say that I have two computers on the network, one with an address of 192.107.101.10 and one with 192.107.101.11. When you convert the addresses and subnet masks to binary, they will be

Computer A—11000000 01101011 01100101 00001010

Computer B—11000000 01101011 01100101 00001011

Subnet Mask—11111111 11111111 11111111 00000000

Anywhere you see the number 1 in the subnet mask, the two computers must match in the same position to be considered on the same subnet and, therefore, to communicate without using a router. If you compare the two, you'll see that they do match with the first three octets and not the last. Therefore, these two computers are on the same subnet.

You might be asking, "Why did I go through the trouble of converting them to binary when I could have figured it out simply by looking at the decimal representation of the addresses?" It is because 255.255.255.0 is the default subnet mask for Class C addresses. You can create a further subnet of a Class C network. This is called *segmenting*. Segmenting networks has a couple advantages. The main advantage is to decrease network traffic, but I won't explain how to segment further even though it makes a great sleeping aid. You won't need to know it for the Windows 95 exam.

In Figure 7.2, you see my example network, this time with IP addresses plugged in. Notice that each subnet has a common Class B address and unique host addresses assigned to each computer. Each router is designed to use a compatible IP address for each subnet that it connects. Because each router connects two subnets, it is assigned two IP addresses. When a computer needs to send a message to another subnet, it uses the router (called a gateway) to forward the message.

Figure 7.2.

Each subnet has its own Class B address.

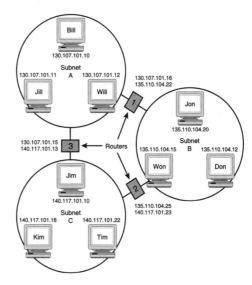

Transmission Control Protocol (TCP)

TCP's job is to ensure that the data is received reliably. IP handles only the sending of the packets and where those packets are supposed to go. It does not tell the sending computer to resend the packet if it was damaged in transit. It is basically the error checking part of the TCP/IP suite. TCP does numerous other things, but error checking is probably the most significant.

7.2.2. Installing TCP/IP

The actual installing of TCP/IP is not as complicated as understanding the concepts of TCP/IP. The install, of course, begins with the Network option in the Control Panel.

7

This section covers the following exam objective: Install and configure network protocols—TCP/IP.

Follow these steps:

1. Double-click the Network option of the Control Panel.
2. Click the Add button.
3. Click Protocol and click Add.
4. Select Microsoft from the list of manufacturers, then select TCP/IP from the list of protocols (see Figure 7.3), and click OK.

Figure 7.3.

Installing Microsoft TCP/IP.

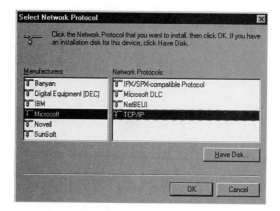

Manual IP Configuration

After you have installed the protocol, you need to configure it. To do so, click TCP/IP under the list of installed components and click the Properties button. The first tab is where you specify the IP address. To specify the IP address manually, click Specify an IP Address. You can type in the IP address and subnet mask that I mentioned earlier (see Figure 7.4). Notice that I configured this computer the same as computer Bill in Figure 7.2.

If you choose the Gateway tab (see Figure 7.5), you can specify the different gateways to outside networks. Those are nothing more than the IP addresses of routers that connect you to other networks. Because computer Bill is on a subnet connected to two other subnets, the two gateways' addresses are the same as the two routers that connect Subnet A to Subnets B and C. Simply type in the IP address of the gateway (router) in the New Gateway block and click Add. The installed gateways are then listed.

Figure 7.4.

Specifying an IP address and subnet mask.

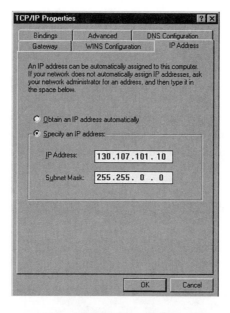

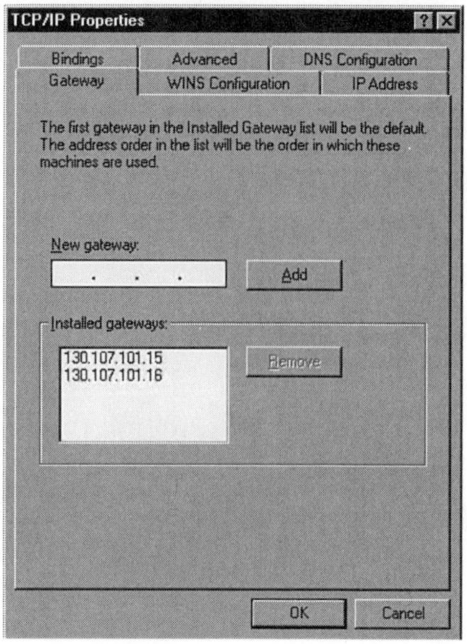

Figure 7.5.

Specifying the gateways used to connect to outside networks.

The gateways are listed in order of precedence. Because Bill needs to make connections to Subnet C more often than Subnet B, the router that connects A and C together (router 3) is specified first. This is also known as the *default gateway*.

Taking Advantage of DHCP

Alternatively, you can configure the IP addresses automatically. This service is called *dynamic host configuration protocol*, or *DHCP*. With DHCP, a server is configured to assign IP addresses on an as needed basis. Let's say you have 20 IP addresses that range from 130.107.101.1 to 130.107.101.21. You could configure the DHCP server to assign these addresses individually to Windows 95 computers when they come online. When assigned the address, the host (Windows 95 computer) keeps the address for a predetermined length of time (which can be configured at the DHCP server). In addition to the IP address, the server also assigns the subnet mask, default gateway, IP address of WINS servers, IP address of DNS servers, and more. Windows NT server is the only Microsoft operating system package that can offer this service.

To configure the Windows 95 computer to use DHCP, simply select the Obtain an IP Address Automatically radio button under the IP Address tab (see Figure 7.6).

Figure 7.6.

Specifying the Windows 95 computer to take advantage of DHCP.

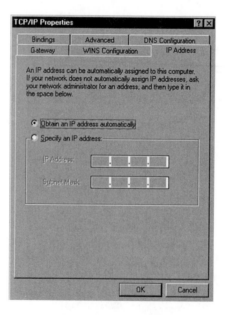

You can use the command-line utility WINIPCFG to find out your TCP/IP configuration, including what IP address your DHCP server assigned you. Simply use the Run command from the Start menu. WINIPCFG can also be used to renew and release DHCP leases.

Windows Internet Naming Service (WINS)

Another service available from Windows NT server is the Windows Internet naming service. Many utilities use NetBIOS computer names to establish a connection, but NetBIOS concepts work predominately by broadcasts.

The computer faces a problem: It needs an IP address to connect to another computer. If it can't find the IP address, it can't make a connection. Typically, computers on the same subnet can find each other fine, but when connecting to computers via routers where broadcasts are usually filtered out, you can run into problems. Therefore, there must be some way of resolving what computer names equal what IP addresses. You could create an *LMHosts* file, which would then have to be copied to each computer, but this would mean more administrative tasks for you. If you're like me, the last thing you need is another task.

WINS fixes this problem for you. With the WINS service installed on your Windows NT server, the server keeps track of what computers have what IP addresses. After you specify the WINS server's IP address on the Windows 95 client, it contacts the server whenever it needs a NetBIOS name resolved.

If you are connecting to a DHCP server to be assigned an IP address, you can also have that DHCP server inform you of the WINS server's IP address. To configure WINS, select the WINS Configuration tab (see Figure 7.7). You can specify two WINS servers. This is a handy option. If you have two WINS servers on your network (for fault tolerance), Windows 95 can be configured for both, in case one server is down at the time. To configure the DHCP server to inform the Windows 95 computer of the WINS server's IP address, simply select the Use DHCP for WINS Resolution radio button.

You must have the computer configured to use DHCP under the IP Address tab (Obtain an IP Address Automatically) before the Use DHCP for WINS Resolution button becomes an option.

7

Figure 7.7.

Configuring the Windows 95 computer to use WINS.

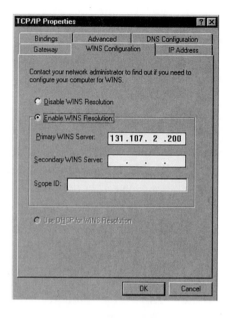

Domain Name System (DNS)

On the DNS Configuration tab, you specify the Domain Name System settings. If your company is connected to the Internet, it probably has a domain name. An example of a domain name is microsoft.com, which is, of course, Microsoft's domain name. Domain names are just another way of connecting to other TCP/IP networks. The same organization that keeps track of IP addresses (InterNIC) keeps track of domain names.

This section partially covers the following exam objective—Configure a Windows 95 computer to access the Internet.

If the Windows 95 computer will be connected to the Internet or if you need some other reason for resolving domain names to IP addresses (such as an intranet), you must configure the Windows 95 computer with some way of resolving these names to IP addresses. You could create a *Hosts* file, which would then have to be copied to each computer, but this would mean more administrative tasks for you. Once again, if you're like me, the last thing you need is another task. Instead, you can put in the IP address of a DNS server. To configure the DNS settings, simply select the DNS Configuration tab (see Figure 7.8). Notice that there are entries for the local computer's name (host). This name does not have to be the same as the NetBIOS name (computer name). There is also a place for you to specify of which domain the computer is a member. It is not necessary to specify a domain name, but Windows 95 requires you to enter a name if you are using DNS name resolution, whether the local machine has an entry on a DNS server or not.

Note | Don't confuse the Internet domain name and a Windows NT domain name. They are not the same. The Internet domain name is a logical grouping of computers for the Internet or an internet. The Windows NT domain name is used for Windows NT security.

Figure 7.8.

Setting up the DNS configuration.

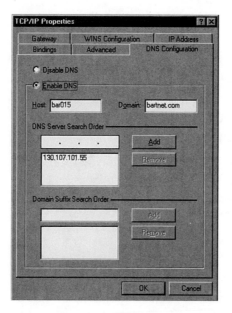

If you are connecting to the Internet, it is important that you get this information correct. Otherwise, your Web browser or other TCP/IP utilities and programs might not work properly. If you are connecting to the Internet using dial-up networking, take a look at Chapter 10.

7

Lab

This lab consists of review questions pertaining to this chapter and provides an opportunity to apply the knowledge that you've learned with this chapter. Answers to the review questions can be found in Appendix B.

Questions

1. Which of the following is the default subnet mask for a Class B network?

    A. 255.0.0.0

    B. 255.255.0.0

    C. 255.255.255.0

    D. 255.255.255.255

2. Which utility can you use to find out what IP address was assigned to a Windows 95 computer by a DHCP server?

    A. Ping

    B. TraceRt

    C. WINIPCFG

    D. Route

3. Which service provides automatic configuration of TCP/IP addresses for computers on a network?

    A. WINS

    B. DHCP

    C. DNS

    D. Ping

4. Which service provides resolution of Internet domain names to TCP/IP addresses?

    A. WINS

    B. DHCP

    C. DNS

    D. Ping

5. Which service provides resolution of NetBIOS computer names to TCP/IP addresses?

   A. WINS

   B. DHCP

   C. DNS

   D. Ping

6. Bob administers a Windows NT and Windows 95 network, which consist of two Windows NT servers (one of which is a WINS server) and sixty-five Windows 95 computers. Bob has called you to consult him on some issues that he would like to take care of. Here are his items and proposed solution. Define whether the proposed solution meets all, some, or none of Bob's objectives.

   Required Result: Ease some administration of TCP/IP tasks on the network.

   Optional Result 1: Automatically assign IP addresses.

   Optional Result 2: Automatically configure computers to help them resolve NetBIOS computer names to IP addresses.

   Proposed Solution: Install and properly configure one of the Windows NT servers with DHCP. Under the TCP/IP settings on the Windows 95 computer, select the Obtain an IP Address Automatically option.

   A. Neither the required result nor the optional results are met by the proposed solution.

   B. The required result is the only result met.

   C. The required result and optional result 1 are met.

   D. The required result and optional result 2 are met.

   E. The required result and both optional results are met.

Exercises

Installing TCP/IP

In this exercise, you will install the TCP/IP protocol. This prepares you for the exam by covering the following exam objective: Install and configure network protocols—TCP/IP.

7

1. Double-click the Network icon in the Control Panel.

2. Click the Add button.

3. Click Protocol and then click Add.

4. Select Microsoft.

5. Select TCP/IP.

6. Click the OK button.

7. Locate TCP/IP in the list of installed components.

8. Select TCP/IP and then click the Properties button.

9. Click Specify an IP Address.

10. In the IP address block, type **131.107.2.200**.

11. In the Subnet Mask block, type **255.255.0.0**.

> **Note** If your network is already using TCP/IP, you should consider using a legitimate IP address and subnet mask for your network.

12. Click OK in the TCP/IP properties box.

13. Click OK in the Network dialog box.

14. After Windows 95 transfers the necessary files, you are prompted to restart the computer. Click Yes.

15. Windows restarts.

Using WINIPCFG

In this exercise, you will use WINIPCFG to verify your configuration of TCP/IP. This will help prepare you for the exam by covering the following exam objective: Diagnose and resolve connectivity problems—WINIPCFG.

1. After Windows 95 restarts, click Start and then Run.

2. Type **WINIPCFG** and press Enter.

3. Note the information.

4. Above the adapter address box, you see a list of adapters. Pull down this list. What adapter(s) do you see?

   If you had a modem installed, and it was connected to another network—for example, the Internet—you would also be able to read the configuration of it.

This can come in handy when troubleshooting. You can see which IP addresses, if any, are assigned to all adapters in the system.

5. Click the More Info button.

6. Note the information.

7. Click the OK button.

8. Click Start, Programs and then MS-DOS Prompt.

9. From the MS-DOS prompt, type **PING 131.107.2.200** and press Enter (you
   can substitute the IP address with yours if you used your network settings).

7

TEST DAY
FAST FACTS

You should know a few things about policies and profiles for the exam. Here are a few fast facts for quick study:

- Local based profiles are stored in the C:\Windows\Profiles*username* folder by default.

- To make profiles mandatory, rename the USER.DAT to USER.MAN.

- Server-based profiles on a Windows NT Server are stored in the user's Home directory.

- Server-based profiles on a Novell NetWare Server are stored in the user's Mail directory.

- Server-based profiles are updated to the server each time the user logs off.

- In order for roving user profiles to work properly, the Windows 95 computer must be running a 32-bit protected-mode networking client, such as Client for Microsoft Networks or Client for NetWare Networks.

- For all settings in the profile to follow the user, the server must support long file names.

- The Policy file should be saved as CONFIG.POL.

- On a Windows NT network, the policy file should be stored in the Netlogon share of the Primary Domain Controller.

Day 8

Locking Down the System: Profiles and Policies

Administering computers on a network has never been easier. Windows 95 comes with the capability for users that share a common machine to have their own personalized settings. Administrators can now lock down parts of the system to keep users from doing damage whether intentionally or not. They can do this through the implementation of system policies.

Objectives

I have found that some people have difficulty with profiles and policies of Windows 95 in detail, so I will spend a little extra time and effort to explain them. Not only should you know profiles and policies for real-world use, but also for testing purposes. If you do not understand them, it could greatly affect your overall score on the exam. Here are the Microsoft exam objectives:

- Develop a security strategy using system policies and profiles.

- Set up user environments using profiles and system policies.

- Diagnose and resolve connectivity problems using Net Watcher.

- Create, share, and monitor a remote resource.

8.1. The Benefits of User Profiles

Profiles give each user of a common machine their own individualized settings. This allows everyone on that common machine to customize it for the look and feel that they want, without having to worry about it affecting everyone else.

Settings stored in the profile include:

- The Start menu
- The Documents folder (most recent documents)
- Shortcuts on the desktop (not files on the Desktop)
- Persistent network connections
- Desktop settings (colors, screen saver, and so on)
- Window configurations

 This section covers the following exam objective: Set up user environments using profiles and system policies.

Additionally, the network administrator can configure the profiles to be located on a network server so that no matter where the user logs on, his settings will be available and downloaded to the computer where he is logging on.

8.1.1. Maintaining Personal Preferences

Let's take a look at how we enable profiles. In Figure 8.1, you see the Passwords option on the Control Panel. There are three tabs. The first tab, Change Passwords, is self-explanatory; the second tab, Remote Administration, we talk about in section 8.3; but the last tab, User Profiles, is where you need to look. Figure 8.2 gives you a look at this tab.

You might notice that you have two options. The top option, All Users of This PC Use the Same Preferences and Desktop Settings, is the default setting. With it set, all users of this machine will have the same identical settings because they will all share the same USER.DAT. Therefore, they all share the same profile.

The second option, Users Can Customize Their Preferences and Desktop Settings, is the setting that enables profiles. Clicking this option enables profiles. After you set it and press the OK button, you are prompted to restart the computer. Upon restart, each user that logs on to the computer is prompted to reconfirm his password. The user is also prompted with the message stating that this is the first time he has logged on to the machine (even though it might not be) and whether the user would like his individual settings retained for use when logging in there in the future. If the user prompts Yes, the computer creates a profile by copying the default profile.

8

Figure 8.1.

The Control Panel, Passwords applet.

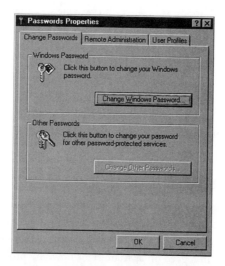

Figure 8.2.

The User Profiles tab of the Passwords applet.

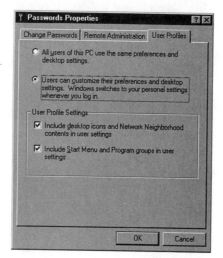

You also should notice two separate options at the bottom of that setting in Figure 8.2:

■ Include Desktop Icons and Network Neighborhood Contents in User Settings

■ Include Start Menu and Program Groups in User Settings

With the first option deselected, everyone on that PC sees the same desktop. Likewise, if the second option is deselected, everyone sees the same Start menu.

The default profile is the settings of the machine at the time that profiles were enabled. If you want to change the default profile after the fact, just bypass the logon banner by pressing Esc or clicking Cancel. After you have bypassed logging on, the default profile is loaded.

Profiles can either be locally based or server-based. The main difference is where the information about the profiles is stored. There are some distinct advantages and disadvantages to each.

8.1.2. Local Profiles

By default, Windows stores profiles in an individual user folder under the C:\Windows\Profiles folder. Every time a new user logs on to a machine with profiles enabled, Windows 95 creates a subfolder that matches his username. Therefore, because I am logged on as Marc right now, my profile is stored at C:\Windows\Profiles\Marc. Take a look at my current configuration in Figure 8.3. Be sure to notice the full path.

Figure 8.3.

The Profiles storage location.

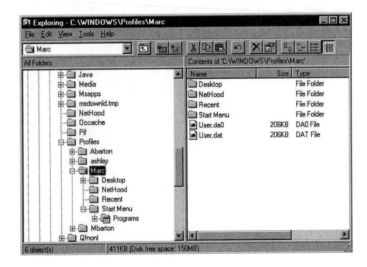

Also notice the directory structure under my profile directory. There are four sub-folders:

- **Desktop**—Items on the desktop
- **Recent**—Shortcuts to the most recently used documents
- **Nethood**—Network Neighborhood contents
- **Start Menu**—Personalized Start menu

If you remember, the Registry is comprised of two files: SYSTEM.DAT and USER.DAT. Both of these files are located in the Windows folder, but after you enable profiles, each user gets his own individual USER.DAT. There is always only one SYSTEM.DAT. With profiles enabled, each user has a USER.DAT and USER.DA0 in his profile folder, as discussed in the previous paragraph. This USER.DAT contains all of his individual settings. When a user logs on to the computer, his USER.DAT is loaded as the user-specific portion of the Registry.

Note

> You can make the profiles mandatory. In other words, after the profile is saved, you can make those settings mandatory. The user can change it, but when he logs off, the changes are not saved.
>
> To make profiles mandatory, rename the USER.DAT to USER.MAN.
>
> If a USER.MAN and a USER.DAT both exist, the USER.MAN profile takes precedence.

8.1.3. Server-Based Profiles

When users need to move from computer to computer, they become known as *roving users*. For this purpose, you can set up the profiles to be stored on a server. This allows the roving users' settings to follow them from computer to computer.

Windows 95 supports roving users by allowing their profiles to be stored on Microsoft Windows NT servers or Novell NetWare servers. The Windows 95 machine must be running a 32-bit protected-mode networking client to connect to the server (such as Client for Microsoft Networks or Client for NetWare Networks). Additionally, the server must support long file names. If not, the only settings that follow the user are those in the USER.DAT (desktop contents, Start menu, recent might not follow).

When the user logs on to a computer, that user's profile is downloaded from the server automatically when the user logs on. Whenever the user makes changes to his profile, it is updated on the server whenever the user logs off.

Due to the differences in the Registries and how they are stored, server-based profiles are not supportive of a user moving from a Windows 95-based PC to a Windows NT-based PC. One reason for this is that they aren't even named alike. For Windows 95, the profile is USER.DAT and for Windows NT it is NTUSER.DAT.

Here is how the process works. First of all, a copy of the USER.DAT always exists on the PC. This is in case a connection on the server can't be made. Take a look at Figure 8.4. Let's say that Sally logs on to computer A for the first time. Because you had properly set up profiles the night before, when she logs off at 8:00 a.m., a copy of her profile is duplicated to the server (1). She then logs on to computer B. The profile is copied from the server to computer B (2). She decides to change her profile by changing the screen saver and adding a persistent network connection. She makes those changes at 10:00 a.m., which changes the time stamp of her USER.DAT. When she logs off of computer B, the time stamp of the local USER.DAT is then compared with the copy of that on the server. Because the USER.DAT on computer B is more recent, it is copied to the server (3) where it overwrites the copy there. When she logs back on to computer A, the comparison once again takes place, and the most recent USER.DAT overwrites the older one.

As you can see, the most current changes and the most current logoff are the ones written to the server. This should be taken into consideration when a user is logged on to several machines simultaneously. If that user makes changes to the profile at different machines, the most recent changes are the ones written to the server. Changes are not merged.

Setting up roving users is relatively easy. Let's take a look at the step-by-step procedures for setting up profiles on a Windows NT and a Novell NetWare server.

For a Windows NT server, follow these steps:

1. Enable Profiles as discussed in 8.1.1.
2. In the Control Panel, open the Network applet.

8

Figure 8.4.

The profile process.

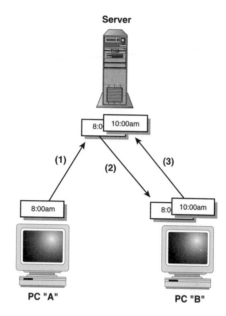

3. Under Primary Network Logon, select Client for Microsoft Networks.

4. On the Windows NT server, set up the user and make sure that a Home Directory is created and specified under the Profiles option of the User Properties.

5. Synchronize the clock of the client PC with the clock of the server.

Synchronizing the clocks is very important. When the user logs on to the network, the date and time stamp of the USER.DAT on the server is compared with the one on the client PC. The one with the most recent date stamp overwrites the older one. If the clocks are not synchronized, you stand a chance of the most recent changes to the profile being overwritten with older settings.

Use the NET TIME command at the command prompt to synchronize the clocks. The proper syntax is

NET TIME *servername* /SET /Y

The *servername* is the NetBIOS computer name of the computer with which you want to synchronize the clock. The /SET option prompts whether you want the computer set to match the server, and the /Y option answers Yes to the prompt automatically.

For a Novell NetWare server, follow these steps:

1. Enable Profiles as discussed in 8.1.1.

2. In the Control Panel, open the Network applet.

3. Under Primary Network Logon, select Client for NetWare Networks.

4. On the NetWare server, set up the user and create a Mail directory.

5. Synchronize the clock of the client PC with the clock of the server.

After these settings are in place on the server of your choice, Windows 95 automatically copies the profile to the Home directory or Mail directory, whichever is appropriate when the user logs off. The profile is a directory tree that is identical to what is locally on the machine under the Profiles folder discussed in 8.1.2.

> **Note**
>
> When using profiles with roving users, make sure that the directory structure between computers on the network are the same. For example, if Windows is installed to C:\Windows on one computer and C:\Win95 on another, the profiles will not work properly.
>
> You should also take this into consideration when dealing with the Start menu. Let's say a user has the Start menu as part of his profile, and Word is a shortcut on the menu. If Word is installed on one computer to C:\Word, and on the other computer it isit is installed to C:\MSOffice\Word, the shortcut on the menu might not work.

8.2. Enforcing Corporate Policies

In corporate America, we have all seen an office, group, or perhaps company-wide policy sent to personnel. This policy might have been on paper and placed in mailboxes, or by some other means such as a flaming email message. Regardless of its means of transportation, it always meant the same thing. It was something that set a standard of how we would do something, or worse yet, not do something. One example may be "Corporate policy dictates that copier paper would not be used to make paper airplanes." Similarly, if you would like to set a policy on what users can and cannot do on a Windows 95 machine, you have the capability. Appropriately, they are called *system policies*.

This section covers the following exam objective: Develop a security strategy using system policies and profiles.

8

Here are some examples of what you can do with system polices:

- Limit access to the Control Panel
- Remove Run from the Start menu
- Show no drives in My Computer
- Disallow users access to the Settings tab in the Display Properties

System policies are basically Registry changes that happen automatically when a user logs on. With corporate policies, they might only affect certain workcenters or certain people. Likewise, you can set system policies on an individual user basis, to a group of users, or on a computer basis.

8.2.1. The System Policy Editor

You make changes to the system policies through the System Policy Editor. System policy files are portions of the Registry and cannot be edited using a text-based editor. Using the System Policy Editor, you can define what Registry changes to make and how to enforce them (by user, group, or computer). You can also combine the policies of users, groups, and machines to get very definitive with the amount of control you would like to enforce.

The System Policy Editor is a powerful administration tool. It is one form of editing the Registry. Like other Registry editing tools, it should be kept out of the reach of children (not to mention anyone else who is not a network administrator).

The System Policy Editor is available on the Windows 95 CD-ROM under the Admin\Apptools\Poledit directory. It can be installed using the Add/Remove Programs applet in the Control Panel. It is not necessary to install the System Policy Editor on every computer. You only need one copy of it on a Windows 95 machine where you can create the policies. Here are the steps for installing the System Policy Editor:

1. From the Control Panel, double-click Add/Remove Programs.

2. Select the Windows Setup tab.

3. Click the Have Disk button (see Figure 8.5).

4. In the Install From Disk box, click Browse.

5. At the bottom of the Open box, select the drive letter that corresponds to your CD-ROM drive.

6. Navigate to the \admin\apptools\poledit directory of the CD-ROM (see Figure 8.6).

7. You should see `poledit.inf` in the file name section (it is not necessary to click `poledit.inf`). Click OK.

8. In the Install From Disk box, you should see the full path. Click OK.

9. In the Have Disk box, you see two options, System Policy Editor and Group Policies. Place a check mark in the box next to System Policy Editor and click Install.

10. Click OK from the Add/Remove Programs dialog box, and you're done.

The System Policy Editor is only available on the CD-ROM version of Windows 95.

Figure 8.5

The Add/Remove Programs dialog box.

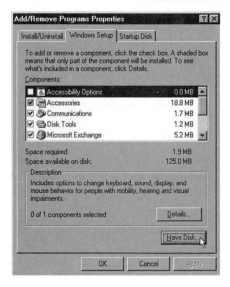

Figure 8.6.

Navigating to the System Policy Editor installation directory.

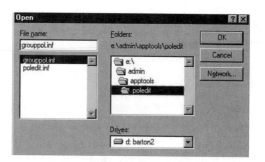

When you install the System Policy Editor, it creates a shortcut to it on the Start menu under Accessories, System Tools. Because the System Policy Editor is such a powerful tool, it's best kept out of sight and out of mind. One example of it being such a powerful tool is that you can directly edit the Registry using the Policy Editor. Only knowledgeable professionals should be editing the Registry. For that reason, most administrators remove the System Policy Editor from the Start menu. To access the System Policy Editor without a shortcut icon, select Run from the Start menu, type **Poledit**, and click OK.

The first time you run the System Policy Editor, it asks you what template you want to load. The templates all have an ADM extension and are not what enables the policies. Templates give you a policy to begin. A template comes on the Windows 95 CD-ROM called ADMIN.ADM, which has the default Windows 95 settings. Nothing is locked down, so it gives users full control of the machine. It is located in the same directory as the System Policy Editor on the Windows 95 CD-ROM.

More sample policy files are located on the Windows 95 Resource Kit CD-ROM:

- MAXIMUM.POL contains suggested policies for maximum network and desktop security.
- STANDARD.POL contains suggested policies for moderate network and desktop security.
- SAMPL1.ADM shows definitions of all custom controls that can be defined in .ADM files.

The most confusing part of the System Policy Editor is that it actually has two capabilities. After you have the System Policy Editor up, select File from the menu (see Figure 8.7) and you see the following options:

- **New File**—Creates a new Policy file
- **Open File**—Opens an existing Policy file
- **Open Registry**—Opens the Registry for editing

Figure 8.7.

The File menu of the System Policy Editor.

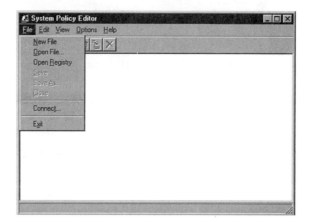

The first two options allow you to create and edit policy files. The policy files are what actually locks the system down. The latter of the three lets you directly edit the Registry of the machine that you are working on or remotely edit the Registry of another computer.

One example of editing the Registry is what we did in Chapter 3, "Windows 95 Blueprint: Internals and Architecture." If you have gone through the Chapter 3 Lab, you might remember that we added a logon banner by modifying the Registry using the Registry Editor (REGEDIT.EXE). In actuality, the System Policy Editor would have been a more appropriate way to add the logon banner. In Figure 8.8, I have selected the Open Registry option of the System Policy Editor's File menu.

Figure 8.8.

The System Policy Editor in Registry mode.

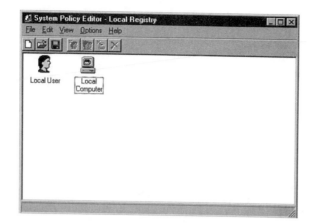

Notice that there are two icons, *Local System* and *Local User*. Local System represents all the system-specific settings in the SYSTEM.DAT. Likewise, Local User represents the user-specific settings in the USER.DAT. By double-clicking the Local System icon, you can see that you have an Explorer type of interface. By clicking the plus signs, you can expand out the settings. I won't go through every single option, but as you can see, you can modify many things in the Registry. Taking a look at Figure 8.9, you can see I have expanded out the System and Logon options. If you look carefully, you'll see the logon banner that we created in Chapter 3.

Figure 8.9.

Creating a logon banner in the System Policy Editor.

Upon exiting the System Policy Editor or by switching to a policy file, you are prompted if you want to save the changes to the Registry (if you made any changes). If you click Yes, the settings take effect immediately. Once again, be careful with any Registry editing tool.

After you select New File from the System Policy Editor's File menu, you see two icons that look similar to the icons when you were editing the Registry, but the titles have changed to Default Computer and Default User.

Before I go any further in talking about how to edit the policy file, let me explain the concept of it. If you look at Figure 8.10, you see a picture of my System Policy Editor. I have created some additional users, computers, and groups. When I save the policy, I save it as a single file called **CONFIG.POL**. When users log on, they are checked to this file and the policy is enforced. You can save the policy file as any name you want, but to enforce it as a policy, it must be saved as CONFIG.POL.

Figure 8.10.

My example of a policy file.

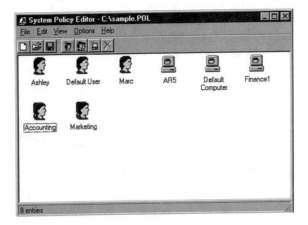

So where do you need to save this file? Windows 95 has the capability to download a copy of the policy changes automatically, depending on where you save it. Where you save it depends on how your Windows 95 computer is configured and what type of network you are on. First of all, it depends on what type of security you have set on the Windows 95 machine. The Network applet of the Control Panel contains an Access Control tab that specifies your security settings. There are two types, share level and user level. I talk more about these two options in Chapter 6, "Linking to Your Network."

If you have share level security enabled, the CONFIG.POL file needs to be stored in the Windows folder of the machine for it to be enforced. If you have user level security enabled, it depends on what type of network you are on.

To set up Windows 95 so that it can automatically download the policy on a Windows NT network, you need to do a couple of things:

1. Ensure that user level security is enabled in the Network applet of the Control Panel under the Access Control tab.

2. Make sure that the Primary Network Logon is set to Client for Microsoft Networks and that the domain is specified in the Client for Microsoft Networks (see Chapter 6).

3. Save the policy file as CONFIG.POL in the Netlogon directory of the Primary Domain Controller of the domain that is specified in the previous step.

To set up Windows 95 so that it can automatically download the policy on a Novell NetWare network, take these steps:

1. Ensure that user level security is enabled in the Network applet of the Control Panel under the Access Control tab.

2. Make sure that the Primary Network Logon is set to Client for NetWare Networks and that the preferred server is specified in the Client for NetWare Networks (see Chapter 6).

3. Save the policy file as CONFIG.POL in the sys\public directory of the preferred server that is specified in the previous step.

It is important to know for the certification exam where the CONFIG.POL file should be placed on both types of networks.

For the policies to be downloaded automatically on NetWare networks, the Windows 95 client must be running Client for NetWare networks. Using VLMs or NETX will not suffice. If Client for NetWare networks is not used, policies must be downloaded manually.

Looking back to Figure 8.10, you can see that you can specify policies to be set by computer, by user, or by groups of users. So what happens if Ashley is on computer AR5 and is a member of the Accounting Group? Well, here is how these options are processed:

1. If the computer has profiles enabled, Windows 95 checks for a user in the policy file that matches the user that is logging on. If this is so, it applies the settings of that user. If it doesn't find a match, the settings for the Default user are applied.

2. If the computer has been set up to support group policies, Windows 95 searches the policy file for all groups for which the user is a member. Any matches found are applied in their priority order.

3. If Windows 95 finds a match in the computer name and one of that name in the policy file, the computer-specific changes to the Registry are applied. If no match is found, the Default Computer settings are applied.

8.2.2. Restrictions Based on Who You Are

User-specific settings in the Registry can be set in two ways, through user policies and group policies. The Default User defines the default settings for all users if they do not have a user in the policy file that matches their user name. Looking at Figure 8.11, you can see the settings that you can specify in the user policy:

- **Control Panel**—Allows you to lock down certain parts of the Control Panel
- **Desktop**—Standardizes desktop settings such as colors, wallpaper, and the like
- **Network**—Locks down capability of sharing or set network configuration
- **Shell**—Locks down the interface, other desktop settings
- **System**—Keeps the settings for MS-DOS and other applications and prevents users from using Registry tools

User Policies

To create a user policy, select Add User from the Edit menu, or click the Add User icon on the toolbar. You are prompted for a name for the user. The name that you use must match the name that the user uses to log on to the computer.

After the user is created, you can edit the settings by double-clicking the user icon. In Figure 8.11, you see an example of a user policy.

Take notice of the squares and the different settings. There are three basic setting options on each policy. Table 8.1 describes each setting.

Figure 8.11.

Configuring a user policy.

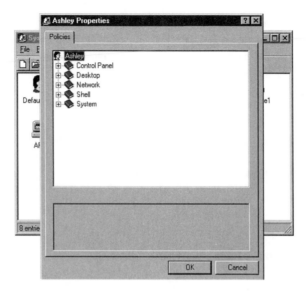

8

Table 8.1. System Policy Editor options.

Option	Description
Checked	Option is applied when user logs on. If it was checked previously, no changes are made.
Cleared	Option is not applied when user logs on. If it was checked previously, the previous setting is not applied.
Grayed	Neutral: No change is made from previous settings.

Previous settings could be either the last time the user was logged on or any settings made by other policies. This is important when processing group policies when a user is a member of more than one group.

After the settings are modified in the System Policy Editor and the Policy file saved in the proper location, the settings specified are applied the next time the user logs on.

For every user that you want to set individual settings for, you must create a separate user that matches that user's name that he uses for logging on to the network.

Group Policies

Group policies give you the capability of specifying the same policy for a group of users. This must be used in conjunction with a security provider that can be either a Windows NT or Novell NetWare server.

Creating and editing a group policy is almost identical to creating and editing a user policy. The only difference is that you name the group policy the same as a group that is already created on the security provider. You cannot create groups and modify group memberships using the System Policy Editor. You must create them using the normal steps using the security provider.

 Note This is very important. If a user logs on and an individual user policy matches his user name, no group policies are applied for that user.

For group policies to work, there must not be an individual user policy for that user. This does not pertain to the Default User.

To make group policies work properly on the client, you must install the GROUPPOL.DLL properly. Every client you want to support for group policies must have the GROUPPOL.DLL properly installed. Listed here are the proper steps to installing the file:

1. From the Control Panel, double-click Add/Remove Programs.

2. Select the Windows Setup tab.

3. Click the Have Disk button (refer to Figure 8.5).

4. In the Install From Disk box, click Browse.

5. At the bottom of the Open box, select the drive letter that corresponds to your CD-ROM drive.

6. Navigate to the \admin\apptools\poledit directory of the CD-ROM (refer to Figure 8.6).

7. You should see grouppol.inf in the file name section (it is not necessary to click on grouppol.inf). Click OK.

8. In the Install From Disk box, you should see the full path. Click OK.

9. In the Have Disk box, you see two options, System Policy Editor and Group Policies. Place a check mark in the box next to Group Policies and click Install.

10. Click OK from the Add/Remove Programs dialog box, and you're done.

Looking back one more time at Figure 8.10, you can see that I have created two groups, Accounting and Marketing. So what happens if I have a user that is a member of the Accounting and Marketing groups? When you have users that are members of more than one group, you need some control over what policies take

8

precedence over others. Under the Options menu of the System Policy Editor, you see a Group Priority option. Selecting it produces something similar to Figure 8.12.

Figure 8.12.

Setting group priority order.

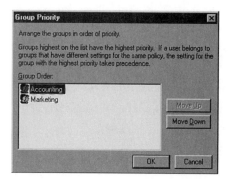

As the dialog box implies, the groups highest on the list take the highest order of precedence. When the group policies are loaded, they are loaded from the lowest priority to the highest priority so that the highest group's policies are enabled. Take a look at Table 8.2 for an example. As you can see, Accounting is the highest on my list. Table 8.2 shows the processing of three examples in the policy file using options that we discussed in Table 8.1. Because the Accounting Group is higher on the list, its settings take precedence.

Table 8.2. Processing groups.

Setting	Marketing	Accounting	End Result
Disable Registry Editing Tools	Checked	Grayed	Checked
Wallpaper = Setup	Checked	Cleared	Cleared
Run Removed from Start menu	Grayed	Checked	Checked

Note

It is very easy to become overwhelmed with figuring out how many individual users to make, versus groups, versus modifying the default user settings.

When using policies, I recommend modifying the Default User settings to enable the policies and just creating individual users and groups to be exceptions to the standard policy set to the Default User.

For example, you can modify the Default User for the more restrictive settings and create an Administrators group with more relaxed settings.

8.2.3. Restrictions Based on Where You Are

Like user and group settings, you can create policies based on the computer name rather than the user or group name. This allows you to set certain settings based on the computer they are logging on to. The settings in a computer policy differ from those in a user or group policy. The computer policy allows you to give the computer specific settings and configurations. Some examples include the following:

- Require Windows alphanumeric passwords
- Require validation by network for Windows access
- Disable caching of Domain Password
- Network path for Windows setup

Once again, you can make settings to the Default Computer, or an individual computer can be created for a computer of a specific name. This allows some specific settings for computers such as lab computers or computers for the use of the general public.

> Microsoft also creates an add-on product called the Zero Administration Kit for Windows that allows you to lock the computer down and limit the access to system files and unauthorized programs. Even though this is not information that you need to know for the certification exam, it is definitely a product that you should look into if you will be supporting Windows 95 in an environment where you might be thinking about implementing policies. For information, visit Microsoft's Web site (www.microsoft.com) and do a search for ZAK.

8.3. Monitoring and Controlling User Access

The System Policy Editor is only one of many ways for you to administer a Windows 95 machine. There are other ways for you to administer a Windows 95 machine remotely on a network. This includes remotely editing the Registry, monitoring network access, and so on.

8

8.3.1. Remote Administration

To administer a Windows 95 machine remotely, you must enable remote administration of that computer. Once again, here is a setting that depends on what type of security you have enabled on the computer. The Passwords applet of the Control Panel is where you specify who can remotely administer the computer.

 This section partially covers the following exam objective: Create, share, and monitor a remote resource.

If the computer has share level security enabled, the Remote Administration tab of the Passwords applet looks like Figure 8.13. You enable the capability to administer the machine remotely by checking the check box. You also have the capability of placing a password so that only those with the password can remotely administer the machine. When they attempt to administer the computer across the network, they are prompted to type in the password.

Figure 8.13.

Setting up Remote Administration in the Passwords option of the Control Panel.

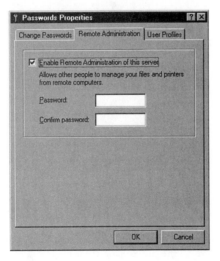

If user level security is enabled, the computer can be administered in the same manner, but the Remote Administration tab of the Passwords applet looks a little different (see Figure 8.14). Instead of placing a password for administration, you specify certain users and groups of users who have permission to remotely administer the computer. The names are received from a security host such as a Windows NT Server or Novell NetWare server (see Figure 8.15).

Figure 8.14.

Setting up remote administration when user level security is enabled.

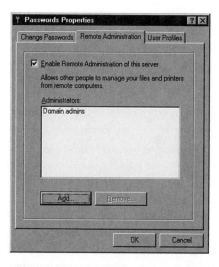

Figure 8.15.

List of users from a Security Provider.

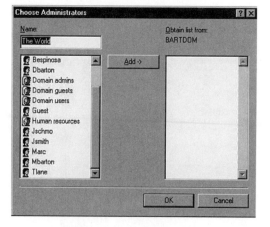

If you set up user-level access in the Network applet of the Control Panel, remote administration is enabled automatically. If you are on a Windows NT network, the Domain Admins group is automatically given the right to remotely administer. On a Novell NetWare network, the Supervisor account on a server running 3.*x* of NetWare or the Admin account for a server running 4.*x* of NetWare is automatically given the right to administer remotely.

After remote administration is enabled, two folders are shared out to the network automatically:

■ **ADMIN$**—Gives administrators access to the hard disk

■ **IPC$**—Provides an interprocess communication channel for computers to communicate

Do not be concerned with these being a way for everyone to access the computer. First, only persons with the administration password (share-level security) or granted permission to administer (user-level security) can access these shares. Second, the $ denotes that these shares are hidden. By hidden, I mean that they do not appear when users are browsing for network resources. To connect to them, you must know the full path, which would be *computername*\admin$. (We discuss UNC naming in the next chapter.)

Two main tools are used when remotely administering a computer: Net Watcher and System Monitor. These tools come with the Windows 95 CD-ROM and can be installed after the fact if you did not install them during setup. To install them, follow these steps:

1. From the Control Panel, double-click Add/Remove Programs.

2. Select the Windows Setup tab.

3. Click Accessories (the word, not the check box) and click the Details button (see Figure 8.16).

4. Scroll down and click the box next to Net Watcher and System Monitor and click OK.

5. Click OK in the Add/Remove Programs dialog box.

Figure 8.16.

Viewing the details of the accessories in Windows Setup.

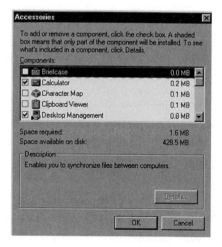

This gives you the necessary tools to administer other Windows 95 computers remotely. For remote administration to be fully possible, a service needs to be installed not only on the computer that you are going to be administering but also on the machine you will be doing the administration from (granted it's a Windows 95 computer). That service is called the Remote Registry Service. Its main use is so that you can remotely edit another computer's Registry, but it also makes the System Monitor possible. To install the Remote Registry Service, follow these steps:

1. From the Control Panel, double-click Network.

2. Click the Add button.

3. Click Service and click the Add button.

4. Click the Have Disk button.

5. Click the Browse button.

6. At the bottom of the Open box, select the drive letter that corresponds to your CD-ROM drive.

7. Navigate to the \admin\nettools\remotreg directory of the CD-ROM.

8. You should see regsrv.inf in the file name section (it is not necessary to click on regsrv.inf). Click OK.

9. In the Install From Disk box, you should see the full path. Click OK.

10. In the Select Network Service box, you should see Microsoft Remote Registry. Click OK.

11. Click OK from the Network dialog dialog box.

> **Note**
>
> For the Remote Registry Service to work properly, you must have user-level security enabled. User-level security is discussed further in Chapter 6, "Linking to Your Network."

You can remotely edit another computer's Registry from the Registry Editor. From the Registry Editor's menu, select Registry. Then select Connect Network Registry. You are then prompted for the computer name. You can either type in the computer's name or click the Browse button to browse for the computer with the Registry you would like to edit remotely.

To administer a machine remotely, access the Network Neighborhood either from the desktop icon or through the Explorer. When you find the computer that you want to administer remotely, right-click it with your mouse. You see Properties as an option. After you click Properties, you see some basic information on the first tab of the computer's property sheet (see Figure 8.17).

Figure 8.17.

Property sheet of a remote computer.

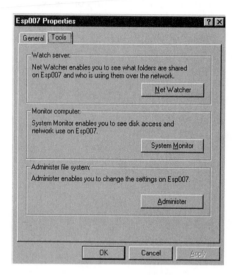

You also might notice the Tools tab of the property sheet. Selecting this Tools tab reveals something similar to Figure 8.18. There are three options: Net Watcher, System Monitor, and Administer.

8.3.2. Net Watcher

The Net Watcher is a utility that allows you to perform some administrative tasks across the network. Some of these tasks include:

- Disconnecting users accessing the remote computer
- Closing files that connected users might have open
- Sharing or stopping sharing of a resource
- Viewing folders being shared to the network including who is connected to them

This section partially covers the following exam objective: Diagnose and resolve connectivity problems using Net Watcher. Additional information covering this objective can be found in Chapter 12, "Monitoring and Optimizing Windows 95," and Chapter 13, "Troubleshooting Windows 95."

Figure 8.18 gives you an example of the Net Watcher and remote administration. The best way to learn the Net Watcher is actually to use it. You will be amazed at some of the remote administration capabilities of the Net Watcher.

Figure 8.18.

Remote administration of a computer using Net Watcher.

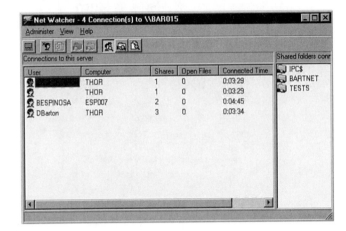

8.3.3. System Monitor

The System Monitor is a tool designed to monitor the different aspects of a computer and report that information in real time in the form of graphs, charts, or figures. It is commonly used to monitor the local computer (while working on the machine that you're monitoring). After the Remote Registry Service is installed, however, you can use it to monitor computers across the network. Figure 8.19 gives you an example of monitoring a computer remotely.

Figure 8.19.

Monitoring a computer remotely using the System Monitor.

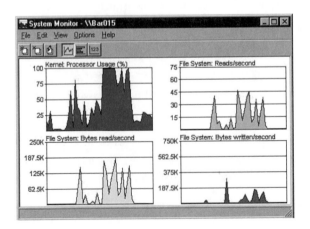

I discuss monitoring a little more in depth in Chapter 12, "Monitoring and Optimizing Windows 95." In that chapter, I give you some examples of items that can be monitored and why you should monitor them.

8.3.4. Administering the File System

Clicking the Administer button allows you to access the entire file system on the remote computer, even the parts that have not been shared to the network. You can access the root of every drive because, after you have configured remote administration on the machine that you want to administer, the root of each drive is shared as a hidden share. One example is the C drive (C:\). It is automatically shared as C$. As I mentioned before, only persons with the administration password (share-level security) or granted permission to administer (user-level security) can access these shares.

Lab

The Lab consists of review questions pertaining to this chapter and is an opportunity to apply the knowledge that you've learned with this chapter. Answers to the Review Questions can be found in Appendix B.

Questions

1. What service must be installed on both the administrator's machine and the machine that you would like to remotely administer?

   A. Remote Registry Service

   B. Remote Administration Service

   C. Server Service

   D. Netlogon Service

2. When saving a policy file to be implemented, what is the proper file name?

   A. `POLEDIT.POL`

   B. `ADMIN.ADM`

   C. `CONFIG.POL`

   D. `CONFIG.ADM`

3. Windows 95 Server-based profiles on a Windows NT network are stored in what directory on the server?

   A. User's Mail directory

   B. User's Home directory

   C. User's Profile directory

   D. User's setup directory

4. Which of the items below is *not* part of a roving user's profile?

   A. Shortcuts on the desktop

   B. Windows color settings

   C. Persistent network connections

   D. Files on the desktop

5. Which of the following Registry files will be copied to the user's profile folder? Choose all that apply.

   A. `SYSTEM.DAT`

   B. `USER.DAT`

8

    C. `SYSTEM.DA0`

    D. `USER.DA0`

6. On a Windows NT network, where should the `CONFIG.POL` file be stored for automatic downloading?

    A. In the Windows directory

    B. In the server's Netlogon share

    C. In the user's Home directory

    D. In the user's Mail directory

7. You are asked to assist in troubleshooting a policy malfunction. The policy file has been created and stored in its proper place on a Novell NetWare server. The policy is implemented and works fine on a Windows 95 machine if the `CONFIG.POL` is in the Windows folder locally, but not when in its proper storage location on the server. What could be the potential problem?

    A. Share-level security needs to be enabled on the Windows 95 computer.

    B. User-level security needs to be enabled on the Windows 95 computer.

    C. A proper Mail directory needs to be configured for the users.

    D. The Remote Registry Service needs to be installed.

8. What file must be properly loaded in order to ensure that group policies work properly?

    A. `GROUP.POL`

    B. `GROUP.DLL`

    C. `GROUPPOL.DLL`

    D. `GROUP.ADM`

9. Windows 95 Server-based profiles on a Novell NetWare network are stored in what directory on the server?

    A. User's Mail directory

    B. User's Home directory

    C. User's Profile directory

    D. User's Setup directory

10. Which user(s) and/or group(s) are given the permission to administer a Windows 95 computer automatically when User level access is enabled? Choose all that apply.

    A. Admin (Windows NT)

    B. Admin (Novell 4.*x*)

    C. Supervisor (Novell 3.*x*)

    D. Domain Admins (Windows NT)

    E. Server Operators (Windows NT)

11. If you would like to view which users are connected to a Windows 95 computer and what resources they are using, which utility would you use to accomplish this remote administration task?

    A. Net Watcher

    B. System Monitor

    C. Remote Registry

    D. Network Monitor

Exercises

In this lab, you will set up policies to be used on a network. You will also create a basic policy and implement it. There is an Alternate Exercise at the end of this one where it is assumed that you have a Windows NT server (Primary Domain Controller) in which you have administrative rights.

Profiles

In this exercise, you will be enabling and testing user profiles. This will prepare you for the exam by meeting the following exam objective: Set up user environments using profiles and system policies.

1. Open the Control Panel and double-click the Passwords icon.

2. Select the User Profiles tab.

3. Click in the circle next to Users Can Customize Their Preferences and Desktop Settings.

4. Click OK and click Yes to restart computer.

5. Log on to the computer.

8

6. Click Yes to If you would like your individual settings retained for use when you log in here in the future.

7. Reconfirm password.

8. Open the Explorer and navigate to the C:\Windows\Profiles folder (where C:\Windows is the directory that you have Windows installed to).

9. Notice the directory structure and contents.

10. To test the profiles, make some changes to the desktop and log off. Log back on as someone else. Did the settings stay intact? If you have properly enabled user profiles, you should see different settings for the different users.

Policies

In this exercise, you will be creating a policy using the System Policy Editor. The policy will be a local-based policy (not using a server). Then, you will test restrictions that you have enforced via the policy. This will prepare you for the exam by meeting the following exam objective: Develop a security strategy using system policies and profiles.

1. Open the Control Panel and double-click the Network icon.

2. Select the Access Control tab.

3. Specify Share level security and click OK. Restart the computer if prompted. (This is to enable policies on the local computer. If you would like to enable policies on the network, see the Alternate Exercise.)

4. From the Control Panel, double-click Add/Remove Programs.

5. Select the Windows Setup tab.

6. Click the Have Disk button.

7. In the Install From Disk box, click Browse.

8. At the bottom of the Open box, select the drive letter that corresponds to your CD-ROM drive.

9. Navigate to the \admin\apptools\poledit directory of the CD-ROM.

10. You should see poledit.inf in the file name section (it is not necessary to click on `poledit.inf`). Click OK.

11. In the Install From Disk box, you should see the full path. Click OK.

12. In the Have Disk box, you see two options, System Policy Editor and Group Policies. Place a check mark in the box next to System Policy Editor and click Install.

13. Click OK from the Add/Remove Programs dialog box.

14. From the Start menu, select Run.

15. Type **POLEDIT** and click OK.

16. Open the ADMIN.ADM template (you might have to navigate back to the `\admin\apptools\poledit` directory of the CD-ROM).

17. From the File menu, select New File.

18. From the Edit menu, select Add User.

19. Type in **Aaron** for the name and click OK.

20. Double-click Aaron.

21. Click the plus sign next to expand Control Panel.

22. Expand Display and place a check mark next to Restrict Display Control Panel.

23. In Settings at the bottom of the window, place a check mark next to Hide Settings Page (you might have to scroll down).

24. Expand out Shell and expand Restrictions.

25. Place a check mark in Remove Run Command.

26. Click OK.

27. Select File from the menu and select Save.

28. Navigate to the Windows folder (where you have Windows 95 installed).

29. In the File name block, type **CONFIG.POL** and click Save.

30. Close the System Policy Editor.

31. Log off and log on as Aaron.

32. Notice that the Run option is no longer available. Also notice that the Settings tab is gone from the Display Properties (Control Panel, Display).

Alternate Exercise

Use this exercise if you have a Windows NT server available. In this exercise, you will be enabling a policy that is considered to be server-based.

1. On the Windows 95 computer, synchronize the clock with the Windows NT server by typing the following command at an MS-DOS prompt (where *servername* is the name of your server):

```
NET TIME \\servername /SET /Y
```

8

2. On the Windows NT server, create a directory called Users and share it to the network with full control permissions.

3. Open the User Manager.

4. Select User from the menu and select New User.

5. Call the user Mike and clear the User Must Change Password at Next Logon box (otherwise the Windows 95 logon will fail).

6. Click the Profile button.

7. Click in the To: box under Home Directory.

8. Type in the network path to the Users directory you just created. Its syntax should be

`\\servername\users\Mike`

This creates Mike a Home directory. Do not be concerned with the drive letter, this option is for Windows NT-based machines. Windows 95 only needs the UNC path. Do not use Local path.

9. On the Windows 95 machine, open the Control Panel and double-click the Network icon.

10. Select the Access Control tab.

11. Specify User-level security and specify the domain name of the NT domain.

12. Click OK and restart the computer when prompted.

13. Log on to the computer.

14. From the Start menu, select Run.

15. Type **POLEDIT** and click OK.

16. Open the ADMIN.ADM template (you might have to navigate back to the `\admin\apptools\poledit` directory of the CD-ROM).

17. From the File menu, select New File.

18. From the Edit menu, select Add User.

19. Type in **Mike** for the name and click OK.

20. Double-click Mike.

21. Click the plus sign next to expand Control Panel.

22. Expand Display and place a check mark next to Restrict Display Control Panel.

23. In Settings at the bottom of the window, place a check mark next to Hide Settings Page (you might have to scroll down).

24. Expand out Shell and expand Restrictions.

25. Place a check mark in Remove Run Command.

26. Click OK.

27. Select File from the menu and select Save.

28. Navigate to the server's Netlogon directory through the Network Neighborhood. (You could type in the UNC path in the file name block, such as \\servername\netlogon\config.pol).

29. In the file name block, type **CONFIG.POL** and click Save.

30. Close the System Policy Editor.

31. Log off and log on as Mike.

32. Notice that the Run option is no longer available. Also notice that the Settings tab is gone from the Display Properties (Control Panel, Display).

33. On the Windows NT server, notice that Mike's Home directory of the server is empty.

34. Log off as Mike.

35. Now look at Mike's Home directory. Is it empty now (you might have to refresh by pressing F5)?

Day 9

Installing and Configuring Printers

Windows 95 printing capabilities have been improved dramatically over previous versions of Windows. Installing a local printer, connecting to network printers, and managing print queues have all been improved. Windows 95 has a few added capabilities such as the Point and Print feature.

Objectives

The exam covers printing in many different facets. Whether it is network printing, troubleshooting printing, or just basic printer setup, questions about printing can pop up anywhere on the exam. The printing related exam objectives include the following:

- Installing and configuring hardware devices
- Printers
- Creating, monitoring, and sharing resources
- Network Printers

9.1. Understanding the Print Process

Understanding and appreciating the Windows 95 printing process requires a little knowledge of how it was handled in Windows 3.11. Printing using Windows 3.11 can be explained as anything but a pleasurable experience. When a user printed from an application, he had to wait until that document was printed before regaining control of the application. Not only that, but Windows 3.11 kicked out data to the printer whether it was there or not. Lastly, if you wanted to print from an MS-DOS application and a Windows application at the same time, you usually ended up with a locked up spooling process or lost print data.

Windows 95 fixes all this. Spooling solves the problem of trying to print from two different types of applications (MS-DOS and Windows) at the same time. Additionally, with the use of enhanced metafile spooling and background printing, you can regain control of the application a lot faster.

9.1.1. Raw and EMF

Windows 95 uses two printer languages during its printing process: *raw output* and *enhanced metafile (EMF) output.*

Raw output is the natural language for the printer; it is its normal language such as escape codes and PostScript. This data is usually printer-specific. This means that raw data generated for one type of printer might not be compatible for another type of printer.

EMF data is generated by Windows 95. It is specific to Windows 95 and is the language that Windows 95 uses to create images.

Metafile spooling can actually speed up the process of printing in several ways. First, it is not printer-specific, so that means that the information can be sent across the network and used by several other Windows 95 machines regardless of the type of printer that they have attached.

Second, most applications written for Windows 95 produce the metafile data automatically. This information can be passed to Windows 95 for spooling to the hard disk and allowing the application to be returned to the user's control. Then she can continue using the application while the printing continues as a background process. Windows uses metafile spooling by default for all print jobs except for PostScript print jobs.

Because EMF is such a new technology, it can cause problems during the print process, especially if older hardware and programs are used. This does not mean you shouldn't use it. As a matter of fact, using EMF can speed up your printing process three to four times faster, but when having trouble with printing, turning off EMF should be one of the first things you should try when troubleshooting.

 Test Tip

It is important to know that turning off EMF spooling is the first step in the print troubleshooting process (other than checking printer cables, checking printer is online, and so on).

9.1.2. Overview of the Process

The printing process is a very modular process. In Figure 9.1, you see the printing process in detail from start to finish. Notice that the figure depicts printing from one Windows 95 computer to another via a network. The computer that you are printing from is called the *workstation*. The Windows 95 computer where the printer is attached is called the *server*.

Figure 9.1.

The Windows 95 print process.

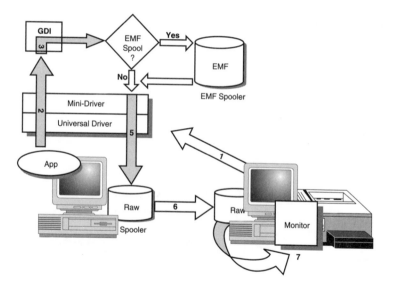

The events happen as follows:

1. When you designate that the application print the document to a printer you've never printed to before, Windows 95 copies the printer driver from the

server (Windows 95 computer with printer attached). The driver is copied to the workstation's (Windows 95 computer you are printing from) hard drive. If the printer driver already exists on the workstation, this process is skipped. If the server contains a newer version of the driver than the one that resides on the workstation, the driver is updated with a copy from the server.

2. The application generates information about the document to be printed. This information is sent through the drivers to the *graphics device interface (GDI)*.

3. The GDI produces an EMF file. This file is not ready for printing; it simply contains Windows 95-specific information.

4. Next, Windows 95 spools the information to the EMF spooler if you have configured it to do so (it is by default). If it is configured to do so, it spools and frees up the application. If it is not set to spool or if the format does not use the spooler, the application waits until the print job is completed.

5. If EMF spooling was used, the EMF spooler passes the document back through the driver where it is converted to raw (printer-specific language). It is then passed to the local print spooler.

6. The local print spooler communicates with the spooler on the server where it passes the raw formatted print job. If you are printing the document to a local printer, this step is skipped.

7. The print spooler on the server then sends the data to the print monitor where it is directed to the correct port for printing. This port can be an LPT or Com port, but it can pass the print job on to a network provider.

> **Note**
> By default, queued print jobs are temporarily stored in \WINDOWS\SPOOL\PRINTERS. Ensure that there is enough disk space for the print jobs wherever the print jobs are set to spool.

9.1.3. Windows 95 Printing Architecture

The printing architecture in Windows 95 differs greatly from that of Windows 3.*x*. With Windows 3.*x*, many different components handled the printing process. This concept is similar to having five or six people trying to cook the same pot of stew. It is slow, unreliable, and difficult to troubleshoot.

With Windows 95, the printing process, especially the spooling process, has been consolidated into a single architecture. This helps to streamline the printing and spooling processes. Additionally, the new architecture allows the spooling process to occur in the background while you continue with your work. See Figure 9.2 for a diagram of the Windows 95 print architecture.

Figure 9.2.

The Windows 95 print architecture.

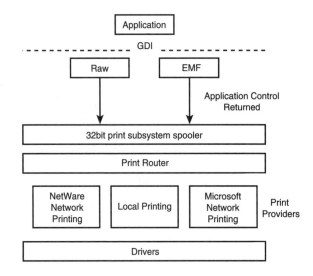

9

The Print Router

The print router's job is to route the print job to the appropriate print provider. If the print job is destined for a local printer, the print router sends the print job to the local print provider. If the print job is destined to the network, the router sends the print job to the appropriate network print provider (Microsoft or NetWare). The router consists of the SPOOLSS.DLL.

> **Note**
>
> If the print router (SPOOLSS.DLL) becomes corrupt or if it fails, you will not receive any error messages that the print job didn't reach the printer. The print process will appear to be working properly, except the print job will never reach the printer.

The Print Provider Interface

The *print provider interface (PPI)* is a modular interface designed to let you install several print providers at the same time. For example, you can have the Microsoft network print provider and NetWare network print provider installed at the same time. The PPI also allows any third-party network vendor to create a print provider for its networking operating system.

The PPI allows for three basic types of print providers:

- **Local printing**—Part of SPOOLSS.DLL that allows sending of print jobs to local ports and the queue management of local printers.
- **WinNet16**—A 16-bit print provider that gives backward compatibility with Windows 3.*x* applications and network drivers.
- **Network**—32-bit print provider that converts data to the appropriate network language specific to that vendor, such as Win32 calls for Microsoft networks.

WinNet16 print provider

Windows 95 includes backward compatibility support for network providers that do not have 32-bit networking support. The WinNet16 provider uses the same driver as the one used with Windows 3.*x*, but the WinNet16 driver does not understand the 32-bit printing calls that Windows 95 makes.

You can overcome this through the use of another DLL, the WNPP32.DLL. The WNPP32.DLL translates these 32-bit calls to 16-bit so that the WinNet16 driver can understand them. This process of translation is called *thunking*. (No, I did not make that one up.)

In Figure 9.3, you see a graphical representation of the architecture behind the WinNet16 print provider. Notice that the IFS manager is also used in the print process. Whenever print calls are made to send a print job to a printer across the network, the IFS manager redirects that call to the appropriate network provider and in the proper format. In this case, a real-mode networking client is used, and the call is passed to the real-mode networking software. Whenever a print call is made to manage the print queue (delete, pause, resume print jobs), the IFS Manager is not needed, and therefore the call is sent directly to the real-mode networking software.

Microsoft network print provider

You use the Microsoft network print provider specifically when the client for Microsoft network accesses printers across the network. Because this is 32-bit, you do not need some of the components that you will see in the WinNet16 print provider.

In Figure 9.4, you see that the Microsoft network print provider and the Microsoft network support library work together to handle the network print calls. In turn, they send the call to the IFS manager for printing jobs or directly to the SMB redirector (VREDIR.VXD).

Figure 9.3.
WinNet16 print provider.

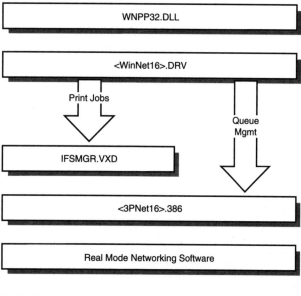

Figure 9.4.
The Microsoft network print provider.

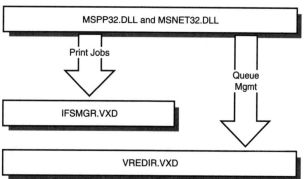

NetWare network print provider

With the client for NetWare networks, the print jobs are handled in the same manner as those with the Microsoft network print provider, but the difference is the

NetWare network print provider (NWPP32.DLL) and the NetWare network support library (NWNET32.DLL). See Figure 9.5 for a comparison.

Figure 9.5.

NetWare network print provider.

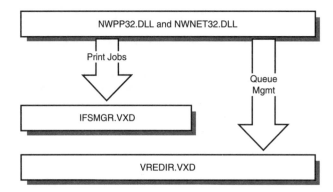

If you have chosen to use the real-mode client software from Novell (NETX or VLM), the print process is handled differently. Windows 95 needs to thunk—there goes that word again—the 32-bit code to 16-bit code so that the real-mode client will understand in a similar manner to that of the WinNet16 print provider (see Figure 9.6).

Third-party print provider

Additionally, third-party vendors can create their own print providers. These print providers must be written so that the print router can submit jobs to an appropriate network file system driver. The third-party vendor must supply the appropriate DLLs and networking software (see Figure 9.7). You can install these third-party print providers by adding a service in the Network applet of the Control Panel.

The amount of functionality of controlling the print queue depends on what the third-party vendor puts into the provider. Any print queue management options that the third-party vendor does not include will be grayed out.

Figure 9.6.

*Real-mode NetWare
client.*

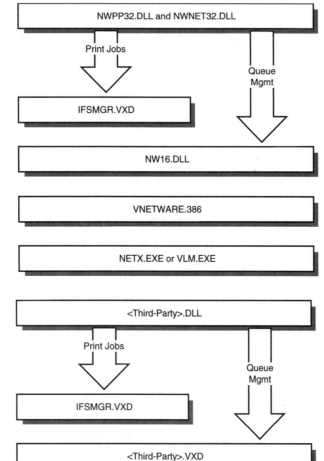

Figure 9.7.

*Third-party print
provider.*

9

9.2. Installing Printers in Windows 95

Installing printers in Windows 95 has been greatly simplified from Windows 3.*x*. In
Windows 95, you can install a printer in several ways; but when all is said and done,
it boils down to three basic methods.

This section covers the following exam objective: Install and configure hardware devices—Printers.

The first method is *Plug and Play*. If the computer supports Plug and Play, as does the printer, all you should have to do is plug in the printer. The level of Plug and Play support determines what happens next. If both the computer and printer are completely Plug and Play compatible, Windows 95 detects the printer and automatically installs the software for it. Sometimes, Windows 95 doesn't detect the printer until the next time the machine starts up. This is a limitation of the computer, not Windows 95.

The second method is using the Add Printer icon in the Printers folder. You can reach the Printers folder through either the My Computer icon or the Control Panel. This icon is one of the many wizards in Windows 95 that simplifies tasks and walks you through the process. You can use the Add Printer Wizard to install either local printers (ones physically connected to the local computer) or network printers (printers shared on the network).

The last method is *Point and Print* printers. Point and Print printers are actually printers shared on the network. The difference between them and any other network printer is the ease of setup. Point and Print printers intend to make the installation require as little intervention by the user as necessary. I'll discuss Point and Print printing later in this chapter.

9.2.1. Printers That Are Friendly

Another important advancement in the printer installation with Windows 95 is the use of friendly names. You can name the printers that you install into Windows 95 using up to 31 characters. This allows you to name printers things like "Bob's Color Printer" or "HP Laserjet next to Water Cooler." Because these names are used to refer to the printer throughout Windows 95, they must be unique. Think what would happen to your print jobs if you had two printers installed using the same name.

Some people might not see this as an important advancement, but end users more easily understand which printers are where when you use friendly names. If you're a network administrator, you know what I mean. If you're not, imagine explaining to 100 users in an email about the 30 printers they will be using with names like HPLJ435 and EPCI122.

9.2.2. The Final Test

The final step in installing a printer in Windows 95 is printing a test page. This is a quick and easy way to make sure you have installed the printer properly. The print test page also contains handy information such as the drivers that are installed. It has sample graphics and text to ensure everything is in working order. Also, if you are printing to a color printer, the Windows 95 logo prints in color.

9.3. Installing a Local Printer

Installing a local printer is a breeze. If your computer and printer both support Plug and Play, just attach the printer and power it up. Windows 95 should detect the printer and automatically install the software for it. If it doesn't, try restarting the computer. If it still doesn't detect the printer, the printer and/or computer does not fully support Plug and Play.

In that case, you need to install the printer manually. You can do this by accessing the Printers folder from either the My Computer interface or the Control Panel. Another way is by pointing to the Settings option of the Start menu. In the Printers folder, you find an icon titled Add Printer (see Figure 9.8).

Figure 9.8.

The Printers folder is where you install printers manually using the Add Printer icon.

When you double-click the icon, the Wizard starts. To confirm that you do indeed want to install a printer, click the Next button. You are then asked how the printer is attached to your computer (see Figure 9.9).

Figure 9.9.

Specify whether your printer is local or shared on the network.

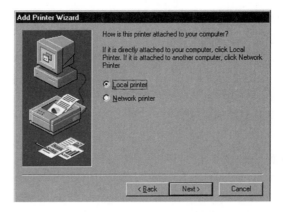

You have two choices of how the printer is connected:

- **Local printer**—The printer is physically attached to the computer in which you are installing it via a serial, parallel cable, or the like. The computer you are installing it on will control the print queue.

- **Network printer**—The printer is physically attached to another computer (Windows 95, Windows NT, NetWare, and so on), and you will be accessing it via the network.

For now, I choose local printer. I will discuss network printing later. After selecting the printer as local, click the Next button. Next, you specify the manufacturer and make of the printer (see Figure 9.10).

Figure 9.10.

Specifying the printer's manufacturer and make.

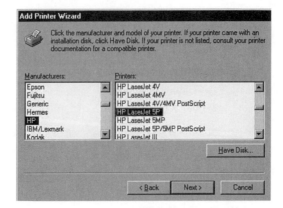

If the printer does not appear in the list of printers or if you have a more up-to-date driver for a printer that is located in the list, click the Have Disk button. Insert the floppy into the drive, specify the path to the driver, and click the Next button.

Next, you specify the way that the printer is attached such as LPT or COM port (see Figure 9.11).

Figure 9.11.

Specifying the port.

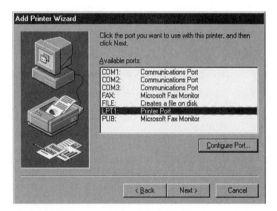

After you have specified the port and clicked Next, you can then specify the friendly name that I discussed earlier. Additionally, you can specify whether this printer should be your default printer or not (see Figure 9.12).

Figure 9.12.

Configuring the printer's friendly name.

The last step in the printer's installation process is to print a test page. When that's done, you're done. That's all there is to installing a local printer.

Let's take a look at installing a local computer in a step-by-step process:

1. Access the Printers folder.

2. Double-click the Add Printer icon and click Next.

3. Select Local Printer and click Next.

4. Choose from the Manufacturers in the left pane and the make of the Printers in the right pane. If your printer appears in the list, go to step 8. If not, go to the next step.

5. Click the Have Disk button.

6. Specify the path to the correct drivers and click OK.

7. Specify the proper printer, if necessary, and click OK.

8. Click the Next button.

9. Choose the port to which the printer is attached. Click Next.

10. Enter a name for the printer (up to 31 characters). If you want the printer to be your default printer, specify it as such. If you want this printer to be the default printer, select the option. Click Next.

11. Choose whether you want to print a test page. Click Finish.

9.3.1. Configuring the Local Printer

After the printer is installed, it appears as an icon in the Printers folder. If you need to make configuration changes to the printer, you can do so by pointing to the printer, clicking the secondary mouse button, and selecting Properties.

With the printer's Properties sheet, you can control just about every aspect of the printer. The first tab, General, contains basic information about the printer (see Figure 9.13). You can specify a comment and what separator page to use, if any.

On the Details tab of the printer's Properties sheet (Figure 9.14), you can specify the Com port and drivers that the printer will use. I discuss the drivers in more detail in the next section. At the bottom of this tab, you see two buttons: *Spool Settings* and *Port Settings*. The Port Settings are the basic information about the port to which the printer is attached (COM, LPT, and so on). The Spool Settings are a little more important.

The Spool Settings are important not only for troubleshooting purposes but also for taking the exam. As for troubleshooting, this is one of the first steps in the process of trying to figure out why a printer is not working properly. The most important setting in this box is the Spool Data Format (see Figure 9.15).

Figure 9.13.

*The General tab
of the printer's
Properties sheet.*

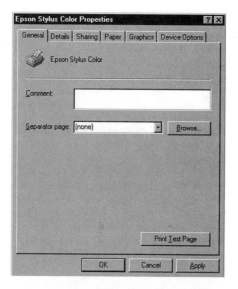

Figure 9.14.

*The Details tab
of the printer's
Properties sheet.*

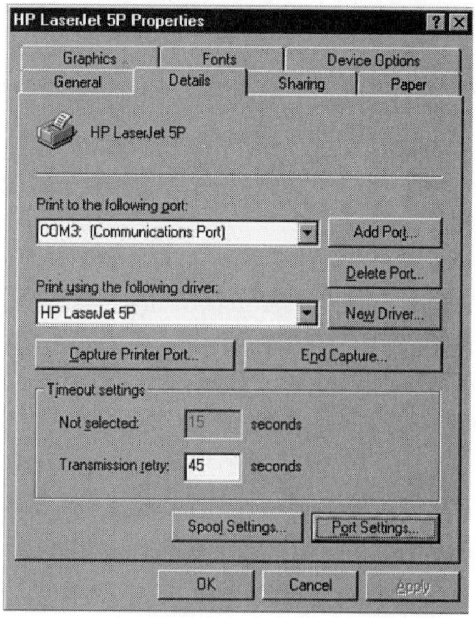

You can choose whether the data format will be RAW or EMF. The default setting is EMF, which lets you print more quickly and regain control of the application faster after printing. Because the EMF spooling process is still relatively new, some older printers or computers might have difficulty using it. Therefore, by selecting RAW as your data format, you, in essence, turn EMF spooling off. You need to be familiar with this as part of the normal printer troubleshooting process for the exam.

Figure 9.15.

Spool Settings.

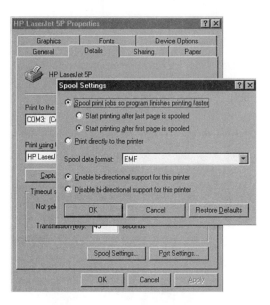

To cut off EMF spooling, select RAW as your data format.

You can configure additional spool settings, such as bidirectional control and how quickly the print job is printed in conjunction with when it is spooled. With bidirectional communications, Windows 95 supports nibble mode (remember that phrase), which provides an asynchronous identification channel between the printer and the computer. This allows the printer to identify itself to Windows 95 using the information stored in the printer's ROM.

Sharing the Printer to the Network

If you want others to have access to the printer that you just installed via the network, select the Sharing tab of the printer's Properties sheet. You can specify the share name, supply comments, and determine access to the printer. In Figure 9.16, you see a printer that is being shared using user-level security. You can specify which users or groups can access the printer via the network.

This section covers the following exam objective: Creating, sharing and monitoring resources—Network Printers.

Figure 9.16.

Sharing a printer using user-level security.

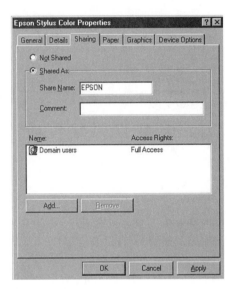

9

When you share a printer on a computer that is configured to use share-level security, you cannot specify which users will have access. As a matter of fact, the User box in Figure 9.16 does not even appear. In its place, you see a box allowing you to specify a password for access. With this method, all users that want to connect to the printer are prompted for the password prior to their gaining access. With either user-level or share-level security, you can specify a comment in the comment box that users can see when browsing for network printers.

The Comment only shows in the browse list whether the user has selected to show details. You can do this by choosing View from the menu and then selecting Details in the window from which you are browsing.

The remaining tabs differ from printer to printer. Because the majority of the settings in these tabs are specific printer capabilities (such as paper tray, color capabilities, and fonts), you might want to review the settings of several different types of printers. I recommend using different manufacturers because most manufacturers include similar capabilities among all of their products.

> When you are studying, it is not necessary to have access to different printers to see the settings for different ones. Simply install them. You don't need to have the printer physically to install it in the Printers folder. (I don't have the HP5 that I installed.)

9.4. Connecting to a Network Printer

Windows 95 makes it fairly easy to hook into a printer that is connected to another computer. In actuality, it is a lot like setting up a local printer, but you can do it with fewer steps. You can accomplish this task in several ways.

The first way is using the Add Printer icon in the printers folder. After you have clicked Next to start the process, you see a choice of how the printer is attached. The first option, Local Printer, is what we explained in the previous section. Because we are discussing a network printer, we select the Network printer option.

After you click Next, you are prompted to enter the UNC path to the printer. You can either type it in or click the Browse button and browse for the printer (see Figure 9.17).

Figure 9.17.

Browsing for a network printer in the Add Printer Wizard.

After you have selected the printer, you might notice that Windows 95 puts in the proper UNC name for you (see Figure 9.18). If you use MS-DOS applications and need access to this printer from them, you need to select the option here. If you do, the next window allows you to capture a printer port.

Figure 9.18.

The UNC name used to connect to a network printer.

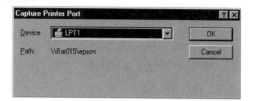

Capturing a printer port allows you to assign a port to the network printer. Because many MS-DOS applications might not understand the UNC name, capturing a printer port fools the application into believing that the print job is going to a local port. Windows, however, passes the print job on to the network printer. To capture a printer port, just specify a printer port and use that port in the MS-DOS application.

The next window asks you what friendly name you want to specify for the printer and provides the capability of assigning this printer as your default printer. Clicking Next takes you to the final screen, which allows you to print a test page.

You might notice that I did not have to specify what type of printer I was connecting to in my scenario. That's because the printer that I was connecting to was a Point and Print printer (which I discuss in 9.7.). If the printer had not been configured as such, I would have had to specify the manufacturer and type of printer as with a local installation.

You can browse for the printer in the Network Neighborhood or Explorer. After you find the printer, you can connect to it by clicking it with the secondary mouse button and selecting Install.

9.5. Understanding Print Drivers

Windows 95 uses a team concept when it comes to drivers. To print to a printer, two drivers are needed. These two drivers are referred to as a *universal driver* and a *mini-driver*. Neither driver can print information to the printer without the other. They must work together as a team.

The universal driver is a generic driver created by Microsoft and designed to work with many types of printers. The mini-driver, which is created by the printer's manufacturer, contains the printer-specific information. When the universal driver is combined with the mini-driver, you can use the printer.

This approach allows the manufacturer to provide a mini-driver with only its printer's specific information. The vendor is free from having to create the entire driver for its printer.

There are three main types of printers and therefore three main universal drivers:

- **Microsoft Universal drivers**—Used for all printers except PostScript printers and some HP Inkjet printers
- **Microsoft PostScript drivers**—Used for all PostScript printers
- **Monolithic drivers**—Used primarily for HP Inkjet and compatible printers

As you can see with the regular universal driver, some HP Inkjet printers are exceptions to the rule that universal drivers are designed for all printers. HP Inkjet printers require the use of a monolithic driver that must be supplied from the manufacturer.

So you see, the mini-driver is combined with the appropriate universal driver to support the printer (see Figure 9.19).

Figure 9.19.

Different universal drivers combine with printer-specific printer drivers to make complete Windows 95 drivers.

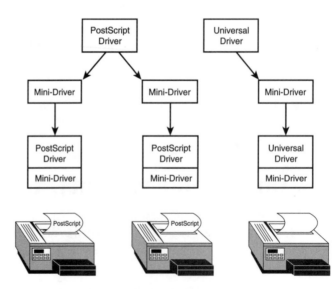

9.5.1. Installing a Printer Driver

You can install printer drivers in two different ways. The first way of installing a driver is through normal setup procedures of the local printer. This is accomplished as previously discussed using the Add Printer icon in the Printers folder.

If you must update the driver, however, you do not need to remove the printer and reinstall it. You can update the driver for a printer using the Properties sheet of that printer. To update the driver, follow these steps:

1. Open the Printers folder.

2. Select the printer that you want to update with the secondary mouse button.

3. Select Properties.

4. Select the Details tab.

5. Click the New Driver button (see Figure 9.20).

6. You receive a message stating that the new driver might change the look of the properties. This is because the new driver might add new capabilities and therefore change the look of the property sheet. Click Yes.

7. Click the Have Disk button.

8. Specify the path to the new driver and click OK.

9. Specify the printer if necessary and click OK.

Figure 9.20.

You can update a driver for a printer by clicking the New Driver button.

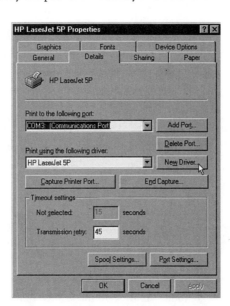

9

9.5.2. The Sleight-of-Hand Method

Another method of installing printer drivers involves connecting to another computer for access to the printer that is attached to it. The neat thing about Point and Print setup is you don't need to specify what type of printer it is. The reason for this is because Windows 95 automatically downloads the driver, if necessary, from the computer that is set up for Point and Print.

9.6. Point and Print

When most people hear a printer being referred to as a Point and Print printer, they believe a special type of printer or an additional option for a printer is required. This couldn't be farther from the truth. The difference between a printer that is Point and Print and a printer that is not is simply the way that the printer is installed on its host computer.

The Point and Print idea serves two purposes. The first purpose involves a printer's ease of installation. To connect to a Point and Print printer, just browse for the printer using the Explorer or Network Neighborhood. After you find the printer, you can click it with the secondary mouse button and select Install. Another way to install the printer is to simply drag it from the window in which you are browsing and drop it in the Printers folder. In both instances, you are asked for minimal information.

The second purpose allows for drag-and-drop printing. To take advantage of this feature, simply drag and drop a document on top of the Point and Print printer's icon, and the system is configured automatically to print the document. This is a handy feature when you need one time or temporary access to the printer.

9.6.1. Configuring a Point and Print Printer

Configuring a Point and Print printer is different on Windows 95, Windows NT, and NetWare computers. This is because the different operating systems handle printing differently and use different drivers.

Windows 95

Any time a printer is installed in Windows 95, it is automatically enabled as a Point and Print printer. No additional configuration is required. When you share the printer to the network, Windows 95 automatically creates a hidden share called PRINTER$, which is the \WINDOWS\SYSTEM folder shared with read-only access. When another computer connects to the printer, it also automatically retrieves the drivers needed from this directory.

Note If at any time you stop sharing that directory or change the name to the share, it ceases to be a Point and Print-enabled printer. This shared folder is necessary so that the drivers are automatically transferred.

When you connect to a Windows 95 machine from another Windows 95 machine, the printer driver is copied automatically. Because it is receiving this driver from the SYSTEM folder in its installed form, the printer settings (such as paper tray, fonts, and so on) carry over also.

When the printer is connected to a Windows NT server or a NetWare server, some additional configuration is needed to support the Point and Print functionality.

Windows NT

With Windows NT, the printer is installed according to normal procedures. Under the Sharing tab of that printer's Properties sheet, you can specify the operating systems of computers that will be connecting to the printer. Windows 95 is one of the options.

After you specify that Windows 95 computers will be connecting to the printer and click OK, Windows NT prompts you for the Windows 95 CD-ROM containing the installation files. It then copies the printer drivers to the hard disk. After the Windows 95 user connects to the printer on the Windows NT computer, the drivers are downloaded automatically.

Note When you connect from one Windows 95 computer to the another, the drivers are downloaded from the SYSTEM directory. The files in that directory are in an installed state. Therefore, printer settings are also copied.

With Windows NT, the driver files are not in an installed state; therefore, you need to specify the printer settings.

NetWare

Point and Print setup on a NetWare server is a little more complicated. First of all, the NetWare server must be running bindery emulation(if you are running NetWare 4.*x* or later, bindery emulation is not installed by default). This is because, for Point and Print to work properly, the printer must be installed into the bindery. A *bindery* is nothing more than a database consisting of objects, properties of those objects, and the values of the properties. Then the drivers must be manually copied to a server share.

To install the Point and Print printer onto a NetWare server, follow these steps:

1. Log in to the server as a Supervisor or an account with Supervisor rights.
2. Using the Explorer or Network Neighborhood, browse to the NetWare print queue.
3. Click the print queue with the secondary mouse button.
4. Point to the Point and Print menu option to expand the menu.
5. Select Set Printer Model and specify the manufacturer and type of printer and click OK. (This option adds the printer to the bindery.)
6. Select Set Driver Path and type in the UNC path to where you will store the drivers to be shared by others and click OK.
7. Copy the printer drivers to the directory that you specified in the previous step.
8. Grant Read and File Scan rights (as a minimum) to the directory in which the drivers are located.

Note If you are not sure which printer driver files should be copied, you can find out the correct files by opening the MSPRINT.INF file. It has a listing of the printers and their associated drivers.

9.7. Managing the Print Queue

You can manage the print queue of the printer either for local printers or for network printers in which you have the proper access rights. To do so, simply double-click the printer icon for the printer that you want to administer (see Figure 9.21). You can use the Printers folder, Explorer, or the Network Neighborhood.

If you are locally logged on to the machine that has the printer attached and you want to manage its print queue, you have full control over that queue. Your capabilities locally include:

- Pause and resume a print job
- Cancel a print job
- Specify a separator page

- Work offline
- Designate default printer

Figure 9.21.

Managing a print queue.

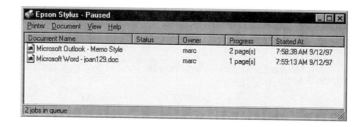

The network management functionality depends on the network operating system that is installed. For example, the capabilities of managing a printer located on Windows NT computer differ from those of a printer located on a NetWare server.

The type of print provider also can vary the capabilities of queue management. You can see this difference between the WinNet16 provider and the Windows 32-bit provider.

Last, the capabilities can vary from user to user depending on the user's level of access to the print queue.

The maximum network management capabilities include:

- View the queue
- Pause the current job
- Resume printing of current job
- Pause the print queue
- Resume the print queue
- Purge all print jobs

Lab

This lab consists of review questions and exercises pertaining to this chapter. Answers to the review questions can be found in Appendix B.

Questions

1. What are the two data formats used in printing with Windows 95? Pick the correct two.

    A. RAG

    B. RAW

    C. EMF

    D. ERD

2. Bi-directional communication in Windows 95 supports _____ mode, which provides an asynchronous identification channel between the printer and the computer.

    A. EMF

    B. RAW

    C. Nibble

    D. Point and Print

3. Windows 95 uses which three types of drivers along with mini-drivers to create a total printer driver?

    A. Microsoft universal

    B. Microsoft PostScript

    C. Monolithic

    D. NetWare Universal

    E. NetWare PostScript

4. The default location for spooled print jobs are:

    A. \WINDOWS\SYSTEM

    B. \WINDOWS\SPOOL

    C. \WINDOWS\SPOOL\PRINTERS

    D. \WINDOWS\PRINTERS\SPOOL

5. After installing the printer and sharing it to the network, what must you do to configure the Windows 95 computer to support Point and Print?

    A. Share the \WINDOWS\SYSTEM folder with Read and File scan rights.

    B. Create a folder for the driver files.

    C. Modify the Details tab of the printer.

    D. Nothing.

6. What rights must you have in order to set up a NetWare server to support Point and Print?

    A. Read and File Scan

    B. User

    C. Supervisor

    D. Change

7. When you connect a Windows 95 computer to another Windows 95 computer configured with a Point and Print printer, the printer configuration settings are copied along with the drivers. True or False?

    A. True

    B. False

Exercises

In this chapter, we discussed how to configure a Windows 95 computer using both a local printer and a network printer. You should become familiar with installing printers and configuring them. The installation practice that you perform should be both with and without Point and Print printing.

Installing a Local Printer

Follow these steps to install a local printer:

1. Click the Start button and choose Settings.

2. Under Settings, choose Printers.

3. Double-click the Add Printer icon.

4. Click the Next button to start the installation.

5. Select Local Printer and click Next.

6. Choose a manufacturer and a printer that you are installing. (If you do not have a printer attached, choose any printer.)

7. Click Next.

8. Select the port that the printer is attached to and click Next. (Once again, if you do not have a printer attached, simply pick any port.)

9. Enter a friendly name for the printer and click Next.

10. When prompted to print a test page, select No.

11. Click Finish, and the files are transferred from the CD-ROM.

12. In the Printers folder, locate the printer you just installed. Right-click the printer and select Sharing.

13. Click Shared As and specify a name in the Share Name box.

14. If you have user-level security enabled, click the Add button and give access to The World.

15. Click OK.

Connecting to a Network Printer

In the following exercise, you will be connecting to the printer that you installed in the previous exercise via the network. This will allow you to simulate attaching to another printer across the network. If you have other printers on your network available to you, you can substitute one of them in this exercise.

1. Right-click the Network Neighborhood icon located on your desktop.

2. Click Explore.

3. Locate your computer.

4. Locate the printer you shared during the previous exercise.

5. Open your Printers folder (Start, Settings, Printers).

6. Click your printer in the Network Neighborhood and drag it into your Printers folder.

7. You are prompted if you will be using this printer with MS-DOS programs. Select No and then click Next.

8. Because you have already installed the drivers, you are asked whether to keep the existing one. Click Next.

9. You are then prompted for a friendly name and whether to make this printer your default printer. Accept the default selections by clicking Next.

10. When prompted to print a test page, select No and click Finish.

Administering a Printer Queue

In the following exercise, you will practice administering a printer queue. Open the Printers folder:

1. Point to the printer that you installed in Exercise 9.1.
2. Right-click and select Pause Printing.
3. Right-click the desktop, point to New, and click Text Document (a new document appears).
4. Press Enter to accept the default name.
5. Drag the document and drop it on top of the printer that you paused.
6. Double-click the paused printer to view the queue.
7. Click the document to select it.
8. Click Document from the menu.
9. Click Cancel Printing.

Also, take some time to familiarize yourself with the administrative capabilities in the printer's queue. Go ahead and print some documents and practice all the queue management functionality.

9

Knowing the different protocols, which clients a Windows 95 dial-up server supports, and which dial-up servers a Windows 95 computer can connect to are important for the exam. Here are some fast facts for quick study:

- Dial-up networking supports the network protocols NetBEUI, IPX/SPX, and TCP/IP.

- The supported line protocols are PPP, SLIP, Windows NT RAS, and NRN NetWare Connect.

- The supported network interfaces are NetBIOS, Mailslots, Named Pipes, RPC (remote procedure call), LAN Manager , TCP/IP, and WinSockets.

- Windows 95 can be a dial-up networking client to another Windows 95 computer, Windows NT, LAN Manager, Windows for Workgroups, LAN Manager for UNIX, IBM LAN servers, and Shiva LanRover.

- As a dial-up server, Windows 95 can support Windows 95, LAN Manager RAS, Windows for Workgroups, Windows NT, and PPP-based clients.

- The briefcase helps keep copies of files synchronized between computers.

- PPP is the most popular line protocol because it supports DHCP.

Day 10

Taking Windows 95 on the Road: Remote Services

As more people began to need computers for their jobs, they needed an easy way to gain access to their data at the home office while they were away. This need is apparent in such positions as sales or perhaps a support position where travel is involved. At any rate, Windows 95 includes just such a feature.

You can use Windows 95 to connect to a computer on your office network using a modem and standard telephone lines. By dialing up the computer on your network, you have access to network resources as if you were sitting at a computer that was physically connected to the network.

Objectives

I discuss many aspects of dial-up networking in this
chapter. In addition to dial-up networking, I also cover
the aspects of using direct cable connections and using
the briefcase to synchronize files. Let's take a look at the
exam objectives:

- Install and configure hardware devices
- Modems
- Configure a client computer to use dial-up
  networking for remote access
- Install and configure network protocols
- PPTP/VPN
- Create, share, and monitor resources
- Unimodem/V

10.1. Understanding Dial-Up Networking

With dial-up networking, Windows 95 gives you the ability to connect to your office or other network from a remote location using a modem and standard telephone lines. In essence, you become a remote node. When connected, it is as if you were back in your office with the computer directly connected to the network, with one exception—speed.

With most modems nowadays, it is standard to get modem speeds such as 14.4, 28.8, 33.6, and 56Kbps. Even though these modems are faster than the modems we were using three to five years ago, they are still slow compared to the standard 10 mbps networks that we have today.

When connected to the network, you have access to every resource that you would normally have if you were back at the office (as long as you have been granted the proper permissions). That means that you can gain access to the files on your server or even print to a network printer. Even though you might have to wait a little longer for that Microsoft Word document to load up, at least you have access to it.

10.1.1. Remote Node Versus Remote Control

Most newcomers to dial-up networking usually get a little confused here. They don't quite understand dial-up networking until they see it in action. This is mainly because they are confusing it with taking remote control of the computer into which they are dialing.

Many software packages out there give you the ability to dial in to another computer and, in essence, take control of it. It is quite a funny sight to watch the monitor of a computer that is being controlled by someone remotely. It is as if a ghost were sitting at the computer. You see every move that the person is making when he or she is controlling the computer from a remote location.

Even though remote control programs do have advantages in certain roles (such as help desk), they have several limitations as well. First, entire screens of information must be passed over the telephone line, giving a very choppy movement, response, and slow screen refreshing. Second, anyone who wants to see what you are doing simply has to turn on the monitor of the computer that is being controlled. Last, they cost extra.

Dial-up networking is *not* taking remote control. When you dial in to a computer on the network, that computer acts as a gateway to the network. When you dial in to an Internet service provider, you are not taking remote control of the server; you are being given access to the entire network. The network in this case is the Internet. The same thing happens when you use dial-up networking to dial in to your network. Unlike the case with remote control programs, the only data that is transferred is the data you are requesting. You do not need to transfer entire screen captures.

> **Note**
>
> Dial-up networking was not designed to run applications over telephone lines. I have seen several network administrators attempt to use dial-up networking to access applications.
>
> In other words, the applications (such as Word and Excel) should be installed on each computer, and the document or spreadsheet should be the only data being transferred. If you attempt to run an application across the connection, you will be disappointed at how slow the application reacts.

When connected, you can map network drives and access network printers and any other available network resources, just as if you are on the network. If you are still a little confused, don't worry. It happens all the time. Just continue reading and try dial-up networking. If you don't understand it now, you will when you try it.

10.1.2. Features

There are many reasons why Windows 95 dial-up networking is an excellent solution to your remote computing. Many Internet service providers (ISPs) have quickly adopted it because of those features. Likewise, you might find it a way of connecting to your network that is easy to use. Some of the features of Windows 95 dial-up networking include

- **It's compatible**—Windows 95 dial-up networking clients can connect to any Microsoft Windows NT, Microsoft LAN Manager, Microsoft Windows for Workgroups, LAN Manager for UNIX, IBM LAN servers, Shiva LanRover, and other dial-up routers that support Microsoft RAS, Novell NRN, SLIP, or PPP protocols.

- **It doesn't care about topology**—Windows 95 supports Ethernet, Token Ring, FDDI, and ArcNet network topologies as a dial-up server.

- **It has more security**—It can be configured to require encrypted passwords.

- **It supports many modems**—Dial-up networking supports any modem capable of using the Unimodem driver system.

- **It can squeeze data**—The software or the modem can compress information sent for increased transfer speeds.

10

■ **It supports slow links**—Included is a slow-link API that informs applications that they are running over a slower link so the applications are a little more patient when waiting for data.

■ **Can be a server**—With the Microsoft Plus! package, Windows 95 can act as a dial-up networking server that allows Microsoft Windows NT, LAN Manager, Windows for Workgroups, and other PPP clients to connect.

■ **Can take advantage of DHCP**—If you recall from Chapter 7, "Linking to Your World," Dynamic Host Configuration Protocol is the capability to dynamically assign TCP/IP addresses and other pertinent TCP/IP information such as DNS and WINS server addresses. This makes it a great option for ISPs to use.

Note

As a Dial-Up Server, Windows 95 only supports a single inbound connection at a time. However, Windows NT Server supports up to 256 simultaneous inbound connections.

10.1.3. Dial-Up Networking Architecture

As with most other components in Windows 95, dial-up networking was built using a layered approach to allow for more flexibility with the design and implementation of the different components. Take a look at Figure 10.1 for a graphical representation.

Request

The diagram basically describes the process of communication between two computers during a dial-up networking session. At the first step, the dial-up networking client computer's application makes a request.

Networking Interface

The networking interface layer takes that request and converts it to a format that the network understands. The supported network interfaces are the following:

■ **NetBIOS** —The two computers establish a two-way connection to send data. The session ensures that the data is received properly.

■ **Mailslots**—This connection is a one-way process. The computer sending the message would not know whether the recipient computer received the message. This is equivalent to shouting a message across a crowded room. You're not sure whether the other person heard you.

■ **Named Pipes**—This is another connection process similar to NetBIOS.

- **RPC (Remote Procedure Call)**—This allows one computer to send a message telling another computer to accomplish some sort of task.

- **LAN Manager API**—Messages sent to an API which in turn tell the computer to accomplish a task. This is similar to an RPC.

- **TCP/IP**—Any use of the TCP/IP suite's protocols and capabilities is supported.

- **WinSockets**—This is another two-way connection, specific to PCs but based on the Berkeley UNIX sockets.

Figure 10.1.

The dial-up networking architecture's process.

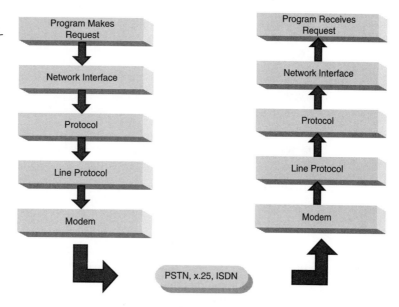

10

You might not need to know each of these interfaces in detail, but you should at least know that they are supported.

Network Protocol

After the request is converted, it then passes through the network protocol layer. Here, the information is readied for shipment as if it were sent across the regular network. The supported protocols are NetBEUI, IPX/SPX, and TCP/IP.

Line protocol

Next, the request passes through the line protocol layer where it is packaged for transmittal over the line (for example, a telephone). This is the equivalent of putting your message in an envelope before giving it to your mail carrier. The supported line protocols are the following:

- **Point to Point Protocol (PPP)** —This is the most popular line protocol. It was created from TCP/IP and is designed for low-speed access. The biggest advantage over other protocols is that you can use it with DHCP for dynamically assigning IP addresses.

- **Serial Line Internet Protocol (SLIP)** —This protocol was also created from TCP/IP. Once a standard, it is being tossed to the side for the more flexible PPP.

- **Windows NT RAS** —This is the protocol designed for earlier versions of Windows NT and is included for backward compatibility. It uses AsyBeui (Asynchronous NetBEUI), which is predominantly slower and less flexible than SLIP and PPP.

- **NRN NetWare Connect** —This is a protocol proprietary to Novell NetWare. It gives Windows 95 the capability to dial in to a NetWare server. It does not, however, give NetWare clients using NRN the capability to dial in to a Windows 95 server. Additionally, only IPX/SPX can be used over a connection using NRN.

SLIP support is not installed by default. To install support for SLIP, you must do so by using the Add/Remove Programs applet in the Control Panel and accessing the ADMIN\APPTOOLS\SLIP folder from the Windows 95 CD-ROM. (Keep in mind that the ADMIN folder is not included on diskette versions.)

You might not need to know each of the line protocols in detail, but you should at least know that they are supported.

Modem

After the message is placed in its line protocol envelope, it is then passed to the mail carrier, which is the modem where it is sent across the wire to the other side of the connection.

So far, we've talked about using standard telephone lines to make this connection. These lines are referred to in the networking arena as *PSTN* or *packet switched telephone network*, but the PSTN is not the only way you can make a connection. You can also use some of the slow connections that you might find connecting two sections of a WAN.

The first of these is x.25. This type of connection is part of a worldwide network made up of x.25 nodes that are responsible for forwarding packets to their destination. At the destination, a *Packet Assembler/Disassembler* (*PAD*) is used instead of a modem.

The other is the more modern and popular *Integrated Services Digital Network* or *ISDN*. This connection can offer you connection speeds of up to 128Kbps. This connection requires a special ISDN adapter or modem.

 Don't get overwhelmed by the different types of connections. This additional information is not usually on the exam.

On the Flip Side

After the request has reached the other side of the connection, the request goes up through the layers again in a reverse order, and the application receives the request.

10.1.4. Communications Architecture

The communications architecture is also a layered architecture similar to the architecture of dial-up networking. In Figure 10.2, you see the different components. The program at the top makes a request to the Unimodem driver.

Unimodem

The Unimodem driver is the main device driver provided by Microsoft. This driver, when combined with mini-drivers from the manufacturer, gives Windows full functionality with the modem.

Figure 10.2.

The different components of the communications architecture.

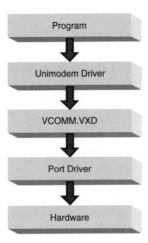

 This section covers the following exam objective: Create, share, and monitor resources—Unimodem/V.

The Unimodem driver then passes the request to the VCOMM.VXD. In Windows 95, all communications ports are virtualized to prevent architectural limits on COM and LPT ports. VCOMM.VXD is the central component in the communication process; it manages all access to communication resources. Because VCOMM.VXD is a 32-bit driver, older 16-bit applications can still use the older COMM.DRV.

 For the exam, you should know the difference between the VCOMM.VXD and the COMM.DRV as stated in the previous paragraph.

Unimodem V

Unimodem V is the newest release of Unimodem. This driver adds the most requested features to support data/fax/voice modems, including wave file playback and recording to and from the handset, and support for speakerphones, Caller ID, distinctive ringing, and call-forwarding.

This section covers the following exam objective: Create, share, and monitor resources—Unimodem/V.

Microsoft has made it possible for independent hardware vendors (IHVs) and original equipment manufacturers (OEMs) to include Unimodem V with voice modem hardware so that applications that support telephony functions can run on their hardware. Independent software vendors (ISVs) can also include Unimodem V with their applications so that they can run on voice modems that might not already include Unimodem V. Users can use Unimodem V with a telephony application or a voice modem if neither includes Unimodem V.

You can download a copy of the updated driver from Microsoft's FTP site. As of this writing, the updated driver is located at **ftp://ftp.microsoft.com/services/whql/drivers/win95/modem/A5582.exe**.

To install the updated driver, follow these directions:

1. Create a blank formatted 3.5"/1.44MB disk.
2. Download the driver to the disk from the preceding site address.
3. Open the Explorer and double-click the file you downloaded. This extracts the driver.
4. Right-click the file Unimodv.inf and then click Install.
5. Restart your computer.

If you already have a modem installed, you need to remove and reinstall it. For more information on installing modems, see section 10.1.1.

10.2. Configuring the Dial-Up Client

Configuring a dial-up networking client involves several different tasks. These tasks include

1. Installing a modem
2. Installing dial-up networking
3. Creating a connection
4. Creating a dial-up server

You can perform these tasks separately or all at once. At any rate, you need approximately 2MB of disk space for the installation of dial-up networking.

10.2.1. Installing a Modem

The installation process is very flexible, and you can go about the task in numerous ways. The first task is to install a modem that you will use for dial-up networking.

This section covers the following exam objective: Install and configure hardware devices—Modems.

If your computer is Plug and Play-compliant and the modem supports Plug and Play, Windows 95 automatically detects the modem when you boot up the computer and install it. If not, you have to install the modem manually.

You can install the modem manually from the Control Panel through the Modems icon. Follow these steps to install the modem:

1. In the Control Panel, double-click the Modems icon.

2. In the Modems Properties box, click the Add button (see Figure 10.3). The Install New Modem box appears.

3. If you want Windows 95 to attempt to detect the modem, make sure that the Don't Detect My Modem option *isn't* checked. In my case, I choose my modem manually by checking it (see Figure 10.4).

4. Choose the manufacturer and the model of the modem (see Figure 10.5). If you do not see the model on the list, you might have to use a driver disk that is supplied by the manufacturer (usually newer modems). If so, click the Have Disk button and specify the path to the location of the drivers. After you have your modem selected, click Next.

5. Specify the communications port that the modem uses (see Figure 10.6) and then click Next.

6. To complete the installation, click Finish.

After completing the installation of your modem, you are returned to the Modems Properties dialog box. You can also further modify the modem's properties by selecting it and then clicking the Properties button (see Figure 10.7). Let's take a look at some of the properties that you can modify.

Figure 10.3.

The Modems Properties dialog box is where modems are added, removed, and configured.

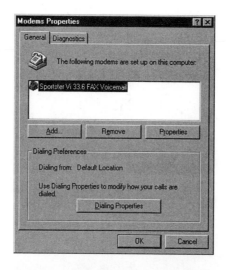

10

Figure 10.4.

Specifying whether you want to select the modem manually or whether you want Windows 95 to attempt to find it.

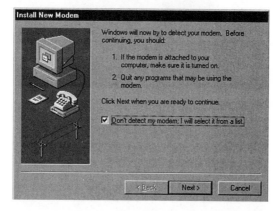

Figure 10.5.

Choosing the manufacturer and model of the modem.

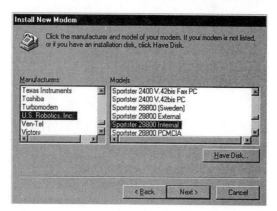

Figure 10.6.

Specifying the communications port that your modem uses can be done here.

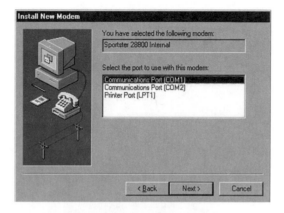

Figure 10.7.

Modifying a modem's properties is accomplished by clicking the Properties button.

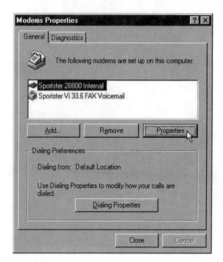

In the properties box, you see two tabs. Under the first tab, General, you can modify the following options (see Figure 10.8):

- **Port**—Specifies which communications port the modem uses.

- **Speaker Volume**—Adjusts the volume of the speaker located in or on the modem. This allows you to hear the modem when it dials the number and establishes the connection.

- **Maximum Speed**—Allows you to specify the maximum speed the modem will use. This can be helpful when connecting to older legacy modems that cannot be contacted when your modem is incompatible with theirs. Specifying a slower speed can assist the modems in establishing communications.

Figure 10.8.

The General tab allows you to modify basic modem settings.

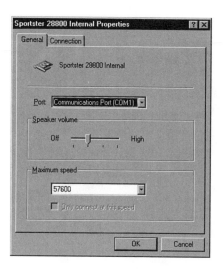

The Connection tab in Figure 10.9 allows you to specify several settings for the modem:

- **Data Bits**—The number of bits that will be transferred at one time. This setting is normally either 7 or 8.
- **Parity**—This is an older setting that modems use to make sure the information was sent correctly. With newer modems, this setting is normally None.
- **Stop Bits**—Stop bits are used to identify the end of a packet. The default setting is 1.
- **Call Preferences**—Settings such as wait for dial tone before dialing, how long to wait for a connection when dialing, and how long to wait before disconnecting if there is no transfer of data.
- **Port Settings**—Settings for FIFO (First In First Out) and UART (Universal Asynchronous Receiver/Transmitter) settings.
- **Advanced**—Error control, flow control, modulation, and any extra (modem commands) settings can be found here. Additionally, you can specify whether a log file (MODEMLOG.TXT) should be recorded.

You might want to know that you can create a MODEMLOG.TXT file for troubleshooting by going to the modem properties and then to the Connection tab. When there, you must click the Advanced button and place a check mark next to the Record a Log File option.

Figure 10.9.

The Connection tab allows you to modify specific modem settings.

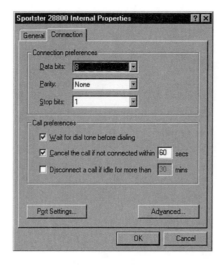

10.2.2. Installing Dial-Up Networking

You can install dial-up networking when installing Windows 95 or through the Internet Connection Wizard. Another way of installing it is through the Add/Remove Programs option of the Control Panel.

This section covers the following exam objective: Configure a client computer to use dial-up networking for remote access.

To install using the latter method, follow these steps:

1. Double-click the Add/Remove Programs icon in the Control Panel.
2. Select the Windows Setup tab.
3. Click the Communications icon (*not* on the check mark box; placing a check mark installs all communications components) (see Figure 10.10).
4. Click the Details button.
5. Place a check mark in the box next to Dial-Up Networking (see Figure 10.11).
6. Click OK from the Communications Details box.
7. Click OK from the Add/Remove Programs dialog box.
8. Restart the computer if necessary.

Figure 10.10.

Click the Communications icon, not the check mark box.

Figure 10.11.

Place a check mark next to Dial-Up Networking.

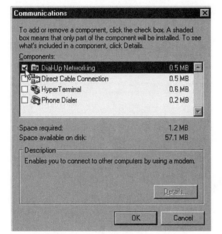

10

10.2.3. Creating a Connection

Creating a connection involves setting up basic information about the computer into which you will be dialing. Upon creation of the connection, you will be able to specify any additional or advanced settings about the connection. To create a connection, follow these steps:

1. Access the dial-up networking folder by choosing Start, Programs, Accessories, and then Dial-Up Networking.

2. Double-click the Make New Connection icon.

3. Specify a name for your connection and the modem that you want to use for the connection (see Figure 10.12) and click Next.

4. Type in the phone number of the computer you will be dialing (see Figure 10.13) and click Next.

5. A confirmation message is displayed (see Figure 10.14). Click Finish.

Figure 10.12.

Specify the Name for your connection.

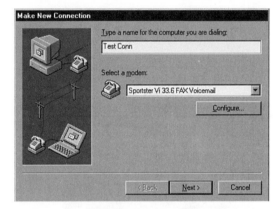

Figure 10.13.

Type in the number for the connection.

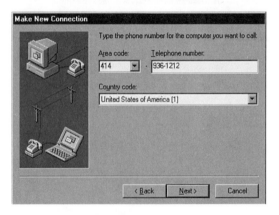

After your connection is made, it is displayed in the dial-up networking folder. You can access this folder at a later date by choosing Start, Programs, Accessories, and then Dial-Up Networking. If additional settings are required, you can set them by clicking the icon in the Dial-Up Networking folder using the right button and then choosing Properties. Let's take a look at some of those settings.

Figure 10.14.

Click Finish at the confirmation message.

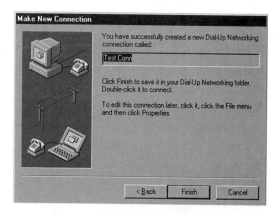

The first thing that you will be able to configure is basic settings, such as the phone number and modem to use (see Figure 10.15). You can set advanced modem properties by clicking the Configure button. These same settings are available through the Modem option in the Control Panel.

Figure 10.15.

Configuring the properties of a dial-up networking connection.

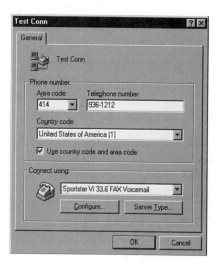

Clicking the Server Type button allows you to specify what type of server you are connecting to, log on options, software compression, use of encrypted passwords, and what protocols to use (see Figure 10.16).

10

Figure 10.16.

Setting Server Types settings.

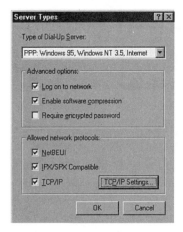

If you have specified that you will be dialing in to a PPP-supported server, you can specify the TCP/IP settings further if you have chosen to use it as a protocol. To do so, simply click the TCP/IP Settings button and specify the proper IP addresses (see Figure 10.17). Notice that you can specify that the computer should be assigned the proper addressing by the server. This is for taking advantage of DHCP (refer to section 10.1.2 and Chapter 7, "Linking to Your World"). This option makes dial-up net-working perfect for Internet service providers. They can use this option because it allows for very little setup on the client side of the connection. The ISP can provide the client's computer with necessary TCP/IP information whenever the client logs on to the network.

 A log file called PPPLOG.TXT is created in the Windows directory and is a useful tool in monitoring PPP sessions. It records the initialization of the basic PPP layers during a PPP session.

If you already have a dial-up server in place, you can test your connection by double-clicking the newly created icon. You see a dialog box where you can specify a user name and password (see Figure 10.18).

Upon typing in the user name and password, click Connect to begin the dialing process. You see several prompts as the connection process progresses. After you are connected, you see a dialog box specifying the connection speed and duration of the connection. If you click the Details button, you are shown which protocols are successfully being used in the connection (see Figure 10.19).

Figure 10.17.

Specifying TCP/IP Settings.

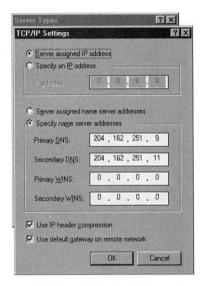

Figure 10.18.

Preparing to make a connection.

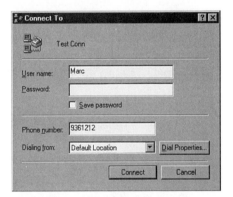

Figure 10.19.

Viewing the details of a dial-up connection.

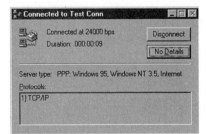

10.3. Configuring a Dial-Up Server

You might have one of the compatible dial-up servers that we specified previously in this chapter as already set up, but if you will be using another Windows 95 computer as your dial-up server, you have to create it.

The first thing you must remember is that, to set up Windows 95 as a dial-up server, you must have the Microsoft Plus! pack installed or handy. The Windows 95 CD-ROM provides the capability to make a Windows 95 computer a server.

 You need Windows 95 Plus! to make a Windows 95 computer a dial-up server.

10.3.1. Dial-Up Security

Before we set up a dial-up server, I want to talk a little about security. Creating any type of remote access to your network creates security holes that you need to make sure are plugged. Even though there is a way around any security measure (security measures are created by humans, and thus humans can break them), the more difficult you can make it to get around security, the less likely a breach will occur.

Here are some things to consider when setting up a dial-up server:

■ Run user-level security on the dial-up server (Windows NT or NetWare server required). This option ensures that whoever logs on to the Windows 95 dial-up server still has to be validated by a better security provider prior to accessing any network resources.

■ Require that encrypted passwords be used (refer to Figure 10.16). Non-encrypted passwords can be easily captured and used by someone else to gain access to the network using sniffers or other similar equipment.

When the Internet is involved:

■ Use firewalls to keep dial-up access and Internet access separate.

■ Disable File and Print Sharing on the dial-up server.

When using third-party programs:

■ Windows 95 supports the use of third-party hardware devices that increase the level of security with additional authentication methods.

■ Use an encryption program to encrypt data when sending information across the Internet.

10.3.2. Configuring the Dial-Up Server

You might be surprised to learn that you don't have a great deal to configure on a Windows 95 dial-up server. After you have the dial-up server installed from the Microsoft Plus! pack, the hard part is over.

After installing Microsoft Plus! pack, it might not appear that any changes were made to the dial-up networking aspects of Windows 95, but this is not true. By opening the Dial-Up Networking folder, you see a Dial-Up Server option from the Connections menu. Upon choosing the Dial-Up Server option, you can configure some basic settings (see Figure 10.20).

Figure 10.20.

Configuring the dial-up server.

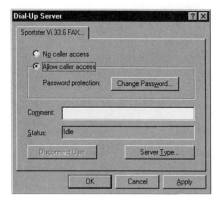

10

You must click the Allow Caller Access radio button so that users can dial in to the dial-up server. Additionally, you can set a password to restrict access to the dial-up server and any network resources that might be connected to it. Upon connection to the server, users are prompted for the password.

Note If you enable password protection but leave the password blank, users who connect must leave the password block blank to connect successfully.

When you click the Server Type button, you see a box similar to that in Figure 10.21. Here, you can specify the type of server, software compression, and password encryption settings. Software compression speeds transfer times, and encrypted passwords increase security.

Figure 10.21.

Specifying Server Types and other settings.

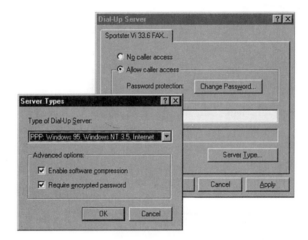

Once again, with the Microsoft Plus! package, Windows 95 can act as a dial-up networking server that allows Microsoft NT, LAN Manager, Windows for Workgroups, and other PPP clients to connect, but it cannot act as a gateway to clients using SLIP or IPX/SPX as protocols.

10.4. Telephony Defined

Telephony in Windows 95 defines a standard of how applications interact with telephony functions such as dialing numbers and calling cards. The *telephony application programming interface* (*TAPI*) was designed to allow a standard way for programmers to define how their applications interact with Windows 95.

The Add a Modem Wizard in the Control Panel creates the default settings. You can modify other telephony settings by double-clicking modems in the Control Panel and then clicking the Dialing Properties button from the General tab (see Figure 10.22).

10.4.1. Location

The location allows Windows 95 to figure out where you are and what settings you want for where you are located. This option can come in quite handy on a laptop when traveling. By specifying a different location, Windows 95 can keep track of who is long distance and how the call should be made. The various settings include what numbers to dial to access an outside line, whether to use a calling card, what numbers to dial to disable call waiting, and tone or pulse dialing.

Figure 10.22.
Defining additional telephony properties.

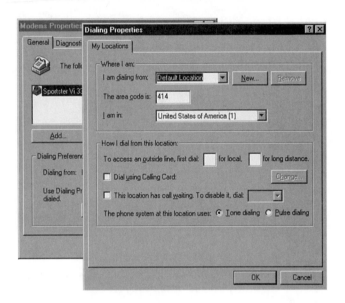

You can give the different locations different names. You just have to remember the name, and the telephony remembers which location should be dialed in which manner.

10.4.2. Calling Card

If you need to use your telephone calling card to make long-distance calls, you can use the same card in the computer to give you long-distance access to your network. Windows 95 includes setup and support for many of the major calling cards. After you have configured the calling card, the information is dialed automatically (see Figure 10.23).

10.5. Private Networking via the Internet

Dial-up networking gives you the ability to connect to your LAN from a remote location. Most dial-up networking happens via regular telephone lines. The cost for access can be high for companies who have people accessing their LANs from very remote locations on a regular basis. Very large telephone bills are a result of this long-distance calling.

Figure 10.23.

Calling card information is dialed automatically from this dialog box.

 Test Tip

This section covers the following exam objective: Install and configure network protocols—PPTP/VPN.

A way to overcome this cost is now available through the use of a Virtual Private Network (VPN). Virtual Private Networking is a new networking technology that you can use to connect to corporate networks securely across the Internet or a LAN. PPTP can also be used as a method to allow selected users to access a private network that is separated from the general corporate LAN by a tunnel server.

Tunneling is a networking term describing the encapsulation of one protocol within another protocol. Tunneling is typically done to join two networks using an intermediate network that is running an incompatible protocol, or is under the administrative control of a third party. Using the tunneling concept, however, we can set up private connections across the Internet through the use of the Point-to-Point Tunneling Protocol (PPTP).

10.5.1. Point-to-Point Tunneling Protocol (PPTP)

PPTP is an add-on that is used to enhance the networking services provided by the Windows NT Remote Access Server (RAS) and Windows 95 Dial-Up Networking. It is not included with either the original release or the OSR2 of Windows 95. It is part of a Dial-Up Networking update (version 1.2 as of this writing) that you must download from Microsoft's Web site. Let's take a look at how it works.

Windows Dial-Up Networking allows a computer to connect to a network of computers over a dial-up connection. While connected to the network, the Windows client behaves exactly as if it had a local network connection, with the exception of speed. Because you're using modem speeds such as a 56Kbps modem, you don't have the speed of a regular network, which averages 10Mbps for most networks. For the most part, Windows Dial-Up Networking uses the Internet standard Point-to-Point Protocol (PPP) to provide network connection over telephone lines. When connected, multiple protocols (NetBEUI, IPX/SPX, TCP/IP and so on) can be used to access the network. PPTP takes Windows Dial-Up Networking to another level. Dial-up networking could give you dial-in access to your network *or* as a connection to the Internet via an ISP. PPTP adds the capability to treat the Internet as point-to-point dial-up networking connection. All data sent over this connection can be encrypted and compressed. Additionally, multiple protocols can be used. For example, you can use IPX/SPX to connect to resources on your office LAN via a TCP/IP network (the Internet).

You might be wondering how this differs from just connecting your LAN to the Internet and then connecting to the LAN from a remote location using the Internet alone. Using VPN and PPTP to connect provides the following advantages over direct Internet connectivity:

- The private networks' IP addresses do not have to be coordinated with the Internet addresses. You can make up whatever IP address scheme you choose on your private LAN.
- All network protocols supported by Dial-Up Networking are supported in a PPTP connection. Private networks that are running combinations of NetBEUI, IPX/SPX, or TCP/IP can be joined.
- RAS security protocols and policies are used to prevent unauthorized connections.
- All network packets being sent over the Internet can be encrypted.

10.5.2. Installing PPTP and VPN Support

So how do you get this new wonderful idea set up on your Windows 95 computer? First of all, you must realize that this doesn't come standard as part of either the retail version (first release) or the OEM version (second release or OSR2) of Windows 95. You must download and install an update to Dial-Up Networking from Microsoft's Web site.

This section covers the following exam objective: Install and configure network protocols—PPTP/VPN.

The Windows 95 Dial-Up Networking 1.2 Upgrade not only adds this additional functionality of PPTP and VPN, it replaces all of the Dial-Up Networking components and installs new versions of the TCP/IP stack and the NDIS layer. A new version of Winsock is included as an optional component to correct name resolution limitations in the original Windows 95 software. This upgrade is also commonly called the ISDN update because it adds ISDN support into Windows 95 Dial-Up Networking.

The Dial-Up Networking 1.2 Upgrade is bundled into a self-installing file called Msdun12.exe. After you run the Msdun12.exe file, all the Dial-Up Networking system components are installed in their proper folders.

To obtain the Windows 95 Dial-Up Networking 1.2 Upgrade, visit the following Web site (as of this writing):

```
http://www.microsoft.com/windows/dowloads/contents/updates/W95DIALUPNETW
```

The Dial-Up Networking 1.2 Upgrade can be applied to existing Window 95-based computers, including the retail release and OEM Service Release 2 (OSR2).

After you have downloaded the previously mentioned file, follow these steps to install it:

1. In the Explorer, navigate to the location where you saved the file and double-click it.
2. Click Yes.
3. Click Yes to the License Agreement.
4. Click Yes to restart the computer.
5. When the computer restarts, it automatically installs the components and once again asks you to restart (this can vary depending on your configuration). Click Yes.

After restarting, you might notice that a couple of things have been added to the system. The following components are added to Network properties:

- Dial-Up Adapter #2 (VPN Support)
- Microsoft Virtual Private Networking Adapter
- NDISWAN -> Microsoft Virtual Private Networking Adapter

These additional adapters give Windows 95 the capability to connect to your PPTP server. They act in the same manner as your Dial-Up adapter that you will use to connect to the Internet.

Also, each installed protocol gains an additional entry. For example, if you have the NetBEUI, TCP/IP, and IPX/SPX protocols installed, the following entries are added:

- NetBEUI -> Dial-Up Adapter #2 (VPN Support)
- TCP/IP -> Dial-Up Adapter #2 (VPN Support)
- IPX/SPX-Compatible Protocol -> Dial-up Adapter #2 (VPN Support)

As you can see, it did not add any additional protocols; it simply bound the existing protocols to the new adapters.

10.5.3. Configuring PPTP and VPN Support

You can configure two types of connections: a connection to the Internet through your ISP and a tunnel connection to the PPTP server on the target network (within the LAN or WAN). Depending on how you will be using PPTP, you might not need to configure both types of connections.

PPTP is most commonly used for enabling secure and encrypted communications to private enterprise networks using a serial (modem) or ISDN connection to the Internet. In this scenario, you must configure both connections: one connection to the Internet through an ISP and one tunnel connection through the Internet to the PPTP server on the target network.

If you are using PPTP, however, to connect to a PPTP tunnel server on your LAN, you only need to configure a connection to the tunnel server.

For the remainder of this section, I concentrate on connecting via the Internet and how I set up my connection.

The first step is to create a connection to your Internet service provider. If you already have created a connection to your ISP, then you can skip this step. This is like any typical dial-up networking connection to an ISP. Here are the steps I used:

10

1. Double-click the Make New Connection icon in the Dial-Up Networking folder.

2. Give your connection a name. As you can see in Figure 10.24, I call it My ISP to keep the confusion to a minimum.

Figure 10.24.

Adding a new Dial-Up Networking connection.

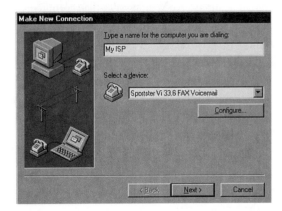

3. After clicking Next, type in the telephone number for your ISP. Once again, click Next.

4. Click Finish.

I can now change any settings for my ISP connection. In my case, the only change I make is to input my ISP's DNS server addresses (see Figure 10.25).

Figure 10.25.

Changing my ISP's DNS addresses.

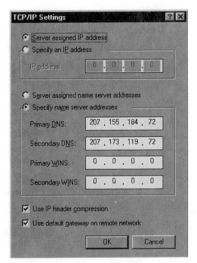

The next step in the process is to create a Dial-Up Networking connection for the PPTP server. Here are the steps I took:

1. Double-click the Make New Connection icon in the Dial-Up Networking folder.

2. Give your connection a name. I called it My PPTP to keep the confusion to a minimum.

3. From your list of modems, select Microsoft VPN Adapter (see Figure 10.26) and click Next.

Figure 10.26.

Selecting the Microsoft VPN Adapter.

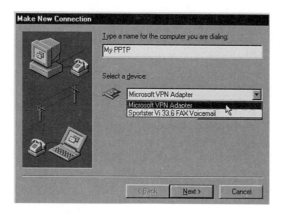

10

4. Type in the host name or IP address of the PPTP server. The host name might be something like thor.bartonet.com. In my case, because I am using a temporary server, I put in its IP address (see Figure 10.27). Click Next.

5. Click Finish.

Figure 10.27.

Entering the IP Address of the PPTP server.

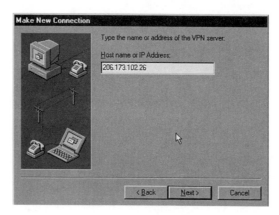

10.5.4. Connecting Using PPTP to Establish a VPN Connection

After you have your connections properly set up, you are ready to attempt to connect. This is a two-step process. The first step is to dial in to your ISP. After that connection is established, you then connect to your PPTP server using the VPN connection that you just created. Let's see the results of my connection.

Connecting to Your ISP

1. In My Computer, double-click Dial-Up Networking.

2. In the Dial-Up Networking box, double-click the connection icon to your ISP.

3. After supplying the proper user name and password, click Connect. In my case, my connection was successful (see Figure 10.28).

Figure 10.28.

Connected to My ISP.

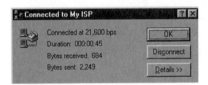

Connecting to Your PPTP Server

1. In the Dial-Up Networking box, double-click the connection icon to your PPTP server.

2. After supplying the proper user name and password, click Connect. In my case, the connection was successful (see Figure 10.29).

Figure 10.29.

Connected to My PPTP server.

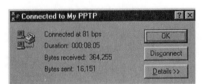

When connected, it is as if you were dialing in to the server directly; instead, you are accessing the server across the Internet! You can access network resources such as files and printers.

10.6. Direct Cable Connection

Windows 95 comes with the capability of connecting to another Windows 95 computer using a direct cable connection between the computers. This can be helpful in several situations.

One situation is when you might have a laptop computer that has numerous files and folders you have been working with while out of town. You want to copy these files and folders to your desktop computer without having to add the laptop to the network or use tons of floppy disks.

Another situation is when you need to migrate a lot of data from one computer to another in preparation for the older computer to receive an upgrade that might take a few days. Neither of these computers is on a network.

When it all boils down, a direct cable connection is simply for transferring a lot of data that otherwise might not be feasible to use regular networks or floppy disks.

You need either a 9-pin or 25-pin serial cable. You can't use any old serial cable. It must be a *null modem cable* because the pin assignments on a straight serial cable are not correct for the data to be transferred. Null modem cables are relatively easy to find and are usually in the same section as printer and other modem cables in your computer store.

To start the direct cable connection, follow these steps:

1. Connect the two computers with the cable.
2. Choose Start, Programs, Accessories, and then select Direct Cable Connection.
3. When the Direct Cable Connection dialog box appears, click whether the computer you are working on is a Host or Guest (see Figure 10.30) and click Next.

Note | You must perform this step on both computers. The guest connects to the host, so be sure to configure the host first.

4. Choose the port where you want to attach the cable (see Figure 10.31) and click Next.
5. Click the Finish button.
6. The connected computer can now see and connect to any shared folders on the host computer.

10

Figure 10.30.

The Direct Cable Connection dialog box.

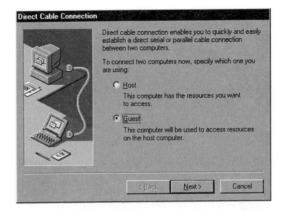

Figure 10.31.

Choosing the port for the direct cable connection.

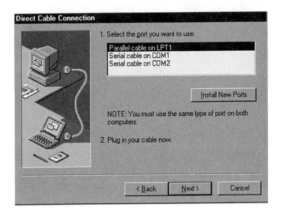

10.7. Taking the Briefcase Home

When working with files on multiple computers, you want to keep track of which files have the most current changes and up-to-date information. Just the slip of a finger could overwrite the newer copy of that file with an older one. Keeping track of files that have copies located on two computers can be relatively easy if you are just dealing with a couple of files. As the number of files grow, though, the possibility of deleting or overwriting the most current copy with an older copy becomes greater.

Along comes the briefcase to assist you in keeping track of these files and their synchronization. For example, let's say you're a salesperson and you own a laptop and a desktop PC. When you are out of the office making sales calls, you make revisions to some sales contracts. When you come back to the office, you also want a copy of these contracts placed on the hard disk of the desktop PC, but copies of these files already exist. How do you know which ones are current and which ones are old? How can you quickly find out and synchronize the files in a breeze?

Follow these steps to create a new briefcase and use it to synchronize a file:

1. Click the desktop with your secondary mouse button and select New, Briefcase.

2. Double-click the Briefcase icon on the desktop.

3. Briefly read through the instructions and click Finish (see Figure 10.32).

4. Create a new text document on your desktop and then drag a copy and drop it on top of the Briefcase window. Notice the document and its status in the Briefcase (see Figure 10.33).

5. Normally, you then copy the Briefcase to another drive. This could be either a floppy or network drive. The Briefcase is then taken with you and you modify the files in the Briefcase.

6. Modify the document in the Briefcase.

7. Save and close the document.

8. When you bring the Briefcase back to the office, open it, and click Update All. You see any files that are unsynchronized.

9. By clicking the document and then clicking the Update button, Windows 95 asks which file you want to replace (see Figure 10.34). Click the appropriate response.

10

Figure 10.32.

Briefcase Setup instructions.

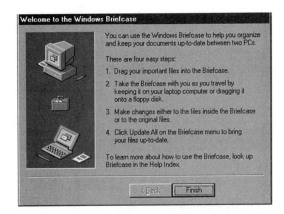

Figure 10.33.

A sample document located in the Briefcase.

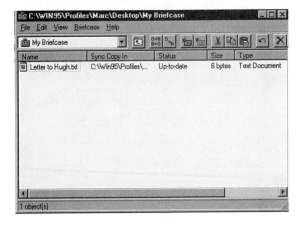

Figure 10.34.

Updating a document.

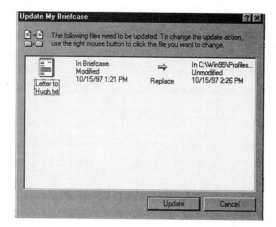

When the document is updated, it makes the document at the original location match the one in the Briefcase, or vice versa, depending on which one is most current.

10

Lab

The lab consists of review questions pertaining to this chapter and provides an opportunity to apply the knowledge that you've learned with this chapter. Answers to the review questions can be found in Appendix B.

Questions

1. Which line protocol is the most popular and flexible to use?

    A. SLIP

    B. Windows NT RAS

    C. PPP

    D. NRN

2. Which wide-area telephone network is the same as your existing telephone service?

    A. PSTN

    B. PPP

    C. x.25

    D. ISDN

3. Which component is considered the central one in communications architecture?

    A. Unimodem

    B. VCOMM

    C. COMM

    D. Mini-VCOMM

4. What type of slow links does Windows 95 support via dial-up networking?

    A. PPP

    B. PSTN

    C. x.25

    D. ISDN

5. What network protocols are supported by dial-up networking?

    A. PPP

    B. NetBEUI

    C. TCP/IP

    D. SLIP

    E. IPX/SPX

6. What extra security measures in the following list should be used in conjunction with configuring a dial-up server? Choose all that apply.

    A. Use user-level security.

    B. Use share-level security.

    C. Use password encryption.

    D. Use user profiles.

7. As a dial-up server, Windows 95 can support all of the following as clients except:

    A. Windows 95 client

    B. NRN NetWare client

    C. Windows for Workgroups client

    D. Windows NT client

8. As a dial-up client, Windows 95 can connect to which of the following servers? Choose all that apply.

    A. Windows 95 dial-up server

    B. NRN NetWare server

    C. Windows for Workgroups

    D. Windows NT server

9. Windows 95 dial-up networking is topology-dependent.

    A. True

    B. False

10

10. A user calls you and wants to know how to make his Windows 95 computer available so that he can dial in to it and access his files from home. He already has Dial-Up Networking installed. What else must he do?

    A. Install Dial-Up Networking Server in the Windows Setup tab from the Add/Remove Programs option in the Control Panel.

    B. Install Dial-Up Networking Server from the Windows 95 CD in the Admin\DUN folder.

    C. Install Microsoft Plus! Pack.

    D. Nothing; Dial-Up server is part of Dial-Up Networking, and thus is already installed.

11. Under Windows 95 architecture, a modem requires two drivers. The first driver is a minidriver provided by the manufacturer; the other is supplied as part of Windows 95 and is called _____.

    A. Unidriver

    B. Unimodem

    C. ModemDrv

    D. WinModem

12. A company asks you to help it decide which type of remote access solution to implement. It has a 25-node network with the clients running Windows 95 and a server running NetWare 3.12. The company has decided that, because only five people need remote access, it wants to use Windows 95 as a dial-in solution. Here are the required and optional objectives that the solution should meet:

    Required Objectives

    A. Access to network shares (files) from a remote location.

    B. Users validated in some form or fashion for additional security when accessing network resources.

    Optional Objectives

    A. Allow all five users simultaneous dial-in access.

    B. Access to network printers from a remote location.

Proposed Solution

Install Dial-Up Networking and the Microsoft Plus! Pack on a single computer. Configure this computer to use the NetWare server as its security provider with user-level security. Assign the individual user's dial-in rights.

    A. The solution meets all of the required objectives and all of the optional objectives.

    B. The solution meets all of the required objectives and some of the optional objectives.

    C. The solution meets some of the required objectives and all of the optional objectives.

    D. The solution meets none of the required objectives and none of the optional objectives.

Exercises

Connecting Two Windows 95 Computers via Direct Cable Connection

For this exercise, you need two computers—one with the Microsoft Plus! pack installed and one with a null modem cable. The null modem cable simulates a modem in this exercise.

Setting Up the Host Computer

1. Open the Control Panel and double-click the Add/Remove Programs icon.
2. Select the Windows Setup tab.
3. Select Communications (the word, not the check box).
4. Click the Details button.
5. Place a check mark in the box next to Direct Cable Connection.
6. Click OK.
7. In the Add/Remove Programs box, click OK.
8. When prompted, specify the location of the Windows 95 source files.
9. Choose Start, Programs, Accessories, and Direct Cable Connection.
10. Click Host and then click Next.
11. Select the cable you are using and click Next.
12. Click Finish.

Setting Up the Guest Computer

1. Follow steps 1–8 in setting up the host computer.
2. Connect the null modem cable to both computers.
3. Choose Start, Programs, Accessories, and Direct Cable Connection.
4. Click Guest and then Next.
5. Select the cable you are using and click Next.
6. Click Finish.
7. You can now map network drives or browse for shared folders on the host computer.

TEST DAY
FAST FACTS

Here are a few fast facts for you to take a look at before test time:

- Microsoft Exchange that comes with Windows 95 is actually a scaled down version of Microsoft Mail.

- The Windows 95 Microsoft Exchange client can connect to a Microsoft Exchange Workgroup Post Office or a Microsoft Mail Post Office.

- To connect Windows 95 to a Microsoft Exchange Server (Windows NT), you must install the Microsoft Exchange client that comes with the server software.

- The Microsoft Mail Postoffice applet in the Control Panel creates new workgroup post offices and administers existing ones.

- Using Microsoft Exchange, you can install Microsoft Fax, which gives you faxing capabilities locally and to others on the network (should you decide to share your modem).

- All outgoing faxes appear in your Exchange Outbox and then in the Sent Items box after the fax has been sent.

Day 11

Exchange Messaging Services

Windows 95 ships with an email messaging and faxing program called Microsoft Exchange, which works closely with the Messaging Applications Programming Interface (MAPI) to provide an interface that can be used with many different types of network messaging. Because Microsoft Exchange can support many different mail and fax services simultaneously, it becomes the central access point from which all network messages and faxes are received or sent.

Exchange is also a single interface for many different MAPI-aware programs and becomes easier for the user to learn because she only has to learn one. If each of these programs had a different interface, the learning curve would take considerably longer.

In this chapter, you will learn how to set up and configure Microsoft Exchange for Windows 95 properly.

Objectives

In preparation for the exam, you should be familiar with basic operations using Microsoft Exchange. Even though the exam objectives for this chapter are almost nonexistent, electronic mail and supporting it on the Windows 95 platform is important. The exam objectives are the following:

■ Create, share, and monitor resources

■ Shared fax modem

11.1. Microsoft Exchange

Microsoft Exchange was designed to be the all-purpose mail interface for Windows 95. Through the Exchange interface, you can access all mail transferred to or from the computer. Microsoft Exchange can support multiple mail services simultaneously; in other words, Exchange can receive mail from a Microsoft Mail server and from a service like the Microsoft Network (MSN). Even though the mail is coming from two different services, you can read it in a single interface.

In addition to the Exchange interface being a single point of access for email, it also lets you fax documents directly from another program like Microsoft Word or Excel using a modem. All incoming faxes also appear in the Exchange interface as incoming mail.

11.1.1. MAPI

The *Messaging Application Programming Interface (MAPI)* is nothing more than a common set of commands and instructions that allows other programs to interface with mail systems. This common programmable interface has several advantages. For one, the Exchange interface can read and send mail through any type of mail service as long as it is written with the MAPI in mind. I'll discuss some of these services, such as Microsoft Mail and Microsoft Exchange Server, in this chapter.

Another advantage is that applications written to be MAPI-aware can take advantage of email because Windows 95 includes not only MAPI support, but also Microsoft OLE 2.0 Component Object Model (COM) interfaces. For example, with Microsoft Word 97, you can send a document as an email attachment to someone directly from the Word application and without having to open the Exchange interface.

11.1.2. Workgroup Post Office

The Microsoft Exchange software that comes with Windows 95 was designed to be used as a workgroup (peer to peer) messaging system. In actuality, it is a scaled-down version of Microsoft Mail. This gives you the email capability on smaller networks where there is no server such as Windows NT or Novell NetWare.

But a central computer has to be in charge of sending the mail back and forth. With the Exchange software, you can set up a Windows 95 computer to become a workgroup post office where all messages are stored.

Even though you might not need a network server such as Windows NT or Novell NetWare, it is not feasible to use the workgroup post office for large numbers of users or a heavy volume of email traffic. This is evident because you cannot connect a workgroup post office to another post office or other messaging systems. If your network has grown to the size where you need to connect several post offices or you need connectivity to another messaging system, it is time you upgraded to a server-based messaging system.

11.1.3. Microsoft Mail

If you decide to use Windows 95 on a network that also has a Microsoft Mail server, you won't have any problems connecting to it. Microsoft Mail is similar to the workgroup post office concept except that Microsoft Mail needs to be loaded on a network server such as Windows NT, Novell NetWare, and so forth.

The Microsoft Mail server program also supports connectivity to other email messaging systems through the use of gateway software. Examples of these include Lotus Notes and Groupwise. Also, you can connect a Microsoft Mail server to other Microsoft Mail servers.

Microsoft Mail is no longer being developed. The last version made was Microsoft Mail 3.5. Microsoft's new solution to the server-based email messaging is the Microsoft Exchange server.

11.1.4. The Microsoft Exchange Server

Here is where most people get a little confused. You see, the version of Exchange that comes with Windows 95 is not *really* Exchange, it is a scaled-down version of Microsoft Mail.

Microsoft released a replacement to Microsoft Mail called Microsoft Exchange, but because it was released after Windows 95, it has no support out of the box. To connect Windows 95 to a Microsoft Exchange server, you must install the client software that accompanies the Exchange server software.

To the users, connecting to a Microsoft Exchange server is only slightly different than connecting to a Microsoft Mail server. To the IS professional though, Exchange and Mail are two completely different mail systems.

11.1.5. Microsoft Outlook

The release of Microsoft Office 97 includes a new mail client called Microsoft Outlook (it is available separately also). Microsoft Outlook performs the same functions as the Exchange client, with some additional utilities. This program offers a calendar, contacts list, task list, and a handy notes option to the mail features. What makes Outlook so outstanding is that it integrates these functions with amazing

11

results. If you have any other Microsoft Office applications installed, they are integrated as well.

> **Note**
>
> A similar tool called Schedule Plus is also available and has similar features, but Outlook is a newer product and has more features and better functionality with mail functions.

You cannot use Microsoft Outlook to create a post office like you can with the Exchange software that comes with Windows 95, but it can connect to any of the mail services that the Exchange client can. Therefore, you can use Exchange that comes with Windows 95 to create a workgroup post office and use Outlook to connect to it and retrieve mail.

> **Note**
>
> Outlook was designed to work best with the Microsoft Exchange server. If you use any other type of mail services, you might not be able to use many of the beneficial features of Outlook.

> **Test Tip**
>
> Schedule Plus and Outlook are not items covered by the exam because they do not come as part of Windows 95. I covered them for your benefit, however.

11.1.6. Other Services

You can also use Microsoft Exchange to connect to other multiple mail services as well. You can also connect to services such as CompuServe Mail and the Microsoft Network.

> **Note**
>
> Sorry, America Online (AOL) uses a proprietary mail system not designed to use the Windows 95 MAPI. Therefore, AOL users can't use Exchange to check their mail.

You should be aware that connecting to these services means additional requirements. For example, to use the Microsoft Network for email, you must have a Microsoft Network account.

11.2. Configuring Email Functions

You need quite a few steps to set up Microsoft Exchange on your Windows 95 machine. First of all, you need some type of email service or post office already configured. Then you can configure the Exchange client to connect to that service or post office. Lastly, you can configure the client's customization features.

The first step is to have your mail service or post office up and running. If not, your installation of the client software will be cut short when it cannot contact the post office. If your mail service will be a mail server such as Microsoft Exchange or Microsoft Mail, you must have connectivity to these servers before installing the client. If your mail service will be a workgroup post office using the Exchange software that came with Windows 95, it too must be set up prior to installing any clients.

11.2.1. Creating a Workgroup Post Office

Windows 95 comes with the capability of creating a workgroup post office. Prior to creating the workgroup post office, you should take a few things into consideration.

First of all, you should decide on the location of the post office. On which computer will it reside? The administrator of the post office needs access to this computer for administrative purposes. Also, keep in mind that with more users, the post office needs more hard disk space for storage. The exact amount of disk space is hard to determine due to all the variables involved. Examples of these variables are how many users, how many messages per user, and so on.

11

 Note The computer where the post office resides must be running during the hours in which users need access to their email. It is not wise to pick a typical end-user machine for storage of the post office. For best results, it should be a computer that is constantly up and running.

Also keep in mind that even though the client can connect to multiple mail services at once, it can only connect to one Microsoft Mail post office at a time. This means that the client cannot be connected to a workgroup post office and a Microsoft Mail server post office simultaneously. The Microsoft Exchange client can connect only to either of these post offices but not to both.

To create a new post office, double-click the Microsoft Mail post office icon in the Control Panel. In Figure 11.1, you see that you have two options from which to choose: Administer an Existing Workgroup Postoffice or Create a New Workgroup Postoffice. Of course, we want to pick the latter.

Figure 11.1.

Creating a new Microsoft Mail workgroup post office.

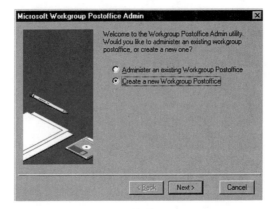

Next, you need to type in the location where the post office will reside (see Figure 11.2). This is a location where all the mailboxes of the users will be stored along with messages and other information. You can select that it be installed locally on the computer that you are performing the installation at, or you can specify the location on another computer using the UNC naming convention. Also, a Browse button is available that allows you to specify the location. Keep in mind that the person who will administer this post office needs to have access to its location.

Figure 11.2.

The location of the post office can be either on the hard disk of the local computer or on a shared folder on another computer.

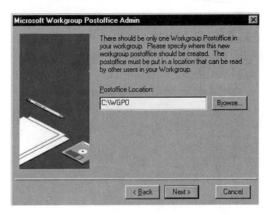

Note The location of the post office has to be in a folder that already exists. The installation program does not create a folder for you. On that same subject, if the post office will reside on another computer, be sure that the folder is already created and shared to the network.

The installation program then allows you to confirm the location of the post office or go back and change it. If the location is correct, just click the Next button to confirm it.

Next, the program prompts you for information about the post office administrator account (see Figure 11.3). This part of the setup process not only identifies the administrator but also creates a mailbox for the administrator. The person who creates the postoffice is automatically the administrator. Be aware of the mailbox name; by default it is Administrator. You need this information when administering the post office. Fill in the appropriate information and click OK.

Figure 11.3.

Specifying the mailbox information for the post office administrator.

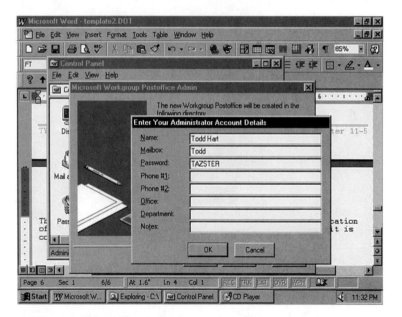

If the folder that you created for the storage of the post office is not already shared to the network, you are prompted with a message to do so. How else will others access the post office? Otherwise, you will be done with the actual post office creation.

11.2.2. Administering a Workgroup Post Office

Prior to setting up any clients to connect to your newly created post office, you want to create mailboxes for the users. To administer your new post office, the steps are similar to creating a new post office. You need to double-click the Microsoft Mail Postoffice icon in the Control Panel. Next, select Administer an Existing Workgroup Postoffice and click the Next button.

You are prompted for the location of your post office. Specify the same location where we recently installed the new post office and click the Next button.

After typing in the administrator's mailbox name and password, click the Next button. You see a window similar to the one in Figure 11.4. In this window, the Postoffice Manager, you can add and remove users. If you choose to add users, you see the same window as when you were setting up the initial administrator account.

Figure 11.4.

The Postoffice Manager interface is where you create and remove users' mailboxes.

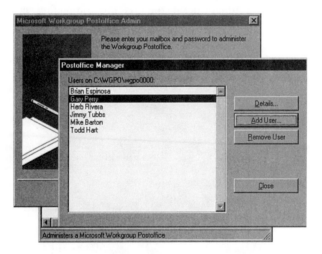

After you have completed administering the post office, click Close. That's all there is to it. As you can see, the workgroup post office doesn't really have any advanced features or capabilities as you have with Microsoft Mail server or Microsoft Exchange server.

11.2.3. Configuring the Exchange Client

Your next step in your emailing journey is to set up the client. The first time you open the Inbox or otherwise start Exchange, you are prompted with the Inbox Setup Wizard (see Figure 11.5). The first question asks whether you have used Exchange before. If any type of Microsoft messaging system was used on the machine that you are setting up, select the Yes radio button; otherwise select No.

Note

If you do not have an Inbox icon on your desktop, you can reach the setup portion of Exchange from the Control Panel. By double-clicking the Add/Remove Programs tab, you can install Microsoft Exchange from the Windows Setup tab.

Figure 11.5.

Starting the setup of Microsoft Exchange.

Next, the wizard prompts you to specify what services you want to use with Exchange. The two options that I have in Figure 11.6 are Microsoft Mail and Internet Mail. I will discuss Internet Mail a little later in this chapter, so for now I only selected Microsoft Mail.

Figure 11.6.

Indicating which services you would like to include with Exchange.

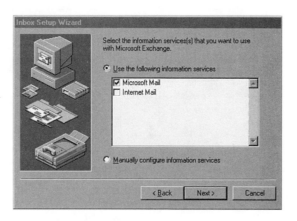

11

Specifying where your post office resides is the next step (see Figure 11.7). Once again, you must have a post office already installed. If not, this is where your installation comes to a screeching halt. After you specify where the post office is located—either by typing in the path or using the Browse option—click Next.

Figure 11.7.

Specify where your post office resides.

Now, the Inbox Setup Wizard wants you to specify who you are or at least what you were called when the post office and/or your mailbox was created. As you can see in Figure 11.8, I have the same list of names that I created during the setup of the post office.

Figure 11.8.

Specifying your mailbox.

After specifying the mailbox and clicking the Next button, the Inbox Setup Wizard prompts you for a password. This is the password that the post office administrator typed in. Therefore, your logon password might or might not match the password for your mailbox; after specifying your password, click the Next button.

Next, the Inbox Setup Wizard asks whether you would like the Inbox to pop up when you log on to the computer (see Figure 11.9). This option causes the Inbox (Exchange Interface) to start up automatically as soon as someone logs on to the machine. The benefit to adding the Inbox to the Startup group simply is that it makes the email interface pop up at the beginning of your logon. The disadvantage is that it increases the amount of time that it takes Windows 95 to load and allow the user control of the interface.

Figure 11.9.

I decide not to add the Inbox to my Startup group.

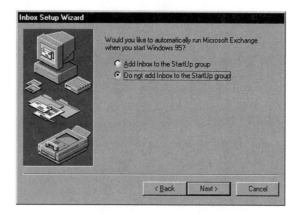

After you have specified the server's location, your job of initial setup and configuration is complete. To access the interface, simply double-click the Inbox icon on your desktop.

11.2.4. Corresponding with Other Exchange Clients

When you first open the Exchange client by double-clicking the Inbox icon on your desktop, you might notice that it defaults to a single-pane view of the Inbox. You can also view the directory of folders for your mailbox by choosing the Folders option of the View menu. In Figure 11.10, you can see the basic structure of the folders on the left with messages displayed on the right.

You can modify the behavior of the Exchange client though the modification of its services. As with any other object in Windows 95, each of the services has its own properties sheet. To access the Exchange Services, choose the Services option under the Tools menu. A list of all the installed services appears similar to Figure 11.11.

11

Figure 11.10.

The Exchange client showing the mailbox folders on the left and the messages on the right.

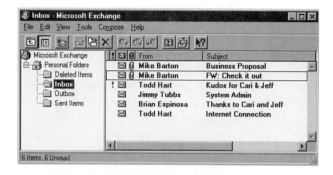

Figure 11.11.

The Exchange Services dialog box displays a list of the installed services.

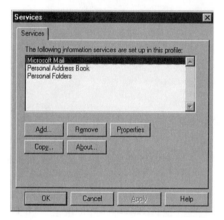

For example, if you want to modify the Microsoft Mail service that is installed by default, select Microsoft Mail in the Services dialog box and then click the Properties button. In the properties box (see Figure 11.12), you can modify such things as the location of your post office, mailbox name, delivery notifications, and so on.

Sending and receiving email with other Exchange clients is quick and easy. Exchange has support of OLE objects so that you can accomplish tasks, such as attaching documents or inserting pictures and sound files directly into your messages. Messages are in Rich Text Format (RTF) so that you can use many features such as different size and style fonts, not to mention adding color to your text (see Figure 11.13).

Figure 11.12.

The Microsoft Mail properties sheet where several modifications can be made.

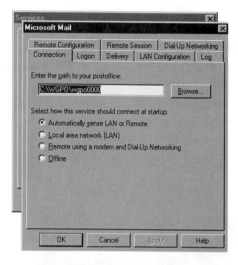

Figure 11.13.

With RTF, you can use different fonts, colors, and other formatting features.

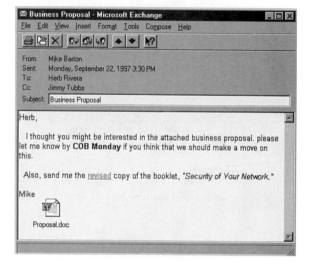

11

Messages are stored in a set of personal folders as seen in Figure 11.10. These folders do not correspond with a set of folders on the hard drive. Instead, the personal folders and messages in them are all contained in a file called a personal folder file. A personal folder file is created by default for the Inbox and Outbox called EXCHANGE.PST. You can create additional personal folder files for archiving messages or organizing messages. To create an additional personal folder file, follow these steps:

1. In the Exchange Client, choose Tools from the menu.

2. Click Services.

3. Click the Add button.

4. Click Personal Folders and click OK.

5. Type in a name and specify the location to store the file and click Open.

6. Specify a name, select your encryption scheme, and specify a password (see Figure 11.14).

7. Click OK.

8. From the Services box, click OK.

Figure 11.14.

Creating additional personal folders.

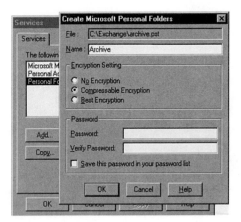

Your newly created set of personal folders appears in the Exchange client, ready for use. You can store messages in the new set of folders by dragging and dropping the messages.

The Exchange client also uses profiles for users. This added capability can have several advantages. First, a user can have multiple profiles. For example, you can use Exchange on a laptop. You might want to use a profile with certain settings while using Exchange at the office and a separate profile when you are away from the office. With these separate profiles, you can specify that Exchange use a Microsoft Mail post office when at the office and another service such as MSN when away from the office.

Using profiles also provides the capability to support multiple users who share the same computer. With each user that uses the computer, a separate profile can be created so that each person can use his or her own mailbox. Basically, a message profile lets you specify different service configurations, different basic settings, delivery order, location information, and more. A profile is created by default when you run the Inbox Setup Wizard for the first time. To create additional profiles:

1. Double-click the Mail and Fax icon in the Control Panel.
2. Click the Show Profiles button.
3. Click the Add button.
4. Complete the Add Inbox Wizard.

The Inbox Setup Wizard walks you through the steps of creating a new profile. These steps are identical to those for creating a mailbox for the first time.

With multiple profiles, you want the Exchange client to prompt you for which profile you want to use at the startup of the client. To specify that the client do this, choose Options from the Tools menu. Click the radio button titled Prompt for a Profile to Be Used (see Figure 11.15).

Figure 11.15.

If multiple profiles are used, you should specify that the client prompt you for which profile to use.

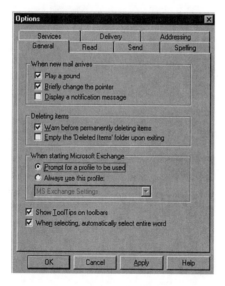

11

11.2.5. Corresponding with Internet Users

Microsoft Exchange also gives you the capability to send and receive mail via the Internet. This capability is added as an additional service. You need to add this service for a couple of reasons:

- The mail server (Microsoft Mail, Microsoft Exchange, and so on) does not support Internet mail for your account, and you must connect to a different mail server within your network for Internet mail support.

- You need to connect to an ISP (not MSN or CompuServe) via dial-up networking for Internet mail access.

To add the service, choose Services for the Tools menu of the Exchange Client. After clicking the Add button, you see a list of services that you can add (see Figure 11.16). Select Internet Mail and click OK.

Figure 11.16.

Adding services to the Exchange client.

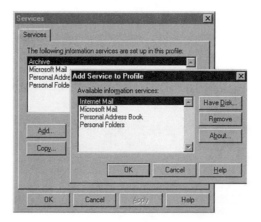

You are then prompted for information pertaining to the setup of your Internet mail connection (see Figure 11.17). You must specify information such as your email address, Internet mail server, and the account on the Internet mail server. You must obtain this information from your Internet mail server or your ISP, whichever is applicable. Additional options include what type of message format your mail server supports and where to forward any outbound mail if the Internet mail server you specified only supports inbound mail.

After you have supplied the necessary information about your server, you then need to specify how you connect to the mail server. Select the Connection tab, and you can specify whether you will be connecting via your local network or via a modem connection (see Figure 11.18). If you specify to use a modem, you can choose from a list of dial-up networking connections you have already created, or you can create a new one by clicking the Add Entry button.

Figure 11.17.

You must specify the necessary information for the Internet mail service.

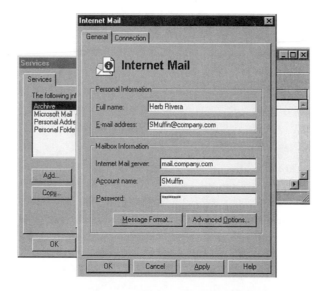

Figure 11.18.

Configuring how the Internet mail service will connect to the mail server.

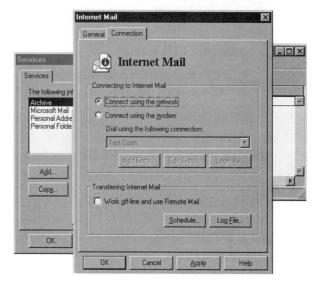

After you have completed the configuration, you can then send Internet-bound email. You can use standard Internet email addressing. So how does the Exchange client know whom to send the mail to? Well, it doesn't really. It just attempts to send all outgoing mail to each service until all the mail is gone or all services have been tried, whichever comes first.

Because I have the Internet service installed along with the Microsoft Mail service, the Exchange client attempts to send my mail to the Microsoft Mail server first. The Microsoft Mail server processes my outgoing mail first, sending any mail addressed in a manner that it understands. Likewise, any mail addressed in a manner that it doesn't understand remains in my Outbox. Then, the Exchange client attempts to send any remaining outgoing mail via the next service (which happens to be the Internet mail service in my case). It continues this scenario until all the mail is sent out.

You can modify the order in which Microsoft Mail tries to send the mail. To do so, choose Options from the Tools menu. The Delivery tab lists the services that are installed. If I want the client to attempt to deliver all outgoing mail to my Internet service first, I simply click the Internet Mail service and then click the up arrow on the right. The services are processed from the top of the list down (see Figure 11.19).

Figure 11.19.

Changing the order of services in which the Exchange client attempts to send outgoing mail.

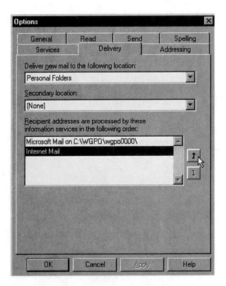

11.2.6. Corresponding with MSN and CompuServe Clients

After you have installed The Microsoft Network or CompuServe client software, you have the ability to send email using these services. For the most part, installing these programs automatically adds their respective services to the Exchange client. You can also add them using the Add option in the Services dialog box as described in 11.2.5.

Note The software for The Microsoft Network or CompuServe must be installed for its services to be shown as one of the available services to add.

Whenever you add services, you can retrieve or send mail to that particular service specifically. By adding services, the Deliver Now option from the Tools menu changes. It becomes Deliver Now Using and, when pointed to, pops up a submenu displaying several options. The first option, All Services, retrieves mail and sends outgoing mail by checking all the installed services. Further down the menu is a list of all the services. You can click a service, and it retrieves and sends outgoing mail to only that particular service. This is a handy option when you are using a dial-up connection for mail, such as The Microsoft Network. This initiates a dial-up session and transfers mail. After you have made the transfer, the call is terminated.

11.3. Faxing from Windows 95

The Exchange client also has the capability to send and receive faxes, which you can also give it to others. In other words, after you have properly set up Microsoft Fax on your machine, you can share it for others to use via your LAN.

11.3.1. Installing Microsoft Fax

You can install Microsoft Fax when you initially install Windows 95 or after it is up and running. As with most components in Windows 95, setup is more easily accomplished during initial installation. You can install the Microsoft Fax through the Add/Remove Programs option in the Control Panel. Even though you are installing an additional component of Windows 95, it is actually a service of Microsoft Exchange. You can configure Microsoft Fax by bringing up the properties of your Exchange and selecting Microsoft Fax as a service. If you want to install Microsoft Fax after installing Windows 95, follow these steps:

1. Double-click the Add/Remove Programs icon in your Control Panel.
2. Select the Windows Setup tab.
3. In the list of components, scroll down until you see Microsoft Fax.
4. Place a check mark in the box next to Microsoft Fax.
5. Click OK.

11

6. Close the Control Panel.

7. Click the Inbox icon located on the desktop using the secondary mouse button.

8. Choose Properties.

9. From the Services tab, click the Add button.

10. From the list of installable services, click Microsoft Fax and click OK.

11. A message appears stating that you need to specify some information before you can send a fax. It asks if you want to specify it now. Click Yes.

12. Specify the necessary information and click OK.

In the last step, you see a dialog box similar to Figure 11.20, which consists of four tabs. The tab that it takes you to, User, is for specifying user-specific information such as name, title, address, and so forth.

Figure 11.20.

The User tab of the Microsoft Fax Properties sheet.

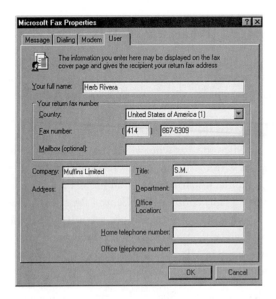

The Message tab (see Figure 11.21) allows you to set options on when to send the fax, whether it will be in editable format, and what kind of default cover page to include. Additionally, you can edit or create new cover pages for your faxes using this tab.

Figure 11.21.

The Message tab of the Microsoft Fax Properties sheet.

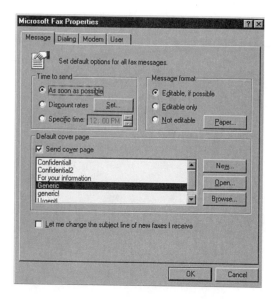

The Dialing tab in Figure 11.22 allows you to set specific settings such as dialing properties specific to your location and toll prefixes. Also, you can set how many times you want Exchange to retry sending a fax that does not go through for some reason and how long it waits between each retry. The last tab, Modem, lets you set specific modem information (which can also be accessed via the Control Panel). The Modem tab also lets you share the fax modem with others on your network.

11.3.2. Sharing the Microsoft Fax with Others

With Microsoft Exchange, you can share your Microsoft Fax with others on the network. This allows others to use the modem installed in your computer and your Microsoft Fax service. There is no need for them to have a modem installed or to have extra software.

This section covers the following exam objective: Create, share and monitor resources—Shared fax modem.

You can share your Microsoft Fax at the Modem tab of the Microsoft Fax Properties sheet (see Figure 11.23) by placing a check mark in the Let Other People on the Network Use My Modem to Send Faxes box. By default, it creates the folder

C:\Netfax, which is shared as Fax. If you have multiple hard disks in your computer, the program asks you which drive to use for the Netfax folder.

Figure 11.22.

The Dialing tab of the Microsoft Fax Properties sheet.

 You must have file and print sharing enabled to share Microsoft Fax.

Using the Properties button for sharing your fax, you can specify the share name and access. Notice with my configuration in Figure 11.24 that I am currently using share-level security. If you are using user-level security, you can specify security as described in Chapter 6, "Linking to Your Network."

Other people can access your modem to use as a fax machine by installing Microsoft Exchange also. After they have it installed, they must specify your modem under the Modem tab of the Microsoft Fax properties.

11.3.3. Sending a Fax with Microsoft Fax

Because Microsoft Fax is so well-integrated with Windows 95, sending a fax couldn't be easier. Just think of Microsoft Fax as another printer. Simply print whatever you want to fax in whatever application you are using. In the Print dialog box, select Microsoft Fax in the list of available printers (see Figure 11.25).

Figure 11.23.

The Modem tab of the Microsoft Fax Properties sheet is where you can share your modem with others.

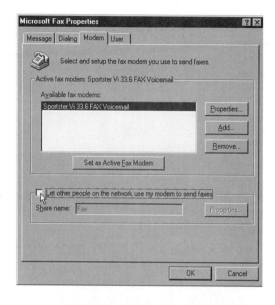

Figure 11.24.

Specifying share information for Microsoft Fax.

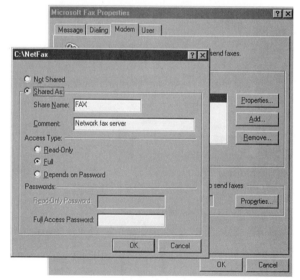

11

Figure 11.25.

*Selecting the
Microsoft Fax as
your printer.*

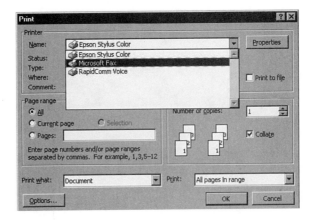

After starting the print (fax) job, you are prompted to input the name(s) of the person(s) you want to receive the fax (see Figure 11.26). Microsoft Fax also has broadcast faxing capabilities. Simply type in the name of the person who you want to receive the fax and click the Add to List button. Then, type in the next fax recipient's name and fax number. You can continue to add as many names and fax numbers to the list as you want. After typing in each name, click the Add to List button. Microsoft Fax dials each fax machine individually and sends the fax.

Figure 11.26.

*Specifying who you
want to receive the
fax.*

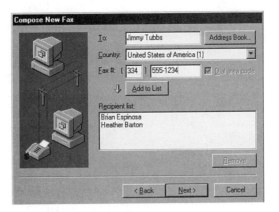

All outgoing faxes are placed in the Outbox of Microsoft Exchange. Any successfully sent faxes are then moved to the Sent items box. Microsoft Exchange notifies you of any unsuccessful faxes by placing a message in your Inbox specifying which fax was unsuccessful.

After clicking Next, you are asked whether you want to send a cover page along with the fax (see Figure 11.27). By default, you have four from which to choose. In addition to a cover page selection, you can also specify some advanced delivery options. Simply click the Options button.

Figure 11.27.

Selecting a cover page.

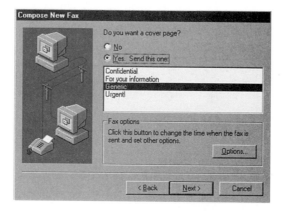

The Send Options for this Message dialog box allows you to pick what time to send the fax, what format to send the fax, and which cover page to use (see Figure 11.28). This is especially handy when you want to send a broadcast fax to several people but would rather do so after business hours.

11

Figure 11.28.

Specifying advanced sending options.

Finally, if you specified that you wanted to use a cover sheet, you are prompted for a subject and note to be placed on it. If you are sending a broadcast fax, this subject and note are placed on the cover sheet of all faxes, so keep it generic.

Lab

This lab consists of review questions pertaining to this chapter and provides an opportunity to apply the knowledge that you've learned. Answers to the review questions can be found in Appendix B.

Questions

1. Who can administer a post office created by Microsoft Exchange?

   A. Any member of that post office

   B. Only members who were designated as an admin after post office creation

   C. Only the person who created the post office

   D. Anyone knowing the administrator password

2. You can connect the Microsoft Exchange client that comes with Windows 95 to a Microsoft Mail server.

   A. True

   B. False

3. What is MAPI?

   A. The manual and automatic programming interface.

   B. A utility used in Microsoft Exchange to assist you in connecting to other Windows 95 computers.

   C. A common set of commands and instructions that allows other programs to interface with mail systems.

   D. The Registry location of Exchange settings.

4. A message profile allows you to specify different service configurations.

   A. True

   B. False

5. You can share the modem that you are using for Microsoft Fax to others on the network so that they can also use it for Microsoft Fax.

   A. True

   B. False

11

6. When you install Microsoft Fax, it is _____.

   A. A Windows 95 Plus feature

   B. A My Computer component

   C. A Network Neighborhood component

   D. A Microsoft Exchange service

7. You can add and delete users to or from a workgroup post office using what tool?

   A. Postoffice Editor

   B. Postoffice Profiler

   C. Postoffice Manager

   D. Postoffice User Manager

8. Which of the following statements are true about a workgroup postoffice? Choose all that apply.

   A. The person who creates the postoffice is the administrator.

   B. You should have multiple postoffices in a single workgroup.

   C. The folder where the postoffice will reside must be created prior to installation.

   D. A user can have his or her Windows 95 Inbox connected to a workgroup Postoffice and an MS-Mail server simultaneously.

9. You have implemented Microsoft Exchange as the email package in a company. There are several computers that are shared by two people. As a solution, you have implemented Exchange messaging profiles so that two users sharing the same computer can both access their individual mailboxes. On Jack and Sue's computer, however, there seems to be a problem. Sue can access her email, but Jack can't. What is the potential problem?

   A. Jack has to log on to another computer to access his email.

   B. The mail server is offline.

   C. Jack's profile is not properly set up to access the mail server.

   D. Jack does not have the proper access rights to his mailbox.

10. When you set up a user to connect to a workgroup postoffice, what information do you need? Choose all that apply.

    A. Postoffice title

    B. Location of the postoffice

    C. User's name and password

    D. Administrator's name and password

Exercises

Creating a Workgroup Post Office

1. In the Windows Explorer, create a new folder called WGPO from the root of the C drive.

2. Double-click the Microsoft Mail Postoffice icon in the Control Panel.

3. Click Create a New Workgroup Postoffice and click Next.

4. Specify C:\WGPO as the location and click Next.

5. Click Next again to confirm.

6. Type in the Administrator information.

7. Click OK.

8. Read message and click OK.

Administer Your New Post Office

1. Double-click the Microsoft Mail Postoffice icon in the Control Panel.

2. Select Administer an existing Workgroup Postoffice and click Next.

3. Click Next to confirm location.

4. Type in your administrator account information and click Next.

5. Click Add User.

6. Create a second mailbox and specify all information.

7. Click OK.

8. Click Close.

Connecting to the New Workgroup Post Office

1. In the Control Panel, double-click the Mail and News icon.

2. Click Add.

11

3. Select Microsoft Mail and click Next.

4. Type in the path to your post office (for example, c;\wgpo\wgpo0000) and click Next.

5. Click the second account you created and click Next.

6. Type your password and click Next.

7. Click Next to accept the default Personal Address Book settings.

8. Click Next to accept the default Personal Information Store settings.

9. Click Finish.

Using the Client

1. Double-click the Inbox icon on the desktop.

2. Type in your password and click OK.

3. Choose Compose from the menu.

4. Click New Message.

5. Click the To button.

6. Click the administrator account and click To.

7. Click your second account and click CC.

8. Click OK.

9. Type in a subject in the subject line.

10. Type a brief message.

11. Choose File from the menu.

12. Click Send.

13. Choose Tools from the menu and click Deliver Now.

14. The sent message should appear in the Inbox. To open it, double-click it.

15. Continue to experiment until you feel comfortable using the client.

Day 12

Monitoring and Optimizing Windows 95

Optimization is the age-old battle of making our
machines run faster and better. Windows 95 handles
most aspects of optimization automatically. With this
self-tuning approach, many configuration settings are
dynamic. For the settings that are not, most of the time
the default settings are the most optimal. With certain
situations, though, you might need to change these
default settings to get Windows 95 running its best for
you. That's what this chapter covers.

Objectives

The exam objectives for this chapter are actually considered part of the troubleshooting objectives, but I feel that they are best explained separately:

- Monitor Windows 95 performance and resolve performance problems using Net Watcher and System Monitor.

- Optimize the system to use Windows 95 drivers.

- Optimize a computer for desktop performance.

- Optimize a computer for network performance.

- Optimize printing.

12.1. Monitoring Windows 95

Windows 95 comes with a tool called the *System Monitor*, which allows you to track most of the system components and any program running at the time. The System Monitor allows you to measure the use of system components to help you identify performance problems with Windows 95.

 This section covers the following exam objective: Monitor Windows 95 performance and resolve performance problems using Net Watcher and System Monitor.

The System Monitor allows you to view system components as objects. Each of these objects is called a *counter*. When you start the system monitor, you tell it which counters you want it to track.

The System Monitor is installed as one of the accessory components of Windows 95. If you did not specify that it be installed at setup, you can install it using the Add/Remove Programs option in the Control Panel. When installed, you can start the System Monitor by locating it in the System Tools menu under Accessories.

12.1.1. Specifying Counters

After you start the System Monitor, you can choose which item(s) you want to monitor. You can add item(s) by selecting Add Item under the Edit menu option (see Figure 12.1). The item(s) are separated into the following categories:

- File System
- IPX/SPX Protocol (if installed)
- Kernel
- Memory Manager
- Microsoft Client For NetWare Networks (if installed)
- Microsoft Network Client
- Microsoft Network Server
- Microsoft Network Monitor Performance Data (if installed)

Figure 12.1.

Specifying which counter(s) to monitor.

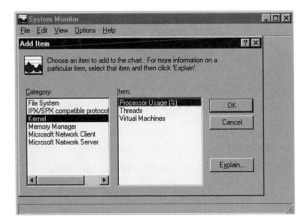

 You do not need to memorize the items in the following tables for the exam, but you should become familiar with them for troubleshooting purposes.

File System

The first category is File System. This is information about the 32-bit file system of Windows 95. You can monitor items such as number of bytes read and written. Table 12.1 gives you a brief explanation of each item that you can monitor.

Table 12.1. File System.

Item	Description
Bytes Read/Second	The number of bytes read from the file system each second
Bytes Written/Second	The number of bytes written by the file system each second
Dirty Data	The number of bytes waiting to be written to the disk
Reads/Second	The number of read operations delivered to the file system each second
Writes/Second	The number of write operations delivered to the file system each second

IPX/SPX-Compatible Protocol

You can also monitor many aspects of the IPX/SPX-compatible protocol. This can reveal much information about IPX/SPX packets, both sent and received. Table 12.2 gives you an explanation of the different items related to monitoring the protocol.

Table 12.2. IPX/SPX-Compatible Protocol.

Counter	Description
IPX Packets Lost/Second	The number of IPX packets received by the computer from an IPX network that was ignored
IPX/Packets Received/Second	The number of packets received by the computer from an IPX network each second
IPX/Packets Sent/Second	The number of packets sent by the computer to an IPX network each second
Open Sockets	The number of free sockets
Routing Table Entries	The number of IPX internetworking routes known
SAP Table Entries	The number of service advertisements known
SPX Packets Received/Second	The number of packets received by the computer from an SPX network each second
SPX Packets Sent/Second	The number of packets sent by the computer to an SPX network each second

The Kernel

You can also monitor the Windows 95 kernel and many aspects of it, including approximate processor usage, number of threads, and number of virtual machines. Table 12.3 provides a brief description of the kernel's many items that you can monitor.

Table 12.3. Kernel.

Counter	Description
Processor Usage	The approximate percentage of time the processor is busy
Threads	The current number of threads present in the system
Virtual Machines	The current number of virtual machines present in the system

Memory Manager

Monitoring the memory manager can produce numerous amounts of valuable information about how the system is running. Examples of items you can monitor include paging and working set information. See Table 12.4 for more information about the different items you can monitor relating to memory management.

Table 12.4. Memory Manager.

Counter	Description
Allocated Memory	The total amount in bytes of Other Memory and Swappable Memory. If this value is changing when there's no activity on the computer, it indicates that the disk cache is resizing itself.
Discards	The number of pages discarded from memory each second. (The pages aren't swapped to the disk because the information is already on disk.)
Disk Cache Size	The current size, in bytes, of the disk cache.
Free Memory	The total amount of free RAM in bytes. This number is not related to the Allocated Memory. If this value is zero, memory can still be allocated, depending on the free disk space available on the drive that contains the swap file.
Instance Faults	The number of instance faults each second.
Locked Memory	The amount of allocated memory that is locked.
Maximum Disk Cache Size	The largest size possible for a disk cache. This is a fixed value loaded at system startup.
Minimum Disk Cache Size	The smallest size possible for a disk cache. This is a fixed value loaded at system startup.
Other Memory	The amount of allocated memory not stored in the swap file—for example, code from Win32D DLLs and executed files, memory mapped files, nonpagable memory, and disk cache pages.
Page Faults	The number of page faults each second. An excessive number of page faults is an indication of low memory.
Page-ins	The number of pages swapped into memory each second, including pages loaded from a Win32-based executable file or memory-mapped files. Consequently, this value does not necessarily indicate low memory.
Page-outs	The number of pages swapped out of memory and written to disk each second.
Swap file Defective	The number of bytes in the swap file that are found to be physically defective on the swap medium. Because swap file frames are allocated in 4,096-byte blocks, a single damaged sector causes the whole block to be marked as defective.
Swap file In Use	The number of bytes being used in the current swap file.

continues

Table 12.4. continued

Counter	Description
Swap file Size	The size, in bytes, of the current swap file.
Swappable Memory	The number of bytes allocated from the swap file. Locked pages still count for the purpose of this metric. This includes code from 16-bit applications and DLLs, but not code from Win32 DLLs and executable files.

Microsoft Network Client for NetWare Networks

If you are connected to a NetWare network, you can also monitor aspects of the Windows 95 machine in relation to the NetWare network. See Table 12.5 for a description of the items.

Table 12.5. Microsoft Client for NetWare networks.

Counter	Description
Burst Packets Dropped	Number of burst packets from this computer lost in transit
Burst Receive Gap Time	Interpacket gap for incoming traffic, in microseconds
Burst Send Gap Time	Interpacket gap for outgoing traffic, in microseconds
Bytes In Cache	Amount of data, in bytes, currently cached by the redirector
Bytes Read Per Second	Bytes read from the redirector per second
Bytes Written Per Second	Bytes written to the redirector per second
Dirty Bytes In Cache	Amount of dirty data, in bytes, currently cached by the redirector and waiting to be written
NCP Packets Dropped	Number of regular NCP packets lost in transit
Requests Pending	Number of requests waiting to be processed by the server

Microsoft Network Client

If you are connected to a Microsoft network, whether it is a peer-to-peer network or connecting to a Windows NT domain, you can monitor networking aspects of the Windows 95 computer's performance. This includes information such as how many transactions are occurring and how much information is being transferred. Table 12.6 gives a brief description for each of the items that can be monitored.

Table 12.6. Microsoft Network client.

Counter	Description
Bytes Read/Second	The number of bytes read from the redirector each second
Bytes Written/Second	The number of bytes written to the redirector each second
Number of Nets	Number of networks currently running
Open Files	Number of open files on the network
Resources	Number of resources
Sessions	Number of sessions
Transactions/Second	The number of SMB transactions managed by the redirector each second

Microsoft Network Server

Because a Windows 95 computer can act as a server on a network, you can monitor aspects of a computer that might be acting as a server. See Table 12.7 for information about the items of a Windows 95 computer that you can monitor and that pertain to it serving information.

Table 12.7. Microsoft Network Server.

Counter	Description
Buffers	The number of buffers used by the server
Bytes Read/Sec	The total number of bytes read from disk
Bytes Written/Sec	The total number of bytes written to a disk
Bytes/Sec	The total number of bytes read from and written to a disk
Memory	The total memory used by the server
NBs	Server network buffers
Server Threads	The current number of threads used by the server

Microsoft Network Performance Data

You can also observe network performance with the System Monitor. See Table 12.8 for specific items that you can monitor. *Mediatype* can be either Ethernet or Token Ring.

Table 12.8. Microsoft Network performance data.

Counter	Description
Mediatype broadcasts/sec	Broadcast frames transmitted over the network adapter per second
Mediatype bytes/sec	Total bytes transmitted over the network adapter per second
Mediatype frames/sec	Total frames transmitted over the network adapter per second
Mediatype multicasts/sec	Total multicast frames transmitted over the network adapter per second

Each category has many counters that you can monitor. You can even monitor more than one counter at a time. In Figure 12.2, you can see that I am monitoring the usage of the processor, how many bytes of data is read per second by the file system, how much memory is allocated, and how much of the swap file is in use. This information is being viewed using a line chart. Other possible charts are bar charts (see Figure 12.3) and numeric charts (see Figure 12.4).

Figure 12.2.

Using the System Monitor to monitor information with a line chart.

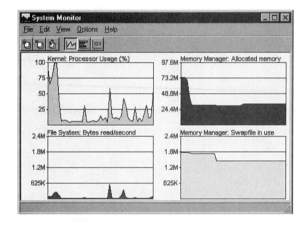

Even though you don't need to memorize each of the items that you can monitor for the exam, you should become familiar with them. At a minimum, you should at least know the categories that you can monitor. One important item to know for the exam is monitoring the kernel, specifically the processor usage.

Figure 12.3.

Using the System Monitor to monitor information with a bar chart.

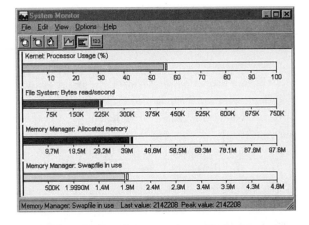

Figure 12.4.

Using the System Monitor to monitor information with a numeric chart.

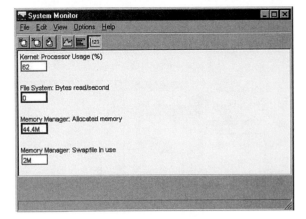

12.1.2. Monitoring the Processor

When monitoring processor usage, it can be common to see processor usage spike almost to 100 percent. Usage spikes above 80 percent are not uncommon when performing tasks such as starting an application or transferring files. As long as the processor usage drops back below 80 percent, the processor is not causing any performance bottlenecks.

When processor usage consistently maintains a level of above 80 percent, however, the processor might not be adequate for the applications being used or the tasks being accomplished on that particular computer. If this is true, the processor needs to be upgraded.

12

12.2. What Makes Windows 95 Run Fast?

In Chapter 3, "Windows 95 Blueprint: Internals and Architecture," you learned the difference between 16-bit applications and 32-bit applications. You also learned the difference between preemptive and cooperative multitasking. If you recall, each 16-bit application consists of a single thread of code to be executed, whereas a 32-bit application can be multithreaded. Even though you can run multiple applications at the same time, many of which can be sending multiple threads of code to be executed simultaneously, the processor can only handle one thread at a time. So, which threads get executed first? Which ones have to wait?

12.2.1. Preemptive and Cooperative Multitasking

As you might remember, Windows 16-bit applications all share the same memory address space and message queue, so they are cooperatively multitasked. But 32-bit programs and MS-DOS programs are preemptively multitasked because they each have their own memory address space. Confused? Take a look at Figure 12.5.

Figure 12.5.

Preemptive and cooperative multitasking with Windows 95.

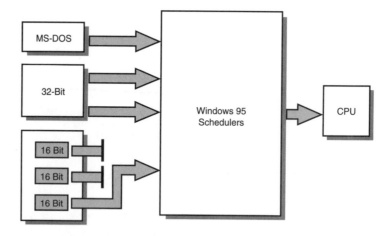

Basically, a process is a running instance of a program. Each process can consist of one or more threads of code to be executed. Each MS-DOS program has one thread per process, but 32-bit programs can have multiple threads per process. Because both MS-DOS and 32-bit programs have their own separate memory address spaces, their threads are preemptively multitasked to the scheduler.

Like MS-DOS programs, 16-bit Windows applications have a single thread per process. When you run more than one 16-bit program at a time, though, they share the same memory address space and therefore the same message queue. This means they must cooperate with each other and take turns sending threads to be processed—hence the name *cooperative multitasking*. As you can see, 32-bit applications can be a little faster to use. Another problem with cooperative multitasking is the way it worked with some of the older operating systems.

With cooperative multitasking, a thread executes until it voluntarily relinquishes the processor. The application determines how long a thread controls the processor. This means that a poorly written program can control the processor, even though it might not be actively using it, causing the other applications to hang up.

With Windows 95, all 16-bit applications are cooperatively multitasked to the scheduler. This means that Windows 95 does not allow a 16-bit application to control the processor because the operating system controls which threads will be processed.

12.2.2. How Tasks Are Scheduled

Windows 95 incorporates a scheduling process that determines which threads have use of the processor. Windows 95 actually has two schedulers, the primary and secondary schedulers. These schedulers determine which threads will be executed based upon their priority.

All threads are assigned a base priority. The thread with the highest priority gets use of the processor. Thirty-two priorities can be assigned (see Figure 12.6). Typically, user applications and noncritical system functions are assigned a priority between 0 and 15, whereas critical system functions are given a higher priority ranging from 16 to 32. Most user applications have threads that begin with a base priority of 7. A thread's base priority can be adjusted as much as two levels up or down to increase system performance.

Figure 12.6.
Thread priorities.

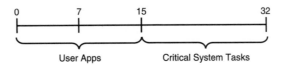

Primary Scheduler

The primary scheduler has a relatively simple job. It basically gives processor time to whichever thread has the highest priority use of the processor. If two or more threads have the same priority, it gives each thread an equal time slice of processor usage (see Figure 12.7). How long this time slice is depends on the computer's configuration.

Figure 12.7.

The primary and secondary schedulers control which thread gets processor time.

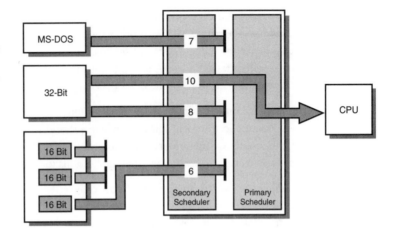

Secondary Scheduler

The secondary scheduler's job is a little more complicated. It constantly evaluates the priority of threads. Upon evaluation, it can increase or decrease the priority of threads to increase system performance. Here are the different reasons why it might dynamically increase or decrease a thread's priority:

- Threads that are waiting for user input (such as the window in the foreground) get a priority increase to make the system more responsive to the user.
- Threads that have been voluntarily waiting get a priority increase.
- Compute-bound threads (such as a spreadsheet calculation) get their priorities lowered.
- All threads periodically get a priority increase to keep the lower-priority threads from holding on to shared resources that a higher-priority thread might need.

Priority Inheritance Boosting

Another feature of the secondary scheduler is priority inheritance boosting. If a low-priority thread is using a resource that a higher-priority thread needs, it can block that higher-priority thread from being processed and possibly lock the system up. With priority inheritance boosting, this problem is prevented.

If this problem occurs, the secondary scheduler raises the priority of the lower priority thread to match that of the higher-priority thread. With both threads at the same priority, the primary scheduler gives each thread an equal time slice. As soon as the thread releases the resource, its priority is then lowered to its original priority, allowing the original higher-priority thread to be processed.

12.3. Optimizing the Desktop

You can optimize Windows 95's performance as a desktop machine in many ways. Windows 95 also tunes itself in many ways without your intervention. This self-tuning approach can be seen through self-adjusting cache sizes, driver optimization, and other aspects.

One of the most important things that you can do to optimize the performance of your Windows 95 computer is to reduce, if not eliminate, the use of older MS-DOS–based real-mode drivers. This is particularly a concern when upgrading from Windows 3.1.

 This section covers the following exam objective: Optimize the system to use Windows 95 drivers.

Windows 95 comes with protected-mode, 32-bit drivers for most devices. Examples of these are network cards, video cards, and CD-ROMs. You can understand why protected-mode drivers are better than real-mode drivers with a basic understanding of what happens when real-mode drivers are used.

After Windows 95 starts up, it switches to protected mode. Any time a real-mode driver is used, it has to switch from protected mode to virtual 8088 mode. This virtual 8088 mode is a simulation of an older 8088 computer so that the real-mode driver can be used. This switch can degrade system performance greatly and must be accomplished several times during a single I/O operation. You must also consider that real-mode drivers are not designed with preemptive multitasking in mind and can greatly reduce the amount of multitasking that you could accomplish if you use protected-mode drivers. With these problems, the solution is simple: Use protected-mode drivers whenever you possibly can.

Most other aspects of performance can be adjusted from the System applet of the Control Panel. In Figure 12.8, you see the Performance tab of the System applet. It reports performance problems, if any. If performance issues need to be resolved, it lists them along with the option to view the details of each issue. You can optimize the file system, graphics, and virtual memory settings of Windows 95 using the buttons located here.

Figure 12.8.

The Performance tab of the System applet.

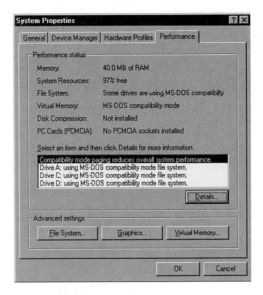

12.3.1. File System

Under the File System option, you can control optimization of the hard disks and CD-ROMs. I will further discuss some troubleshooting options in the next chapter.

Hard Disk

At the Hard Disk tab in the File System Properties dialog box, you can modify the role of the computer and read-ahead optimization (see Figure 12.9). The role of the computer is how the computer is used in most situations. The typical roles control how much RAM is reserved for caching and how often the information stored in the cache is flushed. The three roles to choose from are

- **Desktop Computer**—This configuration is for a normal computer acting primarily as a network client or an isolated computer with no networking capabilities. This configuration should be used if more than the minimum required amount of RAM is used and when the computer is not running on battery power.

- **Mobile or Docking System**—Use this configuration when a computer has very little RAM or when a computer uses battery power. This configuration flushes the cache more frequently.

- **Network Server**—This configuration is for a computer used primarily as a peer server for file and print sharing, is adequate for systems used in this role, and assumes that the computer has adequate RAM. This configuration is best for file and print sharing because it is optimized for high disk activity.

Figure 12.9.

File System Optimization for the local hard disk.

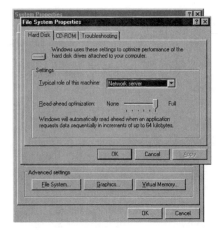

This section covers the following exam objectives:
- Optimize a computer for desktop performance.
- Optimize a computer for network performance.

Read-ahead optimization increases the speed at which information can be accessed from the hard disk. When Windows 95 reads information from the hard disk that is requested, it reads further, gathering information that wasn't requested, assuming that you might request it in the near future. This information is stored in RAM where it can be accessed much faster than if Windows 95 had to go back to the hard disk and find it.

You can adjust how far ahead Windows 95 reads the disk. You can set it so that it doesn't read ahead or so that it reads all the way up to 64K.

Because this built-in function performs the same function as older disk caching programs such as SmartDrive, you should remove any reference to such programs in your AUTOEXEC.BAT and CONFIG.SYS (if you upgraded to Windows 95). Also, if you have used SHARE.EXE in the past, you should also remove any reference to this program.

CD-ROM

Because the file system used for CD-ROMs is different from that of hard disks, performance and caching are handled separately from that of the hard disk. The CD-ROM tab of the File System Properties dialog box allows you to modify caching of CD-ROM information (see Figure 12.10).

Figure 12.10.

CD-ROM opti-mization settings.

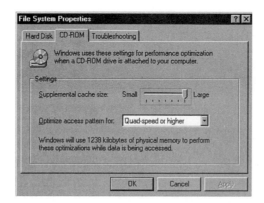

You cannot page the cache of the hard disk read-ahead optimization out of memory. Think about that concept. If information were read from the hard disk, cached into memory (to speed up access to the information), and then paged *back* to the hard disk, what would be the point of reading ahead in the first place?

The information that is cached from a CD-ROM *can* be paged out of memory (to the hard disk). This might seem like a "What's the point?" issue, but it is still faster to read cached information from a hard disk than to read the same information from a CD-ROM because hard disks are still faster than CD-ROMs. The recommended settings for cache sizes are in Table 12.9.

Table 12.9. Recommended CD-ROM cache size.

RAM Installed	Optimize Setting	Cache Size
8MB or less	Single Speed	64K
8MB to 12MB	Double Speed	626K
12MB or more	Quad Speed or higher	1238K

12.3.2. Graphics

The Graphics option from the Performance tab of the System applet allows you to modify graphics acceleration features. If your graphics adapter does not support full functionality, it can cause a wide range of problems, including anything from funny things on the screen, such as wavy lines, to system failure. You can disable certain functions by moving the slider button (see Figure 12.11).

You can set the slider to one of four positions. The first position, closest to None (to the far left), removes all driver acceleration support. This option adds `SafeMode=2` line in the [Windows] section of the `WIN.INI`.

Figure 12.11.

Modifying the graph-ics functionality.

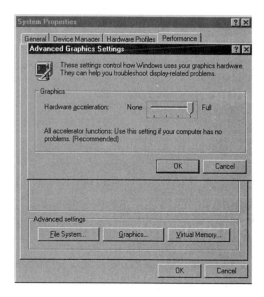

The second position from the left is for less severe errors. These errors usually pop up on your screen and are produced from Windows 95 or an application that you might be running. This adds SwCursor=1 and MMIO=0 to the [Display] section of the SYSTEM.INI. Also it adds SafeMode=1 to the [Windows] section of WIN.INI.

You can use the third position from the left to correct problems with the mouse pointer. This disables hardware cursor support and adds SwCursor=1 to the [Display] section of SYSTEM.INI.

The last and default setting (far right) gives full functionality of acceleration features.

As you can see, this is a perfect example of how Windows 95 uses the older WIN.INI and SYSTEM.INI files for compatibility.

12

Don't worry about remembering all of the WIN.INI settings just mentioned. I've provided you with these settings just for your information and to demonstrate how Windows 95 still uses the WIN.INI for backward compatibility. These settings are most commonly referred to as Full, Most, Basic, and None.

12.3.3. Virtual Memory

The Virtual Memory button lets you modify the settings for the Windows 95 swap file (`WIN386.SWP`). If you recall from Chapter 3, a swap file is created on the hard disk for paging of information back and forth from RAM to the hard disk.

With Windows 3.*x*, you could modify the settings of the swap file to increase performance; but with Windows 95, the swap file is dynamic so that it can grow or shrink to fit the need of the system based on the amount of free hard disk space that is available.

> If the disk that contains the swap file does not have enough free space to allow it to grow as needed, you might notice slower performance, recognize excessive paging, and receive Out of Memory errors. This might pop up in a troubleshooting question.

By default, the Windows 95 swap file is a temporary file, but you can make it permanent. If you make the swap file permanent, it cannot shrink below the size that you have specified, but it can grow in size.

To define the size of the swap file manually, click the Virtual Memory button under the Performance tab of the System applet. In Figure 12.12, you see that you can specify the disk location and the minimum and maximum sizes of the swap file. Additionally, you can even disable using a swap file completely.

Figure 12.12.

Modifying the swap file settings.

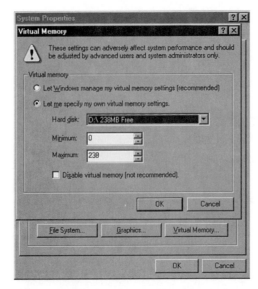

Warning Disabling the use of virtual memory can have disastrous results. Your computer might not work properly or even not at all. After disabling it, you might not be able to restart the computer. You should disable the use of virtual memory only if instructed by a technical support representative.

12.4. Optimizing the Network

Like many other aspects of Windows 95, networking is predominately self-tuning. Here are a few ideas to help you ensure Windows 95's networking performance is at its optimum:

- If the computer will be used as a peer server, ensure that its role is set to Network Server in the System option of the Control Panel as described earlier.

- Use a protected-mode, 32-bit client. For example, use the Microsoft Client for NetWare networks or the Novell 32-bit client rather than Novell VLM or NETX versions of the NetWare client. These versions are 16-bit, real-mode drivers and cannot take advantage of caching and other automatic tuning features.

- If an older network adapter is installed, use the driver that comes with Windows 95. The Windows 95 drivers conform to NDIS 2.x or later, and usually NDIS 3.1. These drivers are smaller and faster. If the network adapter is newer, most likely, the NDIS driver comes with the adapter from the manufacturer.

- When choosing a network adapter driver, if you have a choice between ODI (open datalink interface) created by Novell or NDIS drivers, choose NDIS if you are running a Microsoft client (even the Microsoft Client for NetWare). If you are using Novell client, Novell recommends the ODI driver.

- Remove unnecessary protocols.

12

12.5. Optimizing the Print Process

How you optimize printing varies from computer to computer when dealing with different printing situations. The main way you optimize printing with Windows 95 is how you set spooling and the data format.

This section covers the following exam objective: Optimize printing.

Printing occurs differently when you print to a printer that is attached to a Windows 95 computer and when you print to a printer across a network. Even then, printing varies depending on what operating system the server has installed.

If you recall from Chapter 9, "Installing and Configuring Printers," the print job is spooled in EMF format, rendered in printer-specific format, and sent to the printer. Where this rendering takes place depends on the operating system of the server.

If the server's operating system is Windows 95, the rendering from EMF format to the printer-specific format happens on the server. This frees the client computer from this task and thus gives the user of the client computer a better performance.

If the operating system of the server is Windows NT or NetWare, the rendering from EMF to the printer-specific format happens on the client computer. Even though the user still regains control of the application relatively quickly, the rendering is still a task that is being handled in the background.

Another aspect of optimization is the battle of disk space versus return control of application. To return the user control of the application quickly, the print job is spooled to the hard disk. If the computer is low on disk space, you might have to cut down the amount of spooling; but reducing the spooling increases the amount of time it takes for the user to regain control of the application after printing a document. These are all factors you need to take into consideration when you decide how to optimize your printing.

To optimize the printing, follow these steps:

1. Open the printer folder.
2. Right-click the printer you want to modify.
3. Click Properties.
4. Click the Details tab.
5. Click the Spool Settings button.
6. Click Spool Print Jobs so the program finishes printing faster.

You have two options from which to choose, depending on your particular situation and how printing occurs on a regular basis. Take into consideration whether the printer is local or on the network. If it is on the network, what operating system does the server have? Lastly, if the user prints to several printers, which printer is printed to the most? In Figure 12.13, you see the following options:

- **Start printing after last page is spooled**—This returns control of the application to the user faster at the cost of needing additional disk space. Additionally, from start to finish, the total time that it takes to print the print job takes longer when this option is used. This decreases the amount of work that the computer has to perform at one time by waiting until the entire print job is in EMF format (spooled to disk) before the rendering from EMF to printer-specific format takes place.

- **Start printing after first page is spooled**—This option decreases the total print time and decreases the amount of disk space required by spooling in EMF format and rendering to printer-specific format simultaneously. The downside to this option is that the control of the application is not returned to the user as quickly.

Figure 12.13.

Printer Spool Settings.

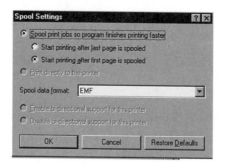

12

Lab

The lab consists of review questions pertaining to this chapter and provides an opportunity to apply the knowledge that you've learned. Answers can be found in Appendix B, "Answers to Review Questions."

Questions

1. When a low-priority thread is tying up a resource that a higher-priority thread needs, the lower thread's priority is increased to match that of the higher thread. This allows each to have an equal time slice until the resource is relinquished. What is this process called?

   A. Priority allocation

   B. Thread equalization

   C. Priority-inheritance boosting

   D. Priority promotion

2. What is the name of the memory swap file in Windows 95?

   A. `MEMORY.SWP`

   B. `386SPART.PAR`

   C. `MEM386.SWP`

   D. `WIN386.SWP`

3. By default, Windows 95 increases and decreases the size of the memory swap file dynamically. True or False?

   A. True

   B. False

4. You are installing a Windows 95 computer on a NetWare network. Of the following clients, which would have optimal performance?

   A. Microsoft Client for NetWare networks

   B. NetWare VLM

   C. NetWare NETX

5. Which of the following applications are multithreaded applications? Choose all that apply.

   A. MS-DOS

   B. Windows 16-bit

   C. Windows 32-bit

6. Which applications are preemptively multitasked in Windows 95? Choose all that apply.

   A. MS-DOS

   B. Windows 16-bit

   C. Windows 32-bit

7. At what percentage of sustained processor utilization should the upgrade of the processor be considered?

   A. 70%

   B. 75%

   C. 80%

   D. 85%

8. You have a computer on your network that is low on disk space. It has a printer attached, and you want to set the printer settings at the optimal setting. Which of the two settings would you choose?

   A. Start printing after the last page has spooled.

   B. Start printing after the first page has spooled.

12

Exercises

Installing the System Monitor

In this exercise, you will install the System Monitor if it is not already installed.

1. If you do not have the System Monitor installed, proceed to the next step. If you do, proceed to Exercise 12.2.

2. To install the System Monitor, click the Add/Remove Programs icon in the Control Panel.

3. Select the Windows Setup tab.

4. Click the word (not the check mark box) Accessories and click the Details button.

5. Scroll down until you see System Monitor.

6. Place a check in the check mark box and click OK.

7. Click OK in the Add/Remove Programs box.

Monitoring the Processor

In this exercise, you will monitor processor utilization while running a complex screen saver. This will prepare you for the exam by meeting the following exam objective: Monitor Windows 95 performance and resolve performance problems using Net Watcher and System Monitor.

1. Right-click a blank area of the desktop.

2. Select Properties.

3. Select the Screen Saver tab.

4. Under the list of screen savers, see if 3Dflower (or 3D Flower Box) is an option.

5. If it isn't, you can download the components from www.bartonet.com/ty95/exercise and follow the instructions on the site.

6. Copy the 3dflower.scr, Opengl32.dll, and Glu32.dll files to your Windows 95 System directory (default location c:\windows\system).

7. If you are prompted that the file already exists, *do not overwrite*. Some OEM implementations of OSR2 come with these files already. *Do not overwrite* them.

8. Choose Start, Programs, Accessories, System Tools, System Monitor.

9. Click Edit from the menu and then click Add Item.

10. Click Kernel and then click Processor Usage.

11. Click OK.

12. Notice how the monitor shows processor utilization as you move the mouse and switch between windows.

13. Right-click a blank area of the desktop.

14. Select Properties.

15. Select the Screen Saver tab.

16. Under the list of screen savers, choose 3Dflower (or 3D Flower Box) and then click the Preview button.

17. Preview the screen saver for about 10 seconds.

18. Move the mouse to disengage the screen saver and then click Cancel in the Display Properties box.

19. View the System Monitor. Notice how the processor utilization was increased by the calculations needed to produce the 3D images.

20. Also notice that after you canceled from the display properties, the processor utilization decreased dramatically.

Day 13

Troubleshooting
Windows 95

Troubleshooting is an art. For the most part, troubleshooting is one of those things that is learned over time
with experience. Humans are creatures of habit. Knowing
that, you can surmise that humans learn things best
through repetition and experience. Troubleshooting is
best learned by using a product firsthand and seeing
things that can go wrong with it. You should spend some
time in a chair, sitting behind the monitor, using
Windows 95. Take what you learn in this chapter and
apply it. It will prove invaluable come test time.

In this chapter, I will discuss some tools and techniques
to troubleshooting Windows 95 problems that might not
have been discussed in other chapters. On the other
hand, you might find some information here that was
already covered in other chapters. This is mainly to cover
the information a little more in depth.

Objectives

Here are the Microsoft exam objectives for the topic of troubleshooting. Although many of these objectives might have been covered in other chapters, it is important to know the troubleshooting information that you will be required to know for the exam:

- Diagnose and resolve installation failures
- Diagnose and resolve boot process failures
- Diagnose and resolve file system problems
- Diagnose and resolve printing problems
- Diagnose and resolve connectivity problems
- Using Net Watcher
- Using Troubleshooting Wizards
- Diagnose and resolve hardware device and device driver problems
- Using MSD

13.1. Troubleshooting Methodology

You should develop a method for handling troubleshooting situations. After you find a method that works, stick to it. Creating a method is not as easy as it sounds, however. Therefore, here are some guidelines to help you out.

These guidelines are time-tested and work for most situations. Using these guidelines will not only help you determine your own method, but they will help you learn troubleshooting should you not be experienced at it already.

13.1.1. Gathering the Facts

The first step to troubleshooting is gathering the facts. You can absolutely not troubleshoot a situation without having some facts. The more facts you have, the quicker and easier you can solve the problem. Keep in mind that a fact has to be something that can be verified as true. Many times administrators let false guesses (fiction) lead them down a time-consuming and dead-end road.

Part of those facts are symptoms. By analyzing the symptoms, you can get closer to the problem that might be causing them. After time in the seat with a product, most administrators can solve a problem solely by the symptoms. The infamous saying, "I've seen this before," can be invaluable when troubleshooting.

Here are just a few of the endless questions you can ask yourself during the information gathering phase of your troubleshooting process. The more facts that you can come up with, the closer you will be to solving the problem:

- **Has it ever worked?**—I know you think I'm joking, but numerous help desks spend countless hours on the phone trying to solve a problem that they think (because the user hasn't informed them) has worked at some time. If it has never worked, try starting over (installation, process, and so on).

- **What changed since the last time it worked?**—A lot of times, you can solve problems simply by asking that question. Quite possibly, whatever was changed might have caused the problem. The fix is usually easy here: change it back.

- **Was anything installed/uninstalled?**—Installations can sometimes have detrimental effects on a computer, especially if the installation replaces that important DLL file to an older version. Equally as damaging is an uninstall that takes away files that other programs, especially the operating system, need.

- **Is all the hardware working properly?**—No one likes a hardware failure, but it does happen. Hardware doesn't live forever, so expect hardware failures. Having a few extras on hand doesn't hurt anything; and if you think it hurts your wallet, think of how much it will cost you to have a computer down until you can get a replacement part.

- **Who touched it last?**—Sounds like a kid's saying, but this can be invaluable. Usually finding the last people to have something to do with the computer can save you time. They know what they have done to it. This is better than you trying to guess what they did. Let's face it, every network has at least one power user or administrator that knows just enough to be dangerous. Although he is still learning and can be an asset, he is still at the stage that he can also be a liability.

13.1.2. Formulating a Hypothesis

Troubleshooting is as much a science as it is an art. Any good scientist knows that before she can prove anything, she must formulate a hypothesis. My dictionary defines a *hypothesis* as "a theory that explains a set of facts and can be tested by further examination."

You can see that gathering the facts in the previous step is needed before you can hypothesize why the problem occurred. With further investigation of the hypothesis, you can come to a conclusion as how to repair the problem.

This step is nothing more than taking the facts and making an educated guess as to what caused the problem. The further testing comes next.

13.1.3. Testing and Documenting

The first part of this two-step phase is testing. Testing is nothing more than taking your educated guess (hypothesis) and seeing if it is correct. Your hypothesis is your judgment, based on the available evidence, of why the problem occurred. One way of testing is either reversing or attempting to repair the cause of the problem and then viewing the outcome.

Reversing is nothing more than undoing what might have caused the problem. If it was a setting of a configuration, set it back the way it was. If it was the installation of something, uninstall it. *Reversing* is nothing more than putting the computer back to a previous state (before the problem occurred).

13

Because reversing is not always feasible (uninstallation of a program you need), repairing the problem is usually more viable. This might be installing the latest patch from the manufacturer, for example. *Repairing* is not changing the computer back to a previous state; it is the negation of the cause's negative effects.

During testing, you can change several things that might not resolve the problem. Be careful of domino situations. These are situations where one thing can have an effect on another, which could have effect on another, and so on. In most cases, when you are done testing (you've solved the problem), you need to put the things that had nothing to do with the problem back the way they were. Nothing is worse than solving one problem and creating another.

The second part of this step is documenting, which is something that most computer professionals hate but is a necessary evil. Documentation can help in several ways.

First of all, if you document what you do to the machine, you have a better understanding of this problem should it arise again. Also, it can help others resolve a similar conflict if they have access to the documentation but do not have access to you. Lastly, it can help you identify recurring problems with a particular computer if you have an idea what has gone wrong with it in the past.

13.2. Troubleshooting Setup

No one likes to have problems during the setup of Windows 95, but the possibility of encountering a problem is there. Some examples of problems include the computer locking up during setup, program groups not converting if you are migrating from Windows 3.*x*, or other problems that might cause you to reinstall Windows 95 completely.

13.2.1. Setup Failure

During Windows 95 setup, two files are created that store information about the progress of the installation. These two files, DETLOG.TXT and SETUPLOG.TXT, are created to assist you during installation problems. A third file, DETCRASH.LOG, is created to keep the setup process moving along.

This section covers the following exam objective: Diagnosing and resolving installation failures.

Detection Log

The detection log is a record of hardware devices that Setup finds during the hardware detection process. It is a text file that you can view using any text editor and is located on the root of the C drive. By looking at the contents of the detection log, you can determine whether Windows 95 is detecting a piece of hardware that you have or not. Take a look at this small example of what you might find in the detection log:

```
Checking for: Advanced Power Management Support
Checking for: Dockable Portable
Checking for: PS/2 Style Mouse
Detected: *PNP0F0C\0000 = [10] PS/2 Style Mouse
    IRQ=12
    IO=310-311
```

As you can see, Setup was searching for advanced power management support and whether the computer is a dockable portable computer. It was unsuccessful in finding support for those two, but after it searched for a PS/2 style mouse, it found one. It also determined the IRQ and I/O Port address for the mouse.

Detection Crash Log

If the detection process causes the system to stop responding, a binary file called DETCRASH.LOG is created in the root directory. After the system does stop responding, you should turn the computer completely off and restart it. Setup automatically restarts after the power is restored to the computer. The DETCRASH.LOG is used in conjunction with the setup log to keep Setup from crashing twice because of the same reason.

Setup Log

The setup log (SETUPLOG.TXT), also created in the root directory, is a record of events that took place during setup including both successful and failure events. When power has been turned off and then back on, Setup reviews the SETUPLOG.TXT and DETCRASH.LOG files to see what caused the installation to fail. It skips whatever caused the system to crash and proceeds with the next step of installation. This, in essence, keeps Setup from crashing twice because of the same problem.

13

| Warning | Do not press Ctrl+Alt+Del to perform a warm boot if Setup crashes. You should turn off the computer and turn it back on. This resets any necessary ISA bus initializations. |

Even though the system might crash several times, you should continue to restart the machine. Setup continues to move past each problem that might have caused the computer to crash.

> **Warning**
>
> During your troubleshooting of setup, be sure not to delete any of these files. Deletion of these files only defeats the purpose for which they were created. For example, if you delete the DETCRASH.LOG file, Windows 95 Setup cannot recognize what caused the previous crash.

13.2.2. Converting Windows 3.*x* Program Groups

If you are upgrading Windows 3.*x* to Windows 95, you might want your Windows 3.*x* program groups to be converted to Windows program folders and shortcuts on the Start menu. If you install Windows 95 into the same directory where Windows 3.*x* resides, Setup converts the program groups by default. If you install Windows 95 into a different directory or if you have problems during setup that prevented the groups from being converted, you can convert them after installation is complete.

Setup runs a program, GRPCONV.EXE, to convert the program groups over. GRPCONV searches all .GRP files listed in the PROGMAN.INI file and then creates shortcuts for those entries in the Applications folder. GRPCONV also searches the SETUP.INI file and creates shortcuts for any items currently specified in the Windows Setup tab in Add/Remove Programs.

GRPCONV actually has two capabilities. The first is obvious—to convert Windows 3.*x* groups to folders and shortcuts on the Windows 95 Start menu. The second capability is that it can recreate the default folders that Windows 95 creates during setup.

> **Note**
>
> Program groups files (ones with GRP extension) are unique to Windows 3.*x*. If you install an application after Windows 95 is installed, no .GRP file or entry in the PROGMAN.INI is created. Using GRPCONV after Windows 95 is installed only recreates the Windows 3.*x* groups that existed before Windows 95 was installed.

To recreate the default Windows 95 folders, follow these steps:

1. In the Windows directory, rename SETUP.OLD to SETUP.INI.

2. From the Start button, choose Run.

3. Type **GRPCONV /s** and press Enter.

You see a dialog box that gives you the status of the rebuilding process (see Figure 13.1). After the folders are recreated, you are returned to the desktop.

Figure 13.1.

Recreating the Windows 95 default menu folders.

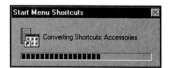

To convert Windows 3.*x* program groups manually, follow these steps:

1. From the Start button, choose Run.

2. Type **GRPCONV /m** and press Enter.

3. You are presented with a dialog box prompting you to select the group you want to convert (see Figure 13.2). Select the group and click Open.

4. You are then prompted whether you are sure that you want to convert the group, click Yes.

Only one group can be converted at a time.

Figure 13.2.

Manually converting a Windows 3.x program group using GRPCONV.

13

13.3. Troubleshooting Startup

Many things could cause Windows 95 to have problems during startup (bootup). Even though I'm sure you're eager to learn every possible reason for startup problems, you aren't required to know every reason when preparing for the exam.

One way of troubleshooting is by viewing the BOOTLOG.TXT file. It is in the root directory of the hard disk that contains a record of the boot process. This hidden, system file contains information helpful in diagnosing setup and boot time errors.

Let's take a look at some specific problems that you might not encounter in the field, but also on the exam.

 This section covers the following exam objective: Diagnosing and resolving boot process failures.

13.3.1. Registry Files Missing

Of the two Windows 95 Registry files, USER.DAT and SYSTEM.DAT, the SYSTEM.DAT file is required for Windows 95 to be operational. All of the Registry files are backed up as files with the extension DA0. If the SYSTEM.DAT is missing, one of two things happens:

- The SYSTEM.DAT is automatically replaced with the SYSTEM.DA0.
- Windows 95 starts in Safe Mode and displays a Registry error. By clicking the Restore From Backup and Restart button, Windows 95 replaces both the SYSTEM.DAT and USER.DAT with the DA0 versions.

If both the SYSTEM.DAT and the SYSTEM.DA0 files are missing, Windows 95 starts in Safe Mode and displays the Registry error message as discussed in the preceding, but clicking the button doesn't get you anywhere. If you encounter this problem, you must restore a copy of the SYSTEM.DAT from backup (backup tape and the like).

13.3.2. Wrong Applications Run at Startup

When you start Windows 95, you might have applications automatically start when they aren't supposed to. Two reasons could explain this occurrence.

One reason can be shortcuts to programs in the Windows Startup folder. To repair this problem, simply open the Windows Start Menu\Programs\Startup folder in the Explorer and delete the program shortcuts for the programs that you do not want to start. If you have profiles enabled, you have to go to the Windows\Profiles*Username*\Start Menu\Programs\Startup folder to remove the unwanted shortcuts. *Username* should be replaced with the logon name of the user.

If you find that no unwanted shortcuts are in the Startup folder but the program is still starting, you might have to make a Registry change. The following Registry entry is the setting that determines which folder Windows 95 uses as the Startup folder. Run the Registry Editor and find this key:

```
Hkey_Current_User\Software\Microsoft\Windows\CurrentVersion\Explorer\Shell Folders
```

The value of Startup= should be Windows\Start Menu\Programs\Startup. Substitute Windows for where you have installed Windows 95. Also, if you have profiles enabled, the path has to point to the Startup folder in your profile path.

13.3.3. Using F8 at Startup

One capability you can use is the Startup menu. This menu is available when you start your computer. To display it, press the F8 key on your keyboard as soon as you see the text, "Starting Windows 95." When the menu displays, you have the following options:

- **Normal**—Starts Windows, loading all normal startup files and Registry values.
- **Logged** (BOOTLOG.TXT)—Runs system startup creating a startup log file.
- **Safe Mode**—Starts Windows, bypassing startup files and using only basic system drivers. You can also start this option by pressing F5 or typing **win /d;m** at the command prompt.
- **Safe Mode with Network Support**—Starts Windows, bypassing startup files and using only basic system drivers, including basic networking. You can also start this option by pressing F6 or typing **win /d;n** at the command prompt.
- **Step-By-Step Confirmation**—Starts Windows, confirming startup files line by line. You can also start this option by pressing F8 when the Startup menu is displayed.
- **Command Prompt Only**—Starts the operating system with startup files and Registry, displaying only the command prompt.
- **Safe Mode Command Prompt Only**—Starts the operating system in Safe Mode and displays only the command prompt, bypassing startup files. Same as pressing Shift+F5.
- **Previous version of MS-DOS**—Starts the version of MS-DOS previously installed on this computer. You can also start this option by pressing F4. This option is only available if **BootMulti=1** in MSDOS.SYS.

13

13.3.4. Creating and Using a Startup Disk

A startup disk is used when you might have difficulty starting the Windows 95 computer. This disk contains the necessary files to boot the computer up to a command prompt. It also contains utilities that you can use for troubleshooting.

You can create a startup disk during initial setup of the Windows 95 computer. If you do not have a startup disk, you can create one by following these steps:

1. Double-click the Add/Remove Programs icon in the Control Panel.

2. Click the Startup Disk tab.

3. Insert a blank floppy and click Create Disk.

> **Warning** The files that are on a startup disk for a standard installation of Windows 95 differ from that of a startup disk for a shared installation. The shared installation startup disk contains additional utilities needed for connecting to the network and so on, whereas the standard startup disk does not.

The startup disk for a shared installation contains all the software required to connect to the network and start Windows 95. One startup disk can be used for computers with the same kinds of network adapters and settings.

For shared installations on computers with hard disks, Setup modifies the Windows 95 startup disk by changing the boot sector and copying new IO.SYS, COMMAND.COM, and MSDOS.SYS files. Table 13.1 compares the files on the different startup disks.

Table 13.1. Windows 95 startup disk files.

Standard	Shared
IO.SYS	IO.SYS
MSDOS.SYS	MSDOS.SYS
COMMAND.COM	COMMAND.COM
ATTRIB.EXE	AUTOEXEC.BAT
CHKDSK.EXE	CONFIG.SYS
DEBUG.EXE	HIMEM.SYS
DRVSPACE.BIN	IFSHLP.SYS
FDISK.EXE	NDISHLP.SYS

Standard	Shared
FORMAT.COM	NET.EXE
EBD.SYS	NET.MSG
EDIT.COM	NETH.MSG
REGEDIT.EXE	PROTMAN.DOS
SCANDISK.EXE	PROTMAN.EXE
SCANDISK.INI	PROTOCOL.INI
SYS.COM	SNAPSHOT.EXE
UNINSTAL.EXE	SYSTEM.DAT
	NDIS 2 ADAPTER DRIVER

The startup disk can help you in several troubleshooting situations. Here are a few examples:

- Repair on a faulty network setup
- Windows 95 hangs up during bootup
- Registry errors
- Boot files (IO.SYS, COMMAND.COM, and so on) missing

With the startup disk, you can boot the computer using the startup disk and then start Windows 95, replace files as necessary, and so on.

13.4. Troubleshooting File System Problems

There are several options for file system troubleshooting in the System option of the Control Panel. If you go to the Performance tab and click the File System button, you are presented with the options in Figure 13.3 under the Troubleshooting tab.

This section covers the following exam objective: Diagnosing and resolving file system problems.

13

Figure 13.3.

File System trouble-shooting options.

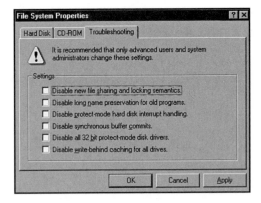

Microsoft warns that enabling any of the file system troubleshooting options seriously degrades system performance, and you should only enable these options if instructed to do so by a product support representative.

Although most of the settings deal with older hardware, drivers, and software; here are some of the common problems and settings that you might need to know.

13.4.1. File Sharing

The Disable New File Sharing and Locking Semantics setting modifies the way file sharing and locking on hard disk occurs. This pertains to whether certain programs or processes can modify files that might be open by another program or process. If you have an older program that requires the use of SHARE.EXE, you can use this option as a temporary fix until the software vendor updates the program.

13.4.2. Long File Name Preservation

Setting the Disable Long Name Preservation for Old Programs settings disables the feature of Windows 95 that preserves long file names when files are opened and then saved by an application that does not recognize long file names.

13.4.3. Write-Behind Caching

Checking the Disable Write-Behind Caching for All Drives option ensures that all data is continually flushed to the hard disk. Write-behind caching greatly improves system performance by caching information that an application wants to save and saving it when the system is less busy. If you want to ensure data is saved to the disk in situations where the data is critical, or power sources are unreliable, enable this option.

13.5. Print Troubleshooting

There are multitudes of reasons why you might come across printing problems. However, most of the reasons can be solved relatively easy. In this section, I have included a quick and easy step-by-step process to assist you in diagnosing printing problems.

 This section covers the following exam objective: Diagnosing and resolving printing problems.

If you have difficulty printing with Windows 95, follow these steps to assist you in narrowing down the problem:

1. Check cable connections and the printer port. Also ensure that the printer is online.

2. Turn off Enhanced Metafile Spooling. To do so, open the properties sheet of the printer with which you are having difficulty. Click the Details tab and then the Spool Settings button. Change the Spool data format to RAW.

3. Verify that printer settings are correct in the printer's properties sheet.

4. Verify that the correct printer driver is installed. You might want to try reinstalling the printer driver even though the correct driver might be installed. This ensures that the driver is not corrupt.

5. Verify that enough hard disk space is available to generate the print job. If spooling is enabled, the print jobs are spooled to the hard disk. Not having free disk space might cause the spooling to fail.

6. Try printing from a different program. If you can, the printing problem resides with the application. Also try printing from different types of applications. For example, attempt to print from both 16-bit and 32-bit applications. You might be able to narrow it down to a system problem that might otherwise appear as an application problem.

7. Print to a file and then copy the file to a printer port. You can specify to print to a file by changing the port for the printer to File. Windows 95 prompts you for the file name. After creating the file, go to an MS-DOS prompt and type

13

COPY *filename* **LPT1:**. Substitute *filename* for the file name that you specified and LPT1 with the port to which you have the printer attached. If this works, your problem probably resides with either the spooler or cabling. If it doesn't, the problem is usually with the driver or is application-related.

> This section covers the following exam objective: Diagnosing and resolving connectivity problems:
>
> ■ Net Watcher
>
> ■ Troubleshooting Wizards

13.6. Network Troubleshooting

Like printing, most network problems can be narrowed down by following a few simple procedures. You can do some general network troubleshooting regardless of what type of network you are connected to. Additionally, you need to be aware of some specific items when connecting to a NetWare network.

13.6.1. General Network Troubleshooting

Here are some questions to assist you in evaluating your network connectivity problems:

1. Has the computer ever successfully been connected? If so, what has changed? If any hardware has been added or changed, try going to the original configuration.

2. Has the network cable been moved or new network cable added? Check cables, connections, and terminators, if applicable.

3. Have any protocols been added, removed, or changed? Check protocol settings and compatibility with the network. For example, are you attempting to use NetBEUI on a NetWare network?

4. Are the network adapter settings correct? Ensure that the network adapter settings are correct. A very common error is a legacy network card set to use certain resources (IRQ, I/O Port, and so on), and the settings are set to different settings in Windows 95. Also, sometimes Windows 95 detects the settings incorrectly. Don't always rely on detected settings. Check the documentation for the adapter for the correct settings.

5. Are the network connections active? Many network cards have indicator lights on them to indicate network activity. If the lights show activity, the connection is active. If not, check the cabling or try a different network cable.

13.6.2. Troubleshooting NetWare Network Problems

The three major problems you might come across when connecting to NetWare networks when using the Microsoft Client for NetWare networks are:

■ **Login Script does not run**—Make sure the correct preferred server is set and that the Enable Login Script Processing is checked in the properties for the Client for Microsoft Networks.

■ **NetWare servers cannot be found**—Whenever you cannot see NetWare servers, there is a good possibility that the problem lies with the frame type that is specified in the Advanced properties of the IPX/SPX compatible protocol. Make sure that the frame type selected matches the type being used on the network. If it is set to Auto, Windows 95 might be having difficulty detecting which frame type to use. Try setting the frame type to the specific type rather than setting it to Auto.

■ **Prompted for password and NetWare password separately**—To fix this problem, make sure your Windows 95 password matches your NetWare password. To change your Windows password, use the Password option in the Control Panel. When the passwords match, you are only prompted once for a password.

13.6.3. Troubleshooting Dial-Up Network Problems

Windows 95 provides a troubleshooter for Dial-Up Networking in online Help. You can access it by choosing Start, Help, and looking under the Troubleshooting heading of the Contents. Try using this troubleshooter before trying the troubleshooting steps included in this section. After attempting to use the Troubleshooter in Help, try some of these items:

■ Verify telephone number, access codes, area code, and country code.

■ Make sure the correct server type is selected (for example, users often choose PPP but dial in to a SLIP server).

■ Ensure the client and server use the same authentication method.

■ Open the Terminal window after dialing to determine whether additional logon information is required.

13

- If you are using an external modem, check the cable and verify that it is connected correctly.
- Check the COM port configuration in Device Manager.
- Make sure compatible protocols are installed.
- Try turning off software compression.

13.7. Remote Troubleshooting

You can also use many of the utilities that you would use locally on a Windows 95 computer to troubleshoot another Windows 95 computer remotely. For you to be able to troubleshoot another Windows 95 computer remotely, the remote capabilities must be enabled on the remote computer.

13.7.1. Remote Administration

You can remotely administer a computer by right-clicking the computer in the Network Neighborhood and selecting Properties. Under the Tools tab, you will find a button titled Administer. Clicking the Administer button gives you the ability to administer the file system completely on the remote computer through your Explorer (see Figure 13.4). You can delete, create, and share folders among other things.

Figure 13.4.

Remotely administering another Windows 95 computer.

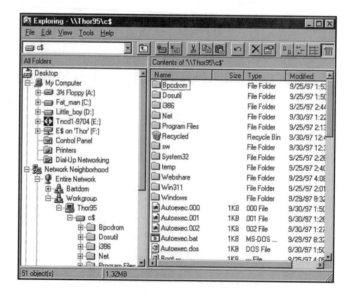

You must have remote administration enabled on the remote computer. To enable remote administration, go to the Passwords option of the Control Panel under the remote Administration tab. For more information about remote administration, see Chapter 5, "Files, Folders, and Disks."

13.7.2. System Monitor

You can also use the System Monitor (discussed in the previous chapter) to monitor another Windows 95 computer remotely. Under the File menu of the System Monitor, you have the option to connect to another computer.

To monitor another Windows 95 computer remotely, you must have user-lever security enabled and the Remote Registry service installed.

13.7.3. Net Watcher

Clicking the Net Watcher button from the Tools tab of a remote computer's properties sheet enables the Net Watcher. The Net Watcher allows you to view which users are connected to the remote, folders that are shared for network access, and files that are currently opened by remote users. For more information about the Net Watcher, see Chapter 5.

13.7.4. Remote Registry Editor

You should use other appropriate interfaces for modifying the Registry, such as the Control Panel, System Policy Editor, and so on. If it is necessary, you can edit another computer's Registry remotely. With the Remote Registry service installed on both computers, you can connect to the remote computer's Registry using the Registry Editor (REGEDIT.EXE).

After you have started the Registry Editor, click on Registry from the menu and select Connect Network Registry. You can then either type in the remote computer's NetBIOS computer name or click the Browse button to find the computer to which you would like to connect.

13

13.8. Troubleshooting Log Files

Windows 95 creates a variety of log files that can be helpful during your troubleshooting process. Here is a summary of log files that Windows 95 creates automatically:

- **BOOTLOG.TXT**—A file in the root directory of the hard disk that contains a record of the boot process. This hidden, system file contains information helpful in diagnosing setup and boot time errors.

- **DETLOG.TXT**—A file in the root directory of the hard disk that contains a list of devices detected during setup. This file is only created once and is helpful in determining hardware detection problems during the setup process.

- **SETUPLOG.TXT**—A file in the root directory of the hard disk that contains a list of messages received during setup and is used for viewing setup errors.

- **IOS.LOG**—A file in the Windows directory that contains error messages from SCSI file system drivers. This file is helpful in tracking down errors from hard disk controllers and drives. An IOS.LOG is also created if any hard drives are using MS-DOS Compatibility mode.

 Test Tip For the exam, make sure you know where the files are located and if they are readable.

13.9. Troubleshooting Resources

Many sources of information are available for you to get information about Microsoft products and Windows 95 in general. These resources include but are not limited to:

- **Troubleshooting Wizards**—Wizards built in to the Help database of Windows 95.

- **Microsoft Diagnostics (MSD)**—This DOS-based utility can be handy in gathering information about the computer.

- **TechNet**—A monthly CD-ROM that is available by subscription.

- *The Windows 95 Resource Kit*—A publication of the Microsoft Press that contains valuable information that is designed for use by IS professionals.

- **Microsoft Web Site**—A Worldwide Web Internet site that Microsoft maintains.

- **Microsoft Download Libraries**—An electronic bulletin board service maintained by Microsoft.

Information available through these different services is often duplicated in each other. For example, much of the information available on the TechNet CD-ROM is available through Microsoft's Web site.

13.9.1. Troubleshooting Wizards

When it comes to troubleshooting, many network administrators and other support personnel seem to overlook a very simple option available to them. Built in to the Windows 95 Help database are many troubleshooting wizards that walk you through important steps. They can be a valuable resource when wondering where to start or what to suspect. If you are new to troubleshooting, this is a good place to start.

To access these wizards, simply choose the Help option from the Start menu. In Figure 13.5, you will see that I used the Contents tab from the Help dialog box. After clicking Troubleshooting, it displays the many wizards. I use the Networking option for this example.

Figure 13.5.

Starting the Network Troubleshooting Wizard.

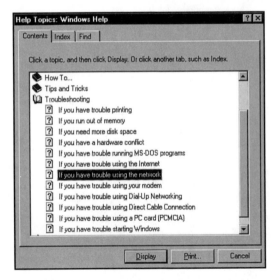

After clicking the Display button, there are many questions the wizard asks to help determine the cause of your problem (see Figure 13.6). You might go through a series of questions before it offers a solution or not.

Let's say, for example, that I am having problems sharing a folder. After clicking the question that pertains to my problem, I am prompted with a possible solution. The Network Troubleshooter asks me to verify that I have sharing enabled (see Figure 13.7). It even gives me a shortcut to display the network properties.

13

Figure 13.6.

The initial questions of the Network Troubleshooter.

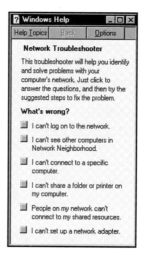

Figure 13.7.

The verification questions of the Network Troubleshooter.

I won't bore you with going through the entire process of troubleshooting a network problem using the Troubleshooting Wizard. There are many different types of questions to be answered depending on what particular problem you might be having. The best way for you to see its capabilities is to use it. As an example, the network troubleshooter might be able to help you figure out why you might not be able to browse the Network Neighborhood.

13.9.2. Microsoft Diagnostics (MSD)

Microsoft Diagnostics is an MS-DOS-based utility designed to provide you with detailed technical information about a computer's hardware and software components. This information can be helpful when you are trying to diagnose and solve problems with Microsoft products including Windows 95.

This section covers the following exam objective: Diagnosing and resolving hardware and device driver problems—MSD.

This tool is not installed by default, but is available on the Windows 95 CD-ROM under the \other\msd folder. You can copy the MSD files to your hard disk, or you can simply run it from the CD. I find it extremely helpful to have it on a floppy disk when out troubleshooting machines where I might not have access to a CD-ROM (or if that's what isn't working).

After you double-click the MSD.EXE file, you see something similar to Figure 13.8. As you can see, MSD has many buttons to choose from. Here is a brief description of each:

Figure 13.8.

Microsoft Diagnostics (MSD).

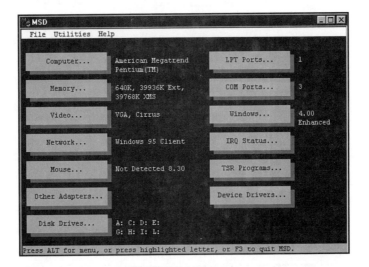

Don't be overly concerned with the following information about MSD. It is not necessary for the exam. I put it here for your benefit.

13

■ **Computer**—Displays computer manufacturer, processor type, and bus type; ROM BIOS manufacturer, version, and date; keyboard type; direct memory access (DMA) controller configuration; and math coprocessor status.

- **Memory**—Displays a map of the upper memory area (UMA)—the memory region from 640K to 1024K. Also displays DOS Protected Mode Interface (DPMI) and Extended Memory Specification (XMS) version numbers as well as available memory statistics.

- **Video**—Displays your video card manufacturer, model and type; video BIOS version and date; and current video mode.

- **Network**—Displays network-specific configuration information.

- **OS Version**—Displays the operating system version, location of MS-DOS in memory (for MS-DOS 5.0 or later only), the drive the system was booted from (for MS-DOS 4.0 or later), the current environment settings, and the path from which MSD was run.

- **Mouse**—Displays the MS-DOS mouse driver version, mouse type, mouse interrupt request line (IRQ) number, and other information specific to the configuration of the mouse.

- **Other Adapters**—Dynamically displays the game card status for up to two game devices or joysticks.

- **Disk Drives**—Displays the size and number of bytes free on local and remote drives.

- **LPT Ports**—Displays the port addresses of all installed parallel ports and dynamically displays the status each port.

- **COM Ports**—Displays the port addresses and current communications parameters of all installed serial ports and dynamically displays the status of each port.

- **Windows**—Displays the Windows version and directory location, as well as virtual device driver (VxD) file names, versions, sizes, and dates.

- **IRQ Status**—Displays the configuration of the hardware IRQs.

- **TSR Programs**—Displays the name, location in memory, and size of each program loaded in memory at the time MSD was run.

- **Device Drivers**—Displays the names of all device drivers installed at the time MSD was run.

After looking at this list of things that MSD can provide, you might be wondering if you can get the same information from the Device Manager (Control Panel—System). You can get *some* of this information from there. However, keep in mind that this tool is an MS-DOS-based utility. Where it really comes in handy is when you can't get Windows 95 up and running. You can run this utility at the command line of a bootable disk and get tons of information about the computer, all without being in Windows 95.

13.9.3. TechNet

The TechNet CD-ROM is a product of Microsoft that contains tons of technical information about Microsoft products as well as the latest drivers and service packs. TechNet is available through a subscription in which one or more CD-ROMs are received every month containing the most up-to-date technical information available.

The information on the CD-ROM is accessed through a program interface such as that in Figure 13.9.

Figure 13.9.
Microsoft TechNet.

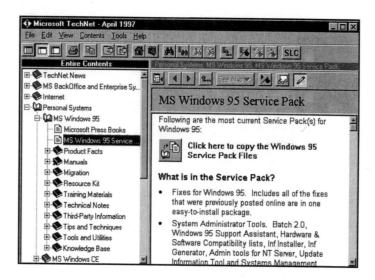

If you want further information about TechNet or want to subscribe, call 1-800-344-2121 or visit Microsoft's Web site at http://www.microsoft.com/technet.

13.9.4. The Windows 95 Resource Kit

The Resource Kit comprises a book and CD-ROM that contain valuable information and utilities helpful in the deployment, implementation, and support of Windows 95. It is available in most major bookstores. If you will be supporting Windows 95, it is a must to have as an available resource. Additionally, it makes an excellent study reference when preparing for the Windows 95 exam.

13

13.9.5. The Microsoft Web Site

The Microsoft Internet Web site located at `http://www.microsoft.com` (see Figure 13.10) is probably one of the most readily available and readily used resources that Microsoft maintains. Unlike the previous resources mentioned, the Web site is free (well, the only cost that you encounter is the cost of the Internet connection).

Figure 13.10.

Microsoft's Web site.

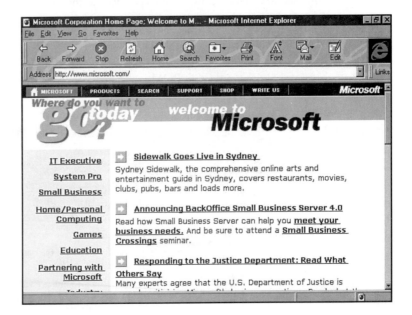

Several areas of the Web site are of helpful for you to use in your troubleshooting process. Probably the most valuable location for getting information on troubleshooting or other support topics is the Microsoft Support. Located at `http://support.microsoft.com/support` (see Figure 13.11), Microsoft Support has a search capability for finding all kinds of technical information on Windows 95 and other Microsoft products.

Figure 13.11.

Microsoft Support.

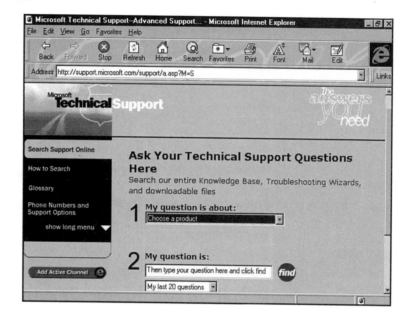

Lab

This lab consists of review questions pertaining to this chapter. Answers to the review questions can be found in Appendix B.

Questions

1. Which log files are needed for Windows 95 to automatically recover from a crash during Setup? Choose all that apply.

    A. `DETLOG.TXT`

    B. `IOS.LOG`

    C. `DETCRASH.LOG`

    D. `SETUPLOG.TXT`

2. Which of the following files contains a list of all devices detected during setup?

    A. `DETLOG.TXT`

    B. `DETECT.LOG`

    C. `DETCRASH.LOG`

    D. `SETUPLOG.TXT`

3. When Setup hangs during the detection of hardware, what should a user do?

    A. Press Ctrl+Alt+Del to reset the computer and allow Windows 95 Setup to continue.

    B. Press Ctrl+Alt+Del to reset the computer and start Windows 95 Setup with the /d switch.

    C. Turn the power off to the computer, return the power, and allow Windows 95 Setup to continue.

    D. Turn the power off to the computer, return the power, and start Windows 95 Setup with the /d switch.

4. Which of the following commands is used to rebuild the default Windows 95 program folders on the Start menu?

    A. `CONVGRP /s`

    B. `CONVGRP /m`

    C. `GRPCONV /s`

    D. `GRPCONV /m`

5. Which of the following commands is used to convert Windows 3.*x* groups to folders on the Start Menu?

    A. `CONVGRP /s`

    B. `CONVGRP /m`

    C. `GRPCONV /s`

    D. `GRPCONV /m`

6. Which of the following files contains a list of messages received during Setup?

    A. `DETLOG.TXT`

    B. `DETECT.LOG`

    C. `DETCRASH.LOG`

    D. `SETUPLOG.TXT`

13

Day 14

Practice Exam

This exam was designed to help you determine your knowledge level. You should take this exam after you have completed the rest of the chapters. Be sure, however, that you are prepared to take this exam. It is most effective the first time that you take it. After taking the exam a few times, you tend to begin to memorize the questions and answers. After memorizing the questions, you may gain a false sense of security. Therefore, wait until you think that you are prepared for the real exam before taking this one.

After taking the exam, you will find the answers at the end of this chapter. Since some questions may be related, don't check your answers until you have completed the entire exam.

Questions

1. Which of the following Windows 95 tools can you use for remote administration?

   A. System Monitor

   B. User Administrator

   C. Net Watcher

   D. Network Monitor

2. You have been asked to configure a Windows 95 computer so that it runs optimally when printing. The user wants to make sure that he regains control of the application as fast as possible so that he can accomplish other tasks while the documents are being printed. Which of the following settings will ensure this?

   A. Start printing after last page is spooled

   B. Start printing after first page is spooled

   C. Print directly to printer

   D. Enable bi-directional support

3. You are upgrading a user's computer from Windows 3.1 to Windows 95. You want the program groups from Windows 3.1 to appear as Start menu items in Windows 95. What would be the easiest way to accomplish this?

   A. Install Windows 95. Under the Taskbar settings, Start Menu Programs tab, you use the advanced option to create subfolders for each program group and create shortcuts for those programs in the appropriate folder.

   B. Install Windows 95 into a new directory and copy all files with the GRP extension from the Windows 3.1 directory to the Windows 95 directory.

   C. Run GROUPCONV and use it to manually convert each GRP file individually.

   D. Install Windows 95 into the same directory that contains Windows 3.1.

4. What subkey of the Windows 95 Registry contains hardware-specific information about your computer?

   A. HKEY_CLASSES_ROOT

   B. HKEY_CURRENT_USER

   C. HKEY_LOCAL_MACHINE

   D. HKEY_USERS

   E. HKEY_CURRENT_CONFIG

5. How many simultaneous remote connections can be made to a Windows 95 machine configured as a Dial-Up Networking server?

   A. 1

   B. 2

   C. 16

   D. 256

6. Which of the following statements is true about processes and threads?

   A. Each process contains only one thread.

   B. Each process contains at least one thread.

   C. Each thread contains only one process.

   D. Each thread contains at least one process.

7. When implementing policies on Windows 95 computers, which of the following would be the appropriate name for the policy file?

   A. USER.DAT

   B. SYSTEM.DAT

   C. CONFIG.POL

   D. SYSTEM.POL

8. Herb created a file named MONEY TRANSFERS.1997. Brian wants to use this file in his 16-bit application, but is having problems locating the file. What alias filename should Brian be looking for?

   A. MONEY~01.1997

   B. MONEY~01.119

    C. MONEYT~1.997

    D. MONEYT~1.119

9. Which of the following line protocols are supported by Windows 95 Dial-Up Networking? Choose all that apply.

    A. NetBEUI

    B. PPP

    C. SLIP

    D. TCP/IP

10. You are installing Windows 95 clients on a NetWare network. You have installed the Microsoft Client for NetWare networks and the IPX/SPX protocol on the Windows 95 machines. They cannot, however, save files on the server using long filenames. What additional step must be accomplished at the NetWare server?

    A. You must load the Long Filename Module.

    B. You must load the LFN namespace.

    C. You must load the OS/2 Module.

    D. You must load the OS/2 namespace.

11. You are running two 16-bit applications, one 32-bit application and three MS-DOS–based applications simultaneously. How many virtual machines are currently being used?

    A. 2

    B. 3

    C. 4

    D. 6

12. Which of the following types or applications are preemptively multitasked in Windows 95? Choose all that apply.

    A. MS-DOS–based applications

    B. 16-bit applications

    C. 32-bit applications

    D. OS/2 applications

14

13. Which of the following files contains specific information about the person logged on to the computer?

    A. USER.DAT

    B. USER.INI

    C. SYSTEM.DAT

    D. SYSTEM.INI

14. What network protocols are supported by Windows 95 Dial-Up Networking? Choose all that apply.

    A. NetBEUI

    B. IPX/SPX

    C. TCP/IP

    D. PPP

15. John has installed a Windows 95 computer on a NetWare network and would like to share a folder on the Windows 95 computer with others on the network. He has properly installed the Microsoft Client for NetWare networks and the IPX/SPX protocol. However, others cannot see the computer on the browse list in the Network Neighborhood. What Windows 95 setting did John possibly leave out?

    A. Enable the computer to be the browse master.

    B. Enable SAP advertising.

    C. Specify the proper domain.

    D. Specify the proper preferred server.

16. Which of the following readable files will provide useful information about the hardware that was detected during setup of Windows 95?

    A. DETLOG.TXT

    B. DETCRASH.LOG

    C. SETUPLOG.TXT

    D. HARDWARE.LOG

17. Which of the following computers *do not* meet the minimum guidelines for Windows 95? Choose all that apply.

A. 386DX, 8MB RAM, 320MB hard drive

B. 386SX, 4MB RAM, 400MB hard drive

C. 386DX2, 16MB RAM, 850MB hard drive

D. Pentium, 8MB RAM, 400MB hard drive

18. Which of the following files is the Registry comprised of? Choose all that apply.

A. SYSTEM.DAT

B. SYSTEM.INI

C. USER.DAT

D. WIN.DAT

19. On a Windows NT domain, where should the CONFIG.POL be stored for automatic downloading of policies?

A. In the Windows directory

B. In the server's Netlogon Share

C. In the user's mail directory

D. In the user's home directory

20. What are the two data formats used in printing with Windows 95? Choose two.

A. RAW

B. RAG

C. ERD

D. EMF

21. You are running an application and it abruptly stops responding. You notice, however, that you can still use the mouse. What should you do to end the application without losing data in other applications that you are running?

A. Switch to the taskbar and close the application.

B. Press CTRL, ALT, and DEL twice.

C. Press CTRL, ALT, and DEL once, select the application and click Shut Down.

D. Press CTRL, ALT, and DEL once, select the application and click End Task.

14

22. Bob administers a Windows NT and Windows 95 network, which consists of two Windows NT servers (one of which is a WINS server), and 65 Windows 95 computers. Bob has called you to consult him on some issues that he would like to take care of. Here are his items and proposed solution. Define whether the proposed solution meets all, some, or none of Bob's objectives.

    Required Result: Ease some administration of TCP/IP tasks on the network.

    Optional Result 1: Automatically assigns IP Addresses.

    Optional Result 2: Automatically configure computers to help it resolve NetBIOS computer names to IP addresses.

    Proposed Solution: Install and properly configure one of the Windows NT servers with DHCP. Under the TCP/IP settings on the Windows 95 computer, select the "Obtain an IP address automatically" option.

    Given the above scenario, which of the following statements are true?

    A. Neither the required result nor either of the optional results is met by the proposed solution.

    B. The required result is the only result met.

    C. The required result and optional result 1 are met.

    D. The required result and optional result 2 are met.

    E. The required result and both optional results are met.

23. Profiles are stored locally on the Windows 95 computer in what location?

    A. \Windows\System\Profiles

    B. \Windows\Netlogon\Profiles

    C. \Windows\Profiles

    D. \Windows\Start Menu\Profiles

24. You have installed Windows 95 onto a computer that contains a Plug and Play–compatible Network card that can use IRQs 5, 9, or 15. Additionally, there is a legacy sound card that has its jumpers set to use IRQ 9. Lastly, there is a Plug and Play video capture board that can use IRQ 3, 5, or 10. With this configuration, which of these IRQs will be assigned first?

    A. 3

    B. 5

C. 9

D. 10

E. 15

25. Scandisk CANNOT fix errors on which of the following types of drives or disks? Choose all that apply.

A. CD-ROM drives

B. floppy disks

C. hard disks

D. network drives

E. RAM drives

26. Windows 95 allocates 4GB of virtual memory for each process. In what memory range do Ring 0 components reside?

A. 3GB – 4GB

B. 2GB – 3GB

C. 4MB – 2GB

D. 0 – 4MB

27. Windows 95 allocates 4GB of virtual memory for each process. In what memory range do Windows 32-bit applications reside?

A. 3GB – 4GB

B. 2GB – 3GB

C. 4MB – 2GB

D. 0 – 4MB

28. Jack has configured Windows 95 computers on his network to use policies using the Policy Editor. He has saved the policy file to the right location and used the proper filename. The policies seem to work for users in which Jack set up based upon their user names. The policies, however, aren't working for users in which he specified using based upon group membership. What step did Jack forget?

A. Install the policy file on each Windows 95 computer.

B. Install the GROUPPOL.DLL on each Windows 95 computer.

14

    C. Create both a user-based policy for each user including the group-based policy.

    D. Create only group-based policies for all users.

29. When using policies on a NetWare network, where should the `CONFIG.POL` file be located?

    A. user home directory

    B. `NETLOGON` share

    C. user mail directory

    D. sys\public

30. Michelle wants to share her printer out for others to use on her network. She has installed File and Print Sharing for Microsoft Networks on her Windows 95 computer. However, she wants to use User-level security so that she can control who has access to her printer without using passwords. Which of the following are also needed to implement this type of security?

    A. Windows NT server

    B. Novell NetWare

    C. Another Windows 95 computer

    D. Nothing

31. A process is comprised of a runnable program, a memory address space, system resources and _____.

    A. a single thread

    B. at least one thread

    C. two or more threads

    D. multiple threads

32. You seem to be having problems saving a file. After checking the drive, you discover that you have several hundred megabytes of free disk space, more than enough to save the file. Additionally, there are only 315 files stored in the root directory. What is the possible cause of this problem?

    A. The filename is too long.

    B. The disk is write-protected.

C. Because of the use of long-filenames, and too many files in the root directory, you have reached the 512 limit.

D. Incompatible disk drivers.

33. Which of the following programs can be used to directly edit the Registry?

A. Regedit.exe

B. Regedt32.exe

C. Edit.com

D. Poledit.exe

34. During the setup of a Windows 95 machine, the machine stopped responding during the hardware detection phase. Before restarting setup, which of the following files should you delete? Choose all that apply.

A. `SETUPLOG.TXT`

B. `DETLOG.TXT`

C. `DETCRASH.LOG`

D. None

35. During a Windows 95 setup, a computer stops responding before it gets to the hardware detection phase. Which of the following files could be used for troubleshooting why the machine may have stopped responding?

A. `SETUPLOG.TXT`

B. `DETLOG.TXT`

C. `DETCRASH.LOG`

D. None

36. You commonly use an HP LaserJet printer connected to a Windows NT server from your Windows 95 computer. It works fine when printing from Windows 16-bit and 32-bit programs. However, it doesn't seem to work with MS-DOS–based applications. What is the probable solution?

A. Capture a printer port.

B. Save the file and copy it to the printer port.

C. Make sure that you have the proper printer drivers installed.

D. Make sure all other programs are closed.

14

37. You have a network that consists of three Windows NT servers, two UNIX-based workstations, and one Novell NetWare server. What would be the appropriate protocol(s) to use on your network (and install in Windows 95)? Choose all that apply.

    A. NetBEUI

    B. IPX/SPX

    C. TCP/IP

    D. DLC

38. Which of the following Registry files will be copied to the user's profile folder? Choose all that apply.

    A. SYSTEM.DAT

    B. USER.DAT

    C. SYSTEM.DA0

    D. USER.DA0

39. You are using a Windows 95 computer on a NetWare network. You have the Client for NetWare Networks properly installed. Additionally you have the IPX/SPX protocol installed. However, you seem to be having problems seeing the NetWare server in the Network Neighborhood. You have verified that other computers can see the server. Which of the following could be the possible problem?

    A. Wrong workgroup specified.

    B. You need File and Print Sharing for NetWare Networks installed.

    C. Wrong Frame Type specified.

    D. NetBEUI is not installed.

40. When connecting to a NetWare 3.12 server, which of the following is the proper way to specify the UNC name?

    A. \\servername\sharename

    B. \\servername\directory

    C. \\servername\volumename

    D. \\volumename\directory

41. What type of docking requires a laptop to be in sleep (or suspend) mode?

  A. Hot Docking

  B. Warm Docking

  C. Cold Docking

  D. None

42. Which of the following protocols allows dial-up networking to use the Internet as a private LAN?

  A. PPTP

  B. PPP

  C. SLIP

  D. TCP/IP

43. What is the main reason why Windows 95 printing is faster than Windows 3.1 printing?

  A. The use of more enhanced printer drivers

  B. Faster memory allocation

  C. Smaller font files

  D. EMF Spooling

44. Bi-directional communication in Windows 95 supports _____ mode, which provides an asynchronous identification channel between the printer and the computer.

  A. RAW

  B. EMF

  C. Nibble

  D. Point and Print

45. A user calls you and complains that her computer is running sluggishly. You inquire and find out that her hard drive is almost constantly active. You investigate to find that she has plenty of free disk space available to last her for quite some time. What would be the proper fix for this problem?

  A. Monitor the hard disk. A possible disk failure may be approaching.

  B. Have her use fewer applications at once.

14

    C. Remove any unneeded applications.

    D. Add more RAM.

46. Which of the following commands is used to rebuild the default Windows 95 program folders on the Start menu?

    A. `CONVGRP /s`

    B. `CONVGRP /m`

    C. `GRPCONV /s`

    D. `GRPCONV /m`

47. Benny calls your technical support line and complains that he cannot run his OS/2 1.x character-based applications on his Windows 95 computer. What must he do to make this possible?

    A. Install the OS/2 Name space.

    B. Install the OS/2 subsystem.

    C. Upgrade to Windows NT Workstation.

    D. Modify the program's property sheet.

48. You seem to be having a problem with a driver that is loading from your `AUTOEXEC.BAT` at startup. How would you troubleshoot this scenario in order to discover the driver that isn't loading?

    A. Press F5 after seeing "Starting Windows 95."

    B. Press F5 after seeing "Starting Windows 95," then select Safe Mode.

    C. Press F8 after seeing "Starting Windows 95," then select Safe Mode.

    D. Press F5 after seeing "Starting Windows 95," then select Step by Step Confirmation.

49. What type of memory model does Windows 95 implement?

    A. Conventional

    B. Expanded

    C. Flat linear

    D. Expanded

50. Which of the following must be installed to make a Windows 95 computer a Dial-Up Networking server? Choose all that apply.

   A. Dial-Up Networking

   B. TCP/IP

   C. NetBEUI

   D. Microsoft Plus!

14

Answers

1. C   Chapter 8, "Locking Down the System: Profiles and Policies" – The Net Watcher utility allows you to perform administrative tasks across the network.

2. A   Chapter 9, "Installing and Configuring Printers" – This setting can be found under the Spool Settings of the Details tab.

3. D   Chapter 1, "Planning and Installing Windows 95" – By installing Windows 95 into the same directory, all program groups will automatically be converted to Start menu items.

4. C   Chapter 3, "Windows 95 Blueprint: Internals and Architecture" – See Table 3.2, Windows 95 Registry keys.

5. A   Chapter 10, "Taking Windows 95 on the Road: Remote Services" – Windows 95 can only receive one inbound call at a time. Windows NT Server can receive up to 256 inbound Dial-Up Networking calls simultaneously.

6. B   Chapter 3, "Windows 95 Blueprint: Internals and Architecture" – MS-DOS and Windows 16-bit programs have a single thread per process. However, Windows 32-bit applications may have more than one thread.

7. C   Chapter 8, "Locking Down the System: Profiles and Policies" – The CON-FIG.POL is created by using the Policy Editor.

8. D   Chapter 5, "Files, Folders, and Disks" – Brian cannot see the file in his 16-bit application because his application does not understand long filenames. Therefore, Windows 95 creates an 8.3 alias.

9. B and C   Chapter 10, "Taking Windows 95 on the Road: Remote Services" – Both the Point to Point Protocol (PPP) and Serial Line Internet Protocol (SLIP) are supported. NetBEUI and TCP/IP are considered *network* protocols.

10. D   Chapter 5, "Files, Folders, and Disks" – The OS/2 namespace gives NetWare the capability to handle long filenames. Without it, you must use 8.3 filenames.

11. C   Chapter 3, "Windows 95 Blueprint: Internals and Architecture" – Windows based applications (both 16-bit and 32-bit) run in the System Virtual machine. Each MS-DOS application gets its own separate virtual machine. So by having one virtual machine (for all Windows based apps) and three MS-DOS virtual machines, you come up with a total of 4.

12. A and C   Chapter 3, "Windows 95 Blueprint: Internals and Architecture" – MS-DOS apps run in their own separate memory address space, which means separate message queues. This means that their threads are handled preemptively. 16-bit applications are handled cooperatively since all 16-bit applications share the same message queue. 32-bit applications run in their own separate memory address space which means separate message queues. This means that their threads are handled preemptively multitasked. OS/2 applications will not run under Windows 95. The question specifically states "in Windows 95."

13. A   Chapter 8, "Locking Down the System: Profiles and Policies" – The USER.DAT is the portion of the Registry that contains all user-specific configuration information.

14. A, B, and C   All of the *network* protocols listed are supported. PPP is considered a *line* protocol.

15. B   Chapter 6, "Linking to Your Network" – In order for others to see your computer on the network with this configuration, you must enable SAP advertising.

16. A   Chapter 1, "Planning for and Installing Windows 95" – DETLOG.TXT contains query and response information about the hardware detection.

17. B   Chapter 1, "Planning for and Installing Windows 95" – This machine does not meet the minimum processor requirements; all other machines can be upgraded.

18. A and C   Chapter 8, "Locking Down the System: Profiles and Policies" – The SYSTEM.DAT makes up system-specific configurations, and likewise, the USER.DAT makes up the user-specific portion.

14

19. B   Chapter 8, "Locking Down the System: Profiles and Policies" – The proper location is in the NETLOGON, a Windows NT network. The *user's home directory* is where *profiles* are stored on a Windows NT network. Most people seem to get these two locations confused. *The user's mail directory* is where their profiles are stored on a *NetWare* network.

20. A and D   Chapter 9, "Installing and Configuring Printers" – Both RAW and EMF data formats are supported by Windows 95.

21. D   Chapter 3, "Windows 95 Blueprint: Internals and Architecture" – By pressing CTRL, ALT and DEL once, the Close Program dialog box appears. Once there, you can choose the application and click the End Task button to close the program.

22. C   Chapter 7, "Linking to Your World" – The Required result and Optional result 1 are met since DHCP is implemented. However, Optional result 2 is not met. If WINS were installed and the DHCP server configured to inform the Windows 95 computers of the WINS server's address, then all options would have been met.

23. C   Chapter 8, "Locking Down the System: Profiles and Policies" – Profiles are stored in a folder called Profiles which is inside the Windows folder. Within the Profiles folder, there will be a separate folder for each person.

24. C   Chapter 4, "Plug and Play" – Legacy devices that are not flexible (hardwired or jumpered) are assigned resources ahead of other devices. Because the sound card is jumpered to IRQ 9, it will be assigned first.

25. A and D   Chapter 5, "Files, Folders, and Disks" – Scandisk can fix errors on floppy disks, hard disks, and RAM drives. Additionally, it can also fix errors on Memory cards. CD-ROMs cannot be repaired due to the read-only nature of that technology. Network drives cannot be repaired because there stands a chance that the file systems are different. An example of this may be evident in a scenario where Windows 95 is connected to a Windows NT server whose file system may be NTFS.

26. A   Chapter 3, "Windows 95 Blueprint: Internals and Architecture" –
Windows 95 allocates the 3GB to 4GB range for Ring 0 components. The
2GB to 3GB range is where core system components and Windows 16-bit
applications reside. Windows 32-bit applications reside in the 4MB to 2GB
range.

27. C   Chapter 3, "Windows 95 Blueprint: Internals and Architecture" –
Windows 95 allocates the 3GB to 4GB range for Ring 0 components. The
2GB to 3GB range is where core system components and Windows 16-bit
applications reside. Windows 32-bit applications reside in the 4MB to 2GB
range.

28. B   Chapter 3, "Windows 95 Blueprint: Internals and Architecture" – You
must install the GROUPPOL.DLL on all Windows 95 computers. Without this
file installed, policies based upon individual users will work, but group policies
will not.

29. D   Chapter 8, "Locking Down the System: Profiles and Policies" – The
proper location is in the sys\public directory. The *user's mail directory* is where
their *profiles* are stored. Most people seem to get these two locations confused.
The *NETLOGON share* is the storage location for policies on a *Windows NT*
network. Likewise, the *user's home directory* is where *profiles* are stored on a
Windows NT network.

30. A   Chapter, 6, "Linking to Your Network" – You must use a security
provider to be able to use user-level security. Since her computer has File and
Print Sharing for Microsoft Networks, she needs to use a Windows NT server
(or NT Workstation) as her security provider. Another Windows 95 computer
will not give her the capability since it has no way of creating a user database.
In order for her to use a NetWare server, she must have File and Print Sharing
for NetWare Networks installed.

31. B   Chapter 3, "Windows 95 Blueprint: Internals and Architecture" – A
process consists of at least one thread. Windows 16-bit and MS-DOS programs have only one thread per process. However, Windows 32-bit programs
may have multiple threads per process.

14

32. C   Chapter 5, "Files, Folders, and Disks" – Each directory entry uses 32 bytes to store its information. Because the root directory is 16K in size, it can contain a maximum of 512 directory entries. Since long filenames take up more than one directory entry, you may reach your 512 limit without having 512 files and directories.

33. A and D   Chapter 3, "Windows 95 Blueprint: Internals and Architecture" and Chapter 8, "Locking Down the System: Profiles and Policies" – Regedit.exe is the program used to view and edit the Registry. Poledit.exe is the Policy Editor used to create policy files. It can also be used to open and edit the Registry.

34. D   Chapter 1, "Planning for and Installing Windows 95" – You shouldn't delete any of these files. Windows 95 uses these files to determine what may have caused setup to fail, so that it doesn't happen again. Deleting these files may cause Windows 95 to continue to hang because of the same problem.

35. A   Chapter 1, "Planning for and Installing Windows 95" – SETUPLOG.TXT lists everything that took place during setup, and whether it was successful or not. DETLOG.txt isn't created until the detection process happens. DETCRASH.LOG is a binary file that is not viewable.

36. A   Chapter 9, "Installing and Configuring Printers" – By capturing a printer port, such as LPT1, you can send the print job from the MS-DOS program to LPT1. Windows 95 will then "relay" the print job to the printer. Most people would tend to think that the printer driver might be the problem. However, if the printer driver was an incorrect or corrupted one, then the Windows-based application wouldn't work either.

37. B   Chapter 6, "Linking to Your Network" – Because there are Novell NetWare servers, you should use the IPX/SPX protocol which was designed by Novell.

38. B and D   Chapter 8, "Locking Down the System: Profiles and Policies" – Both the USER.DAT and USER.DA0 will be copied because the USER.DAT contains the user-specific settings of the Registry. The USER.DA0 is a backup copy of the USER.DAT.

39. C   Chapter 6, "Linking to Your Network" – If the Frame Type is not properly specified, then the computer will not be able to see the server, although all other items are installed. Adding the File and Print Sharing will not help the situation.

40. C   Chapter 6, "Linking to Your Network" – The proper way is using the \\servername\volumename. The entry that uses share name is used for Windows NT network. Both entries that use the directory are invalid.

41. B   Chapter 4, "Plug and Play" – Hot docking can be performed with the machine completely powered up. Cold docking requires that the computer be completely powered off. This leaves warm docking as your answer.

42. A   Chapter 10, "Taking Windows 95 on the Road: Remote Services" – The Point to Point Tunneling Protocol can be used to create a Virtual Private network connection to a PPTP/VPN-configured server.

43. D   Chapter 9, "Installing and Configuring Printers" – Enhanced MetaFile Spooling allows Windows 95 to spool the print job to the hard disk so that the application can be returned to the user's control. Meanwhile, the printing process can continue in the background, while the user continues his work.

44. C   Chapter 9, "Installing and Configuring Printers."

45. D   Chapter 3, "Windows 95 Blueprint: Internals and Architecture" – This problem is usually caused by not having enough RAM installed in the computer to support the type of work and the type of applications being used. Therefore, the result is excessive paging of information, causing the high disk activity.

46. D   Chapter 13, "Troubleshooting Windows 95" – You will be presented with a dialog box prompting you for the location of the program group you would like to convert.

47. C   Chapter 1, "Planning for and Installing Windows 95" – Windows 95 does not support OS/2 applications. If Benny wants to be able to run these applications, he must upgrade to Windows NT workstation (which will support the application he is trying to use).

14

48. D   Chapter 13, "Troubleshooting Windows 95" – By selecting Step by Step Confirmation, you can select Yes or No to each item as it loads.

49. C   Chapter 3, "Windows 95 Blueprint: Internals and Architecture" – Windows 95 follows a scheme very similar to Windows NT. The rest of the possible answers are all terms used with the old memory model.

50. A, B, and D   Chapter 10, "Taking Windows 95 on the Road: Remote Services" – You must have Dial-Up Networking, and TCP/IP installed in order for Dial-Up Networking to work for outbound calls. In order for the Windows 95 computer to act as a Dial-Up server, you must install the Microsoft Plus! Pack.

MCSE

Appendix A

Technical Glossary

(A)

API (application programming interface)   A set of functions that provide application programmers with access to common system functions.

applet   A component of the Control Panel. Each icon starts a program that is not considered an application and is therefore called an applet.

ARP (Address Resolution Protocol)   A protocol that TCP/IP hosts use to discover the hardware address of a destination node when only the IP address is known. A hardware address refers to a unique address on the network for the network adapter (network card). Windows 95 includes a command-line tool for examining the system's local ARP cache. For more information, type **ARP -?** at a command prompt.

ARPA (Advanced Research Projects Agency)   A government agency responsible for developing robust internetworking technologies that led to the ARPAnet, a predecessor to today's Internet.

(B)

backup domain controller (BDC)   A computer running Windows NT Server on a network that is configured to help distribute the load of validation and other tasks from the primary domain controller. See also *primary domain controller.*

batch (Installation)   The automated installation of Windows 95 using a batch file to input needed information that the user normally asks to be supplied.

bindery Where NetWare 2.*x* and 3.*x* servers store all account, security, and other related information. The bindery was replaced with the NDS with NetWare 4.*x*. See also *NDS*.

bindery emulation The process of a NetWare 4.*x* server emulating the way that NetWare 2.*x* and 3.*x* servers provide and store security information. Available on NetWare 4.*x* servers for backward compatibility.

BIOS (basic input/output system) A program stored in the firmware of a computer that contains basic information and drivers needed to get the computer up and running. Firmware is another way of referring to the software that is stored in a ROM chip. This information is nonvolatile, meaning it will remain when power to the computer is off.

boot sector The sector on the hard disk that contains basic information about the operating system. This sector is the first sector on the hard disk that is read during the boot process of a computer.

browse master A system that maintains the list of all NetBIOS resources for a particular entity, whether a subnet or a domain. Browsers contact the Master Browser for the list of available NetBIOS resources, and Master Browsers are determined via the election process.

browser A NetBIOS client that attempts to contact other NetBIOS resources on a network, using the Browse List maintained by one or more browse masters. The Browse List contains a list of active systems, identified by their NetBIOS network names.

bus An architecture for communication between multiple devices, whether on a systemboard or across a network. A bus architecture is a shared medium, where all devices on the bus must contest for communication time, and all devices can hear all transmissions.

(C)

cache Where commonly used data from one data storage medium is stored on another, faster medium. See *caching*.

caching The process of storing commonly used data from one data storage medium in another, faster medium. This greatly increases the speed at which the computer can access information. By caching recently used information that can be used in a faster medium (such as RAM) rather than accessing it directly from the slower medium (such as hard disk), access times can be greatly reduced.

Class (A, B, C)   A type of IP address that determines the range of digits available to a particular installation. A Class A number is preallocated only the leftmost octet of the dotted-decimal IP address, leaving the rightmost three fields free for suballocation (for example, 143.0.0.0). Similarly, a Class B address is preallocated the leftmost two octets (143.122.0.0), and a Class C address is preallocated the leftmost three octets (143.122.89.0). A Class A number can have a maximum of 16,777,214 nodes, a Class B number 65,534, and a Class C 254. The InterNIC currently assigns IP network numbers.

client   Any computer that accesses a server for services or data.

cluster   An operating system allocates disk space for files in units of one or more sectors; these units are called *clusters* or *allocation units*. Clusters can vary in size depending on the size of the disk. On a disk, a 1-byte file is allocated one cluster of disk space, wasting the unused area of the cluster. A file that is 3.2 clusters large is given four clusters. Overall, a smaller cluster size means less waste. The cluster size of FAT file systems are significantly larger than those of the FAT32 file system of OSR2 (Release 2) of Windows 95.

cold boot   The process of restarting a computer by cutting off the computer's power and then turning it back on.

cold docking   The process of docking a laptop or notebook computer into or out of a docking station with the computer turned off.

command-line switch   An addition to the normal command-line of a program. When running the program at a command prompt or using the Start-Run utility, you can specify that the program run in a different way, usually by adding a forward slash (/) and a letter or phrase. An example would be FORMAT /S. This command formats the disk specified and then adds the system files to make it bootable. Without the /S, the command would simply format the disk specified.

compressed volume file (CVF)   A single data file that comprises the entire contents of the compressed portion (or volume) of the hard disk. This data file is created when using the Windows 95 or other Microsoft equivalent disk compression utility.

CONFIG.POL   The file that makes up a Windows 95 policy. This file is usually stored in the Windows directory of the local computer. If this policy will be a server-based policy, it will be stored in the NETLOGON share of a Windows NT server or the Public folder of a NetWare server.

Control Panel   A software utility that allows you to modify the settings and behavior of Windows 95. These settings and/or properties are stored in the Registry.

conventional memory   The first 640K of memory.

cooperative multitasking   The process of running more than one application at a time where each application sends a single thread of code at one time to be processed by the processor. A thread can control the processor until the thread is done with it. The program that is sending the thread controls how long the thread has control of the processor and when it should relinquish it.

cross-linked files   An error caused when two files are linked to the same areas of the hard disk. Only one file can occupy the area at one time. To fix these errors, run ScanDisk.

CSMA/CD   Short for *carrier sense-multiple access/collision detection*, CSMA/CD is a bus contention communication method used by network technologies such as EtherNet. In a CSMA/CD network, workstations first determine whether a transmission is taking place (Carrier Sense) before trying to transmit. After the wire is free, any workstation can attempt to transmit packets (Multiple Access). If, however, multiple workstations attempt to transmit at the same time, a collision occurs (Collision Detection), and the workstations wait a random time period to retry communication. CSMA/CD networks are not suitable for real-time data transmission because no workstation is guaranteed the capability to transmit its packets; but CSMA/CD networks have proven simple and reliable enough for most data transmission needs.

(D)

data link layer   The second level of the OSI network model, this layer is responsible for the formation and transmission of packets over layer one, the Physical layer. This layer has no facility for connection-oriented communication. EtherNet and Token Ring are examples of data link layer protocols.

defrag   See *disk defragmenter*.

demand paging   The process in which Windows 95 moves files to and from memory to and from the hard disk. This process frees up memory to be used by other applications.

Desktop   The background area of the screen that contains the My Computer, Network Neighborhood, Recycle Bin, and other icons. This area directly relates to a folder on the hard disk that allows folders and files to be created directly on the desktop. The default location for this folder is c:\windows\desktop.

device driver   A program that provides an interface between a piece of hardware and the operating system.

DHCP (dynamic host configuration protocol)   A method for dynamically allocating IP addresses. DHCP can be run on servers such as Windows NT, UNIX, and NetWare and can dynamically provide IP addresses and stack configuration to several different network clients, thus avoiding the process of manually configuring the stack on each workstation. DHCP supports the leasing of addresses to specific machines for set periods of time.

dial-up networking   A program in Windows 95 that allows connection to a network via modem and has full functionality as if the computer were connected to the network using a network card.

direct hardware call   The process in which a program calls on a hardware device directly, bypassing the functions of the operating system.

disk compression   A Windows 95 feature that allows you to free up hard disk space by compressing the data so as not to take up as much space.

disk defragmenter (or Defrag)   A utility that is run to defragment the hard disk. Fragmentation happens as files are removed from the hard disk leaving blank areas that are noncontiguous. When files are written to these noncontiguous blank areas, they become fragmented. Running Defrag repairs this problem.

DLL (dynamic link library)   A library file containing functions that many different programs can use, allowing those programs to be smaller and to load only the shared execution code into memory when needed.

DNS (domain name service)   The standard for resolving IP addresses to canonical host names on TCP/IP systems. DNS relies on static tables that map addresses to host names, although standards for Dynamic DNS, designed to be used in conjunction with DHCP and NetBIOS naming, are under development. See *WINS*.

domain   A logical structure that allows for centralized administration of user and group objects and resources, as well as centralized authentication and rights management. A domain must have at least one Windows NT Server system serving as a domain controller. See *workgroup*.

domain controller   See *primary domain controller* and *backup domain controller.*

domain name server   A server on a network whose job it is to resolve Internet domain names such as www.microsoft.com to an IP address.

domain naming service (DNS)   The service that runs on a server such as Windows NT, UNIX, or NetWare that resolves Internet domain names to IP addresses.

dual-boot   The configuration of a computer where more than one operating system can be booted. An example would be when both Windows NT and Windows 95 reside on the same computer; both are operational and can be booted.

DX   A specification of X86 processors. An example might be 386DX. The DX denotes that the processor contains an enabled math coprocessor used to help speed the processing of extensive math calculations and graphics.

dynamic link library   See *DLL.*

(E)

EISA (extended industry standard architecture)   An enhanced version of the ISA bus standard, using a 32-bit bus with bus mastering that can transfer data at up to 66MB per second, while still maintaining backward compatibility with ISA cards. EISA is a relatively rare bus standard, found mostly in older server-class systems. EISA bus devices can be configured automatically using software utilities. See *ISA, Micro Channel,* and *PCI.*

EMF spooling   The process in which Windows 95 processes print jobs in a nonspecific printer format. This speeds up the time in which the control of the application is given back to the user because EMF spooling can happen in the background while the user continues with his work.

EtherNet   A system for CSMA/CD networking, originally developed by Xerox in the 1970s, now adopted in many implementations as an industry standard data link layer networking protocol. See *CSMA/CD.*

excessive paging   The process in which high hard-disk activity occurs. This is usually caused by a lack of RAM.

expanded memory   Memory in addition to conventional memory that some older MS-DOS programs use. This memory is installed on expanded memory boards and comes with an expanded memory manager. This memory is not part of the memory that is normally installed into PCs.

extended memory   Memory above 1MB on computers with X86 processors. Extended memory is required by Windows and Windows-based programs.

(F)

FAT (file allocation table)   A file system, originally developed for MS-DOS, which is still used by DOS, Windows 95, and Windows NT systems. FAT indexes all files and extensions in a table, called the FAT. FAT requires little system overhead, making it simple and fast to implement, but it includes little fault tolerance, wastes disk space with inefficient block allocation, and suffers heavily from disk fragmentation.

FAT32   The new version of FAT that comes with OSR2 (Release 2) version of Windows 95. It repairs many problems and limitations of the original FAT but at the cost of compatibility. You lose backward compatibility because Windows 95 is the only operating system that supports FAT32.

FDDI (fiber-distributed data interface)   A fiber-optic network technology used for high-speed WAN interconnectivity, using a token-based access method. FDDI is commonly used for high-speed, fault-tolerant interconnection between LANs in a wide-area network.

firewall   A system that limits access to a network from an outside network. A firewall is most commonly used to limit access to a network from computers on the Internet.

folder   A container of objects. A folder usually contains other folders, files, or shortcuts. In Windows 95, the folder is the equivalent to a directory of other operating systems.

fragmentation   The process of spreading the extents of a file across the free space on a hard disk, rather than placing them in contiguous blocks. Fragmentation generally occurs when a file system inefficiently plans space for file saves and the growth of existing files. Fragmentation affects different file systems differently. Fragmentation can also take place within the virtual memory address space of an operating system but does not seriously affect operating systems with efficient memory managers.

frame type   One of several different standards for the layout of an EtherNet frame, based on the type of protocols that the frame can carry. Examples of frame types are 802.2, 802.3, and Ethernet II.

FTP   A protocol for performing file downloads and uploads over TCP/IP, supporting both raw binary and ASCII file transfer. This is one of the more common ways of transferring files across the Internet.

(G)

gateway   A device that provides access to outside networks. A gateway can be a hardware device, such as a network router, or a software service, such as routing provided by a Windows NT Server.

general protection fault (GPF)   An error that occurs when a program tries to access the protected memory address space of another program. Any time this happens, it is possible that the accused program can violate system integrity. Instead, a GPF is issued.

GUI (graphical user interface)   The shell of Windows 95. It is the idea of creating a picture-oriented interface rather than a text-based one as with MS-DOS. Icons represent objects such as files and directories, along with executable programs. Manipulation and navigation are controlled by some form of pointing device.

(H)

handheld computer   A computer that is smaller than a laptop or notebook computer and generally small enough to hold in one hand. These computers, also commonly known as *palmtops*, usually run a smaller version of Windows 95 called Windows CE (short for Compact Edition).

hexadecimal   A shorthand system for representing binary numbers. Hexadecimal uses digits 0 through 9 and the letters A through F, whereas binary employs only 0 and 1. A number such as 183 is 10110111 in binary, but B7 in hexadecimal.

HMA (high memory area)   The first 64K of extended memory.

hot docking   The process of docking a laptop or notebook computer into or out of a docking station with the computer completely powered and running.

HPFS *High performance file system* that resides in IBM's OS/2 operating system.

HTML (Hypertext Markup Language)   A text-based language used to create Web pages that can be seen with a Web browser such as the Microsoft Internet Explorer or Netscape Navigator.

HTTP (hypertext transfer protocol)   An Internet protocol used to transfer files formatted in HTML. This protocol is most commonly used to browse Web pages created using HTML.

(I)

I/O port   A unique memory address through which input and output to a hardware device takes place.

IDE (integrated device electronics)   A standard interface for mass storage drives on PC systems, based on the original PC hard disk controller interface. EIDE (Enhanced IDE) improves still further on the IDE model.

IFS Manager (installable file system manager)   The component in Windows 95 that manages interoperability of the different file systems. These file systems include VFAT (virtualized file allocation table), CDFS (CD-ROM file system), and the network redirector.

INF   A file that provides information to the Setup program about a device, such as configuration information. These files are normally provided by the manufacturer. INF files can also assist in the installation of Windows 95 through automated setups. These INF files provide information normally given by the user when installing Windows 95.

INI files   Initialization files that are used by Windows 3.x for storage of configuration information. In Windows 95, these files are used for backward compatibility with older Windows 3.x applications.

Internet   A worldwide network of computers once called the ARPAnet. Today, the Internet is a great resource for information and communication.

Internet domain name   A name such as www.bartonet.com that is used for reaching another computer to access information when its IP address is not known.

interrupt   A signal to the system's CPU to gain processor time to execute an I/O or other function. Operations that generate excessive interrupts can negatively affect system performance. Interrupts can be signaled either by hardware access or by software command.

IPX/SPX (Internet packet exchange/sequenced packet exchange)   A LAN protocol designed by Novell Corporation for use with NetWare. IPX/SPX is a routable protocol that occupies the Transport and Network layers of the OSI model. IPX/SPX provides dynamic address configuration and high-speed networking, at the cost of chattiness and the inability to route packets beyond a set hop limit. IPX/SPX can be used for NetBIOS communications.

ISA (industry standard architecture)   The bus designed for AT-class systems, still commonly in use today. ISA buses have a 16-bit data path, with a maximum transfer rate of 10MB/sec, with no bus mastering. ISA buses do not, by default, have the capability to perform automatic adapter configuration, though the Plug and Play standard does allow for automatic configuration of those devices that support the standard, on a system with a Plug and Play BIOS.

ISDN (integrated services digital network)   ISDN gives you access to a network with end-to-end digital connections. ISDN uses existing copper telephone wiring to send digital signals at high speeds over multiple pathways (channels). ISDN enables voice, data, video, and graphics to be sent over a single, ordinary telephone line at speeds up to 64Kbps on a single channel or 128Kbps by combining two channels.

ISP (Internet service provider)   A company that markets services such as dial-up access to the Internet, Web page hosting, Internet mail, and so on.

(K)

kernel   The core of an operating system that provides essential services such as management of the processor.

(L)

LAN (local-area network)   Generally, a LAN consists of several network computers connected within the same building. Most LANs have one or more servers.

LFNBK.EXE Long filename backup utility used to back up information about the files stored on a Windows 95 computer, specifically the information about the long filenames. This utility is generally run before using a disk utility (that doesn't understand long filenames) that might be needed to fix disk problems.

LLC The logical link control, in the data link layer of the OSI networking model.

local profile Individual user information stored locally on the computer, as opposed to being stored on a server.

login script or **logon script** A batch or script file containing certain settings or tasks to accomplish for a user or group of users to execute after the user logs on to a network. An example is mapping certain network drives upon logon/login.

long filename A filename that can consist of up to 255 characters including spaces and multiple period separators.

lost cluster A portion of the hard disk that can contain useful data that has been logically lost. See Chapter 8.

(M)

MAC (media access control) The unique hardware address of an EtherNet workstation; every EtherNet interface has a unique MAC address.

mailslot A type of interprocess communication between computers. In Windows 95, mailslots are provided for backward compatibility with existing Microsoft LAN Manager installations.

mandatory profile A profile that configures a computer in a specific way for a user. The user can change this configuration, but after the user logs off of the computer, the changes are not saved. You can make a profile mandatory by renaming the USER.DAT to USER.MAN.

MAPI (messaging application program interface) A set of calls that programmers can use to add mail-enabled features to their Windows-based applications.

mapped network drive A network connection to a shared resource for access to files. This network connection is translated into a drive letter.

memory address   A specific location in memory where information is stored. Each location is referred to by its address.

Message Queue   Part of the message-passing model that Windows 95 uses to control programs. Each time an event occurs in an application, such as a keystroke, that keystroke generates an interrupt. Interrupts are then transformed into messages and are stored in the message queue, where they wait to be processed.

Micro Channel   A proprietary bus architecture designed by IBM, using 32-bit width and automatic adapter configuration via software configuration files. Micro Channel supports bus mastering and can support communication rates ranging from 10MB/sec to 160MB/sec. Micro Channel is no longer common in PCs, but can be found in other IBM computer systems.

Mini-driver   A small portion of hardware-specific code provided by the manufacturer to be combined with the Windows 95 universal driver to allow communication between the device and the operating system.

modem   A device used to communicate between computers. Different types of modems can be used such as dedicated line modems, cable modems, and so on. The most common type of modem in use today is the analog modem that uses standard telephone lines.

monolithic driver   A driver that is entirely created by the manufacturer of a piece of hardware or program. These drivers do not use the Windows 95 universal and mini-driver concept.

MS-DOS VM (MS-DOS Virtual Machine)   The simulation of a complete MS-DOS–based environment in which to run MS-DOS–based applications.

(N)

NCP (NetWare Core Protocol)   The protocol used for NetWare file, print, bindery, and NDS (NetWare Directory Services).

NDIS (Network Device Interface Specification)   The network driver model used by LANMAN and NT-based network clients, such as Windows for Workgroups, Windows 95, and Windows NT. See *ODI*.

NDS (NetWare Directory Services)   The replacement for the bindery, NDS uses an advanced X.500-based directory service to maintain a tree-hierarchy database of all network resources, including users, groups, servers, volumes, and printers, for ease of management and administration. NDS also provides distributed authentication and security management, as well as fault tolerance. NDS requires higher hardware and network overhead than other network implementations but provides functionality not found in many other operating systems (though Windows NT 5.0 promises the Active Directory, a similar service). See also *bindery*.

NET TIME   A command used to check the time on another computer. This command also allows for synchronizing the clocks of computers on a network. To synchronize a Windows 95 computer's clock with another, type in the following command at an MS-DOS prompt: **NET TIME *computername* / SET /Y**.

Net Watcher   A program included with Windows 95 that allows for monitoring access to another Windows 95 computer. Information such as what resources are shared, who is connected to them, and what resource they have in use can be found using the Windows 95 Net Watcher.

NetBEUI (NetBIOS enhanced user interface)   Originally an enhanced version of the NetBIOS protocol designed by Microsoft and IBM, NetBEUI is now a highly efficient but unroutable protocol that replaces the original role of NetBIOS. NetBEUI can be used for NetBIOS networking in small, single-subnet workgroups, and provides efficient throughput and dynamic addressing. See *NetBIOS*.

NetBIOS (network basic input/output system)   Originally a subnet-only network protocol designed by IBM in the early 1980s, NetBIOS is now a standard for network APIs that can be transported over other protocols, such as NetBEUI, IPX/SPX, and TCP/IP. See *NetBEUI*, *IPX/SPX*, and *TCP/IP*.

network   Two or more computers connected together for communications purposes.

network drive   Drive letters that correspond to a folder on another computer. Theses are also commonly known as *mapped network drives*.

Network Neighborhood   A component of Windows 95 that allows users to browse for network resources regardless of the network vendor of most of the networking components on the network.

network provider   The component that allows Windows 95 to communicate with the network. The included network components include providers for Microsoft networks and NetWare networks.

NETX   A real-mode networking client created by Novell. This network client was predominately used with NetWare 3.*x*.

nibble mode   The concept of sending smaller pieces of data to a printer to be printed rather than sending one large file.

NIC (Network Interface Card)   A generic term for any device, whether an adapter card or simply a port on a gateway device that connects a computing system to a network.

NTFS (New Technology File System)   The file system of Microsoft Windows NT.

null modem cable   A cable used to connect two computers using standard serial ports. A standard serial cable cannot be used for this process because of pin assignments on the cable. A null modem cable usually simulates a direct modem connection without the use of modems.

(O)

octet   Each of the four groupings of a TCP/IP address. For example, for the TCP/IP address 101.456.789.001, the numbers *456* make up a single octet. The name is derived from the fact that a TCP/IP address is 32-bit. When the numbers are split into the four groups, each grouping consists of 8 bits.

ODI (open data interface)   A standard for implementing a network protocol stack, used by NetWare and other network stacks.

OEM (Original Equipment Manufacturer)   A common way of referring to the original manufacturer of a piece of hardware or software.

OLE   *Object linking and embedding*, OLE provides distributed object communication services.

OS/2   The IBM operating system that competes with Microsoft's MS-DOS and Windows products.

OSI (open systems interconnection) model   A reference model for implementing network protocol stacks. No real-world network stack is entirely OSI-compliant, but the OSI model remains a standard for describing how network stacks function.

(P)

packet   A unit of information to be transmitted over a network connection of some sort. Packets generally consist of the data being transferred, a header containing an ID number, the address of the sender, the address of the intended recipient, and error-correction information.

paging table   A table used by the Virtual Memory Manager to determine where information is really stored, in physical RAM or on the hard disk in the Virtual Memory file.

partition   A division of the hard disk. Hard disks can be divided up into smaller pieces, like a pie, creating additional local drive letters.

pass-through authentication   The process that Windows 95 uses to validate a user's access to locally stored information. This type of security requires a security provider like Windows NT or Novell NetWare.

PCI (peripheral component interconnect)   A system bus designed by Intel but administered as a current industry standard, using 64-bit data width, with automatic adapter configuration and bus mastering. It supports data rates of up to 264MB/sec, although most PCs currently cannot transmit data at this rate across the bus.

PCMCIA   Personal Computer Memory Card International Association standard for credit card-sized hardware used in laptop and other portable computers.

PIC (programmable interrupt controller)   A device in a personal computer that handles the signaling between hardware and applications. An example of this signaling is with a keystroke. With the keystroke, something needs to notify or interrupt the application. Here is where the PIC comes in.

Ping (packet Internet grouper)   A TCP/IP utility used to troubleshoot TCP/IP connections.

Plug and Play (PnP)   A set of standards and design philosophies based upon the concept of configuration of hardware devices with little or no help from the user.

PostScript driver   A printer driver that uses the Adobe printer description format.

PPI (print provider interface)   An open and modular interface that allows multiple print providers to be installed at once. These print providers can be for local printing or network printing.

PPP (point-to-point protocol)   A protocol designed to allow the encapsulation of other protocols, such as TCP/IP, over a modem connection.

PPTP (point-to-point tunneling protocol)   A new networking technology that supports multiprotocol virtual private networks (VPN), enabling remote users to access corporate networks securely across the Internet.

preemptive multitasking   The process of running more than one application at a time where each application sends at least one thread of code to the processor at one time for processing. A thread can control the processor until a thread with a higher priority is executed. This allows much better response and higher data throughput than cooperative multitasking.

primary domain controller   An NT Server that maintains the primary copy of a Domain's SAM database. A PDC is required to create an NT Domain, though some authentication services can be provided by backup domain controllers (BDCs). See *backup domain controller*.

primary mouse button   By default, the left mouse button. It is used to select objects (single click), open objects (double click), and move objects (click and drag), among other functions.

primary network logon   The logon chosen among multiple network providers that is most commonly used to access resources. You can choose your primary network logon in the Network applet of the Control Panel.

program information file (PIF)   A file that gives specific information about MS-DOS-based applications. This file controls certain aspects about the applications' environment and behavior. To modify or create a PIF, simply edit the Properties sheet for the MS-DOS application. You can have multiple PIFs for a single MS-DOS application.

Program Manager   The main interface of Windows 3.*x*. This interface is replaced by the Windows 95 desktop, Start menu, and taskbar.

properties sheet   A place where you can modify the attributes, characteristics, or behavior of an object. You can get to most objects' properties sheets by right-clicking the object and then choosing Properties from the shortcut menu that appears.

protocol   A standard for communication, defining rules for transmitting data in a fashion understandable to all parties supporting that protocol.

(R)

RAS   A dial-up server service that allows Windows 95 to connect over telephone lines, ISDN, or X.25 networks.

read-only   An attribute of a file that prevents it from being modified or deleted. This is also an access right that can be specified when users are accessing shared information across a network.

redirector   A component that determines whether requests for mapped resources should be sent to the local file system or to the network stack, thus making access of those resources transparent to applications.

REGEDIT.EXE   The command for running the Windows 95 Registry Editor.

Registry   A database that contains information used by the operating system and its applications, ranging from dynamic hardware configuration and system runtime information to application customization settings.

remote administration   Administration of a computer by an administrator located at another computer across the network.

remote registry service   A service that allows modification of the Registry by administrators from another computer across the network.

remote resource   Any resource such as files or printers that can be accessed on another computer via the network.

REN   Command for renaming files at a command prompt. The syntax is REN *oldfilename newfilename*.

Resource Kit   A technical guide for installing, configuring, and supporting Windows 95 created by Microsoft and published by the Microsoft Press.

ROM   Read-only memory. Generally, read-only memory is nonvolatile, meaning that the information stored in it is not lost when the power is turned off as opposed to RAM (random access memory), which is volatile.

root keys   The main keys in the Registry, which are HKEY_CLASSES_ROOT, HKEY_CURRENT_USER, HKEY_LOCAL_MACHINE, HKEY_USERS, HKEY_CURRENT_CONFIG, and HKEY_DYN_DATA.

router   A computing device designed to route network traffic from one subnet to its destinations. Any system with two or more NICs and the proper software can act as a router, although systems designed and dedicated to network routing are far more efficient and cost-effective.

roving users   Users that commonly use more than one computer on the network. Windows 95 supports roving user profiles which allows roving users' individual settings to be available wherever they log on.

RTF   Rich text format. A way of formatting documents so that other operating systems can understand them.

(S)

SAP Advertising   Server Advertising Protocol. One process in which servers on an IPX network notify other computers of their presence.

ScanDisk   A utility used to repair common hard disk errors, such as cross-linked clusters and lost allocation units.

SCSI (small computer systems interface)   A bus architecture for mass-storage and other devices, commonly used in servers and other systems where performance and extensibility are important.

secondary mouse button   By default, the right mouse button. This button is commonly used to bring up a shortcut menu that allows quick access to items such as Cut, Copy, Paste, or an object's properties sheet.

security provider   When a user attempts to connect to a Windows 95 computer's shared resource, it can pass that request to a computer (the security provider) running a server operating system, such as Windows NT or NetWare that holds a list of users. Windows 95 must be configured for user-level security.

server   Any system designed and tuned to provide centralized network services, such as network authentication, file and print, or application services. Alternately, any system capable of sharing data or services on a network might be perceived as a server.

server-based profile Individual user information stored centrally on a server. This gives the advantage of the profile being available anywhere on the network, no matter where the user logs on to the network.

Service Pack A medium used by Microsoft to give updates to common problems experienced with one of its products. These updates provide new drivers and functionality.

shared-level security A type of security configuration where each shared resource is assigned a password and any user knowing that password can connect to that resource.

shell A term used to refer to the interface of an operating system.

shortcut A quick and easy way to reach commonly used folders, utilities, and files.

SLIP (serial line Internet protocol) An industry-standard protocol that can be used with Windows 95 Dial-Up Networking.

SMB (Server Message Block) The protocol used by NT for file, print, and other services. See *NCP*.

SNMP (Simple Network Management Protocol) A protocol used to allow network management of remote system and network resources.

spooler A service that receives a print job from an application and in turn sends it to the print device. This allows the application to be returned to the user faster by not tying up the application.

SPX See *IPX/SPX*.

Start button The button that is located in the lower-left corner of the Windows 95 desktop by default. Most activities can be accomplished or initiated at the Start button.

Start menu The primary entry point into the operating system. This takes the place of the Program Manager of Windows 3.*x*.

subnet mask A 32-bit value that distinguishes the network ID portion of an IP address from the host ID portion.

swap file A file on your hard disk that Windows 95 uses to swap information temporarily from RAM into so that it can free up valuable RAM storage space. If the information is needed again, Windows 95 swaps the information from the swap file back into RAM.

SX A specification of X86 processors. An example might be 386SX. The SX denotes that the processor contains a disabled math coprocessor used to help speed the processing of extensive math calculations and graphics.

System Monitor A utility in Windows 95 to monitor information about Windows 95 such as memory usage, swap file usage, processor usage, and so on.

System Policy Editor A utility that allows for creating and editing policy files. This program is not installed by default and can be located in the Admin folder of the Windows 95 CD-ROM.

System VM The virtual machine within which all Windows-based applications and system processes run. MS-DOS–based applications run separately in their own virtual machines.

SYSTEM.DAT The system-specific settings of the Registry. This is one of two files that make up the Registry in Windows 95.

(T)

taskbar The bar located at the bottom of the screen by default. It replaces the Task Manager of Windows 3.*x* and allows for quick and easy access to all applications that are running.

TCP/IP (transfer control protocol/Internet protocol) The standard protocol for communications over the Internet, TCP/IP is a protocol that supports efficient routing over large internetworks and generally requires static configuration of addressing information (although newer standards like DHCP eliminate this need). See *DHCP*.

telephony A standard way that applications interact with telephone and dialing functions of Windows 95.

Telnet A protocol for terminal emulation communications over TCP/IP.

thread The smallest possible unit of execution. Each process has at least one thread, but a process can have multiple threads to allow more efficient processing of complex tasks.

Tracert A TCP/IP utility that allows you to trace the route to another computer.

(U)

UDP (user datagram protocol)   A TCP/IP component that allows a datagram to be sent without establishing a connection with another computer.

UNC (uniform naming convention)   A standard for providing uniform resource names, which are valid no matter where the resource is located or what type of resource the name describes.

UniModem   The universal modem driver in Windows 95. It uses modem description files to control how it interacts with the communications driver VCOMM.

Universal Driver   A driver created by Microsoft and included with Windows 95 that is used in conjunction with a manufacturer-supplied mini-driver.

UNIX   Another operating system typically written in C with a hierarchical file system and integration of file and device I/O. The name *UNIX* was intended as a pun on Multics and was written *Unics* at first (UNiplexed Information and Computing System).

upper memory   Memory ranging above 640K (conventional memory) and below 1MB (extended memory). This memory range (384K) is used by system hardware, such as the display adapter. Unused portions of upper memory are referred to as *upper memory blocks* (UMB).

user interface   A term used to refer to the shell of an operating system, the part with which the user interacts.

user profile   The individual settings of a user on a computer such as color settings, mouse settings, network connections, and so on.

user-level security   A type of security configuration where each shared resource is assigned a list of users and what type of access the user attempting to access the resource via the network (not locally) can have. The names are acquired from a security provider on the network. Each time a user attempts (requests) to connect to that resource, the request is passed to the security provider for validation.

USER.DAT   The user-specific settings of the Registry. This is one of two files that compose the Registry in Windows 95.

USER.MAN   The same as **USER.DAT**, except that the file has been renamed with the MAN extension. This makes all settings mandatory. Even though the users can change these settings, all changes are not saved when the user logs off of the computer. This is also referred to as mandatory profiles.

(V)

validation   The process of being approved to log on to the network and/or use a resource.

VCACHE   A hard drive caching program that runs in protected mode and accomplishes the same task as some older disk caching programs such as SmartDrive.

VFAT (virtualized file allocation table)   The native file system of Windows 95 that is used on hard disks and allows for 32-bit disk access.

virtual device driver   A 32-bit, protected-mode driver that manages or controls a system resource which can be accessed by more than one application at a time.

virtual machine   The simulation of a complete MS-DOS–based environment in which to run MS-DOS–based applications. Multiple virtual machines can run at the same time.

Virtual Memory Manager   A Windows 95 component that handles all aspects of memory management including the paging of information into and out of the swap file.

VLM (Virtual Loadable Module)   A real-mode networking client created by Novell. This network client was predominately used with NetWare 4.x.

(W)

WAN (wide-area network)   A series of interconnected LANs that provide networking services to a large campus or series of installations. See *LAN*.

warm boot   Rebooting a computer by pressing Ctrl+Alt+Del rather than restarting the machine by turning the power off.

warm docking   The process of docking a laptop or notebook computer into or out of a docking station with the computer in some sort of suspended mode.

Windows 3.x   A way of referring to the most recent versions of Windows prior to Windows 95.

Windows CE (compact edition)   A version of the Windows operating system for handheld/palmtop computers that resembles Windows 95.

Windows Explorer   The Windows utility for managing the files and folders in Windows 95. This utility replaces the File Manager of Windows 3.*x*.

WINIPCFG.EXE   A command-line utility that can find out information about the TCP/IP configuration of a Windows 95 computer. This is especially helpful when a computer is assigned an IP address automatically by a DHCP server.

Winntroot   A way of referring to the directory location where Windows NT is installed on a computer. An example would be C:\WINNT.

WINS (Windows Internet Name Service)   A service for resolving NetBIOS names to TCP/IP addresses, WINS uses dynamic address configuration rather than static tables. See *DNS*.

workgroup   An organization of systems using peer-to-peer network resources. Workgroups lack centralized administration of accounts and access privileges. See *domain*.

(X)

X86   Term for Intel's 80×86 line of processors, beginning with the 286 (although most system requirements which state an x86 processor actually require a 386 or higher). Later versions of these processors use names rather than numbers to enhance their capability to carry a trademark. The line includes the 286, 386, 486, Pentium, Pentium Pro, Pentium MMX, and Pentium II processors.

Appendix B

Answers to Review Questions

Chapter 1

Question 1

Which of the following machines do not meet the minimum guidelines for Windows 95? Choose all that apply:

A. 386DX, 8MB RAM, 320MB Hard Drive

B. 386DX2, 4MB RAM, 400MB Hard Drive

C. 386SX, 16MB RAM, 850MB Hard Drive

D. Pentium, 8MB RAM, 400MB Hard Drive

Answer:

C. The machine needs to be a 386DX or higher. This particular machine is only a 386SX (see section 1.2.1).

Question 2

Which of the following Setup options does not create a working copy of Windows 95?

A. Floppy

B. CD-ROM

C. Network

D. Shared

E. Batch

Answer:

C. The network installation decompresses and copies the Windows 95 files from the CD-ROM to the hard drive to be shared out to the network (see section 1.3.1).

Question 3

A company has asked you to help determine which operating system to migrate to in its different workcenters. The company has already decided that it will be either Windows 95 or Windows NT. It has four workcenters. In the first workcenter, four people will do word processing, spreadsheets, and other general administrative work. In the second workcenter, 20 people will be working with accounting information, payroll, and accounts payable. They will also be doing some minimal word processing. In the third workcenter, around six to ten people will be working with computer-aided design and graphics. The fourth workcenter will consist of ten machines shared by manufacturing personnel who will need them from time to time to do word processing and basic spreadsheets.

Using this scenario, which operating system would be appropriate for the first workcenter?

A. Windows 95

B. Windows NT Workstation

Answer:

A. Windows 95 would be appropriate for the first workcenter, where users will be doing basic word processing and spreadsheets (see section 1.1.2).

Question 4

Using the scenario given in Question 3, which operating system would be appropriate for the second workcenter?

A. Windows 95

B. Windows NT Workstation

Answer:

B. Windows NT would be appropriate for the second workcenter, where additional security is needed for the accounting functions (see section 1.1.2).

Question 5

Using the scenario in Question 3, which operating system would be appropriate for the third workcenter?

A. Windows 95

B. Windows NT Workstation

Answer:

B. Windows NT would be appropriate for the third workcenter, where programs requiring additional processing power and a more stable operating system are needed (see section 1.1.2).

Question 6

Using the scenario in Question 3, which operating system would be appropriate for the fourth workcenter?

A. Windows 95

B. Windows NT Workstation

Answer:

A. Windows 95 would be appropriate for the fourth workcenter, where users will be doing basic word processing and spreadsheets (see section 1.1.2).

Question 7

Which of the following files would contain useful information about hardware found during Windows 95 Setup?

    A. `DETCRASH.LOG`

    B. `SETUPLOG.TXT`

    C. `DETLOG.TXT`

    D. `HARDWARE.LOG`

Answer:

    C. `DETLOG.TXT` is a file created during Windows 95 Setup that contains information about all hardware found during the detection process (see section 1.7.1).

    `DETCRASH.LOG` and `SETUPLOG.TXT` are files used to recover if Windows 95 crashes during setup. `HARDWARE.LOG` is a fictitious file.

Question 8

To upgrade the desktop settings and program groups from Windows 3.11 to Windows 95, copy all files having GRP and INI extensions to the folder containing the Windows 95 files.

    A. True

    B. False

Answer:

    B. To migrate the settings, you must specify that Windows 95 be installed to the same directory that contains Windows 3.11 during setup (see section 1.4).

Question 9

Which of the following statements are true about installing Windows 95?

A. Windows 3.1 can be upgraded to Windows 95 by installing into the same directory.

B. Windows 3.11 can be upgraded to Windows 95 by installing into the same directory.

C. Windows NT Workstation 3.51 can be upgraded to Windows 95 by installing into the same directory.

D. Windows NT Workstation 4.0 can be upgraded to Windows 95 by installing into the same directory.

Answer:

A. and B.   Previous versions of Windows can be upgraded simply by installing Windows 95 into the same directory. However, due to differences in drivers and configuration files, Windows NT cannot be upgraded to Windows 95 (see section 1.3).

Chapter 2

Question 1

You can modify the behavior of a Windows 95 object through its _____.

A. Settings

B. Attributes

C. Switches

D. Properties sheet

Answer:

D. Windows 95 objects are modified through the use of a properties sheet. Right-click the object and select Properties (see section 2.1.1).

Question 2

What keyboard keys do you press to access the Start menu?

   A. Alt+Tab

   B. Shift+Enter

   C. Ctrl+Esc

   D. Shift+Up Arrow

Answer:

   C. Ctrl+Esc pressed simultaneously will access the Start menu. You can then use your arrow keys to navigate this menu (see section 2.1.1).

Question 3

A user is experiencing problems navigating through the Start menu. She is having difficulty opening up an application that she uses daily because she has to go through a series of menus to get to it. How would you make it easier for her to get to her application?

   A. Create a shortcut on the desktop that points to her application.

   B. Drag the icon representing the program directly from a window and drop it on the Start button.

   C. Create an icon for it on her taskbar.

   D. Both A and B.

   E. Both A and C.

Answer:

   D. You could create a shortcut on the desktop or drag it onto the Start button. Dragging it on top of the Start button creates a shortcut at the top of the Start menu (see sections 2.1.4 and 2.1.5).

Question 4

You want to modify the Start menu. What two paths can you take to access it in order to edit it?

   A. Click Start, point to Settings, and select Taskbar. Then, select the Start Menu Programs tab.

B. Open the Explorer and navigate to its default path, C:\Windows\ Programs Menu.

C. Right-click the Start button and click Explore.

D. Both A and B.

E. Both A and C.

Answer:

E. Both A and C are correct. By going to the Taskbar properties, you can modify the menu. Additionally, Exploring the Start button will automatically open the Explorer with the Start menu already expanded where you can also modify the menu (see section 2.1.5).

Question 5

When you delete a shortcut, it also deletes the application (or other object) that it points to.

A. True.

B. False.

Answer:

B. False. Deleting a shortcut only gets rid of the pointer. It does not affect the application (or the object it points to) (see section 2.1.4).

Question 6

What ways can you access the Control Panel?

A. Click Start, point to Settings, and select Control Panel.

B. Open the Explorer and navigate to Control Panel.

C. Double-click the My Computer icon.

D. All of the above.

E. Both A and C.

Answer:

D. All options, A, B, and C will get you to the Control Panel. Most people do not realize that they can access it through the Explorer (see sections 2.1.2, 2.2.1, and 2.2.2).

Question 7

A user complains that he has lost his taskbar. Upon investigation, you find that his taskbar is visible when no applications are open, but the minute one is, it disappears and the application is full screen. Taking the mouse to the bottom of the screen does not result in a reappearing taskbar. What could be the best possible solution to the problem?

A. Click the Restore button for the application.

B. In the Control Panel, double-click Display. Remove the check mark from Hide Taskbar.

C. Right-click the taskbar and select Properties. Remove the check mark from Auto Hide.

D. Right-click the taskbar and select Properties. Place a check mark in Always on Top.

Answer:

D. By default, the taskbar is configured as Always on Top, which keeps it in view no matter how many windows are open (see section 2.1.3).

The question stated that taking the mouse to the bottom of the screen would not produce the taskbar. If the Auto Hide option had been on, this would have produced the taskbar.

Question 8

You have just installed Windows 95 on an end user's machine. You would like to configure the computer so that common system files are out of view from the user in the Explorer without affecting the operability of the files. What is your best possible solution?

A. Do nothing.

B. Select the files that you want hidden, right-click them, and select Properties. In the Properties dialog box, place a check mark in the box next to Hidden.

C. Select the files that you want hidden, right-click them, and select Properties. In the Properties dialog box, select the Miscellaneous tab, and select Administrative view only.

Answer:

A. Windows is set this way by default. If you would like to see where the option is, select View from the menu in Explorer. At the bottom of the menu, select Options. The option is at the top of the box titled Hidden Files (see section 2.2.1).

Question 9

Jack, a user on your network, prefers using the My Computer instead of the Explorer to view his files, but he doesn't like how many windows he has open after getting to the file he wants. What way would be the best solution to Jack's problem?

A. Open My Computer. From the View menu, select List.

B. Right-click My Computer and select Properties. In the properties dialog box, select the Folders tab and click next to Browse folders by using a single window that changes as you open each folder.

C. Open My Computer. From the View menu, select Options. In the Options dialog box, select the Folders tab and click next to Browse folders by using a single window that changes as you open each folder.

D. Open My Computer. From the View menu, select Details.

Answer:

C. When you open another object in My Computer, it creates a separate window with the contents. If you select Options from the View menu, you can change the Folder option. Your choices are Browse folders using a separate window for each folder OR Browse folders using a single window that changes as you open each folder. (2.2.2)

Question 10

You have installed a new video card in a Windows 95 machine and have installed the new drivers. Where is the appropriate place to do so?

A. Click Start, point to Settings, and select Control Panel. Double-click the Drivers icon.

B. Right-click the desktop. Click the Settings tab. Click the Change Display Type button.

C. Click Start, point to Settings, and select Control Panel. Double-click the Display icon. Click the Settings tab. Click the Change Display Type button.

D. Both B and C.

E. Both A and B.

Answer:

D. Both B and C are correct ways to get to the display drivers (see section 2.3).

Question 11

A user has a shortcut to a document on the desktop and would like to know an easier way to print it. What would be the best answer?

A. Double-click the icon and select the printer icon from the toolbar.

B. Right-click and select print.

C. Open the My Computer icon and drag the shortcut on top of the printers folder.

D. Both B and C.

Answer:

B. Right-clicking the shortcut with the mouse and selecting print is by far the quickest and easiest way to print the document (see section 2.1.1).

Chapter 3

Question 1

What type of application can have multiple threads per process?

    A. An MS-DOS application

    B. A Windows 16-bit application

    C. A Windows 32-bit application

Answer:

    C. Only Windows 32-bit applications are multithreaded applications (see section 3.4.3).

Question 2

A user is working on a 486DX2 with 16MB of RAM. He is working in several 16-bit Windows-based applications when the one he is currently using stops responding to the keyboard and the mouse. What would be his proper course of action?

    A. Restart the computer.

    B. Press Ctrl+Alt+Del twice to bring up the Close Program dialog box and terminate the proper application. All other 16-bit applications will resume normal operation.

    C. Press Ctrl+Alt+Del to bring up the Close Program dialog box and terminate all programs. Restart the programs as appropriate.

    D. Press Ctrl+Alt+Del to bring up the Close Program dialog box and terminate the proper application. All other 16-bit applications will resume normal operation.

Answer:

    D. Because all the programs that he is working with are 16-bit, by terminating the hung up program, the other 16-bit programs will continue to function correctly (see section 3.4.5).

    Answer B is incorrect because pressing Ctrl+Alt+Del twice will restart the computer (read answers carefully). Answer C is incorrect because it is not necessary to terminate all the applications.

Question 3

What key in the Windows 95 Registry stores information such as which drivers are loaded, what hardware is installed, and how ports are mapped?

A. `HKEY_CLASSES_ROOT`

B. `HKEY_LOCAL_MACHINE`

C. `HKEY_DYN_DATA`

D. `HKEY_CURRENT_CONFIG`

Answer:

B. The `HKEY_LOCAL_MACHINE` stores configuration information dealing with hardware, drivers, and other machine-specific information (see section 3.5.2).

Question 4

You are running three Win16 applications, two Win32 applications, and two MS-DOS applications on a Windows 95 computer. How many virtual machines are running on that computer?

A. 3

B. 4

C. 5

D. 7

Answer:

A. One System VM is running in which all Windows functions, Win16 applications, and Win32 applications run. For each MS-DOS–based application running, a separate MS-DOS VM is running. That makes one System VM and two MS-DOS VM for a total of three (see section 3.4.2).

Question 5

Windows 95 Virtual Memory allocates memory in what size blocks?

A. 2K

B. 4K

C. 16K

D. 64K

Answer:

B. In Windows 95 Virtual Memory, the allocation size is 4K (see section 3.1).

Question 6

A user calls you and complains that her computer is running sluggishly. You inquire and find out that her hard drive is almost constantly active. You investigate to find that she has plenty of free disk space available to last her for quite some time. What would be the proper fix for this problem?

A. Monitor the hard disk. A possible disk failure may be approaching.

B. Have her use fewer applications at once.

C. Remove any unneeded applications.

D. Add more RAM.

Answer:

D. This user's problem occurs because she doesn't have enough RAM in the computer for what she is trying to accomplish with it. Excessive paging of information causes the thrashing of the hard disk (movement of information from memory to the disk and vice versa). Adding more RAM will decrease the amount of paging Windows 95 will have to do to run the applications (see section 3.3.1).

Question 7

Which applications in Windows 95 are preemptively multitasked?

A. MS-DOS applications

B. Win16 applications

C. Win32 applications

D. Both A and C

Answer:

D. Both MS-DOS applications and Win32 applications are preemptively multitasked. Win32 applications each run in separate memory address spaces. MS-DOS applications do this similarly because each MS-DOS application runs in its own MS-DOS VM (see section 3.4.4).

Win16 applications cannot be preemptively multitasked in Windows 95 because they share the same memory address space and therefore must be cooperatively multitasked.

Question 8

A user who is having problems with his MS-DOS application contacts you. It appears that his machine runs fine in MS-DOS mode, but he needs the ability to cut and paste between this application and a Windows-based application. The application runs inside Windows 95, but behaves differently. Which of the following would you suggest?

A. From the Properties dialog box of this application, go to the Miscellaneous tab and set the Idle Sensitivity at its lowest level.

B. From the Properties dialog box of this application, go to the Program tab. Click the Advanced button and place a check mark in the box titled Prevent MS-DOS–Based Program from Detecting Windows.

C. From the Properties dialog box of this application, go to the Program tab. Click the Advanced button and place a check mark in the box titled Suggest MS-DOS Mode as Necessary.

D. From the Properties dialog box of this application, go to the Screen tab. Click the Advanced button and place a check mark in the box titled Fast ROM Emulation.

Answer:

B. The program needs to run in Windows 95. If it runs in Windows 95 but behaves differently in MS-DOS mode, set it so that it doesn't detect whether Windows is present.

Idle sensitivity doesn't pertain to this particular problem. Idle sensitivity deals with suspending a program. Suggesting MS-DOS mode as necessary is not an option. The user needs this application to run within Windows. This problem also doesn't have anything to do with video, so the fast ROM emulation wouldn't be correct.

Question 9

Which one of the following statements is true?

    A. A process contains only one thread.

    B. A process consists of at least one thread.

    C. A process contains two threads.

    D. A process consists of at least two threads.

Answer:

    B. A process consists of at least one thread. MS-DOS and 16-bit applications have only one thread per process. 32-bit applications can have multiple threads per process (see section 3.4.4).

Question 10

You are running an MS-DOS application, two 16-bit Windows applications, and a 32-bit Windows application. The MS-DOS application fails. Which of the following statements is true?

    A. Only the MS-DOS application is affected.

    B. The MS-DOS application and the 16-bit applications will stop responding.

    C. The MS-DOS application and the 32-bit applications will stop responding.

    D. All applications will stop responding.

Answer:

    A. Because every MS-DOS-based application runs in a separate Virtual Machine, they do not affect other MS-DOS applications or Windows applications (both 16-bit and 32-bit)(see section 3.4.6).

Chapter 4

Question 1

What type of docking requires that the portable computer be in a suspended or sleep mode?

A. Hot docking

B. Warm docking

C. Cold docking

D. Boat docking

Answer:

B. Hot docking is docking with the computer up and running, and cold docking is with the computer completely off (see section 4.4.1).

Question 2

Legacy devices cannot be used in a PnP computer.

A. True

B. False

Answer:

B. PnP-compatible computers cannot only support PnP devices, but must also be backward compatible with legacy devices (see section 4.1.3).

Question 3

Which of the following components is in charge of handling all aspects of the configuration process?

A. Configuration Manager

B. Resource Arbitrator

C. Bus Enumerator

D. Registry

Answer:

A. The Configuration Manager handles all aspects of the configuration process by working closely with the Resource Arbitrators and Bus Enumerators (see section 4.3.3).

Question 4

Which of the following components resolves conflicts between devices?

    A. Configuration Manager

    B. Resource Arbitrator

    C. Bus Enumerator

    D. Registry

Answer:

    B. The Resource Arbitrator allocates resources and resolves conflicts when necessary (see section 4.3.6).

Question 5

Which of the following components is responsible for building the hardware tree?

    A. Configuration Manager

    B. Resource Arbitrator

    C. Bus Enumerator

    D. Registry

Answer:

    C. The Bus Enumerator is responsible for identifying all of the devices attached to its specific bus and then assigning a unique identification number to each device (see section 4.3.1).

Question 6

Which of the following components is used to manually intervene in the event of an unresolved resource conflict?

    A. Configuration Manager

    B. Device Manager

    C. Registry editor

    D. Configuration editor

Answer:

B. The Device Manager can be reached through the System applet of the Control Panel and can be used to configure devices manually (see section 4.3.7).

Question 7

A user solicits your assistance. He has just installed a new component in his machine and seems to be having problems. He has the following devices installed that can use the listed IRQs:

Mouse on COM 1

Floppy Drive

Printer on LPT1

Modem that can use IRQ 3, 4, or 5

Network card that can use 5 or 7

Sound card that can use 3 or 5

IDE controller that can use 14 or 15

All the devices are legacy devices. Can the resource conflict be resolved?

A. Yes

B. No

Answer:

B. The devices required for boot will be resolved first. This means that the IDE device will get either 14 or 15. Let's say 15. Next, any legacy devices are resolved before PnP devices (of which we have none). The mouse on COM1 will use IRQ 4. The floppy drive will use IRQ 6, and the printer will use IRQ 7. That leaves 3 and 5. The three devices leave no possible combination. Your recommendation should be for this person to purchase some PnP-compatible upgrades (see section 4.3.6).

Question 8

Which component is responsible for creating the hardware tree?

A. BIOS

B. Device Manager

C. Bus Enumerator

D. Resource Arbitrator

Answer:

C. The Bus Enumerator is responsible for assigning a unique identification number to each item on its bus (see section 4.3.1).

Question 9

As part of the Plug and Play operating system, certain resources need to be assigned to devices so that they can communicate with the processor. Which of the following are they? Choose all that apply.

A. Direct Memory Access (DMA) channels

B. Interrupt Requests (IRQ)

C. Peripheral Component Interconnect (PCI) numbers

D. Input/Output (I/O) ports

E. Memory

F. Small Computer Standard Interface (SCSI) ID numbers

Answer:

A., B., D., and E.   These resources are used by hardware devices to communicate with the processor. For an operating system to meet the Plug and Play standard, it must be able to assign these resources to hardware devices and to resolve conflicts when they arise (see section 4.3.5).

Question 10

Which component is responsible for allocating specific resources and resolving conflicts when two or more devices request the same resource?

A. BIOS

B. Device Manager

C. Configuration Manager

D. Resource Arbitrator

Answer:

D. The Resource Arbitrator assigns IRQ, DMA, IO Port, and Memory resources to devices and resolves conflicts that might arise when two or more devices ask for one of these resources at the same time (see section 4.3.6).

Question 11

For a computer to be Plug and Play-compliant, its BIOS must be able to do which of the following? Choose all that apply.

A. Notification of dynamic changes in system configuration

B. Creation of the hardware tree

C. Allocation of IRQs

D. Configuration of system boot devices

Answer:

A. and C.   The BIOS must configure boot devices at system startup prior to the loading of the operating system. Additionally, it should be able to notify the operating system of any dynamic changes, such as the docking (or undocking) of a laptop computer (see section 4.1.1).

Chapter 5

Question 1

What program takes the place of SmartDrive in Windows 95?

A. DrvSpace

B. VCache

C. DiskCache

D. DiskSpace

Answer:

B. VCache is the caching replacement for SmartDrive that was used for previous versions of Windows (see section 5.3.1).

Question 2

When renaming a long filename that contains spaces at the command prompt, what should you use before and after the filename to designate that the spaces are part of the filename?

    A. Asterisks

    B. Number signs

    C. Quotes

    D. Parentheses

Answer:

    C. The filename must be surrounded by quotes; if not, Windows 95 thinks that the spaces are being used to separate the commands and usually returns a file not found error (see section 5.3.3).

Question 3

To support long filenames, what additional component(s) must be loaded on a Windows NT server? Choose all that apply.

    A. OSR2 Name Space

    B. OS/2 Name Space

    C. LFNBK

    D. Nothing

Answer:

    D. Windows NT servers support long filenames out of the box. No additional components need to be loaded (see section 5.3.3).

Question 4

To support long filenames, what additional component(s) must be loaded on a Novell NetWare server? Choose all that apply.

    A. OSR2 Name Space

    B. OS/2 Name Space

C. LFNBK

D. Nothing

Answer:

B. For NetWare servers to support long filenames, the OS/2 name space must be loaded. If not, only 8.3 filenames can be stored on the server (see section 5.3.3).

Question 5

A user comes to you and states that she just ran ScanDisk and Defrag to optimize her system, but she also states that her files no longer have long filenames and some of her files are corrupt. What could she have possibly done wrong?

A. She ran ScanDisk before she ran Defrag and should have run Defrag first.

B. She shut her system down while one of the utilities was running.

C. She ran the utilities in Windows when she should have run them in MS-DOS mode.

D. She used 16-bit real-mode versions and should have used the 32-bit protected-mode versions.

Answer:

D. The user should have used the 32-bit, protected-mode versions of the utilities that came with Windows 95. The 16-bit, real-mode versions do not support long filenames (see section 5.3.3).

Question 6

With the Windows 95 Backup program, you can back up to what type of devices? Pick all that apply.

A. Floppies

B. Another hard disk

C. Mapped network drive

D. Tape drive

Answer:

All. You can back up to any of the types of media specified in the possible answers of the question using the Windows 95 backup utility (see section 5.5).

Question 7

A filename in Windows 95 can be how many characters long?

  A. 250

  B. 255

  C. 256

  D. 260

Answer:

B. Individual filenames can be up to 255 characters long, including spaces (see section 5.3.3).

Question 8

What is the largest partition that can be compressed with Windows 95 without any additional software installed?

  A. 256MB

  B. 512MB

  C. 1GB

  D. 2GB

Answer:

B. The DriveSpace that comes with Windows 95 can only compress partitions or drives smaller than 512MB (see section 5.4.3).

Question 9

What is the largest partition that can be compressed with Windows 95 with Microsoft Plus software installed?

A. 256MB

B. 512MB

C. 1GB

D. 2GB

Answer:

D. The DriveSpace that comes with the Microsoft Plus package can compress partitions or drives up to 2GB in size (see section 5.4.3).

Chapter 6

Question 1

The naming convention used to connect to resources is called what?

A. Universal Naming Convention

B. Universal NetBIOS Connection

C. United Name Convention

D. Underling Naming Correction

Answer:

A. The Universal Naming Convention is the naming convention used for connecting to resources. An example would be \\thor\datastor (see section 6.2.1).

Question 2

Windows 95 supports which of the following network protocols? Choose all that apply.

A. Net1

B. TCP/IP

C. IPX/SPX

D. NetBEUI

E. NetX

Answer:

B., C., and D.   Windows 95 supports all of the three protocols. The other protocols are fictitious (see section 6.1.3).

Question 3

Windows 95 can use which of the following computers for security hosts? Choose all that apply.

A. Windows 95

B. Windows NT Workstation

C. Windows NT Server

D. Novell NetWare

Answer:

B., C., and D.   The only computer in the list that Windows 95 cannot use as a security host is another Windows 95 computer. The security host must have the capability of maintaining a database of users and using that database to validate them (see section 6.3.2).

Question 4

When connecting to a Windows NT server, which UNC name would be used?

A. \\sharename\directoy

B. \\servername\sharename

C. \\servername\volumename

D. \\volumename\directory

Answer:

B. Windows-based computers use the \\servername\sharename format (see section 6.2.2).

Question 5

When connecting to a Novell NetWare server, which UNC name would be used?

A. \\sharename\directoy

B. \\servername\sharename

C. \\servername\volumename

D. \\volumename\directory

Answer:

C. NetWare servers use the \\servername\volumename format (see section 6.2.2).

Question 6

You can have File and Printer Sharing for Microsoft networks and File and Printer Sharing for NetWare networks installed simultaneously.

A. True

B. False

Answer:

B. You can only have one File and Printer Sharing service installed at one time because of the differences between Microsoft and NetWare networks in the communications process (see section 6.3.3).

Question 7

Security based on a password at each resource is called what?

A. Resource-level security

B. Password-level security

C. Share-level security

D. User-level security

Answer:

C. Share-level security is designed so that each share can be assigned a level of access to everyone who connects to it. For additional security, you can assign a password for different levels of access (see section 6.3.2).

Question 8

John has a network consisting of 10 Windows 95 computers and two Windows NT servers. Several printers are attached to the Windows 95 computers. He would like to share the printers so that others can use them, but he wants to set security so that not everyone has access to all printers (for example, check printers). He would like to have the highest level of security available to him but with the easiest administration. What type of security should he use?

A. Resource-level security

B. Password-level security

C. Share-level security

D. User-level security

Answer:

D. User-level security would be his best bet. It provides a way of controlling access through group memberships, which are handled at the server. Additionally, it is better to assign who has access to which resource rather than assigning passwords and giving them out as with share-level security.

Question 9

With the frame type of IPX/SPX set to automatic, what frame type will be used if Windows 95 cannot detect the frame type?

A. 802.2

B. 802.3

C. Ethernet II

D. Token Ring

Answer:

A. 802.2 is the frame type used by NetWare 3.12 and later versions and is therefore the default frame type (see section 6.5.1).

Chapter 7

Question 1

Which of the following is the default subnet mask for a Class B network?

A. 255.0.0.0

B. 255.255.0.0

C. 255.255.255.0

D. 255.255.255.255

Answer:

B. In actuality, the proper default mask is indicated by the letter of each answer with the exception being d. 255.255.255.255 is not a valid subnet mask (see section 7.2.1).

Question 2

Which utility can you use to find out what IP address was assigned to a Windows 95 computer by a DHCP server?

A. Ping

B. TraceRt

C. WINIPCFG

D. Route

Answer:

C. By using the Run command from the Start menu, you can use WINIPCFG to tell you your TCP/IP configuration including your address that was assigned by a DHCP server (see section 7.2.1).

Question 3

Which service provides automatic configuration of TCP/IP address for computers on a network?

A. WINS

B. DHCP

C. DNS

D. Ping

Answer:

B. DHCP is short for *dynamic host configuration protocol.* DHCP is a service for dynamically assigning TCP/IP address to computers (see section 7.2.1).

Question 4

Which service provides resolution of Internet domain names to TCP/IP addresses?

A. WINS

B. DHCP

C. DNS

D. Ping

Answer:

C. DNS is short for *domain name service* and is a service that provides resolution of Internet domain names (see section 7.2.1).

Question 5

Which service provides resolution of NetBIOS computer names to TCP/IP addresses?

A. WINS

B. DHCP

C. DNS

D. Ping

Answer:

A. WINS is short for *Windows Internet naming service* and is a service that provides resolution of NetBIOS computer names to TCP/IP addresses (see section 7.2.1).

Question 6

Bob administers a Windows NT and Windows 95 network, which consists of two Windows NT servers (one of which is a WINS server) and 65 Windows 95 computers. Bob has called you to consult him on some issues that he would like to take care of. Here are his items and proposed solution. Define whether the proposed solution meets all, some, or none of Bob's objectives.

Required Result: Ease some administration of TCP/IP tasks on the network.

Optional Result 1: Automatically assign IP addresses.

Optional Result 2: Automatically configure computers to help them resolve NetBIOS computer names to IP addresses.

Proposed Solution: Install and properly configure one of the Windows NT servers with DHCP. Under the TCP/IP settings on the Windows 95 computer, select the Obtain an IP Address Automatically option.

A. Neither the required result nor the optional results are met by the proposed solution.

B. The required result is the only result met.

C. The required result and Optional Result 1 are met.

D. The required result and Optional Result 2 are met.

E. The required result and both optional results are met.

Answer:

E. By installing and properly configuring DHCP on a Windows NT server, Windows 95 can take advantage of its capability to automatically assign IP addresses. Also, a DHCP server can configure other aspects of IP configuration, including informing the client computer of the IP address of the WINS server. This option allows for the computers to meet Optional Result 2.

Chapter 8

Question 1

What service must be installed on both the administrator's machine and the machine that you would like to remotely administer?

A. Remote Registry Service

B. Remote Administration Service

C. Server Service

D. Netlogon Service

Answer:

A. The Remote Registry Service must be installed on both the administrator's computer and the computer to be administered remotely (see section 8.3).

Question 2

When saving a policy file to be implemented, what is the proper filename?

A. `POLEDIT.POL`

B. `ADMIN.ADM`

C. `CONFIG.POL`

D. `CONFIG.ADM`

Answer:

C. `CONFIG.POL` is the correct filename for a policy file that will be saved and implemented (see section 8.2.1).

Question 3

Windows 95 Server-based profiles on a Windows NT network are stored in what directory on the server?

A. User's Mail directory

B. User's Home directory

C. User's Profile directory

D. User's setup directory

Answer:

B. On a Windows NT network, a user's profile is stored in his or her Home directory that is properly set up on the server (see section 8.1.3).

Question 4

Which of the items below is *not* part of a roving user's profile?

A. Shortcuts on the desktop

B. Windows color settings

C. Persistent network connections

D. Files on the desktop

Answer:

D. Files stored on the desktop cannot follow a user on the network (roving user). Only shortcuts on the desktop will be copied to the server as part of the user's profile (see section 8.1).

Question 5

Which of the following Registry files will be copied to the user's profile folder? Choose all that apply.

A. `SYSTEM.DAT`

B. `USER.DAT`

C. `SYSTEM.DA0`

D. `USER.DA0`

Answer:

B. and D.   Both the `USER.DAT` and `USER.DA0` are copied to the user's profile folder (see section 8.1.2).

The `SYSTEM.DAT` and `SYSTEM.DA0` are part of the computer-specific portion of the Registry and do not make up any portion of the user profile.

Question 6

On a Windows NT network, where should the `CONFIG.POL` file be stored for automatic downloading?

A. In the Windows directory

B. In the server's Netlogon share

C. In the user's Home directory

D. In the user's Mail directory

Answer:

B. The `CONFIG.POL` should be stored in the server's Netlogon share directory (see section 8.2.1).

The Windows directory is where local-based policies are stored. The Home and Mail directories deal with profiles, not policies.

Question 7

You are asked to assist in troubleshooting a policy malfunction. The policy file has been created and stored in its proper place on a Novell NetWare server. The policy is implemented and works fine on a Windows 95 machine if the `CONFIG.POL` is in the Windows folder locally, but not when in its proper storage location on the server. What could be the potential problem?

A. Share-level security needs to be enabled on the Windows 95 computer.

B. User-level security needs to be enabled on the Windows 95 computer.

C. A proper Mail directory needs to be configured for the users.

D. The Remote Registry Service needs to be installed.

Answer:

B. User-level security needs to be enabled on the Windows 95 computer (see section 8.2.1).

If the policy works properly with the `CONFIG.POL` in the Windows directory locally on the computer, share-level security is enabled. With share-level security enabled, the proper storage location of the `CONFIG.POL` is in the Windows folder. The Mail directory does not need to be set up properly, simply because it deals with profiles, not policies. The Remote Registry Service is used to administer the computer remotely.

Question 8

What file must be properly loaded to ensure that group policies work correctly?

A. `GROUP.POL`

B. `GROUP.DLL`

C. `GROUPPOL.DLL`

D. `GROUP.ADM`

Answer:

C. The `GROUPPOL.DLL` must be properly installed for group policies to work (see section 8.2.2).

Question 9

Windows 95 Server-based profiles on a Novell NetWare network are stored in what directory on the server?

A. User's Mail directory

B. User's Home directory

C. User's Profile directory

D. User's setup directory

Answer:

A. The proper storage location of a user's profile on a Novell NetWare network is in the user's Mail directory (see section 8.1.3).

On a Windows NT network, a user's profile is stored in his or her Home directory.

Question 10

Which user(s) and/or group(s) are given the permission to administer a Windows 95 computer automatically when user-level access is enabled? Choose all that apply.

A. Admin (Windows NT)

B. Admin (Novell 4.*x*)

C. Supervisor (Novell 3.*x*)

D. Domain Admins (Windows NT)

E. Server Operators (Windows NT)

Answer:

B., C., and D.   If you are on a Windows NT network, the Domain Admins group will automatically be given the right to remotely administer. On a Novell NetWare network, the Supervisor account on a server running 3.*x* of NetWare or the Admin account for a server running 4.*x* of NetWare is automatically given the right to remotely administer (see section 8.3).

Question 11

If you would like to view which users are connected to a Windows 95 computer and what resources they are using, which utility would you use to accomplish this remote administration task?

    A. Net Watcher

    B. System Monitor

    C. Remote Registry

    D. Network Monitor

Answer:

    A. The Net Watcher utility would be used to accomplish such a task (see section 8.3.2).

Chapter 9

Question 1

What are the two data formats used in printing with Windows 95? Pick the correct two.

    A. RAG

    B. RAW

    C. EMF

    D. ERD

Answer:

B. and C.   RAW information is the data type that is ready to be printed. EMF data is the Windows 95 internal graphics data type (see section 9.2).

Question 2

Bidirectional communication in Windows 95 supports _____ mode, which provides an asynchronous identification channel between the printer and the computer.

    A. EMF

    B. RAW

    C. Nibble

    D. Point and Print

Answer:

    C. Nibble mode allows the printer to use the channel to communicate device identification information located on the ROM of the printer (see section 9.3.1).

Question 3

Windows 95 uses which three types of drivers along with minidrivers to create a total printer driver?

    A. Microsoft universal

    B. Microsoft PostScript

    C. Monolithic

    D. NetWare Universal

    E. NetWare PostScript

Answer:

    A., B., and C.   Windows 95 uses the Microsoft universal driver for all printers except PostScript and printers such as the HP Inkjets. The Microsoft PostScript driver is used with PostScript printers. Lastly, the monolithic drivers are used with HP Inkjet printers (see section 9.4).

Question 4

The default location for spooled print jobs is:

    A. \WINDOWS\SYSTEM

    B. \WINDOWS\SPOOL

C. \WINDOWS\SPOOL\PRINTERS

D. \WINDOWS\PRINTERS\SPOOL

Answer:

C. The default location is \WINDOWS\SPOOL\PRINTERS (see section 9.2.2).

Question 5

After installing the printer and sharing it to the network, what must you do to configure the Windows 95 computer to support Point and Print?

A. Share the \WINDOWS\SYSTEM folder with Read and File scan rights.

B. Create a folder for the driver files.

C. Modify the details tab of the printer.

D. Nothing.

Answer:

D. To set up a printer on a Windows 95 computer as a Point and Print printer, just install it as normal and share it to the network. Everything else is automatic (see section 9.6).

Question 6

What rights must you have to set up a NetWare server to support Point and Print?

A. Read and File Scan

B. User

C. Supervisor

D. Change

Answer:

C. Supervisor rights are needed to configure the NetWare server. If not, the Point and Print menu selections will not appear when you right-click a printer (see section 9.6).

Question 7

When you connect a Windows 95 computer to another Windows 95 computer configured with a Point and Print printer, the printer configuration settings are copied along with the drivers. True or False?

A. True

B. False

Answer:

A. True. Because the drivers are copied from the computer's working copies, the settings are carried with it (see section 9.4).

Chapter 10

Question 1

Which line protocol is the most popular and flexible to use?

A. SLIP

B. Windows NT RAS

C. PPP

D. NRN

Answer:

C. The Point-to-Point Protocol (PPP) is the most popular. It is the most flexible because it supports DHCP (see section 10.1.3).

Question 2

Which wide-area telephone network is the same as your existing telephone service?

A. PSTN

B. PPP

C. x.25

D. ISDN

Answer:

A. The Packet Switching Telephone Network (PSTN) is the same as the telephone service you use daily (see section 10.1.3).

Question 3

Which component is considered the central component in communications architecture?

A. Unimodem

B. VCOMM

C. COMM

D. Mini-VCOMM

Answer:

B. VCOMM is an irreplaceable component that manages all access to communications resources (see section 10.1.4).

Question 4

What type of slow links does Windows 95 support via dial-up networking?

A. PPP

B. PSTN

C. x.25

D. ISDN

Answer:

B., C., and D. PPP is the only one of the four that is not a slow link connection that Windows 95 supports. PPP is a line protocol, not a slow link type (see section 10.1.3).

Question 5

What network protocols are supported by dial-up networking?

A. PPP

B. NetBEUI

C. TCP/IP

D. SLIP

E. IPX/SPX

Answer:

B., C., and E.   Windows 95 supports NetBEUI, IPX/SPX, and TCP/IP. The tricky part to that question is the use of the work network. PPP and SLIP are not network protocols; they are line protocols (see section 10.1.3).

Question 6

What extra security measures in the following list should be used in conjunction with configuring a dial-up server? Choose all that apply.

A. Use user-level security

B. Use share-level security

C. Use password encryption

D. Use user profiles

Answer:

A. and C.   User-level security should be enabled on the host computer. Additionally, requiring the use of encrypted passwords will help to increase security. The catchy part of this question is with the last answer. You can use Policies to help with security, but not Profiles (see section 10.4.1).

Question 7

As a dial-up server, Windows 95 can support all of the following as clients except:

A. Windows 95 client

B. NRN NetWare client

C. Windows for Workgroups client

D. Windows NT client

Answer:

B. Windows 95 cannot be a gateway for SLIP or IPX networks. NRN NetWare clients are required to use IPX/SPX (see section 10.3.2).

Question 8

As a dial-up client, Windows 95 can connect to which of the following servers? Choose all that apply.

A. Windows 95 dial-up server

B. NRN NetWare server

C. Windows for Workgroups

D. Windows NT server

Answer:

All. All of the these operating systems can act as a dial-up server for a Windows 95 computer (see section 10.1.2).

Question 9

Windows 95 dial-up networking is topology-dependent.

A. True

B. False

Answer:

B. Windows 95 dial-up networking is topology-independent and supports Ethernet, Token Ring, FDDI, and ArcNet (see section 10.1.2).

Question 10

A user calls you and wants to know how to make his Windows 95 computer available so that he may dial into it and access his files from home. He already has Dial-Up Networking installed. What else must he do?

A. Install Dial-Up Networking Server from Windows Setup tab from the Add/Remove Programs option in the Control Panel.

B. Install Dial-Up Networking Server from the Windows 95 CD in the Admin\DUN folder.

C. Install Microsoft Plus! Pack.

D. Nothing, Dial-Up server is part of Dial-Up Networking, and thus already installed.

Answer:

C. Dial-Up Networking server is only available as part of the Microsoft Plus! Pack. In order to have a Windows 95 computer configured as a dial-up server, it must be installed (10.3).

Question 11

Under Windows 95 architecture, a modem requires two drivers. The first driver is a minidriver provided by the manufacturer; the other is supplied as part of Windows 95 and is called _____.

A. Unidriver

B. Unimodem

C. ModemDrv

D. WinModem

Answer:

B. The Unimodem driver is the main device driver provided by Microsoft. This driver, when combined with minidrivers from the manufacturer, gives Windows full functionality with the modem (10.1.4).

Question 12

A company asks you to help them decide what type of a remote access solution to implement. They have a 25-node network with the clients running Windows 95, and a server running NetWare 3.12. They have decided that since only five people need remote access, they would like to use Windows 95 as a dial-in solution. Here are their required and optional objectives of what the solution should meet:

Required Objectives

A. Access to network shares (files) from a remote location

B. Users validated in some fashion for additional security when accessing network resources.

Optional Objectives

A. Allow all five users simultaneous dial-in access.

B. Access to network printers from a remote location.

Proposed Solution

Install Dial-Up Networking and the Microsoft Plus! Pack on a single computer. Configure this computer to use User-Level security using the NetWare server as its security provider. Assign the individual user's dial-in rights.

A. The solution meets all of the required objectives and all of the optional objectives.

B. The solution meets all of the required objectives and some of the optional objectives.

C. The solution meets some of the required objectives and all of the optional objectives.

D. The solution meets none of the required objectives and none of the optional objectives.

Answer:

B. With Dial-Up Networking and Microsoft Plus! Pack installed, Windows 95 can act as a dial-in server, meeting the first required objective. With User-Level security enabled, the second required objective is met since there is a security host (the NetWare server) available. The first optional objective cannot be met using Windows 95. Windows NT Server is the only Microsoft product that supports more than one simultaneous inbound call (it supports 256). The second optional objective is met because, as a dial-up client, users can access both files and printers on the network.

Chapter 11

Question 1

Who can administer a post office created by Microsoft Exchange?

A. Any member of that post office

B. Only members who were designated as an admin after post office creation

C. Only the person who created the post office

D. Anyone knowing the administrator password

Answer:

C. Whoever creates the post office is automatically designated as the post office administrator (see section 11.2.2).

Question 2

You can connect the Microsoft Exchange client that comes with Windows 95 to a Microsoft Mail server.

A. True

B. False

Answer:

A. The Microsoft Exchange client that comes with Windows 95 can connect to workgroup post offices and Microsoft Mail servers (see section 11.1).

Question 3

What is MAPI?

A. The manual and automatic programming interface.

B. A utility used in Microsoft Exchange to assist you in connecting to other Windows 95 computers.

C. A common set of commands and instructions that allows other programs to interface with mail systems.

D. The Registry location of Exchange settings.

Answer:

C. This is the part of Windows 95 that allows you to have a common interface for all mail functions (see section 11.1.1).

Question 4

A message profile allows you to specify different service configurations.

A. True

B. False

Answer:

A. It allows you to specify different basic settings, delivery order, location information, and more (see section 11.2.4).

Question 5

You can share the modem that you are using for Microsoft Fax to others on the network so that they can also use it for Microsoft Fax.

A. True

B. False

Answer:

A. With Microsoft Exchange, you can share your Microsoft Fax with others on the network. This allows others to use the modem installed in your computer and your Microsoft Fax service. You can share your Microsoft Fax at the Modem tab of the Microsoft Fax Properties sheet (see section 11.3.2).

Question 6

When you install Microsoft Fax, it is actually _____.

A. A Windows 95 Plus feature

B. A My Computer component

C. A Network Neighborhood component

D. A Microsoft Exchange service

Answer:

B. Even though you are installing an additional component of Windows 95, it is actually a service of Microsoft Exchange (see section 11.3.1).

Question 7

You can add and delete users to or from a workgroup post office using what tool?

A. Postoffice Editor

B. Postoffice Profiler

C. Postoffice Manager

D. Postoffice User Manager

Answer:

C. You can access the post office manager interface by double-clicking the Microsoft Mail Post icon in the Control Panel and then specifying that you would like to administer an existing post office (see section 11.2.2).

Question 8

Which of the following statements are true about a workgroup postoffice? Choose all that apply.

A. The person who creates the postoffice is the administrator.

B. You should have multiple postoffices in a single workgroup.

C. The folder where the postoffice will reside must be created prior to installation.

D. A user can have his Windows 95 Inbox connected to a workgroup Postoffice and an MS Mail server simultaneously.

Answer:

A., B., and C.   (A) Whoever creates the post office for the first time creates the first mailbox. In doing so, he creates the administrator's mailbox and therefore becomes the administrator. (B) You can only be connected to one workgroup post office at a time. There is no way of connecting two or more post offices together. Because of this, you should generally create only a single post office. If the need is there for a larger implementation, use another product such as MS Mail, or even better, MS Exchange. (C) The post office setup utility does not have the capability of creating a folder for its location during the installation. You should create it before starting the setup.

Question 9

You have implemented Microsoft Exchange as the email package in a company. There are several computers that are shared by two people. As a solution, you have implemented Exchange messaging profiles so that two users sharing the same computer can both access their individual mailboxes. On Jack and Sue's computer, however, there seems to be a problem. Sue can access her email, but Jack can't. What is the potential problem?

    A. Jack has to log on to another computer to access his email.

    B. The mail server is offline.

    C. Jack's profile is not properly set up to access the mail server.

    D. Jack does not have the proper access rights to his mailbox.

Answer:

    C. This is the most likely problem. The other problems can be eliminated because of the fact that Sue can access her mail. To fix this problem, log on to the computer as Jack, and right-click the Inbox icon located on the desktop. By selecting Properties, you can then modify Jack's messaging profile (see section 11.2.4).

Question 10

When you set up a user to connect to a workgroup postoffice, what information do you need? Choose all that apply.

    A. Postoffice title

    B. Location of the postoffice

    C. User's name and password

    D. Administrator's name and password

Answer:

    B. and C. During the setup of the user's Inbox, you are prompted for the locatio of the postoffice (so it knows where to go to get the mail) and the user's name and password (so it will have access to the mailbox) (see section 11.2.3).

Chapter 12

Question 1

When a low priority thread is tying up a resource that a higher priority thread needs, the lower thread's priority is increased to match that of the higher thread. This allows each to have an equal time slice until the resource is relinquished. What is this process called?

A. Priority allocation

B. Thread equalization

C. Priority inheritance boosting

D. Priority promotion

Answer:

C. The secondary scheduler handles this process. After the resource has been relinquished, the thread's priority is decreased to its original priority (see section 12.2.2).

Question 2

What is the name of the memory swap file in Windows 95?

A. `MEMORY.SWP`

B. `386SPART.PAR`

C. `MEM386.SWP`

D. `WIN386.SWP`

Answer:

D. The `WIN386.SWP` file is located in the Windows folder by default (see section 12.3.3).

Question 3

By default, Windows 95 increases and decreases the size of the memory swap file dynamically.

A. True

B. False

Answer:

A. True. This dynamic sizing is referred to as the growing and shrinking of the swap file (see section 12.3.3).

Question 4

You are installing a Windows 95 computer on a NetWare network. Of the following clients, which would have the most optimal performance?

A. Microsoft Client for NetWare networks

B. NetWare VLM

C. NetWare NETX

Answer:

A. The Microsoft Client for NetWare networks would be the most optimal because it is a 32-bit, protected-mode client. The NETX and VLM clients are 16-bit, real-mode clients. Also available is Novell's Client 32, which is also a 32-bit, protected-mode client (see section 12.4).

Question 5

Which of the following applications are multithreaded applications? Choose all that apply.

A. MS-DOS

B. Windows 16-bit

C. Windows 32-bit

Answer:

C. Windows 32-bit applications are the only applications that are multi-threading. MS-DOS and Windows 16-bit applications are single-threaded applications (see section 12.2.1).

Question 6

Which applications are preemptively multitasked in Windows 95? Choose all that apply.

   A. MS-DOS

   B. Windows 16-bit

   C. Windows 32-bit

Answer:

A. and C.   Both MS-DOS and Windows 32-bit applications occupy their own separate memory address space. Because Windows 16-bit applications share the same memory address space, they are cooperatively multitasked (see section 12.2.1).

Question 7

At what percentage of sustained processor utilization should the upgrade of the processor be considered?

   A. 70%

   B. 75%

   C. 80%

   D. 85%

Answer:

C. When the utilization of the processor is consistently above 80 percent, the processor might not be adequate for the tasks being accomplished and might need to be upgraded (see section 12.1.2).

Question 8

You have a computer on your network that is low on disk space. It has a printer attached, and you want to set the printer settings at the most optimal setting. Which of the two settings would you choose?

   A. Start printing after the last page has spooled.

   B. Start printing after the first page has spooled.

Answer:

B. This setting allows less disk space to be needed for spooling, but the user does not regain control of the application faster than with the first option (see section 12.5).

Chapter 13

Question 1

Which log files are needed for Windows 95 to automatically recover from a crash during Setup? Choose all that apply.

A. DETLOG.TXT

B. IOS.LOG

C. DETCRASH.LOG

D. SETUPLOG.TXT

Answer:

A., C., and D.   All of these files are needed with exception to the IOS.LOG. DETLOG.TXT is needed so that Windows 95 knows which devices have already been detected. DETCRASH.LOG is used in conjunction with the Setup log to keep Setup from crashing because of the same reason twice.

Question 2

Which of the following files contains a list of all devices detected during setup?

A. DETLOG.TXT

B. DETECT.LOG

C. DETCRASH.LOG

D. SETUPLOG.TXT

Answer:

A. The DETLOG.TXT file contains a list of all devices detected during setup.

Question 3

When Setup hangs during the detection of hardware, what should a user do?

A. Press Ctrl+Alt+Del to reset the computer and allow Windows 95 Setup to continue.

B. Press Ctrl+Alt+Del to reset the computer and start Windows 95 Setup with the /d switch.

C. Turn the power off to the computer, return the power, and allow Windows 95 Setup to continue.

D. Turn the power off to the computer, return the power, and start Windows 95 Setup with the /d switch.

Answer:

C. Completely turning off the power allows ISA buses and other components to reset, whereas performing a warm boot by pressing Ctrl+Alt+Del does not. After power has been returned, Windows 95 Setup continues installation, bypassing the problem that caused the crash.

Question 4

Which of the following commands is used to rebuild the default Windows 95 program folders on the Start menu?

A. CONVGRP /s

B. CONVGRP /m

C. GRPCONV /s

D. GRPCONV /m

Answer:

C. You will notice a dialog box that gives you the status of the rebuilding process. After the folders are re-created, you are returned to the desktop.

Question 5

Which of the following commands is used to convert Windows 3.x groups to folders on the Start menu?

A. CONVGRP /s

B. CONVGRP /m

C. GRPCONV /s

D. GRPCONV /m

Answer:

D. You are presented with a dialog box prompting you to select the group that you would like to convert. Select the group that you would like to convert and click Open.

Question 6

Which of the following files contains a list of messages received during Setup?

A. DETLOG.TXT

B. DETECT.LOG

C. DETCRASH.LOG

D. SETUPLOG.TXT

Answer:

D. SETUPLOG.TXT is a file in the root directory of the hard disk that contains a list of messages received during setup and is used for viewing setup errors.

Index

Q-R

REGISTRATION CARD

TY MCSE Windows 95 in 14 Days

Name _____ Title _____

Company _____ Type of business _____

Address _____

City/State/ZIP _____

Have you used these types of books before? ☐ yes ☐ no

If yes, which ones? _____

_____

How many computer books do you purchase each year? ☐ 1–5 ☐ 6 or more

How did you learn about this book? _____

Where did you purchase this book? _____

Which applications do you currently use? _____

_____

Which computer magazines do you subscribe to? _____

_____

What trade shows do you attend? _____

_____

Comments: _____

_____

_____

Would you like to be placed on our preferred mailing list? ☐ yes ☐ no

☐ **I would like to see my name in print!** You may use my name and quote me in future Sams products and promotions. My daytime phone number is: _____

Sams Publishing   201 West 103rd Street ◆ Indianapolis, Indiana 46290 USA

Fax to **317-581-4663**

Fold Here

‖‖‖

BUSINESS REPLY MAIL
FIRST-CLASS MAIL PERMIT NO. 9918 INDIANAPOLIS IN

POSTAGE WILL BE PAID BY THE ADDRESSEE

SAMS PUBLISHING
201 W 103RD ST
INDIANAPOLIS IN 46290-9058